Business and Professional Writing

Business and Professional Writing
A Basic Guide

SECOND CANADIAN EDITION

Paul MacRae

broadview press

BROADVIEW PRESS – www.broadviewpress.com
Peterborough, Ontario, Canada

Founded in 1985, Broadview Press remains a wholly independent publishing house. Broadview's focus is on academic publishing; our titles are accessible to university and college students as well as scholars and general readers. With over 600 titles in print, Broadview has become a leading international publisher in the humanities, with world-wide distribution. Broadview is committed to environmentally responsible publishing and fair business practices.

The interior of this book is printed on 100% recycled paper.

Library and Archives Canada Cataloguing in Publication

Title: Business and professional writing : a basic guide / Paul MacRae.
Names: MacRae, Paul, 1946- author.
Description: Second Canadian edition. | Includes bibliographical references and index.
Identifiers: Canadiana (print) 2019005364X | Canadiana (ebook) 20190053666 | ISBN 9781554814725 (softcover) | ISBN 9781770487079 (PDF) | ISBN 9781460406632 (HTML)
Subjects: LCSH: Business writing—Canada—Handbooks, manuals, etc. | LCSH: Business report writing—Handbooks, manuals, etc. | LCSH: Business communication—Canada—Handbooks, manuals, etc.
Classification: LCC HF5718.3 .M32 2019 | DDC 808.06/665—dc23

Broadview Press handles its own distribution in North America:
PO Box 1243, Peterborough, Ontario K9J 7H5, Canada
555 Riverwalk Parkway, Tonawanda, NY 14150, USA
Tel: (705) 743-8990; Fax: (705) 743-8353
email: customerservice@broadviewpress.com

Distribution is handled by Eurospan Group in the UK, Europe, Central Asia, Middle East, Africa, India, Southeast Asia, Central America, South America, and the Caribbean. Distribution is handled by Footprint Books in Australia and New Zealand.

Broadview Press acknowledges the financial support of the Government of Canada for our publishing activities.

Edited by Michel Pharand

Book design by Chris Rowat Design

PRINTED IN CANADA

Contents

Acknowledgements

No work appears out of a vacuum, and this book is no exception. Since 2005, I have taught a course on business and professional writing, English 225, at the University of Victoria. I inherited that course from professors Claire McKenzie and Norma Depledge; I also inherited from them many of the key concepts in this book, including the eight Cs of good professional writing, the AIDA format for persuasive writing, and the format for "bad-news" letters, among others. I am sincerely grateful to them.

I'd like to acknowledge University Canada West, a private university now in Vancouver but originally based in Victoria. I taught several courses, both in-classroom and online, at UCW, and designed two of the courses: one on writing for the media and a second on writing for business and the professions. *Business and Professional Writing: A Basic Guide* is based on the online textbook I wrote for UCW's business-writing course, and I am grateful to UCW for agreeing to allow Broadview Press to publish this version of it.

I would like to thank Broadview Press for taking this book out of the online world and putting it into actual print, and particularly Don LePan and Marjorie Mather. Broadview editor Karen Taylor went well beyond what I would consider the call of duty in editing the manuscript and I am very grateful to her for her many suggestions and corrections. And many thanks, as well, to my wife Sheila, who carefully and kindly proofread the manuscript and made many, many helpful suggestions.

Finally, I would like to thank the hundreds of University of Victoria students I have had the pleasure of teaching over the past decade. I would particularly like to thank the students who kindly agreed to let me use their formal reports as examples of very good work: Cole Funk, Carl Marais, Jessie Zhang, and David Wang for their report on bike-sharing, and Marissa Louie, Emma Choo, and Youssef Abdelaziz for their report on hotel websites. I have learned as much from my students as, I hope, they have learned from me.

When I began to teach writing in 2005, after more than 30 years in journalism, I made a startling discovery: I didn't know what my students didn't know about writing, and I didn't know what I didn't know about teaching writing.

As a former journalist, I often assumed at first that my students knew more about writing than they actually did. But I also often assumed I knew more about what students needed than I actually did. I quickly learned that what was obvious to me wasn't obvious to my students, and what was obvious to my students wasn't obvious to me. And so, over the years, my course materials and teaching evolved to fill the gaps in both my students' knowledge and my own.

Business and Professional Writing: A Basic Guide is the result of this learning process. This book contains everything that, I believe, students *need* to know to become strong writers in the professional and business world. But I have also tried to include background material that, based on a decade's teaching and learning, I found most students *didn't* know.

Above all, I hope this book will be useful to you, both in your writing for university or college and after you leave university for the world beyond. I wish you the best of luck! But, in university and in the work world, "luck" is almost always based on hard preparatory work.

So let's get started....

—Paul MacRae

Preface

Welcome to *Business and Professional Writing: A Basic Guide*. It's called a "basic" guide because that's what it is. It's what you *need* to know, without a lot of bells and whistles, for your first few writing assignments in the real world.

The bells and whistles in a textbook are cool, but as a student you're juggling course work and probably a part-time job, while still trying to have a social life. Do you really have time to read more than what you absolutely need to know?

Also, in the real, working world, you aren't going to be handed a major assignment, like a news release or formal report, without some previous training and knowledge learned on the job. In addition, in your first real-world writing assignments, you'll almost certainly have co-writers who are more experienced to train and guide you.

That said, being familiar beforehand with how to structure and format a formal report, say, or how to write a strong news release, or how to send an angry customer a "bad news" letter that won't lose the customer's goodwill, means you won't look like a complete newbie, and might even impress the boss!

So, in this book, we'll keep it simple. We'll be looking at some basic formats for correspondence, promotional materials (brochures, news releases, and the like), informal reports, and formal reports. We'll look at how to design attractive documents. And we'll look at how to make your writing as powerful, persuasive, and grammatically correct as possible.

Incidentally, "professional" writing in this book refers to writing within the professions like law, medicine, architecture, business, government, and so on, not "professional" writing in the sense of publishing your writing for money. However, the writing taught in this book is practised by professional writers.

Let's discuss grammar for a moment. The grammar section is Chapter 3. If you are already terrific at grammar, then by all means skip that chapter. But if your grammar, spelling, and general written communication skills are even a bit dodgy, then you should spend quite a bit of your precious study time working on making your grammar perfect. Why?

It's not hard to learn the various professional writing formats—letters, brochures, news releases, reports, and so on, that we cover in this book. But if the writing you put into the formats isn't good—which means grammatically correct, easy to read, and clear—then your efforts will not succeed as you'd hoped.

Also, you want to write well because, as we'll discuss in more detail later, your writing reflects *you*. If your writing has grammatical and spelling errors or is hard to read, the literate reader will assume you aren't careful and detail oriented. They might also think you aren't too bright. In other words, you may look uneducated or sloppy or both. And that means you may not get the job you applied for, or gain the customer you hoped to persuade, or win the voters you hoped would elect you or your candidate, or clinch the commission you were counting on. So always keep this in mind: the quality of your writing reflects the quality of *you* to the world.

But good writing isn't just a matter of how you appear to the world; the quality of your writing also influences the quality of your thinking. Clear writing shows clear thinking; muddled writing reflects a muddled mind. It's obvious which type of mind employers, clients, and customers prefer. Fairly or not, they will judge your mind based on the quality of your writing.

Therefore, this book aims above all to give you the tools you need to become a fine *writer*. Then you can apply that fine writing to any task at all, from writing Aunt Mary to applying for your dream job to writing a formal report that will knock the socks off your boss or clients.

Introduction to Business and Professional Writing

In this chapter you will learn

- The importance of good professional communication and
- What the text will cover.

THE IMPORTANCE OF GOOD COMMUNICATION

We live in what has been called a "post-literate" age. Before television, radio, movies, and the Internet, reading was the major source of information and entertainment for most educated (i.e., literate) people. As a result, even if these literate people never took a grammar course (although many of them did), in their extensive reading they "absorbed" the rules of good writing and followed those rules in what they wrote. They were excellent writers almost by default.

However, when television appeared in the 1950s, computers and video games in the 1980s, and the Internet in the 1990s, the emphasis shifted from *written* media to *visual* and *aural* media for both entertainment and information. In schools, the importance of accurate spelling and grammar has given way to encouraging "creativity." For many years, "progressive" educators have believed that forcing students to learn the persnickety rules of writing, spelling, and grammar would hamper their ability to express themselves freely and creatively.

Nothing could be further from the truth. Indeed, without a thorough knowledge and mastery of the rules underlying any discipline, creativity is impossible. And in no other discipline but writing in English are the underlying principles of that discipline so thoroughly ignored.

For example, physicians aren't allowed to do surgery "creatively"; they need to have a detailed knowledge of the various parts of the human body and how those parts all work together. Architects and engineers don't design buildings and bridges without learning the basic, persnickety principles of construction and materials. Nobody in these professions believes that mastering the basic rules of anatomy and the tensile strength of materials will hamper professionals' "creativity."

Quite the opposite: mastery of the basics is the essential ingredient for creativity. And yet, many school systems have decided that budding writers can produce creative work without a thorough grounding in the basic rules of English grammar, spelling, and syntax.

The result of this flawed educational philosophy, plus the move away from print toward visual and aural media, has been several generations of students—not all students, for sure, but far too many—who, when they write, often can't spell, who don't know the fine points of grammar, and who, contrary to the educators' expectations, can't clearly express themselves in print, much less create great written work.

From the point of view of professional and business communication, all this would be unfortunate but not disastrous if professional communication had also moved away from written to visual and aural media. In fact, quite the opposite has occurred. The Internet and visual media may have helped to kill good writing, but the Internet and visual media have also made clear and accurate written communication in business and professional life more important than ever.

As a company vice-president has noted, "One of the most amazing features of the information revolution is that the momentum has turned back to the written word." And the need for clear written communication is true not just for business but for virtually all the professions. As one analyst has written, "Engineers tell us that they spend 20 to 40 per cent of their work time writing memos, letters, emails, reports, and proposals." So, even if our schools—not all but many—no longer emphasize correct and clear writing, this kind of writing is not just expected but demanded in the world of work communication.

OUR COMMUNICATION SAYS SOMETHING ABOUT US

Not only is good written and spoken communication as important as it ever was but, as noted in the Preface, how well you communicate reflects heavily on *you*, as an individual, company, or organization.

For example, a company website may be visually pleasing. But if the page is riddled with grammatical errors that company will lose credibility with potential customers and, therefore, sales as well. For example, look at the following web-page advertisement for a car-rental company (the company name has been changed to protect the grammar-challenged):

Thank you for asking XXX Car Rentals to quote for your car rental requirements. We are pleased to say XXX Car Rentals has invested many man-hours, in gearing our whole rental operation to work for our customers. We pride ourselves on the high level of customer service we achieve, we are also sure you will find us good value for money.

At XXX Car Rentals we are aware that car rental can be a stressful time for the best of us, that's why we have made our service very easy to use. In fact we call it hassle free. So allowing you to start enjoying your holiday the moment you drive off in your rental car, or even getting to that all important business meeting faster. If you need to cancel your trip for any reason, XXX Car Rental will refund your money back in full, with no penalties. We are sure once you have tried our service; you will be delighted and will never look back.

Think of all the extras you are getting with XXX Car Rental, and when comparing quotes from other rental agencies, check that they include all that we offer, at no additional cost to you.

The advertisement is riddled with small grammar and wording errors. Later in this chapter, you will be asked, as an exercise, to find the errors and correct them to produce the advertisement as it should have been written.

For now, ask yourself this question: would you feel confident renting a car from this company? If XXX Car Rental can't get the small details of its web advertising right, will it get the details of car rental and auto mechanics right? Perhaps the company is superb at renting top-quality, perfectly running cars in a timely fashion. That doesn't matter if poor writing undermines the company's credibility with the firm's target audience—the people (usually literate) who can afford to rent a car for a holiday or business trip.

So our communication, in business, in the professions, in government, even just with work colleagues and friends, tells our audience a great deal about us. If we care about the details of our communication, probably we'll care about the details of our work as well. Therefore, to show ourselves in the best possible light, we need to write well and accurately.

And, in business and the professions, we *do* most definitely want to show ourselves in the best possible light. Why? If for no other reason, the financial success of the business or profession we work in—and therefore our livelihood—depends on the confidence clients and customers place in us.

Reputation is hugely important in business and the professions, in part because large sums of money are often involved, in part because much of business and professional communication is *persuasive*: we are trying to persuade someone or some group to perform an action we desire.

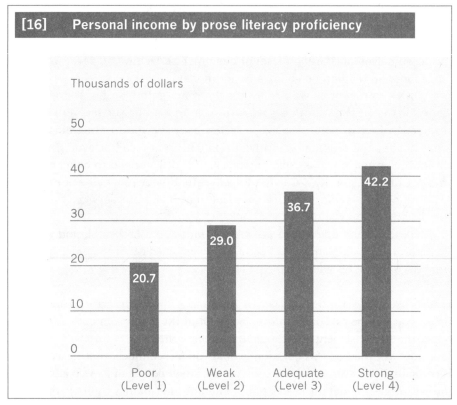

Figure I.1 Prose Literacy and Personal Income
Source: Adapted from TD Bank Financial Group, *Literacy Matters: A Call for Action* (Toronto: Toronto Dominion Financial Group, 2006), 12.

We want our audience to buy something from us, sign a contract with us, vote for us, agree to an action we desire. Because most people's first impulse is to resist this kind of persuasion, we need every tool at our disposal if we want to succeed. One of those tools is excellent communication.

There are added benefits to learning to write well—a higher income and increased chances of finding a job.

A report by the TD Bank on literacy notes that those with high literacy skills earn, on average, $42,239 a year, based on 2003 figures from Statistics Canada. This is *double* the $20, 692 average income of those with poor literacy skills (see Figure I.1).[1]

The report also observes that those with strong literacy skills are more likely to find a job than those who don't write well (see Figure I.2).

---

1   TD Bank Financial Group, *Literacy Matters: A Call for Action* (Toronto: Toronto Dominion Financial Group, 2006), 12. This report can be found using the search terms "Brant Skills Centre," "Literacy matters," and "2012." Figures in the TD report were taken from Statistics Canada data.

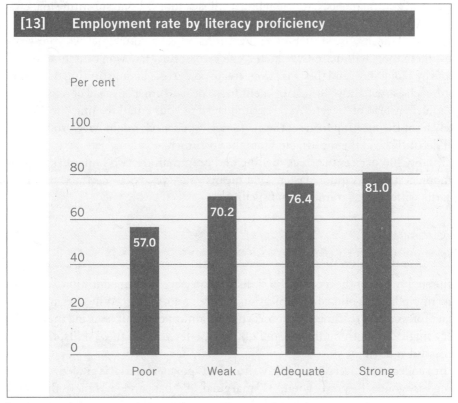

Figure I.2 Literacy and Employment Rate

Source: Adapted from TD Bank Financial Group, *Literacy Matters: A Call for Action* (Toronto: Toronto Dominion Financial Group, 2006), 11.

THERE ARE NO SHORTCUTS TO GOOD WRITING

In the past, top business executives and professionals didn't need to write well or correctly—they had staff to do that. Today, thanks to computer word processing, even executives and CEOs now need to do at least some of their own writing and proofreading.

These communications might be emails to a superior or to employees, letters to clients, or reports to higher management or to a client. Writing errors in any of these documents might make the recipient wonder about your or your company's basic competence.

Ah, you might say, but computers have spellcheck and grammar check. Unfortunately, although useful tools, spellcheck and grammar check won't catch errors such as the following: "We where gang to the stair for a battle of milch." All of these words are spelled correctly; they're just the wrong words, so spellcheck won't catch them. And grammar check, too, is at best a fallback tool—it's no substitute for actually knowing good grammar.

So, by all means, use spellcheck and grammar check to double-check your writing—these tools will definitely catch some errors. But they won't catch all of the errors by a long shot, and they may even create new errors by substituting the wrong word, such as "defiantly" instead of "definitely," or "costumer" instead of "customer," or "grate" instead of "greet." As a result, instead of your email reading "I will definitely be at the meeting to greet the customer," spellcheck might have produced "I will defiantly be at the meeting to grate the costumer."

Totally, 100 per cent correct spelling and grammar are two human skills that computers still can't quite master. That means you—yes, you—need to know how to write with perfect grammar and spelling.

WHAT WE WILL LEARN

Quite simply, one of the most useful skills you can learn in your education, whatever your discipline, is good communication, written and spoken. Why? Regardless of what profession you ultimately choose, you will almost certainly be using these skills every single day, both on the job and off. The better you use these skills, the more successful you will be.

In a college or university setting, written and spoken material is graded, with "A" being very good, "B" pretty good, "C" marginal, "D" bad, and "F" fail. In the world of business and the professions, however, there are no Bs, Cs, and Ds. In the work world, anything less than an "A"—and preferably an "A+"—is an "F." It's something to think about. Communication is one of the constants of business and professional life, and it's in your interest to make all of your communication as close to perfect as possible.

In *Business and Professional Writing: A Basic Guide*, we'll be looking at the following topics in this order:

- **Plain language** (also called plain English): making your writing as clear, concise, concrete and specific, and coherent as possible.
- **The seven Cs** of good professional writing: writing prose that is clear, concise, concrete and specific, complete, courteous, coherent, and constructive.
- **The eighth C**, correct: using proper grammar, the foundation of good writing.
- **Copy-editing**: putting the finishing touches on your written work so it's perfect.
- **Document design**: making your written material as attractive to readers as possible.

- **Business and professional correspondence**: using various letter formats and conventions, with an emphasis on persuasive letters and "bad-news letters"—letters that tell clients or customers that you can't do what they are asking while keeping their good will. (Unless you choose a line of work that involves almost no writing at all you *will* be writing letters.)
- **Job-search letters and résumés**: writing effective cover letters and résumés. These are among the most important documents you will ever write, as they might (or, if poorly done, won't) land you the job of your dreams.
- **Promotional materials**: producing brochures and news releases (chances are very good you *will* be writing a news release or two in your working life, so this is worth knowing) and writing for social networking sites such as Facebook and Twitter.
- **Public speaking**: making an effective oral presentation—chances are very good that, at some point in your career (and maybe quite often), you will need to speak in public.
- **Group tasks**: giving group talks and taking minutes.
- **Informal reports**: structuring and writing these indispensable tools of business and professional life—luckily, this lesson is relatively easy to learn.
- **Formal reports**: producing these significant documents, just in case a report-writing task comes your way.

And, throughout the book, in the text boxes, you'll find various tips and tricks to improve your communication.

This book aims to give you the basic written and verbal skills you need to walk into any professional job and succeed, at least as far as written and spoken communication is concerned.

In the next chapter, we'll look at one particular and vitally important feature of good business and professional communication: plain English.

Exercise

Rewrite the car rental ad below, fixing the grammatical errors and making the ad more concise and direct. Can you identify the grammatical problems by name? One possible answer is in the Appendix, page 391, but don't peek until you've done the exercise.

Thank you for asking XXX Car Rentals to quote for your car rental requirements. We are pleased to say XXX Car Rentals has invested many man-hours, in gearing our whole rental operation to work for our customers. We pride ourselves on the high level of customer service we achieve, we are also sure you will find us good value for money.

At XXX Car Rentals we are aware that car rental can be a stressful time for the best of us, that's why we have made our service very easy to use. In fact we call it hassle free. So allowing you to start enjoying your holiday the moment you drive off in your rental car, or even getting to that all important business meeting faster. If you need to cancel your trip for any reason, XXX Car Rental will refund your money back in full, with no penalties. We are sure once you have tried our service; you will be delighted and will never look back.

Think of all the extras you are getting with XXX Car Rental, and when comparing quotes from other rental agencies, check that they include all that we offer, at no additional cost to you.

Part I
The Basics of Strong Writing

In Part I you will learn about

- The difference between professional writing and academic writing,
- The seven Cs of good writing,
- The importance of correct grammar, and
- The importance of accurate copy-editing.

Chapter 1
Plain Language

In this chapter you will learn about

- The difference between academic and business writing and
- The importance of writing in plain language.

BUSINESS COMMUNICATION VERSUS ACADEMIC WRITING

The Preface briefly discussed the formats we will learn in this book—correspondence, report formats, and the like—but also the importance of good writing within each format. If the writing in a report, say, is inferior, that report will fail no matter how well it's formatted. So in Chapters 1 and 2 we'll discuss how to develop strong writing, and Chapter 3 will be all about grammar.

To be a good communicator in business and the professions, you may have to unlearn some of the techniques that might have made you a good academic writer. Here is what you are likely to find in good academic writing.

- The information is often highly complex.
- The language is often highly specialized.
- Sentences tend to be long and complex, in keeping with the complex subject matter.
- Paragraphs are long enough to explore each complex idea deeply.
- The style is formal—it avoids "I" and "you," although "we" is sometimes acceptable, and it doesn't use contractions (e.g., you will write "does not" instead of "doesn't").

- Academic citation and works-cited styles, like APA, MLA, or other academic formats, are highly detailed and strictly followed.
- Grammar rules are strictly followed (e.g., the "Oxford" comma is preferred, colons are used after full sentences and before lists, and so on. We'll discuss these rules in Chapter 3.).

Most professional, non-academic writing, on the other hand, is very different.

- Ideas are expressed as simply and concisely as possible.
- Specialized words and jargon are avoided if possible (it's not always possible, and specialized language may be necessary for some audiences).
- Sentences have one main idea, with perhaps one or at most two supporting ideas.
- Paragraphs are short—four to eight lines would be typical.
- The style is more informal than in academic writing; first ("I," "me," "we"), second ("you"), and third person ("he," "her," "they," etc.) are all allowed, as are contractions ("don't" rather than "do not" is acceptable).
- Grammar rules are (slightly!) relaxed (for example, sentence fragments are sometimes allowed for rhetorical effect, but in moderation, comma use is not rigid, and so on).

Academic and business writing styles are different because they have different audiences. The academic writer and reader is a specialist in a particular discipline, and specialized language is part of that discipline. The audience for a business or professional document is more often a generalist one, and this audience calls for a less specialized vocabulary and less complex set of concepts.

But, more importantly, the business or professional audience doesn't want to spend a lot of time figuring out what the wording in a particular report or memo is trying to say—time is money! The meaning of professional writing should be immediately clear, unlike academic writing, which is sometimes obscure.

On the page, too, academic writing looks different from business and professional writing. An academic essay or published article may consist of page after page of print, in long, grey paragraphs, perhaps broken by the occasional picture, chart, or diagram. As a *visual* experience, an academic essay can be hard going; however, the hard going is, the academic writer hopes, rewarded by the essay's stimulating intellectual content. That said, academic writing in some disciplines is moving toward a plainer style!

A business or professional document aims to be much more attractive, visually speaking. That means using white space, lists, pictures, charts and graphics, headings and subheadings, and many other techniques for easy readability that we will be discussing below in this chapter on plain language and in Chapter 5 on document design.

PLAIN LANGUAGE

Business, legal, government, and professional writing can, over time, sink into a morass of technical jargon and convoluted syntax that is almost unintelligible to the general public. In other words, this writing has become the communication of experts for other experts. This bureaucratese wouldn't be a problem if these documents didn't have to be read by non-experts, but that is often not the case.

For example, legal documents such as contracts, mortgages, and wills need to be both read and understood by people who aren't lawyers. Government communications often contain important information about laws and regulations on everything from legal business practices to the size and type of pipe fittings in a new house. If the business owners and tradespeople who have to follow building regulations, for example, can't understand the regulations—and they often can't—then there's a problem.

In short, hard-to-read texts cause more

- misunderstandings
- errors
- complaints
- enquiries
- staff time lost to problem solving.[1]

Therefore, many businesses and governments around the world are moving to put their communications into what is called plain language or plain English.

Features of Plain Language

What is plain English? It has a number of features:

- It uses *concrete and specific examples* rather than abstractions to be as clear as possible.

---

1 Plain Language Online Training Program, "Introducing Plain Language," *PlainTrain*, http://www.lisibilite.net/PlainTrain/IntroducingPlainLanguage.html. The *PlainTrain* website is an excellent resource on plain language and its application. The British passport office and Royal Mail examples come from an article at www.plainenglish.co.uk entitled "Chrissie speaks out for women in plain English."

Worth Knowing
The British passport office found that 52 per cent of passport applicants couldn't complete the form properly. When the form was rewritten in plain English, 97 per cent of applicants were able to fill it out correctly, for a saving of 370,000 hours of administration time per year. Similarly, the UK's Royal Mail used mail-forwarding forms that had an 87 per cent error rate among users and cost £10,000 a week for corrections. When the forms were rewritten the error rate fell and the Royal Mail saved £500,000 in only nine months.

Additional Resources
The following websites offer useful information on plain language:

1. US federal government writing guidelines: http://www.plainlanguage.gov/index.cfm

2. *PlainTrain*, a website teaching plain language: http://www.lisibilite.net/PlainTrain/Digest.html

3. George Orwell's essay "Politics and the English Language" on the need for plain language: https://biblio.wiki/wiki/Politics/Politics_and_the_English_Language

4. Centre for Literacy: http://www.centreforliteracy.qc.ca/node/188

- *It avoids unfamiliar words and technical jargon.* For example, it prefers "know" to the jargonistic "fully cognizant."
- It uses *active rather than passive verbs* for clarity, directness, and conciseness. Active verbs use fewer words: "The man ate the sandwich" (five words) versus "The sandwich was eaten by the man" (seven words).
- *It avoids wordy expressions* ("in order to do business" = "to do business"; "at the present time" = "now").
- *It avoids repetitiveness* ("please return my stapler back to me" = "please return my stapler").
- *It avoids nominalizations*—verbs used as nouns. So, instead of "He gave an introduction to the next speaker," you would write "He introduced the next speaker." In the first example sentence, "introduction" is a nominalization. Chapter 2 has more on nominalizations.

Plain language also aims to make text as easy to read as possible by

- using *white space* to make documents more readable;
- making *document-design elements easy to read*;
- using *headings and well-labelled graphics*, if appropriate; and
- using *easy-to-read lists, tables, and indexes* whenever possible.

In the next section we'll look at examples of how plain language can make communication clearer.

Examples of Plain Language

The government of British Columbia has for several years been rewriting cumbersomely worded and sometimes incomprehensible legislation into language the average person can understand. The result? The government saves time and money because civil servants don't have to field so many calls and letters asking what the laws and regulations mean.

Here's how the BC government described this effort:

Why is it important to use plain language? . . . It is more efficient, more effective, and leads to better public relations. Less time is needed to find and understand the information, less time is needed to deal with people who did not understand the information, and fewer errors are made.

Plain language

- Improves compliance, which reduces enforcement costs.
- Expresses thoughts clearly, which reduces the likelihood of a legal challenge.
- Responds to the needs of the audience—people don't feel their time is unnecessarily wasted.
- Ultimately reduces costs for the public.[2]

The United States's government's website on plain language states the benefits of plain language as follows:

- fewer calls from customers (by about 80%),
- less time for users to solve a problem (about half the time),
- fewer errors by customers (from 40% to 20%), and
- higher rates of compliance with government regulations (more than twice as high).[3]

For example, a 1992 Canadian Security Intelligence Service (CSIS) report originally read like this:

> Economic espionage may be defined as the illegal or clandestine acquisition of critical Canadian economic information and technology by foreign governments or their surrogates.

Here is this sentence rewritten in plain English:

> Economic espionage means foreign governments or their agents illegally obtaining critical Canadian economic and technological secrets.[4]

Here is another example, from a last will and testament. The first version is in legalese; the second version is in plain language.[5] Which is easier to understand?

---

2 Government of British Columbia, "Key elements of plain language." This URL is no longer accessible, but it has been quoted in this presentation: Minnesota Hospital Association. *Plain Language Emergency Overhead Paging: Implementation Toolkit* (St. Paul, MN: Minnesota Hospital Association, November 2011), 22.

3 See Plain Language Action and Information Network (PLAIN). *"Plain Language: The Bottom Line," Plain Language.gov: Improving Communication from the Federal Government to the Public.*

4 Plain Language Online Training Program, "Using appropriate words," *PlainTrain.*

5 Adapted slightly from David C. Elliott, "Writing Wills in Plain Language" (paper, Canadian Bar Association, Alberta Branch, Wills and Trusts Section, June 1990).

Version 1

> (d) if my spouse should predecease me or should survive me but die within a period of thirty days after my death:
>
> (i) subject to the rights under the *Exemptions Act*, to pay out of the capital of my general estate my legally enforceable debts, funeral and all expenses in connection with the administration of my estate and the trusts created by my Will charging first the residue, then specific bequests, then devises. My Trustee shall also pay all estate, income, inheritance and succession duties or taxes whether imposed by Alberta or Canadian law or by any other jurisdiction that may be payable in connection with any property passing or deemed to pass by any governing law on my death or in connection with any insurance of my life or any gift or benefit given or created by my Will conferred by me either during my lifetime or by survivorship or by this Will and whether such duties or taxes be payable in respect of estates or interests which fall into possession at my death or at any subsequent time. Such payments shall be made at such time and in such manner and subject to such security as my Trustee in my Trustee's discretion determines.

Version 2

> If Mary dies before or within 30 days after I do, I want John to
>
> (a) pay out of the capital of my general estate
>
> > (i)   my legally enforceable debts,
> > (ii)   my funeral expenses,
> > (iii) the expenses incurred in administering my estate,
> > (iv)   the trusts created by this Will (charging first the residue, then specific bequests, then devises) and
>
> (b) pay any tax or duties which my estate is liable to pay.

Businesses, too, are finding that contracts and documents in plain English save them time and money and their customers and clients time and hassle. For example, an insurance company announcement used to read as follows:

We have recently implemented an enhancement to our computer system that will enable us to provide better service to our valued customers. This has resulted in a slight delay in the processing of your renewal. The difference you will notice is in the payment schedule. Your annual policy premium has been divided over 11 (eleven) months, and as a result your monthly payment will have increased due to the reduced number of monthly instalments.

Here it is in plain language:

We are a little late in sending your renewal documents because we have made a change in our computer system in order to provide better service. Your annual premium will now be divided over 11 months instead of 12, so the monthly payment will increase slightly.[6]

The first sentence of the announcement could be even more concise: "Your renewal documents are slightly delayed because we have changed our computer system to provide better service." In this example, we have removed a nominalization: from "made a change" to "changed."

> **Quick Tip**
> If your reader has to read what you've written more than once to get the meaning, it's not plain language.

As you can see, in all cases the plain language version is both more concise and much more readable. All of these elements of plain language—both the writing and the presentation—should be part of any business or professional communicator's toolkit. How to employ this toolkit is discussed further in Chapter 2 on the seven Cs.

Meanwhile, here's a rule of thumb for plain language: If your reader has to read what you've written more than once to get the meaning, it's not plain language.

---

6 Plain Language Association International, "Samples of Plain Language rewrites and organizational change," http://www.plainlanguagenetwork.org/Samples.

Exercises

1. Look at the example of the will, above. What are the key differences between the original will and the rewritten version? (See page 393 for the answer.)

2. Rewrite the following paragraphs into plain English.[7] Rewritten versions are available in "Appendix: Answers," page 393, but don't peek until you've tried the exercise.

   a. When in the process of freeing a vehicle that has been stuck results in ruts or holes, the operator will fill the rut or hole created by such activity before removing the vehicle from the immediate area.

   b. After notification of NMFS, this final rule requires all CA/OR DGN vessel operators to have attended one Skipper Education Workshop after all workshops have been convened by NMFS in September 1997. CA/OR DGN vessel operators are required to attend Skipper Education Workshops at annual intervals thereafter, unless that requirement is waived by NMFS. NMFS will provide sufficient advance notice to vessel operators by mail prior to convening workshops.

   c. Investigators at the contractor will review the facts in your case and decide the most appropriate course of action. The first step taken with most Medicare health care providers is to re-educate them about Medicare regulations and policies. If the practice continues, the contractor may conduct special audits of the provider's medical records. Often, the contractor recovers overpayments to health care providers this way. If there is sufficient evidence to show that the provider is consistently violating Medicare policies, the contractor will document the violations and ask the Office of the Inspector General to prosecute the case. This can lead to expulsion from the Medicare program, civil monetary penalties, and imprisonment.

---

7 These examples come from *PlainLanguage.gov*. See Plain Language Action and Information Network (PLAIN). "Before-and-After Comparisons," *Plain Language.gov: Improving Communication from the Federal Government to the Public*, https://www.plainlanguage.gov/examples/before-and-after/.

Chapter 2
The Seven Cs of Good Professional Communication

In this chapter you will learn to

- Write clearly,
- Write concisely,
- Write concretely and specifically,
- Write completely (include all necessary information),
- Write with courtesy (including gender neutrality),
- Write coherently,
- Write constructively,
- Identify four types of sentence structure,
- Join sentences correctly for variety, and
- Use punctuation correctly.

INTRODUCTION

The eight Cs are a checklist of the qualities of good professional and business communication that you should apply to your writing. They are another, more detailed way of approaching plain English.

In this chapter we will look at seven of the eight Cs: how to write in a way that is

1. clear,
2. concise,
3. concrete and specific,

4. complete,
5. courteous,
6. coherent, and
7. constructive.

The eighth C, grammatically correct, is discussed in Chapter 3. One thing to notice from the start: the Cs overlap. Writing that is clear is also coherent and concrete and specific, and vice versa. The rest of this chapter describes the seven Cs in detail.[1]

1. CLEAR

Another word for "clear" is "transparent." Good writing is transparent: the audience never, ever, has to go back over a sentence or paragraph to puzzle out what the writer meant because the material is always clearly and logically (i.e., coherently) presented (see "Coherent" below). How do we do this? There are six basic ways:

  I. Avoid jargon and technical or obscure words.
  II. Make your writing concrete and specific.
  III. Use active rather than passive verbs.
  IV. Avoid long strings of prepositional phrases ("word salads").
  V. Make pronoun references crystal clear.
  VI. Avoid dangling and misplaced modifiers.

I. Avoid Jargon and Technical or Obscure Words

Do you know what "alembic" means? Probably not, and few readers will have this word in their vocabulary. Yet "alembic" appears in the novel *Charlie Johnson in the Flames*, a thriller written for general readers by academic and former Canadian politician Michael Ignatieff. "Alembic" refers to the tube between two retorts in a chemistry experiment, although Ignatieff was using the word in a more metaphorical sense.

How about "eponymous," a word that occasionally appears in writing for the general public? Is "eponymous" part of most readers' vocabularies? Likely not. An eponymous hero is one whose name is also the title of a work, such as *Anne of Green Gables*.

There was a time when parents and teachers would say, "Look it up in the dictionary" if you asked the meaning of a word. However, as popular culture moves away

---

1 Much of the material in this chapter is adapted from *APT to Do Anything: Workplace Communication,* 2014, by Norma Depledge, Claire McKenzie, and Paul MacRae, a course pack prepared for business-communication classes at the University of Victoria.

from print toward visual media, many readers of today have smaller vocabularies than their better-educated grandparents, and business and professional writers today must accept this limitation. Most readers don't want to consult the dictionary every few paragraphs just because a fancy word (like "alembic" or "eponymous") makes the writer appear intelligent.

As for jargon, technical terms, and the like, if you must use them then you must also define them, unless you are sure your audience is completely familiar with these terms. Never assume your readers know what an unusual word means—chances are, they don't. Keep it simple.

II. Make Your Writing Concrete and Specific

No writing technique is more powerful than being concrete and specific. For example, look at this sentence:

Federal MP George Smith made an exciting speech in Parliament yesterday.

What does this tell us, concretely and specifically, about Smith's speech? Nothing. We don't even know what he was speaking about.

If Smith made an exciting speech, then the writer should be concrete and specific about what Smith said and what made his speech exciting. How about this:

Slamming his fist on his desk, face red with outrage, MP George Smith accused the government of covering up allegations that Afghani prisoners of Canadian forces were abused while in custody.

There's more on concrete and specific writing in Section 3 of this chapter. Meanwhile, note that the more concrete and specific a piece of writing is, the clearer it is as well.

III. Use Active Verbs

Active verbs have *the subject* of the sentence *doing the action*, as in "The rabbit [subject] ate [action] five carrots [object]." Passive verbs have the *doer of the action* as the *object* of the sentence: "Five carrots [subject] were eaten [action] by the rabbit [object, but doer of the action]."

The "natural" or default order for English sentence structure is doer (subject) and what he/she/it did (verb), then the object (what the rabbit ate, in this example). So, the *natural* order for an English sentence uses an *active* verb.

Note that the active verb structure also uses fewer words than the passive structure (which includes added words, usually a form of the verb "to be"). In the carrot example above, the active sentence has five words; the passive sentence has seven. Active verbs are, therefore, not only clearer than passive verbs but also more concise.

> **Worth Remembering**
> The "natural" order of an English sentence is
>
> **Subject + Verb + Object.**

In karate training, students are told that their fists must be tightly clenched when they throw a punch; if the fist isn't tight, the bones of the hand will break. The same is true of writing: tight, concise writing is punchy, powerful writing. That means most of your verbs should be active except when

- *you want to introduce variety in sentence structure*;
- *the doer of the action isn't precisely known* (e.g., "Three people were admitted to hospital yesterday with severe burns"); and
- *the doer of the action isn't as important as the action itself* (e.g., "Interest rates were raised half a point yesterday").

While we're on the subject of active verbs, your verbs should also be active in the sense of colourful, exciting, and appealing to the senses whenever possible. "He ate the orange" is correct as a sentence, but "ate" is a pretty boring verb. How about "He

> **Worth Remembering**
> Active verbs really should be "active"!

devoured the orange"? Or "He munched the orange with gusto"? Similarly, "He drank his glass of cola quickly" is ho-hum. Better: "He gulped down his glass of cola."

If you can find a more colourful form of a familiar verb, while keeping it active, your writing will be stronger and more interesting. That said, don't go so overboard on description that you end up with the kind of purple prose found in, for example, Harlequin romances and bad adventure novels.

IV. Avoid Strings of Prepositional Phrases (the "Word Salad")

Prepositions are short (usually) linking words, such as "in," "on," "with," "over," and so on, that begin a prepositional phrase. The following sentence has four prepositional phrases (in italics with prepositions underlined):

The results *of the chemistry tests of the students at the University of Toronto* were excellent.

Any sentence with a long string of prepositional phrases could be called a word salad; the sentence's meaning gets buried in a jumble of unnecessary words.

The sentence can be rewritten to reduce the number of prepositional phrases from four to two:

Student chemistry test results *at the University of Toronto* were excellent.

That's 11 words instead of 16 (and therefore also more concise); it's also easier to understand (clear). Note that most prepositional phrases can be turned into words that function as adjectives (by modifying or describing nouns). In the example above, instead of "the results *of the tests*," you can write "the test results."

However, be careful you don't create a word-salad string of adjectives (or of nouns modifying other nouns) instead. If the example sentence had been rewritten as "The University of Toronto student chemistry test results were excellent," you'd have a word salad of modifiers (they are underlined) before the subject (which is "results"). In general, more than three modifiers before the noun they modify creates an adjectival word salad, and you need to reintroduce a prepositional phrase or two.

Incidentally, not all prepositional phrases can be shortened. For example, "University of Toronto" shouldn't be reduced to "Toronto University" because "University of Toronto" is the institution's proper name.

V. Make Pronoun References Crystal Clear

Look at this sentence: "The *manager* asked her *executive assistant* to finish the report before *she* left for the day." To whom does the pronoun "she" refer? Is the report needed before the *manager* leaves for the day, or before the *executive assistant* leaves for the day? The sentence's meaning is not clear because the pronoun reference "she" is not clear.

Pronouns are place-keeper words; they stand in for (the Latin "*pro*" means "for") a noun. As such, they are generic but often very convenient. For example, "it" could refer to literally any single thing, from a nation to an atom. "They" could refer to literally any number of things (as long as that number is more than one), from the three people in a musical trio to all the soldiers in a nation's army. And so on.

As a writer, you must make sure that, if you use a pronoun as a place keeper, readers never, ever have to puzzle about who or what that pronoun refers to. If in doubt, repeat the noun: "The manager asked her *executive assistant* to finish the report before the *assistant* left for the day." The grammar language term for this problem, by the way, is unclear pronoun reference.

Similarly, what's wrong with the following sentence? "Each cabinet minister must be responsible for the security of their briefcase." This construction is used so often that it's come to be considered correct grammar by many people—but not by everyone.

Those who reject this usage, called the singular "they," argue that the pronoun ("their") is plural, but the noun the pronoun refers to ("minister") is singular. In grammar language, this problem is called faulty noun-pronoun number agreement, abbreviated as NPNA.

The rule is that pronouns must always agree in number—singular or plural—with the nouns they refer to. Advocates of the singular "they" argue that the phrasing is natural to English speakers and that it makes sense to use it where attempts to avoid it would make your sentence needlessly complicated. That said, because some consider the singular "they" unprofessional, you may want to avoid it altogether in professional contexts.

What about this fix? "Each cabinet minister must be responsible for the security of *his* briefcase." It's got the correct pronoun number, but many cabinet ministers these days are women, so using "he" is not gender neutral (something we'll discuss in detail in the "Courteous" section).

To avoid using the singular "they," you have three options:

- *make the noun plural* ("Cabinet *ministers* must be responsible for the security of *their* briefcases"),
- *make the pronoun singular* ("Each cabinet *minister* must be responsible for the security of *his or her* briefcase"), or
- *take out the pronoun entirely* ("Briefcase security is every cabinet minister's responsibility").

VI. Avoid Dangling and Misplaced Modifiers

A dangling modifier is a word or phrase that modifies (gives additional information about) a subject that doesn't exist in the sentence, as in "Flying into Vancouver, the mountains were beautiful." As written, the sentence implies it is the mountains that are flying into Vancouver!

What the sentence intends to mean is that "we" thought the mountains were beautiful as we flew into Vancouver, but it's missing the "we," the subject, who is "flying into Vancouver." The fix for a dangling modifier is to add the proper subject, a noun that could be in an airplane admiring the view: "Flying into Vancouver, *we/ Simon/the passengers* thought the mountains were beautiful."

A misplaced modifier is a word or phrase that, because it is poorly placed in the sentence, appears to modify the wrong noun.

An example: "I have a treaty signed by Napoleon *in my office*." Obviously, because he's long dead, Napoleon didn't sign the treaty in the speaker's office (unless it's an office from the early 1800s, when Napoleon was alive, which is unlikely). Therefore, "in my office" is a misplaced modifier.

To avoid sounding ridiculous, the sentence should read, "*In my office*, I have a treaty signed by Napoleon" or "I have *in my office* a treaty signed by Napoleon." The fix for a misplaced modifier is to move it closer to, and preferably next to, the noun or pronoun it actually modifies.

Dangling and misplaced modifiers are often amusing, and sometimes laugh-out-loud funny ("I came across a family of raccoons in my pyjamas"). But in a business or professional context, a misplaced or dangling modifier may not be so funny, and it *will* cost you credibility if you're trying to be serious.

Review
....

Clear writing

   i. avoids jargon and unfamiliar words,
   ii. is concrete and specific,
  iii. uses active verbs,
  iv. avoids strings of prepositional phrases,
   v. makes pronoun references clear, and
  vi. avoids dangling and misplaced modifiers.

2. CONCISE

Conciseness and clarity go together. The more concise a piece of writing, the more likely it is to be clear. Wordy writing is also less powerful (punchy) than tight writing. The following guidelines (some the same as for clear writing) will make your prose more concise:

   I. Use active verbs.
  II. Avoid the verb "to be" whenever possible.
 III. Don't turn verbs into nouns ("nominalizations").
 IV. Avoid long strings of prepositions (those "word salads" again).
  V. Avoid repetition and redundancy.

I. Use Active Verbs

We discussed using active verbs in "1. Clear," Section III. Using active verbs also helps you avoid "to be" verbs, as discussed in the next section.

II. Avoid the Verb "To Be" Whenever Possible ("isy's")

"To be" is a weak verb form, in part because it indicates a state of being rather than action. In other words, "to be" verbs are static rather than dynamic, passive rather than active. And they are often unnecessary.

"To be" verbs can be called "isy's," and they are found in the passive forms of verbs. Make the verb active and the isy's usually disappear. Presto! A more concise sentence.

Look at this sentence:

The meeting *is* going *to be* attended by students in the economics faculty next week.

This sentence has two "isy's": "is" and "to be." How about this: "Economics students *will attend* the meeting next week." On the conciseness index, that's eight words compared to 15, one "isy" ("will") instead of two.

That said, even active sentences can fall into the "isy" trap, as in "The gardener *is* of the opinion that we should prune the roses." Better: "The gardener *thinks* we should prune the roses." That's eight words instead of 12. The wordy construction in this example, by the way, is called a "nominalization"—which means a verb (or other part of speech) turned into a noun—and how to avoid nominalizations is discussed in the next section.

"To be" verbs are sometimes called "helping verbs" or "auxiliary verbs" because they help change the tense of a verb from, say, present to past or present to future, and so on. For example, "I went" is past tense because I did that at some time in the past. "I am going" is present progressive tense: I am going right now. "I was going" is the past progressive tense.

The helping verbs, including "to be" and "to have," are used to create gradations in time, so they can't and shouldn't be eliminated when they are doing this job. These verbs should, however, be used only when necessary.

"To be" constructions such as "there is," "there are," and "it is" can also almost always be trimmed. "*There are* five ducks in the pond" = "Five ducks *are* in the pond." Even better: "Five ducks *splashed* in the pond" (a more dynamic active verb).

Similarly, "*It is* easy to jump rope" is less concise and punchy than "Jumping rope *is* easy." Sometimes, however, "there is," "there are," and "it is" are unavoidable, as in, "There are five ways to peel an apple."

That said, if you see the phrase "there is," "there are," "it is," or anything similar at the start of a sentence, consider eliminating it to increase conciseness and clarity.

And while we're on "there is" and "there are," you should be aware that "there" is never the subject of a sentence. "There" is a place-keeper word; it is a generic pronoun representing a noun, and that noun, not "there," is the subject of the sentence.

For example, in "There *are* five ducks in the pond," the subject of the sentence is "ducks," plural. So the verb after "there" must be "are," plural.

> **Worth Remembering**
> Sentences beginning with "it is," "there is," and "there are" can almost always be rewritten to eliminate the "isy's." Note, however, that, for some audiences, a writer might use the occasional "isy" to create a conversational style. (See if you can find a few of these in this section.)

If the sentence reads "There *is* a duck in the pond," the subject of the sentence is "duck," singular, and the verb is also singular.

III. Don't Turn Verbs into Nouns (Nominalizations)

Nominalizations occur when you use a verb or other part of speech as a noun, and they have the effect of making your sentences less concise. They often involve "isy's"—the "to be" helping verbs that you usually want to avoid if possible. Nominalizations weaken your writing.

Here's an example: "The teacher *made the comment* that the class was sleepy." "The comment" is the noun form of the verb "comment." So why not cut to the chase and use the verb alone for a much more concise and punchy sentence? "The teacher *commented* that the class was sleepy." That's eight words instead of ten.

Another example: "Morgan asked the managers *to make a decision* about the new sales strategy." More concise: "Morgan asked the managers *to decide* on a new sales strategy."

Incidentally, there's a nominalization (italicized below) in the first sentence of this section: "They *have the effect* of making your sentences less concise." How about this: "They *make* your sentences less concise." Same meaning, but in six words instead of ten!

IV. Avoid Long Strings of Prepositional Phrases ("Word Salads")

We discussed avoiding prepositional word salads in "1. Clear," Section IV.

V. Avoid Repetition, Redundancy, and GWS

One of the most overused and unnecessary phrases in the English language is "in order to," as in "*In order to* finish this job, we need to work overtime." How about the simpler "*To* finish this job, we need to work overtime"?

The second sentence means exactly the same thing, and you've gotten rid of two words—"in order"—that do no useful work whatsoever.

Other wordy phrases you don't need are "due to" (= "because"), "the fact that" (= "because"), and many others. So, "*Due to the fact that* we were hungry, we ate" becomes the much more concise "*Because* we were hungry, we ate."

Similarly, do you really need to "join together" something? Doesn't "join" imply putting together? Can you "return back" an unwanted purchase? Or would "return" alone do?

If the cat was "coloured brown," do we need to say "coloured"? Isn't "brown" by definition a colour? "*The use of* photos and graphics made the website very attractive"—do we need to say "The use of"? Why not the more concise "Photos and graphics made the website very attractive"?

A variation of redundancy is "goes without saying," or GWS. GWS refers to words, phrases, or sentences that are so obvious they don't need to be said.

Here is an example of GWS: "Pictures and graphics make the website attractive *for the viewer.*" If the website is attractive, that implies a viewer, so you don't need to say "viewer."

Important Exception
Do repeat a word if you need to make a pronoun reference clear. Here's the example from "1. Clear," Section V, on unclear pronoun reference: "The manager asked her executive assistant to finish the report before *she* left for the day." To whom does "she" refer? In this case, repetition of the noun is necessary: "The manager asked her executive assistant to finish the report before the *assistant* left for the day."

Similarly, "In addition, the website is free of jargon, *allowing the average reader to clearly understand the information presented.*" If the website is free of jargon, then it's GWS that the average reader can clearly understand the information.

So, keep an eye out for words that do no work (i.e., are redundant or repetitious or GWS) and—unless you are using the longer construction for rhetorical effect—eliminate them for more concise, punchier writing.

Review

Concise writing

    i. uses active verbs,
   ii. avoids "to be" and similar constructions,
  iii. avoids nominalizations,
  iv. avoids long strings of prepositions, and
   v. avoids repetition and redundancy.

3. CONCRETE AND SPECIFIC

Concrete words appeal to the senses—they describe things we can see or hear or feel or smell or touch, thereby painting a vivid mental picture (e.g., "sports car" as opposed to "transportation"). Specific words are more limited and defined than more general terms (e.g., "Aston Martin DB5" as opposed to "sports car"). Your writing should be concrete and specific whenever possible.

For example, "This is a lot of fun!" doesn't tell us anything—"this" could be a million activities that are fun. "Riding a zip line in the rainforest is a lot of fun!" allows us to *see* the activity. Why? The description is concrete.

And we can make the description more specific, too. Where is the rainforest? What sort of feeling do we mean by "a lot of fun"? Better: "Riding a zip line in the Ecuadorian rainforest is exhilarating."

Another example: "small town" isn't very specific. The mental picture of a "small town" in Canada will be different from the mental picture of a "small town" in, say, China, so "small town" by itself really doesn't tell us anything useful. "A rural Prairie town of 2,000 people" is specific—you've now defined and limited the term "small town." This version is also more concrete—it creates more of a mental picture.

How old is an "old man"? For a 20-year-old, 50 seems "old." For a 50-year-old, 70 seems "old." For someone in his 70s, 90 is "old." The phrase "old man" doesn't mean much unless you make it more specific: "a 60-year-old man."

Concrete and specific go together, and, as the painter Salvador Dalí put it, "We are all hungry and thirsty for concrete images." If you examine your own reactions to writing and speech, you will discover this is true. The communication most of us prefer—that we are "hungry and thirsty for"—is filled with concrete and specific detail.

So "The fire was huge" doesn't appeal to the senses as much as "Towers of flame rose 20 metres above the treetops, throwing off vast billows of smoke and ash." The first sentence presents an abstract idea of the fire (huge); the second appeals to the senses by being concrete and specific. It creates a vivid mental picture.

Another example: "On long car trips with my parents, I spent most of my time reading comics" isn't as concrete or specific as "On long car trips with my parents, I spent most of my time with Archie and Jughead." Written the second way, the reader should get an instant mental picture of the comic book characters, not just an image of a generic comic book.

How about this one: "He boarded the aircraft." An "aircraft" could be anything from a fighter jet to a passenger liner. "He boarded the stretch Boeing 737" gives a more specific and vivid mental picture of the plane (assuming you know what a Boeing 737 looks like).

"Nitrogen is the most common gas in Earth's atmosphere" doesn't give us as much information as "At 78 per cent of the air by volume, nitrogen is the most common gas in the Earth's atmosphere."

Here are the first three paragraphs of the novel *Damascus Gate* by Robert Stone. Note how Stone uses concrete and specific detail to create a mental picture of a morning in Jerusalem that seems utterly *real*.

> **Worth Thinking About**
>
> A celebrated historian, essayist, and orator of the nineteenth century, Thomas B. Macaulay (1800–59) was famous for being concrete and specific in his written descriptions and speeches. Biographer John Clive gives an example of Macaulay's concrete and specific style, comparing it to a more abstract presentation of the same idea from journalist Sir James Mackintosh (1765–1832).
>
> In praising the Industrial Revolution, Mackintosh describes this progress as "All the marvellous works of industry and science."
>
> Macaulay makes the same point, but much more vividly, using concrete and specific language:
>
> *Our fields are cultivated with a skill unknown elsewhere, with a skill which has extorted rich harvests from moors and morasses. Our houses are filled with conveniences which the kings of former times might have envied. Our bridges, our canals, our roads, our modes of communication, fill every stranger with wonder.*

THAT MORNING Lucas was awakened by bells, sounding across the Shoulder of Hinnom from the Church of the Dormition. At first light there had been a muezzin's call in Silwan, insisting that prayer was better than sleep. The city was well supplied with divine services.

He climbed out of bed and went into the kitchen to brew Turkish coffee. As he stood at the window drinking it, the first train of the day rattled past, bound over the hills for Tel Aviv. It was a slow, decorous colonial train, five cars of nearly empty coaches with dusty windows. Its diminishing rhythms made him aware of his own solitude.

When the train was gone, he saw the old man who lived in one of the Ottoman houses beside the tracks watering a crop of kale in the early morning shade. The kale was deep green and fleshy against the limestone rubble from which it somehow grew. The old man wore a black peaked cap. He had high cheekbones and a ruddy face like a Slavic peasant's. The sight of him made Lucas imagine vast summer fields along which trains ran, long lines of gray boxcars against a far horizon.[2]

You probably won't need this level of concrete and specific detail in your business writing. But in all your writing you should remember that humans are sensory beings first, thinking beings second. Most of us are more interested in concrete, specific description that appeals to the senses than in abstract, intellectualized generalizations that appeal only to the mind.

Review

Concrete and specific writing

  i. uses concrete terms that appeal to the senses and
 ii. uses terms that are limited and defined.

4. COMPLETE

In writing for the news media, the classic news "lead" paragraph answers most or all of the following six questions: who, what, where, when, why, and sometimes how (the "Five Ws plus H"). In other words, the lead paragraph is complete, or almost. It gives readers all the necessary information about what to expect; they aren't left wondering what the piece is about. If they have any unanswered questions (and they usually do), a complete lead paragraph promises that all questions will be answered as the reader goes along.

The same is true of professional communication. Writing or speaking that leaves readers wanting more information is not complete. Communication that isn't complete wastes everyone's time because the reader has to ask supplementary questions and the writer has to answer them. It just makes sense to put all the necessary information in your writing right from the start. Incidentally, complete communication is also clearer communication.

Suppose your company sends out this memo: "The finance committee will meet at 10 a.m." What's missing here?

Well, for a start, the memo doesn't say where the committee is meeting, nor is the date of the meeting clear. Now, in practice, everyone may know the finance committee always meets in Room 232 at 10 a.m. on Tuesdays. But, just to be complete

---

2 Robert Stone, *Damascus Gate* (New York: Houghton Mifflin, 1998), 3.

(and therefore absolutely clear), the memo should read "The finance committee will meet in Room 232 at 10 a.m. on Tuesday, Nov. 18."

How about this sentence: "The majority of Dell shareholders voted to merge with Apple Computer." What's the first question the CEO of Dell is going to ask when she receives this news?—"What kind of majority?" If 90 per cent of shareholders voted for the merger, that indicates strong support. If only 51 per cent voted for the merger, then the shareholders are badly split on this move. The original sentence is not complete—it doesn't give all the information that the CEO of Dell would want.

Or how about this sentence: "Some of our delivery trucks have faulty brake mechanisms." The first question the boss would ask is, "How many of the trucks?" One or two? Half the fleet of 20 trucks? The missing detail hides the difference between a minor inconvenience for the company and a serious delivery problem.

So, in all of your communication, whether professional or not, whether written (letters, emails, reports) or spoken, aim to include *all* the necessary information. In other words, be complete.

Review

Complete writing answers all of the six basic questions:

    i. Who?
   ii. What?
  iii. Where?
   iv. When?
    v. Why?
   vi. How?

5. COURTEOUS

Courteous communication, as one of the seven Cs, is about being polite in the social sense ("yes, Sir," "thank you very much," that sort of thing). But courteous in the context of business and professional writing is much more than that. Writing courteously means following these guidelines:

    I. Be gender neutral.
   II. Put the audience first ("you" rather than "we").
  III. Be tactful.
   IV. Follow the traditional forms of courtesy.
    V. Use a reader-friendly format.

Let's look at these five in detail.

i. Be Gender Neutral

Good writing today is gender neutral, but even fairly recently that wasn't always the case. In the not-so-distant past, university anthropology courses were sometimes called "The Study of Man" or "The Study of Mankind." Similarly, a professional-communications textbook used to be called *Technically Write: Communication for the Technical Man*. The text is now entitled *Technically Write*, period.

The person who ran a meeting used to be the "chairman" or "chairwoman"; today that will usually be written as "chair" or "chairperson." Of course, if the gender of the chairperson is known, then "chairman" or "chairwoman" is acceptable. But "chair" or the slightly more awkward "chairperson" is now preferred in almost all cases as the most gender-neutral title.

In other words, given that humanity includes more than just men, communicators must be courteous and inclusive in their writing and speech.

Avoiding this mistake can be tricky for writers in some situations:

"A good military officer never forgets his duty to the nation."

Until a few decades ago, military officers (and most other professionals) were almost invariably male. Today, in this more enlightened age, military officers, cabinet ministers, company officers, postal workers, police officers, doctors, nurses, firefighters, and even heavy-construction workers can be either gender.

Therefore—and just to repeat what we studied in being clear—you are better to rewrite the military duty sentence (and all others of its kind) in one of four ways:

1. *Use "his or her"*: "A good *officer* never forgets *his or her* duty to the nation." However, this solution often sounds awkward (it certainly does in this example).
2. *Make the singular noun plural*: "Good *officers* never forget *their* duty to the nation." In most cases, this solution is best.
3. *Take the gender reference out entirely*: "An *officer* never forgets the importance of duty to the nation."
4. *Use the singular "they"*: "A good *officer* never forgets *their* duty to the nation." This choice is grammatically controversial and is considered an error by many readers, so it is probably best to avoid in professional writing.

Another acceptable way to get gender balance without the awkward "he or she" or "he/she" construction ("he/she" is not yet fully accepted in formal writing but is becoming increasingly common) is to alternate "she" and "he" in your text, as you will sometimes find in this book.

For people whose genders don't match "she/her" or "he/him" pronoun sets, "they/them" is the most common choice of pronouns, but others (such as "zie/hir" and "ev/em") exist. It is courteous to use the specific pronoun set a given individual uses. This book takes the position that until common business- and professional-writing usage embraces these de-gendered terms, or a form of them, they should be used with restraint in other contexts.

II. Put the Audience First—"You" not "We"

Courteous, in the business-communication sense, also means *focusing all of your attention on the client or customer.* To say, "*We will send* your shipment of pencils to arrive on November 25" puts the emphasis on "we," the company's agents, rather than the customer. A "you" or customer-centred letter would read: "*You will receive* your shipment of pencils on November 25."

Another example: "*We have scheduled* your appointment for August 3 at 2 p.m." This is a more "you"-centred sentence: "*Your appointment* is scheduled for August 3 at 2 p.m." "*You* did fine work today" is more "you" oriented than "*We* really appreciate the fine work you did today."

Whenever possible (and it often isn't possible, of course, but when it is), keep the "we" out of your professional communication and focus on "you"—the client, customer, or audience.

That said, there are times when you want to put the emphasis on "we" rather than "you."

Here's a "you" message that is not courteous: "*You* forgot to include your cheque with your order, so we can't send you the merchandise." It suggests blame and is bound to get the customer's back up. In this case, you should use the "we" form: "*We* will be happy to send the merchandise when we receive your cheque."

It's the same message—we didn't get your cheque—but stated in a more courteous, positive, and tactful way, without implying or outright stating the customer did something wrong. It's possible the customer did send the cheque! Accounting may have lost it, or perhaps the postal system delivered the letter to the wrong address. So to avoid blaming or angering the client, focus the message on "we" rather than "you." In most other cases, put the other person ("you") first.

III. Be Tactful

Part of putting the audience first is being tactful, which means considering the other person's feelings. If you have a negative message to deliver, find the most courteous and tactful way of expressing it.

We do this all the time in social life. "How do you like my new hat?" Instead of "It makes you look like a drunken moose," you say, "Um, it's lovely, although perhaps a more neutral colour would better complement your skin tone."

Instead of criticizing an employee directly—"You were incredibly rude to that customer"—the supervisor might shift the focus to the company and its policies: "We try to be courteous to even the most difficult customer." In this case, the boss should use the "we" approach to avoid openly suggesting blame.

Have you ever thanked a sales person and been told, "No problem!" The implication here is that you *could* have been a problem—which, when you think about it, isn't very tactful or polite. A more courteous and tactful response is a simple "You're very welcome" or "It was a pleasure serving you."

IV. Follow the Traditional Forms of Courtesy

Courteous also, of course, means courteous in the traditionally accepted sense of polite and respectful, avoiding the use of coarse language and the like. For example, business letters invariably begin "Dear Sir:" or "Dear Ms. Okimora:" or something similar, and they end with "Yours sincerely," or "Yours truly," or something similar. These traditional forms of greeting and closing are part of courtesy in professional communication. Chapter 5 on document design discusses the traditional forms of courtesy used in a business letter.

V. Make Formats Reader Friendly

A major part of being courteous is writing and speaking clearly, coherently, and concisely—to do so is reader friendly, i.e., courteous. In other words, all of the seven Cs are courteous because they make communication clear, more concise, and so on and therefore easier to read.

It is also courteous, in the reader-friendly sense, to format documents so they are easy to read and understand. You'll find details on creating reader-friendly, and therefore courteous, documents in Chapter 5.

These five types of courtesy might seem like small things, but they add up and make it more likely that your customer or client or audience will respond positively to your communication.

Review

Courteous writing

  i. is gender neutral,
 ii. is "you" or audience centred,
iii. is tactful,
 iv. follows the traditional forms of courtesy, and
  v. is reader friendly.

6. COHERENT

Coherent writing is writing that hangs together—the order of the words and the argument make logical sense, and each sentence and paragraph flows easily into the next. How can you make your writing coherent? Follow these guidelines:

I. Construct paragraphs carefully about one topic.
II. Write sentences with one main idea.
III. Use transitional words to unite sentences and paragraphs into a logical and coherent whole.
IV. Be consistent in formatting numbers.
V. Begin lists with the same grammatical construction.

I. Construct Paragraphs Carefully

In all good writing, paragraphs develop one topic, and this topic is clearly signalled by a topic sentence.

Imagine a piece of writing as a train and each paragraph as a boxcar on the train. Boxcars are labelled with what's inside—grain, oil, coal, chemicals, and so on—so that oil and grain, say, aren't put into the same boxcar. Similarly, in business and professional writing, you don't want to put two key ideas in the same paragraph. The topic sentence, usually the first sentence, is the label stating what the paragraph is about. For example, the first sentence of this paragraph is the topic sentence for the paragraph; the topic is that paragraphs are like labelled boxcars.

As mentioned in Chapter 1, in academic writing, paragraphs tend to be long—perhaps ten sentences or even more. There's a topic sentence with the main idea of the paragraph, but there can be many supporting subtopics and examples in an academic paragraph.

In business writing, if you've got a paragraph like that—long, with lots of ideas and examples—then you should break that long paragraph down into two or more shorter paragraphs. The topic sentence for the first, shortened paragraph will serve as the topic sentence for the shorter, following paragraphs as well.

II. Write Sentences that Express One Main Idea

Just as paragraphs develop one topic, signalled by the topic sentence, so business sentences also present one idea within that topic—they don't veer off into tangled webs of related ideas as academic sentences sometimes do.

This doesn't mean that business sentences are all short, as in "I went for a walk on the beach. I saw a dog. The dog was black and white. It was chasing sticks in the water." A series of short, simple sentences like this would be incredibly boring.

Sentence variety is important (see Chapter 3 for ways to create sentence variety). But within that variety, each sentence develops one *main* idea, not two or three.

Here's a sentence that has too many ideas:

> Miriam Parker was planning to write about her recent trip to Beijing, where she saw many examples of Chinese painting through the centuries, examples that, she felt, reflected the changing social conditions in China over time.

This sentence would be acceptable in academic writing, but there are two ideas here:

1. Ms. Parker planning to write about her trip to Beijing to look at Chinese art and
2. her observations about how Chinese art reflected historical periods in China.

For business-writing purposes, we should break the longer sentence into two sentences, reflecting two ideas:

> Miriam Parker was planning to write about her recent trip to Beijing, where she saw many examples of Chinese painting through the centuries. These paintings, she felt, reflected the changing social conditions in China over time.

Worth Considering
Give your sentences the "breath" test. If you can't read the sentence in one breath, it's too long.

In other words, for business and professional writing, aim for several short sentences, with one idea per sentence (with variety of sentence structure!), rather than long, complex, rambling sentences.

III. Use Transitional Words to Unite Sentences and Paragraphs

Transitional words are the glue that joins sentences and paragraphs into a pleasing, logical, and coherent unity. Here's a paragraph without transitions:

> Our company's sales have gone down 30 per cent. Our cash flow situation has become critical. This loss of profits could threaten our company's future. We need to take action to prevent bankruptcy. We need to work harder to get sales. We need to cut our production costs.

As you can see, the writing is choppy and, although it makes its point, could be more coherent. We get this coherence by adding transitions (in italics):

> *In the past month*, our company's sales have gone down 30 per cent. *As a result*, our cash flow situation has become critical. *Worse*, this loss of revenue could even threaten our company's future. *Therefore*, we need to take action

to prevent bankruptcy, *including* working harder to get sales and cutting our production costs.

Sentences, too, need transitions, for example: "Jorge spent 12 hours last night watching a *Big Bang Theory* marathon. He failed his English exam." We can, sort of, see the connection between these two sentences, but basically they are not coherent.

The fix? Add a transition: "Jorge spent 12 hours last night watching a *Big Bang Theory* marathon. *Therefore*, he failed his English exam." "Therefore" is a transitional word showing causality, which is discussed just below.

In other words ("in other words," incidentally, is a transitional phrase), coherent writing needs transitions linking its sentences and paragraphs.

Transitions can be classified into seven logical types: *illustration*, *addition*, *contrast*, *similarity*, *causation*, *showing time*, and *showing space*.

- *Illustration* transitions are words and phrases such as "for example," "first of all," "such as," and so on. Illustration transitions show how X is an example of or similar to Y.
- *Addition* transitions are words and phrases such as "also," "furthermore," "secondly," "in addition," and so on. Addition transitions show how X and Y are linked or add something to each other.
- *Contrast* transitions are words and phrases such as "although," "however," "on the contrary," "on the one hand...on the other hand," and so on. Contrast transitions highlight how X is different from Y.
- *Similarity* transitions are words and phrases such as "in the same way," "similarly," "just as," and so on. Similarity transitions highlight how X is similar to Y.
- *Causation* transitions are words and phrases such as "because," "consequently," "as a result," "therefore," and so on. Causation transitions show that X caused Y or Y resulted from X.
- Transitions *showing time* include "after," "later," "while," "since then," and so on. Time transitions highlight how X and Y are related in time.
- Finally, transitions *showing space* include "above," "in front of," "next to," and so on. Space transitions emphasize how X and Y are related in space.

Exercise: Identifying Transitions

The example paragraph above about a company's poor sales, which is reprinted below, uses several types of transitions. For example, "in the past month" is a transition showing time. Can you identify the types of transitions for the other bolded words or phrases in the example? You'll find the answers in the Appendix, page 393.

In the past month, our company's sales have gone down 30 per cent. **As a result**, our cash flow situation has become critical. **Worse**, this loss of revenue could even threaten our company's future. **Therefore**, we need to take action to prevent bankruptcy, **including** working harder to get sales and cutting our production costs.

IV. Formatting Numbers

A big part of coherence is consistency—doing the same thing in the same way throughout a written document, whether it's the writing or the page layout. When the elements on a page are consistent, readers know what to expect and sense your writing has been carefully thought out.

So, for example, you may decide to use the American spelling for words like "honor," "armor," and "color." In that case, all your "-or" words should use that style. If you've opted for British/Canadian spelling—"honour," "armour," and "colour"—you should stick to that spelling style throughout the document. If your verbs are mostly in the past tense ("he said"), then don't switch into the present tense ("he says") without a good reason.

With coherence in mind, we need consistent guidelines on the use of numbers. For example, do you spell numbers out (four, thirty-six) or use numerals (4, 36)? This section outlines some widely accepted guidelines for numbers in professional and business writing.

- *Spell out the numbers one to ten; use numerals for numbers 11 and above.* "We ordered four large dinners from takeout." "He has 23 books on loan from the library." Some style guides suggest using numerals for 10 and above and spelling out the single-digit numbers (one to nine), as in "She has 10 cats." Whichever rule you follow—"ten" (the style used in this book) or "10"—be consistent.
- *In general, for technical documents such as engineering, scientific, or economic reports, feel free to break the above rule.* "For this project, you will need 6 two-by-fours and 8 #6 screws."
- *Never start a sentence with a numeral.* Either write the number out or rewrite the sentence to start with some other word. For example, "33 people applied for the job" should be written "Thirty-three people applied for the job." Similarly, "2012 sales figures indicate a sharp decline in the third quarter" should be rewritten "Sales figures for 2012 indicate a sharp decline in the third quarter."

- *Don't start a sentence with a large, written-out number.* "Three thousand two hundred and thirty-four people applied for the job" follows the previous rule (never start a sentence with a number in figures) but is hard to read. In this case it's better to recast the sentence so the number isn't at the beginning: "The job attracted 3,234 applicants." Highly technical, number-intensive documents, e.g., engineering reports, can be an exception to this rule.
- *Spell out numbers that aren't precise figures.* "I've told you a thousand times not to exaggerate." "He always has a hundred projects on the go." In addition, you would usually spell out numbers before terms such as "dozen," "hundred," and "thousand": "We ordered four dozen eggs." "He has four hundred chickens." But for more complex or large, precise numbers, use numerals: "The battalion ate 325 dozen eggs while on manoeuvres." That said, this rule is flexible depending on what looks reasonable in context.
- *Use figures for currency.* "I had only $4 in the bank." "The Smiths spent $360,000 renovating their new house." Non-precise numbers in the millions and higher are usually expressed by a mixture of numerals and spelled out numbers: "Canadian civil servants spent $3 million on lattes last year." Currency figures in the thousands and above can be clearer if you use a hyphen, although this is an option for business writing depending on an organization's style. Why a hyphen? If a line ends with $3 and the next line begins "million," the reader might first assume the cost is only $3. The hyphen signals that the figure is more than $3. Note that if the number is not a money unit, you should spell out the number if it is ten or below, unless it is a decimal fraction: "Canada sent three million cases of milk to Zimbabwe" but "Canada sent 3.5 million cases of milk to Zimbabwe."

  For large numbers, million and trillion are usually spelled out—"The government spent $3.2 million on plastic figurines"—unless an exact figure is needed: $3,256,383.
- *Use numerals for ages, years, dates, percentages, and addresses.* "My son, aged 5, won the race." "This man is 73 years old." "Millie lives at 12 Elderberry Street." "I was born in 1974." "The range was from 2 to 6 per cent." Use hyphens if the number is part of a compound adjective (see Chapter 3 on grammar): "The 73-year-old man retired after 50 years as a carpenter."
- *Use decimals if fractions are hard to read in print.* "The shed is 3.25 metres wide" rather than "The shed is 3¼-metres wide." Most word processors will automatically convert, say, 1/4 into ¼, and in most cases the numeral is readable, so this rule is flexible.

V. Begin Lists with the Same Grammatical Construction

As part of coherent communication, all items in a list must have the same grammatical structure. That is, all items must begin with a noun, a verb, an adjective, a participle, or some other part of speech. Another word for this type of coherence is parallelism.

Why parallelism? Even if readers aren't grammarians, they can sense when coherence is missing; the list just seems wonky, somehow. Also, not using parallel structure often creates a break in logic or at least a shift in focus. If nothing else, parallelism in lists is a sign of elegant, carefully thought-out writing.

For example, is the following list parallel?

When using your colouring book and crayons,

- *stay* within the lines,
- *don't break* the crayons, and
- *colours* should be vivid.

> **Worth Noting**
> Lists that form a complete sentence end with a period or other appropriate punctuation. Always.

This list isn't parallel because the first two bulleted items begin with a verb ("stay" and "don't break"), and the third begins with a noun ("colours"). This lack of parallel structure creates an illogical and grammatically incorrect sentence: the noun "colours" can't be "using your colouring book"—that's a dangling modifier (see "1. Clear," above). The list is parallel if written this way:

When using your colouring book and crayons,

- *stay* within the lines,
- *don't break* the crayons, and
- *choose* only vivid colours.

In this case, the first word in each item is a verb (although the verb "break" has the negative "don't" initially), the subject of the sentence (which is implied by the three commands but not stated) is "you," and the items all have the same grammatical structure.

To start your list with nouns, say, write it this way (although it's clumsier than the verb version):

When you use your colouring book and crayons,

- *colours* shouldn't cross the lines;
- *crayons* should be handled carefully, so they don't break; and
- *vivid colours* should be preferred. [In this case, the first part of the list item is still a noun, even if it has an adjective, "vivid," as well.]

Review

Coherent writing

    i. has one idea per paragraph,
    ii. has one idea per sentence,
    iii. uses transitions to create a logical whole,
    iv. is consistent in its use of numbers, and
    v. begins lists with the same grammatical element.

7. CONSTRUCTIVE

The seventh of the Cs is constructive. Constructive writing avoids unnecessary negativity. In your professional writing, whenever possible, you want to emphasize the positive, not the negative. You want to put forward what you *can* do, not what you *can't* do. Similarly, you want to tell customers and clients what they *can* do, not what they *can't* do.

For example, a sign outside an apartment building reads: NO CHILDREN, NO PETS. This building sounds pretty unwelcoming, doesn't it? But suppose the sign is rewritten to read: "This building welcomes adults without pets." Oh, you think, if I'm an adult and I don't own a pet, I'd be welcome here. It conveys the same message as the first sign, but without the negative connotation. It is, in other words, constructive.

> **Worth Remembering**
> Never, ever (unless absolutely unavoidable) say what you *can't* do; say what you *can* do.

How about this: NO SMOKING. We see a lot of this wording because it is direct, even blunt: it says, "We don't want you smoking." And fair enough. A lot of people are bothered by second-hand smoke.

THANK YOU FOR
OBSERVING OUR
NO SMOKING
POLICY

But if you are running, say, a hotel, and you want to emphasize the positive to keep your guests' good will (remember, some of your clients will be smokers), a better notice is this: "All of our rooms are smoke free." Similarly, the sign to the right (on the previous page), which thanks customers, is more constructive than the one on the left, which issues an order.

If you operate a delivery company, do you really want to present this negative image to your customers: "We do not offer next-day delivery"? It's far better to advertise what you can do: "We can deliver your package within two days." Or, if the delivery is running late, don't tell the customer "Sorry, but your package won't arrive until Wednesday." Say, "Your package will be delivered on Wednesday!"

Constructive writing also avoids words such as "sorry," "regretfully," "unfortu-nately," and the like. These negative words all imply that you have either failed or cannot offer a service customers might like, even if what you *do* offer is excellent.

For example, you'll often hear this negative wording in automated phone mes-sages: "We're sorry, but all our operators are busy." Haven't you often thought, "Well, if you were *really* sorry, you'd have more operators!"

In the same way, you may have been passed over by a bus with a sign saying, "Sorry, this bus is out of service." Again, haven't you thought, "If you were *really* sorry, you'd pick me up and I wouldn't have to wait another 15 minutes."

These "sorry" messages remind you of what the company *can't* do for you: provide a telephone operator when you want one or offer a bus that picks you up when you need a ride. Surely it's better for the com-pany to say, much more honestly (because, again, if it was truly sorry it would hire more staff or put on more buses) what it *can* do: "All our operators are busy. We will be with you as soon as possible." Or just, "This bus is out of service."

Have you ever had someone say to you, "Sorry for putting you to all this hassle." The message is that helping that person was an arduous chore that would have been better avoided. He could have said, instead, "I really appreciated your help." The tone is much more positive and much more welcome: you are being thanked sincerely.

Figure 2.1 Sorry? Really?

Similarly, in discussing courteous communication, we mentioned the case of thank-ing a sales person and being told, "No problem!" This form, although very common and intended to be polite, is neither courteous nor constructive. The courteous and constructive response is, again, "You're welcome!" or "It was a pleasure serving you."

Constructive is also used in the sense of "constructive criticism," which means criticism that identifies problems and proposes solutions rather than blindly judging, blaming, or condemning.

Saying to someone "You are a terrible writer" or "Your handling of the Higgins account was dreadful" doesn't help that person to become a better writer or account manager. The criticism is not constructive. Constructive criticism would be something such as this: "If you used fewer passive verbs, your writing would be stronger" or "Spending more time with Higgins will give you a better idea of what he is looking for." In both cases, you tell the person what *can* be done to improve.

Just to repeat, here is the basic rule for constructive communication: Say what you *can* do, not what you *can't*.

Sometimes You Have to Say "Sorry"

Being constructive—avoiding words such as "unfortunately" and the like—doesn't mean that you shouldn't apologize if you have genuinely made a mistake. For example, in 2008 Michael McCain was the president of Maple Leaf Foods, a Toronto-based meat-packing company that was the source of an outbreak of listeriosis that killed 22 Canadians.

McCain was upfront about his company's role in the outbreak, rather than trying to minimize the responsibility or cover it up. McCain said, "It's our best efforts that failed, not the regulators or the Canadian food safety system. I emphasize: this is our accountability and it's ours to fix, which we are taking on fully. We have and we continue to improve on our action plans." With this admission, Maple Leaf Foods was able to restore some of its good reputation.

When a company or individual genuinely makes a mistake, the best course of action—the most constructive course of action!—is to admit the mistake, take responsibility, and vow to do better next time.

Review

Constructive writing

  i. emphasizes the positive,
  ii. states what you can do, not what you can't do,
  iii. avoids negative words such as "unfortunately," "sorry," and the like,
  iv. focuses on how to improve when delivering criticism, and
  v. says sorry when necessary!

CONCLUSION

Good business and professional writing is clear, concise, concrete and specific, complete, courteous, and constructive. Although we've summed these up as the "seven Cs," in fact, these seven principles overlap quite a bit. A sentence that is not complete will also be less clear, coherent, and courteous. In Chapter 3, we'll look at the eighth—and perhaps most important—C, grammatically correct.

Meanwhile, here is a checklist of the seven Cs to consult before sending your writing out into the world:

1. Clear Writing

    i. avoids jargon and technical or obscure words,
    ii. is concrete and specific,
    iii. uses active rather than passive verbs,
    iv. avoids long strings of prepositional phrases ("word salads"),
    v. makes pronoun references crystal clear, and
    vi. avoids dangling and misplaced modifiers.

2. Concise Writing

    i. uses active verbs,
    ii. avoids the verb "to be" (and similar constructions) whenever possible,
    iii. avoids turning verbs (and adjectives and adverbs) into nouns ("nominalizations"),
    iv. avoids long strings of prepositions (those "word salads" again), and
    v. avoids repetition and redundancy.

3. Concrete and Specific Writing

    i. uses concrete terms that appeal to the senses ("horse" rather than "transportation") and
    ii. limits and defines terms by using specific words ("Clydesdale" rather than "horse").

4. Complete Writing

answers all reasonable questions, including who, what, where, when, why, and how.

5. Courteous Writing

   i. is gender neutral,

   ii. puts the audience first ("you" rather than "we" or "I"),

   iii. is tactful,

   iv. follows the traditional forms of courtesy ("Dear Sir" and the like), and

   v. uses a reader-friendly format.

6. Coherent Writing

   i. constructs paragraphs carefully around one topic,

   ii. has sentences with one main idea,

   iii. uses transitional words to unite sentences and paragraphs into a logical and coherent whole,

   iv. is consistent in formatting numbers and in spelling, and

   v. makes list items parallel in grammatical structure.

7. Constructive Writing

   i. emphasizes the positive,

   ii. states what you can do, not what you can't do,

   iii. avoids negative words such as "unfortunately," "sorry," and the like,

   iv. focuses on how to improve when delivering criticism, and

   v. says sorry when necessary.

On the next page, you'll find a quiz on the seven Cs.

Quiz on the Seven Cs

The sentences below contain errors in terms of the seven Cs. That is, they may not be clear, concise, concrete and specific, complete, courteous, coherent, or constructive. Find the errors and correct them. If you can explain why the sentence is wrong, that's even better. The answers are on page 393 in the Appendix at the end of the book, but don't peek until you've tried the quiz on your own.

1. She decided to evaluate the program, which would take five months.
2. The entrance exam was failed by two-thirds of the applicants.
3. We will re-evaluate our marketing strategy after the new chairman is hired.
4. There is a steady flow of people crossing back and forth across the road while the cars are waiting in lines up to 300 metres.
5. A fair percentage of the company's tool-and-die stampers have developed mechanical problems.
6. If you can't use the new iPod, please return it back to me.
7. Checkout procedures at the Luxor Hotel chain are especially designed for the businessman in a hurry.
8. In order to provide a mechanism by which customers may air their problems concerning product quality, the company has established the following procedure for registering grievances for all purchasers.
9. There was a traffic accident at Bay and Main streets yesterday.
10. Belleville, Ontario, is a small city.
11. Children under 42 inches tall cannot go on this ride.
12. Many English majors are skilled at reading and writing; however, commerce majors enjoy impressive salaries after graduation.
13. Your speech shouldn't be too long.
14. The owner's manual for your new Excelsior clock radio is enclosed herein to assist you in utilizing all the convenient and useful features of your new device.
15. The debate between the prime minister and his political opponent was about the merits of sweater vests.
16. We are pleased to inform you that we have selected you for an interview for the sales associate position.
17. Alicia's pet fish died yesterday. She went shopping.
18. Unfortunately, your order of plastic marmot figurines cannot be delivered before August 14.
19. He distributed annual reports to the audience bound in red and green covers.
20. A new photocopier is needed by the employees in our office.

Chapter 3
The Eighth C: Learning Grammar Language

In this chapter you will learn to

- Understand the importance of correct grammar,
- Identify the eight parts of speech,
- Understand sentence structure,
- Identify three types of clauses,
- Identify four ways of joining clauses, and
- Use punctuation correctly.

INTRODUCTION

Anyone taking a course in business and professional communication should already be a grammatically correct writer—correctness is the eighth C, and all the Cs are essential for good communication. But just to review: Why is grammar so important?

The short answer is that grammar makes communication clearer. Consider the following well-known example of bad grammar: "The panda eats, roots, shoots, and leaves." Is this what the writer was trying to convey—a panda that munches something, then roots around in the ground, shoots at something, and finally departs?

The writer was trying to describe the panda's diet: "The panda eats roots, shoots, and leaves." But the writer broke a simple grammatical rule, and therefore the sentence lost its clarity. What grammatical rule? *Never put one comma between a subject and its verb or between a verb and its object.*

In the panda example, there's a single comma between the verb "eats" and the sentence object, "roots, shoots, and leaves."

The sentence would be awkward but still make sense if it read: "The panda eats, *slowly and carefully*, roots, shoots, and leaves." In this case, there are *two commas* between the verb and the object— the commas enclose the adverbial phrase "slowly and carefully." (One function of an adverb is to add additional information to—or modify—a sentence's verb.)

The adverbial phrase is enclosed in two commas because it is an "interrupting" phrase—"slowly and carefully," as positioned here, interrupts the typical order of the sentence: "The panda [subject] eats [verb] roots, shoots, and leaves [object]." (For more on these "interrupters," including non-essential or non-restrictive clauses, phrases, and words, see the section on "Relative Causes.")

There is another reason, apart from clarity, for business and technical writers to be perfect grammarians: as we've said before, like all your writing, your grammar reflects on you and your credibility. Sloppy grammar implies a sloppy person, even if you are actually very neat and tidy. Impeccable grammar implies that the writer is conscientious, detail oriented, and credible, all qualities highly valued in business and the professions (and, indeed, almost everywhere).

Therefore, for those who need a refresher on grammar (and almost all of us do), the following sections summarize some of the most important principles of the eighth C of good business and professional (and, really, all) writing: being correct.

GRAMMAR LANGUAGE

To master grammar, you need to know at least some grammar language—the terminology that describes how the English language works.

For example, many students don't know what a "preposition" is or a "subordinate clause" or a "conjunctive adverb." These are part of grammar language. If you are approaching business and professional writing with less than perfect grammar, you need to learn at least some grammar language in order to become perfect.

Why? Imagine you are on a beach, perhaps as a tourist in Mexico. What do you see? Apart from other tourists, you see sand. Ocean. Palm trees. Maybe some shrubs. A few rocks. It's lovely, but you quickly lose interest in the scenery and go back to your novel.

But what would you see if you were a biologist? Biology has a specialized language to describe plants and animals, and, for the biologist, the Mexican beach would be a much more complex place than you, the tourist, see. The biologist could identify the many different types of plants on the beach: what *kind* of palm tree is it? What *kinds* of shrubs? Those small pink flowers—what are they? What kind of seaweed washes up on the beach? What little creatures make those small holes in the sand?

The biologist's experience of the beach is much richer than the tourist's because the biologist has a detailed language for the many natural features of the beach. Therefore, she literally *sees more*. Putting this another way, parts of the beach are *invisible* to the tourist but *visible* to the biologist, thanks to her specialized knowledge and language.

The same could be said of a geologist. The tourist sees sand and rocks. The geologist sees much, much more: the *types* of sand, which point to the possible geological history of this particular beach, the different *kinds* of rocks, and so on. Once again, knowing geology language gives the geologist a much richer experience of the beach than that afforded the tourist with no geological knowledge.

Here's the connection to grammar and grammar language: without a specialized language to analyze and discuss grammar, you will not be able to *see* what makes grammar correct or incorrect. Grammar problems will, in other words, be invisible to you.

Learn some grammar language, however, and suddenly the grammar problems become not just visible but blindingly obvious! And, on an even more positive note, with a command of grammar language you can tell the difference between writing that is just good and writing that is very, very good.

With a command of grammar language, you will be able to read a paragraph and *see* that there is a topic sentence, or not, and that the paragraph sticks to that topic, or doesn't. You will be able to *see* that the sentences are properly constructed, or not. You will be able to *see* whether all of the words are spelled and used correctly and which words are not quite right. You will be able to *see*, rather than guess, whether the punctuation is correct.

In other words, with a command of grammar language, you will find the world of grammar opening up to you—and with it the world of good writing. It's worth learning this language!

Learning grammar language demands hard work at the beginning, just like learning a foreign language (let's say Spanish) is hard work at the beginning. However, over time, with study and practice, speaking Spanish becomes easier until, one day, you no longer have to fumble around to find the right Spanish word for any given situation. Speaking Spanish has become second nature to you. You are fluent in Spanish.

The same is true of grammar language. There's hard work to be done in this chapter, including some memorization of terms. But once you've mastered grammar language, the world of writing will open up to you—good grammar will become "visible."

We've said learning grammar language takes hard work, and it does. But other specialized languages are much harder to master. For example, medical students have to memorize hundreds of terms—the parts of the human body, diseases, drugs, and much more—before they can call themselves physicians. Grammar students don't need to memorize nearly as many terms as an aspiring doctor, and the grammar terms can be put into easy-to-learn lists. Here are the lists in the rest of this chapter:

> **Worth Remembering**
> A young lawyer asked a more experienced lawyer if it was necessary to know Latin to practise law. The older man replied, "No, it's sufficient to have forgotten it." The same is true of grammar. Once the rules of grammar have become second nature, you no longer have to think about them (or, not much); you just apply them. At that point, you can "forget" grammar and just write.

- eight parts of speech,
- three types of clauses,
- four types of conjunctions,
- ten uses for commas,
- two uses for semicolons, and
- four uses for colons.

That's pretty much it. Assuming you have the absolute basics of grammar—verb tenses and the like, which this book doesn't cover—the list above is all you need to know to become perfect at grammar and punctuation.

PARTS OF SPEECH

In the same way that the vast range of Western music, from classical to hip-hop, is made from only seven basic notes—A to G plus their sharps and flats—so all English sentences are made up of only eight basic elements, called the parts of speech: nouns, pronouns, adjectives (including articles), verbs, adverbs, prepositions, conjunctions, and interjections.

> **Worth Remembering**
> Although there are only eight parts of speech, many words function regularly as more than one part of speech. To categorize a word, look at its role or function and its position in a sentence.
>
> "I love a good Book (noun)."
> "Book (verb) him, Danno."
> "She had Book (adjective) knowledge but not street smarts."

If you think of a sentence as the brick for building larger structures, such as paragraphs, then the parts of speech are the clay and straw that go into making the bricks. The eight parts of speech are the following:

1. **Nouns** name a person, place, thing, or idea (girl, city, school, justice). Proper nouns name a particular person, place, thing, or title (Jill Adams, Vancouver, the University of Waterloo, Chief Justice Beverley McLachlin) and are capitalized.

2. **Pronouns** are generic terms—place-keeper words—for nouns. "*Pro*" in Latin means "for." So a pronoun stands in "for" a noun. There are many kinds of pronoun, but here are the most common:
   a. personal pronouns (I and me, we and us, you, he and him, she and her, it, they and them);
   b. possessive pronouns (my and mine, your and yours, their and theirs, its);
   c. demonstrative pronouns (this, that, these, those);
   d. indefinite pronouns (anyone, some, many, most);
   e. relative pronouns (who, whom, whose, what, which, that); and
   f. interrogative pronouns (who, whom, whose).

3. **Adjectives** describe or give additional information about (the grammar-language term is "modify") a noun or pronoun, e.g., *red* car, *elderly* cat, he was *muscular*. **Articles**—*the*, *a*, and *an*—are a special type of adjective.

4. **Verbs** show action: "While Adam *delved* and Eve *span*, who then *played* the gentleman?" as the old saying goes. (The verbs are italicized.) Verbs also show an action of the mind or a state of being: "I *think*, therefore I *am*."

5. **Adverbs** give us additional information about (modify) verbs ("Betty ran *slowly*."); adjectives ("He had an *unexpectedly* cultivated voice."); other adverbs ("Young adults *very* often return to the home country to seek their roots."); or entire clauses ("*Specifically*, we recommend several steps to increase youth employment."). Most (not all) adverbs end in "ly," so it's usually easy to tell them apart from adjectives. But note that "elderly," in the adjective example above, modifies a noun, not a verb, and is therefore an adjective even though it ends in "ly."

   Adverbs answer questions. How? When? Where? Why? Under what conditions? With what result? The adverb in "Betty ran *slowly*" tells us how Betty ran. "We went to the store *yesterday*" has an adverb showing when. "He has gone *away*" has an adverb showing where. And so on.

6. **Prepositions** are short (usually) linking words that express relationships between nouns or pronouns and other words in a sentence. Examples of prepositions are "in," "of," "over," and so on. In the sentence "Sam fell *into* the swimming pool," the preposition is "into." It shows the relation between the noun "pool" and Sam's fall.

Noun	horse
Pronoun	they
Adjective	yellow/the
Verb	run
Adverb	slowly
Preposition	of
Conjunction	and
Interjection	yikes!

So it is "positioned" before ("pre") this noun ("pool") and before any words modifying this noun (in this case, "swimming" and the article "the").

7. **Conjunctions** join words, phrases, clauses, and sentences. There are only four types of conjunctions, so it's easy to remember them: coordinating conjunctions, subordinating conjunctions, conjunctive adverbs, and conjunctive punctuation alone. We'll look at these four types of conjunctions in more detail in the section on clauses and conjunctions determining punctuation.

8. **Interjections** are words such as "oh" and "holy smoke" and "yikes" and "drat" that express emotion. They are not essential to the meaning of the sentence—although they may be essential to the emotional message of the sentence!—and almost always take commas around them. "*Goodness me*, you've grown an inch since the last time I saw you!" "*Darn*, I forgot my keys." An interjection can also stand alone, forming an exclamatory sentence. "Holy guacamole Batman!" "Wow!" Some interjections may be X-rated and therefore not for polite company.

Review

There are only *eight* parts of speech:

1. nouns,
2. pronouns,
3. adjectives (including articles),
4. verbs,
5. adverbs,
6. prepositions,
7. conjunctions, and
8. interjections.

SENTENCES AND CLAUSES

As noted, the basic building block of all writing in English (and in all languages) is the sentence. Strong, correct sentences make for strong, correct paragraphs, and strong, correct paragraphs make for strong, correct articles, reports, letters, essays, and so on.

A full sentence, in English grammar language, has a subject, a verb, and, usually but not always, an object—also called subject and predicate—all coming together to communicate a complete idea. A full sentence is also called a "simple" sentence or an "independent" sentence.

Subject + verb (+ object) + complete idea = complete/full/simple sentence.

"The rain in Spain falls mainly on the plain" is a complete sentence: it has a subject ("rain"), a verb ("falls"), an object ("on the plain"), and offers a complete idea: that most of the rain in Spain falls on that country's plains.

Not all sentences have an object: "He ran" lacks an object, but it still offers a complete idea and is therefore a sentence in good standing. However, in most sentences, "he ran" would be followed by where he ran to ("He ran to the store."). But don't let the length of a sentence confuse you as to whether or not it has an object. Here is a longer sentence without an object: "He ran only occasionally but swiftly."

When sentences are joined with other sentences, however, they take on a new name in grammar language: they are called "clauses." Just as, depending on her role within the family, a "daughter" can also be a "sister," a "niece," a "granddaughter," and so on, a sentence joined to other sentences changes its name to become a clause. The sentence's new name reflects its new role as part of a "family" of clauses coming together to form a complex sentence.

There are basically three types of clauses, which will be explained in detail:

1. independent clauses,
2. subordinate or dependent clauses, and
3. relative clauses.

Do you have trouble with punctuation? If you understand these three types of clauses and how they fit together to make complex sentences, you will solve 90 per cent of your punctuation problems, and most grammar problems as well. What could be easier? So let's look at these three types of clauses in more detail.

1. Independent Clauses

Independent clauses are full sentences, e.g., "The rain in Spain falls mainly on the plain," that have been joined with other sentences (now also clauses) to make a more complex structure.

"*The rain in Spain falls mainly on the plain,* <u>but</u> *it's still too dry here,* <u>and</u> *I wish it rained more*" has three independent clauses (each in italics) in the same sentence. Every grammatically correct sentence must have at least one independent clause. The independent clause is the anchor of any sentence.

Note that a sentence can have two or more independent clauses; the example above has three. In this case, in grammar language, the independent clauses are joined by "coordinating conjunctions," discussed in the section "Conjunctions." In the example sentence, the underlined words "but" and "and" are coordinating conjunctions that join the three independent clauses.

> **Worth Remembering**
> Every grammatically correct sentence must contain at least one independent clause. The independent clause is the "anchor" of the sentence.

2. Subordinate or Dependent Clauses

In grammar language, a **subordinate or dependent clause** is a clause that begins with a subordinating conjunction, explained in the section "Conjunctions." The box to the right has a list of the most common subordinating conjunctions.

> **Worth Knowing**
> Subordinating conjunctions include the following:
>
> | | |
> |---|---|
> | after | although |
> | as | as if |
> | as long as | as though |
> | because | before |
> | even if | even though |
> | if | in order that |
> | provided that | rather than |
> | since | so that |
> | though | unless |
> | until | when |
> | whenever | where |
> | wherever | whether |
> | while | |

The subordinate clause is almost but not quite a full sentence—it has a subject, a verb, and usually an object. But, thanks to the subordinating conjunction, this clause no longer offers a *complete* idea. The subordinating conjunction tells the reader that the sentence needs more information to convey the complete idea.

For example, "Aisha visited the museum" is a full sentence and could be an independent clause. However, "*While* Aisha visited the museum" is a subordinate clause because it begins with the subordinating conjunction "while," which points to missing information. It's like waiting for the other shoe to drop—what happened while Aisha visited the museum?

To communicate the complete idea, an independent clause (underlined below) is needed: "*While* Aisha visited the museum, Rebecca went to the movies."

"Rebecca went to the movies" is an independent clause—it has a subject, verb, object, and complete idea—so the independent clause and the subordinate clause are now part of a grammatically correct sentence.

If the subordinating conjunction was switched to read "Aisha visited the museum *while* Rebecca went to the movies," then "Aisha visited the museum" becomes the independent clause that anchors this sentence.

> **Worth Knowing**
> Additional resources on subordinating conjunctions can be found at
>
> https://owl.purdue.edu/
>
> http://web2.uvcs.uvic.ca/elc/StudyZone/330/grammar/subcon.htm

Subordinate clauses are also called "dependent" clauses in grammar language because they need—are dependent upon—an "independent" clause to complete the idea the sentence is trying to convey.

3. Relative Clauses

A **relative clause** tells us more about (modifies) a noun or pronoun, e.g., "The woman *who ran the office* was very competent." "Who ran the office" is additional information about the woman. In "The mouse *that ran across the room* was very cute," the relative clause "that ran across the room" gives more information about the noun "mouse."

Relative clauses begin with a relative pronoun: "who/whom," "whoever/whomever," "that," "which," and "whose." "What," "when," and "where" can also be relative pronouns.

Relative pronouns act like subordinating conjunctions: they "subordinate" a clause because they point to missing information—the noun or pronoun that "who" or "that" or "which," for example, refers to. Therefore, like subordinate clauses, relative clauses can't stand on their own. They need to be part of an independent clause because they do not communicate a complete idea.

In "The man *whose hat I borrowed* is angry at me," the subordinate clause "whose hat I borrowed" is more usefully considered a relative clause because it begins with a relative pronoun. The punctuation rules for clauses using relative pronouns are explained in the section on comma use.

Note that not all clauses beginning with "who" or "that" or "which" are relative clauses. "Who went through the door?" is an independent clause (an interrogative sentence or question, actually) with "who" as the subject. This group of words is a relative clause only if it modifies a noun or pronoun: "The man *who went through the door* was severely injured."

Consider this sentence: "While Adam delved and Eve span, *who then played the gentleman?*" Is "who then played the gentleman?" a relative clause?

Actually, it's an independent clause and "While Adam delved and Eve span" is a subordinate clause beginning with a subordinating conjunction (again, more on conjunctions below). It's a grammatically correct sentence, and every correct sentence needs an independent clause, which, in this case, is a question: "Who then played the gentleman?" There is no relative clause in this sentence.

What about this sentence, commonly heard in fast-food restaurants: "Can I help who's next?" For those attuned to grammar language this sounds wrong. But why? (We will leave aside, for the moment, the issue of "can" asking about "ability" to help and "may" asking about "permission" to help.)

Recasting the sentence might help solve the mystery. It could be stated as "Can I help the next customer?" "Customer" is what "who" refers to in "Can I help *who's next?*"

So "who's next?" is a relative clause, but the clause is not "relative" to a noun or another pronoun; it's a bit like a dangling modifier. It would be correct to say, "Can I help *the customer* who's next?" Then the relative clause "who's next" has a noun to be relative to. But "Can I help the next customer?" is more concise. (You could also use a different pronoun, "whoever," which carries with it the idea of "whichever person" is next.)

Relative clauses have a few extra complications:

1. **Who/whom versus that/which**: Use "who" or "whom" when referring to *people* or *favoured pets* (e.g., Lassie or Flipper). Use "that" or "which" when referring to *things*, *animals*, *ideas*—anything not human.

    So don't write, "The executive *that* ran the office was competent." It should be, "The executive *who* ran the office was competent." This sentence is correct, however: "The mouse *that* ran across the room was very cute." And this: "Plato's *Republic* offers political ideas *that* should be considered seriously."

2. **Who versus whom**: Use "who" when the relative pronoun is the subject of the relative clause and "whom" when the relative pronoun is the object of a relative clause. In grammar language, these are called the subjective case and the objective case.

In the sentence "The executive *who* ran the office was competent," the relative pronoun "who" is the subject of the relative clause (underlined). Therefore, you should use the subjective form "who" rather than the objective form "whom."

However, you must use the objective pronoun "whom" in the following and in sentences like it: "I was impressed by the competence of the executive *whom* I met yesterday." In this example, "executive," the word the relative pronoun "whom" refers to, is the object of the relative clause "I met yesterday." You can test which case to use by substituting "he" and then "him" or, of course, "she" and then "her" for the idea of "the executive." Which of these makes sense: "I met he or she yesterday" or "I met him or her yesterday." The pronouns that stand for subjects, "he" and "she," are wrong, so you want the objective case.

> **Worth Pondering**
> Is there a case where you might refer to an executive or any other that refers to a human being as "which"? Yes—if you are referring to the *word* "executive" rather than a *person* who is an executive. In that case, a sentence might read: "...the relative clause refers to 'executive,' which is the subject of the sentence." In this context, "which" is correct. Grammar language can be tricky.

> **Worth Consulting**
> For more on using pronouns correctly, see the Purdue Online Writing Lab (OWL) site at
>
> https://owl.purdue.edu/owl/purdue_owl.html.

In other words, in relative clauses, follow the usual rules for the use of "who" (subjective case, as in "*Who* ate my homework?") or "whom" (objective case, as in "My homework was eaten by *whom*?"). Note that relative pronouns in prepositional phrases always use the objective case (e.g., "by *whom*" or "in *whom* we trust").

Be careful, though, that the relative pronoun after the preposition is not functioning as the subject of a clause: "My homework was eaten by the dog *that* wanders our neighbourhood." Or see the example above: "While Adam delved and Eve span, *who* then played the gentleman?" Usually, the easiest test is to see whether a verb or a noun follows the relative pronoun. If it's a verb ("wanders" in the "dog" example), chances are you need the subjective case. If it's a noun or pronoun ("I" in the "executive" example), test out the objective case.

Relative clauses	Essential	Non-essential
Human (or favoured pet)	Who or whom	Who or whom + commas
Not human	That	Which + commas

3. **Essential versus non-essential clauses**: There are two types of relative clause, apart from subjective (beginning with "who") and objective (beginning with "whom"): relative clauses can be essential (also called restrictive) or non-essential (or non-restrictive).

An **essential relative clause** is one that is *essential* to the meaning of your sentence; that is, it *restricts* to one particular meaning the part of the sentence to which it "relates."

A **non-essential relative clause** offers *additional information* about a noun or pronoun but doesn't restrict that part of the sentence's meaning. If the non-essential relative clause were taken out, the sentence would still have the meaning you intended. If an essential relative clause were removed, however, the sentence would not have the meaning you intended. Examples are below.

a) **Essential clauses**: If the relative clause is *essential* to the meaning of the sentence, and *refers to a human being* (or favoured pet, like Flipper), use "who" or "whom." If the relative clause *does not refer to a human being*, use "that."

"That is the executive <u>who runs the office</u>" refers to a particular executive, the one who runs the office, and no other. The relative clause *restricts* the meaning to that particular executive. If the relative clause refers to a non-human, use "that": "Simba was the lion <u>that ran away from the zoo</u>." It's *that* lion, the one that ran away, and no other, so the relative clause is essential to the meaning of the sentence.

b) **Non-essential clauses**: If the relative clause is *not essential* to the meaning of the noun or pronoun, use "who" or "whom" for a person or favoured pet (in other words, it's the same pronoun for both the essential and non-essential relative clauses) and "which" for anything else.

Worth Knowing
Non-essential relative clauses are *always* separated from the main part of the sentence by commas.

If the non-essential relative clause is in the middle of a sentence, then you *must put commas around that clause*: e.g., "The executive, <u>*who* was tall</u>, ran the office" or "The mouse, <u>*which* was grey and white</u>, ran across the room." The underlined clauses are not essential to the meaning of these nouns or to your basic point, which is that the man ran the office and that the mouse ran across the room. So these relative clauses offer additional, non-essential information.

If the non-essential relative clause is at the end of a sentence, it only needs one comma: "I live in this house, <u>*which* is at the corner of Elm and Maple streets</u>." But: "This house, <u>*which* is at the corner of Elm and Maple</u>, is where I live." The key point is that non-essential relative clauses need either one comma or two, depending on where they are in the sentence, to set them off from the essential part of the sentence.

> **Worth Thinking About**
> To a considerable extent, the writer decides whether a relative clause is essential or non-essential and signals this by punctuation and word choices. These sentences, too, are correct:
>
> The executive who was tall ran the office.
> The mouse that was grey and white ran across the room.

> **Worth Thinking About**
> The "that/which" rule for essential and non-essential relative clauses is frequently broken, even in professional writing, but to be crystal clear that a clause is essential or not essential to the meaning of your sentence, use "that" and "which" properly.

The Independent Clause Revisited

We've said that independent clauses can be combined in many ways. They can be combined with other independent clauses, with subordinate clauses, and with relative clauses to create sentence variety and express more complex ideas than a simple sentence could.

But remember, in the vast majority of cases, and no matter how complex, *every grammatically correct sentence must have at least one independent clause as its "anchor."* The exception is when you are deliberately using a sentence fragment to make a point. Because you can. ("Because you can" is not a full sentence but is being used to emphasize a rhetorical point.)

At one time, grammar was taught using diagrams. Suppose we have this sentence: "Sally went to an aerobics class while Rupert, who was very strong, lifted weights." Here is a diagram that illustrates how a complex sentence with an independent clause, a subordinate clause, and a relative clause might look:

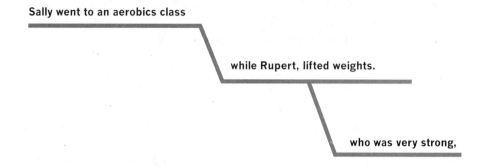

Any sentence can be diagrammed this way, and it's a useful exercise.[1]

A diagram makes clear how the sentence is structured, keeping in mind, again, that sentences must have an independent clause as the "anchor."

The "glue" that joins independent clauses into more complex sentences is the conjunction, which we'll discuss next. (Note that "which we'll discuss next" is a non-essential relative clause referring to "conjunction"; therefore, "which" is preceded by a comma.)

CONJUNCTIONS

The basic, default sentence is the full sentence: subject, verb, maybe an object, and a complete idea. And, theoretically, you could write a whole novel using only full sentences. The old Dick and Jane elementary school reading primers were famous for using simple sentences: "See Dick run. See Jane run. See Dick run with Jane."

> **For more on conjunctions,** use the online search terms "grammar.ccc" and "conjunctions."

But this kind of writing is very boring, so good writers combine sentences to make more interesting patterns that include subordinate and relative clauses. To create these more complex sentences, we use conjunctions.

Fortunately, conjunctions aren't difficult to master because there are only four ways of joining simple sentences into more complex sentences. How sentences are joined also determines what punctuation you use, so what follows is vital information for a writer.

In grammar language, here are the four ways of joining simple sentences, which are usually referred to as independent clauses:

1. Use a coordinating conjunction (for, and, nor, but, or, yet, so = FANBOYS).
2. Use a subordinating conjunction (e.g., while, because, although).

---

1   An excellent introduction to sentence diagramming is *Grammar by Diagram: Understanding English Grammar through Traditional Sentence Diagraming*, by Cindy L. Vitto (Broadview Press, 2006).

3. Use a conjunctive (or linking) adverb and a semicolon, colon, or dash (e.g., however, meanwhile, therefore).
4. Use punctuation alone (semicolon, colon, or dash).

In the following sections we'll see how to put the three types of clauses together using the four types of conjunctions.

1. Coordinating Conjunctions

There are only *seven* coordinating conjunctions: **for**, **and**, **nor**, **but**, **or**, **yet**, and **so**. They can be remembered easily by the acronym FANBOYS.

Coordinating conjunctions join grammatical elements of equal weight, such as nouns, verbs, adjectives, prepositional phrases, and clauses.

In the following examples, coordinating conjunctions join equal grammatical elements that are *not* clauses: "salt *and* pepper" (two nouns), "Batman *and* Robin" (two proper nouns), "In my opinion *and* in that of my colleagues" (two prepositional phrases), "angry *and* disgusted" (two adjectives), and "firmly *and* fiercely" (two adverbs).

> **Worth Knowing**
> There are only *seven* coordinating conjunctions (FANBOYS):
>
> for   and   nor   but
> or   yet   so

Coordinating conjunctions also join **independent clauses**. The sentence "<u>Johnny bought groceries</u>, *but* <u>Jill went to the movies</u>" has two independent clauses (underlined) joined by the coordinating conjunction "but." Note that coordinating conjunctions do *not* join independent and subordinate clauses or independent and relative clauses because subordinate and relative clauses are not of equal grammatical weight with independent clauses. (You may, however, find a coordinating conjunction in front of a subordinate clause when three clauses—two independent clauses and one subordinate clause—are joined.)

In academic writing, the coordinating conjunction between two independent clauses, even if they are short clauses, always takes a comma before the conjunction, as in "<u>I wrote the essay</u>, *but* <u>Subash did the editing</u>." That said, academic sentences tend to be long and complex, with plenty of commas.

However, business, professional, technical, and media writing try to avoid lots of commas, which can act as grammatical speed bumps that slow the reader down. And non-academic writing prefers short, snappy sentences and a speedy reading pace.

Therefore, in the world of business and the professions, *the comma before the coordinating conjunction is optional* if the independent clauses being joined are fairly short. For longer sentences, you should consider using the comma to give the reader a "breather."

For example, "I wrote the novel and my agent helped me sell it to a publisher," without a comma before "and," is okay for professional writing, unless you need your prose to be hypercorrect, say for a job application or a formal report. But what about a sentence such as this: "I wrote the novel based on my experiences as a reporter in the former Soviet Union using an Apple Airbook portable computer running on lithium batteries, *and* my agent helped me sell it to a publisher."

For this mouthful, you need a comma after "batteries" to give the reader a break. But you should also consider dividing this monster into two (or even three) shorter sentences: "I wrote the novel based on my experiences as a reporter in the former Soviet Union. I used an Apple Airbook portable computer running on lithium batteries. When the manuscript was finished, my agent helped me sell it to a publisher."

Consider this sentence: "I wrote the novel *and* sent it to a publisher." Is the "and" in this sentence a coordinating conjunction connecting two independent clauses?

In grammar language, no, it is not. The second part of the sentence has a verb and object, but no subject. Therefore, it doesn't convey the complete idea that "I" did this. It is not an independent clause on its own.

"I," the subject of "sent it to a publisher," is in the previous clause, "I wrote the novel," which *is* an independent clause. These two clauses do not have equal grammatical weight. In this example, the "and" is a coordinating conjunction for the two *verbs* in this sentence—"wrote" and "sent"—not for two independent clauses. Therefore, you would not put a comma before this "and" in either academic or professional writing.

> **Worth Consulting**
> More details about coordinating conjunctions can be found using the search terms "UVic," "study zone," and "coordinating conjunctions."

That said, you might want to use a comma before a coordinating conjunction, even if doing so is not necessary or "technically" correct, to give what follows a bit of extra emphasis or to highlight the contrast between two ideas. This is called an end-of-sentence modifier. (Remember, you can "break the rule" about writing in complete sentences for the same reason—to accentuate a phrase or word.) For example, you might write this: "Professional writing tries to avoid long, windy sentences, *but* doesn't always succeed."

In this sentence, there's a comma before "but" to emphasize the contrast between the ideal (avoiding wordy sentences) and the reality (sometimes wordy sentences). Again, this type of highlight comma is unconventional, but occasionally useful to make your point. (We used a highlight comma to emphasize "occasionally useful.")

For business and professional writing, putting a comma before a coordinating conjunction between two short independent clauses, or not, is up to you but, as always, try to be consistent. Also, consider both what your reader will expect (e.g., how formal is this writing?) and what will make your writing easy to understand (e.g., does a comma between the two independent clauses help your meaning or hinder it?).

Independent clause, [optional comma] [*coordinating conjunction*] **independent clause.**

Note: The comma before a coordinating conjunction that joins two independent clauses is optional in professional writing. If a comma helps the meaning or point of your sentence, use it. If the comma seems to create an unnecessary break, then don't use it.

2. Subordinating Conjunctions

Subordinating conjunctions do just that: they take perfectly good independent clauses and "subordinate" them—turn them into subordinate (also called dependent) clauses. Subordinating conjunctions include "because," "while," "since," "if," "whenever," "whereas," and so on (see the box in "Subordinate or Dependent Clauses" for a more complete, but not totally complete, list of subordinating conjunctions).

A subordinating conjunction makes the idea of the clause incomplete, as in, "*While* Jill went to the movies...." While Jill went to the movies, what else happened? It's not a complete idea. In other words, if you feel you're waiting for the other shoe to drop in a sentence, then it's probably got a subordinating conjunction.

Note that the sentence "Jill went to the movies" without "while" is a perfectly good simple sentence and could be a perfectly respectable independent clause. Add the subordinating conjunction, however, to produce "*While* Jill went to the movies" and the sentence no longer expresses a complete idea. It's become a subordinate clause.

> **Additional Resources on Subordinating Conjunctions**
> Use search terms "Purdue," "subordinating conjunctions"
>
> Use search terms "UVic," "study zone," "subordinating conjunctions"

Knowing you've got a subordinating conjunction in your sentence helps you decide what punctuation to use. We'll discuss this in more detail in the section "Punctuation," but, basically, if the subordinate clause *follows* the independent clause, you don't need a comma. If the subordinate clause *precedes* the independent clause, use a comma.

Independent clause [*subordinating conjunction*] subordinate clause.

[*Subordinating conjunction*] subordinate clause,[comma] independent clause.

3. Conjunctive (Linking) Adverbs

A third way to join independent clauses is to use words such as "however," "moreover," and "therefore" plus appropriate linking punctuation. In grammar language these words are called **conjunctive adverbs** or **linking adverbs** ("conjunctive" is a fancy way of saying "linking"). For example, "George went to the store; *however*, Jill went to the movies." "However" is a conjunctive adverb.

Conjunctive adverbs are transitional words, which we discussed in Chapter 2 on coherence. That is, they link independent clauses based on several logical connections, including

- **time** (consequently, meanwhile, afterward),
- **contrast** (however, on the contrary, nonetheless),

- **similarity** (likewise, similarly),
- **causation** (therefore, as a result, hence),
- **addition** (in addition, furthermore),
- **summary** (in short, in brief, in conclusion), and
- **illustration** (for example, namely).

Note that, unlike subordinating conjunctions, conjunctive adverbs can be part of an independent clause or simple sentence: "*However*, Jill went to the movies" is a complete sentence even though it is related, presumably, to a previous complete sentence.

When conjunctive adverbs are used to combine independent clauses, *they are preceded by a semicolon, colon, or dash and followed by a comma*. Always. This rule is not optional. For example, "What you say may be true; however, I am too angry to care." "The company had a slump—namely, it lost its triple-A rating."

> **Worth Knowing**
> Conjunctive adverbs include the following:
> furthermore   moreover
> likewise   however
> nonetheless   nevertheless
> consequently   therefore
> otherwise   (and many more)

What about these sentences, though? "What you say may be true. I do not, however, agree with you." Why doesn't "however" take a semicolon in this case?

In the second sentence, "however" is not a *linking* adverb because it is no longer linking two independent clauses: "I do not, however, agree with you" is a complete sentence and can stand on its own.

In this example, "however" is an "interrupting" word (although still an adverb)—a word that adds nuance to a sentence and refers back to the ideas expressed in at least one other complete sentence. Equally, we could express these two ideas in this way: "What you say may be true. *However*, I do not agree with you." In this example, "however" is not a *conjunctive* adverb because the two sentences aren't joined into one. See the section on commas in "Punctuation" for more on using commas with interrupting words and phrases.

> **Additional Resources on Conjunctive Adverbs**
> Use search terms "grammar untied" and "conjunctive adverbs."

> Independent clause;[semicolon] [*conjunctive adverb*],
> [comma] independent clause.

4. Semicolons, Colons, Dashes

Full sentences can also be joined by punctuation alone. In other words, as long as we have this "joining" punctuation, we don't really need the conjunctive adverbs discussed previously to join two independent clauses together. Usually, we use a semicolon: "George went to the store; Jill went to the movies."

Independent clauses joined with a semicolon have ideas that are closely related; the ideas are, as it were, cousins. It wouldn't make sense to use a semicolon in this sentence: "George went to the store; the Northern Lights are beautiful." The ideas aren't related. This would work: "George went to Nunavut; he thought the Northern Lights were beautiful."

Colons and dashes can also join independent clauses (and be used with linking adverbs) but should be employed sparingly and for some sort of dramatic effect: "George helped with the chores—Jill went to the movies." Here the dash emphasizes Jill's irresponsibility in not helping George while there was work to be done; the second part of the sentence isn't just about the fact that Jill saw a film.

In joining sentences, colons can be used to introduce another full sentence that explains or expands on something in the preceding sentence: "George helped with the chores: at only age 7, he was already a helpful son."

There is more about the correct use of the colon in "Punctuation."

Review

There are *three* types of clauses:

1. independent,
2. subordinate (or dependent), and
3. relative.

Independent clauses can be combined to make more intricate sentences in only *four* ways:

1. coordinating conjunction;
2. subordinating conjunction;
3. conjunctive adverb + semicolon or (other "joining" punctuation); and
4. semicolon, colon, or dash.

Quiz on Sentences (answers are on page 396)

1. Name the three types of clauses, define them, and give an example of each type of clause.
2. There are only four ways of combining independent clauses correctly. Name them and give an example of each.

CLAUSES AND CONJUNCTIONS DETERMINE PUNCTUATION

A student taking English poetry was putting commas into her essays more or less at random. Her teacher asked why she was doing this. She replied, "Because my prof last term told me to use more commas." She'd been adding commas, but she didn't know where commas were supposed to go. The result was a grammatical mess.

Fortunately, you can easily determine where punctuation goes in your writing: by understanding the three types of clauses and the four types of conjunctions. Where periods, commas, semicolons, and colons go depends on how the sentence is structured. Learn sentence structure and you won't make mistakes in punctuation. So let's discuss punctuation and its relation to clauses and conjunctions.

The "Natural" Order for Sentences

The "natural" or default order for an English sentence is *subject* first, then *predicate* (verb and object). Similarly, the "natural" order of clauses in English is *independent clause* followed by a *dependent clause*, just as the engine goes ahead of the boxcars in a train (see Figure 3.1). (Not all languages follow this order. German, for example, at the end of a sentence the verb puts.)

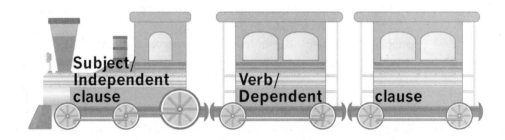

Figure 3.1 The "Natural" Order for an English Sentence

The subject of the sentence is the "engine"; the predicate (the verb and object, if there is an object) is formed by the "boxcars." Similarly, an independent clause is the "engine" of a complex sentence; the subordinate and relative clauses are the "boxcars."

Here's one of the basic rules of punctuation: If the sentence follows the "natural" order, like a train with the engine followed by boxcars, then *no comma is needed between the independent clause and subordinate clause*. But if the boxcars are put ahead of the engine, *you need a comma* after the boxcars. In grammar language, this comma is called an "introductory" comma, and it's used when a sentence is out of the "natural" order.

For example: "*Aisha visited the museum* <u>while Rebecca went to the movies</u>." This is an independent clause (italics) followed by a subordinate clause (underlined). There is no comma after "museum."

But if we change the order—put the "boxcar" ahead of the "engine," the subordinate clause ahead of the independent clause—then a comma is needed: "<u>While Rebecca went to the movies,</u> *Aisha visited the museum.*"

The same is true when it comes to subject and predicate. "I went to the museum in the morning" follows the "natural" order; no comma is needed. But if one or more of the predicate "boxcars" is ahead of the subject "engine," you usually need a comma: "In the morning, I went to the museum."

The introductory comma rule doesn't always apply if the out-of-order word or phrase is short, as in "Today I'm going to the store" or even "In the morning I went to the museum"—it's a grey area. For long phrases and clauses out of order, however, the introductory comma is almost always required.

Summary

Subject + predicate comprised of a verb and sometimes an object and modifying words [*no comma needed*]

Words from the predicate,[comma] subject + predicate comprised of at least a verb [*introductory comma*]

Independent clause + dependent clause [*no comma needed*]

Dependent clause,[comma] + independent clause [*introductory comma*]

End-of-Sentence Modifiers

Even if a dependent clause or phrase follows an independent clause (in other words, even if the sentence is in the "natural" order), sometimes a comma can be used if the dependent clause

- is not essential to the meaning of the sentence or
- offers a distinct shift in the idea of the sentence.

For example, the writer of these sentences wanted to stress the sharp change in meaning between the independent and the dependent clauses:

- "He was still upset about the outcome of the match, even though his side won."
- "Toast is very good with butter, although butter can be fattening."

In grammar language, these are called "end-of-sentence modifiers," and the comma helps to highlight the change in emphasis or idea at the end of the sentence. That said, putting a comma with an end-of-sentence modifier is not a fixed rule—you can choose to use the end-of-sentence comma or not depending on the effect you are trying to achieve.

PUNCTUATION

We have already discussed using commas and semicolons with independent, sub-ordinate, and relative clauses and with the four kinds of conjunctions. This section offers a few more simple rules for using punctuation correctly.

Commas

Commas are used in the following ten situations. Other sources will give different numbers of comma-use situations, but they will include all of the following:

1. **After an introductory word, phrase, or dependent clause**: "In the case of commas, it's best to follow the rules." "Although lemon is tasty, I prefer sugar in my tea." The introductory comma is used when the parts of a sentence are out of the "natural" order, that is, when part of the predicate (a "boxcar") goes before the subject (the "engine") or when a subordinate clause precedes an independent clause.
2. **In academic and formal professional writing, before a coordinating con-junction** (FANBOYS), i.e., a conjunction that joins independent clauses: "John ran to the store, *but* Jill did her homework." Note, again, that, in non-academic and informal writing, and particularly in joining short independent clauses, this comma is optional.
3. **For a series or list of items**, such as "George ate Spam, toast, eggs, and asparagus for breakfast." This example uses the "Oxford" comma—a comma before the final conjunction "and"—and the Oxford comma is required in academic writing. However, a comma is, in non-academic writing, *optional* after the second-last item in the series: "George ate Spam, toast, eggs and asparagus for breakfast." The rule: Decide whether you'll use the Oxford comma or not in a piece of writing and then be consistent. Note that professions such as journalism and advertising tend not to use this comma, but lawyers, accountants, and other professionals whose writing needs to be unambiguous tend toward using it. A 2011 *Globe and Mail* poll found that 65 per cent of respondents said they used the Oxford comma, 24 per cent said they didn't, and 11 per cent said they didn't care. *The Globe and Mail* advises its own journalists not to use the comma.
4. **To introduce dialogue or a quotation in dialogue form**: He said, "I want my rights respected!" Note, however, that quotations not in dialogue form do not take commas:
    - The newspaper editorial wrote that the "Safe Pets" initiative was promising.
    - An income statement is "a type of summary flow report that categorizes and lists revenues and expenses over a given period."

5. **To set off non-essential or "interrupting" words, phrases, or clauses**: "Apple, which was founded in 1976, began by selling the Apple I for $666.66" or "A copy of our analysis, along with our interpretation of its results, is enclosed." These are words, phrases, or clauses that, if removed, would not change the meaning of the sentence. For example, in "George, *who likes toast*, went to the store," the italicized relative clause isn't essential to the meaning of the sentence: that George is going to the store. Another example: "George walked to the store, *which was five blocks away*." The distance to the store is not key to the meaning of the sentence.

   Some elements need commas around them because they interrupt the normal flow of a sentence: "I am tired, *however*, of Ellen's buffoonery."

   On the other hand, if the word, phrase, or clause is *essential* to the overall meaning of the sentence, then don't use a comma, as in "The cat *that scratched me* was tawny." It's that cat and not some other cat that scratched you; therefore, the relative clause "that scratched me" is essential to the meaning of your sentence and doesn't take a comma. Other examples: "George walked to the store *that was five blocks away*" (which store he walked to is now important) and "The man *who likes toast* went to the store for butter" (which man went to the store is defined as the one liking toast).

   Ultimately, it is what the writer considers essential that determines how he or she punctuates a sentence. This is correct, too: "The cat, *which was tawny*, scratched me." In this case, the writer thinks the colour of the cat isn't essential to the basic message of the sentence (that she got scratched by a cat), so the clause uses "which" and is enclosed by commas.

6. **When you are talking about the same noun twice but using different words**: "<u>*Hamlet*</u>, *Shakespeare's most famous play*, can be four hours long" or "Larry Campbell, <u>the former Vancouver mayor</u>, is now in the Senate." "*Hamlet*" = "Shakespeare's most famous play," and "the former Vancouver mayor" = "Larry Campbell." In grammar language, this renaming of a noun is called an **appositive**, so the surrounding commas are called **appositive commas**. Appositives are usually not essential to the main idea of the sentence, hence the commas.

   But suppose you write your sentence this way: "Former Vancouver mayor Larry Campbell is now in the Senate." In this case, the formerly appositive information is now a person's title or role; it is essential to the meaning of your sentence, and, therefore, it doesn't take the appositive commas.

   Similarly, you could write, "Stephen Harper, *the Canadian prime minister*, attended a pancake breakfast in Calgary." "The Canadian prime minister" is an appositive and needs the commas. You would use commas if your sentence read, "The Canadian prime minister, *Stephen Harper*, attended a pancake breakfast in Calgary." In this case, "Stephen Harper" is the appositive and needs commas. But what if your sentence read: "Canadian Prime Minister Stephen Harper attended a pancake breakfast in Calgary"? In this case, "Canadian Prime Minister" is now Mr. Harper's title or position and essential to the meaning of the sentence; it is no longer an appositive and doesn't take commas.

Why? You wouldn't write either "Former Vancouver mayor is now in the Senate" or "Prime Minister attended a pancake breakfast in Calgary." So these phrases are not appositives.

7. **When an element at the end of the sentence offers a shift in the idea of what's gone before or is an aside not essential to the meaning of the main clause**: "The illness is slow, while recovery is fast" or "Many fail to consider the importance of grammar to writing, if they think about grammar at all." The grammar-language term for this is an "end-of-sentence modifier," which we discussed previously.

> **Worth Consulting**
> The search terms "Purdue," "Owl," and "commas" lead to a useful site on comma usage.

8. **When you have a series of modifying adjectives** such as the following: "The big, tough, brawny wrestler won his match." If you could put "and" between the adjectives—"The big *and* tough *and* brawny wrestler won his match"—then use a comma instead of the "and." However, you wouldn't use a comma for the following: "I would recommend an inexpensive quartz watch." Yes, you could write "I recommend an inexpensive and quartz watch." But these two adjectives, "inexpensive" and "quartz," are not created equal. The adjective "quartz" is essential to the noun "watch" and should go right next to the noun it modifies. (You wouldn't naturally flip these adjectives: "I recommend a quartz inexpensive watch.") So, in this case, a comma is wrong. (Note that you can put the adjectives in the first example in any order: "The tough, brawny, big wrestler won his match.")

9. **To separate dates, addresses, or geographical names**: "He lived at 345 Smith Avenue, Kamloops, B.C., Canada, from January 31, 2011, to April 9, 2014." In effect, what you're doing here is putting commas in a list.

10. **After the salutation and closing in personal (non-business) letters**: "Dear Aunt Mary," an example of a salutation, and "Yours truly," an example of a closing, both take commas. Note that *business letters* use a colon after the greeting ("Dear Mr. McIntosh:"), but a comma after the closing ("Yours sincerely,").

You should not use a comma in the following situations:

1. **Between two independent clauses without a coordinating conjunction between them** (in grammar language, this is called a comma splice and is

a major grammatical sin): "George went to the store, Jill went to the movies." Use one of the four types of conjunction to fix this all-too-common grammatical error:

- George went to the store, *but* Jill went to the movies. [coordinating conjunction and comma (optional because these are short clauses)]
- George went to the store *while* Jill went to the movies. [subordinating conjunction]
- George went to the store; *however,* Jill went to the movies. [conjunctive adverb and semicolon]
- George went to the store; Jill went to the movies. [semicolon alone]

2. **Between a subject and its verb or a verb and its object**: "A 14-year-old, is not allowed to drive" is not correct because the comma separates the subject "14-year-old" from its verb "is not allowed." But this is correct: "A 14-year-old, because he or she is not considered mature, is not allowed to drive." In the second example, the clause "because he or she is not considered mature" interrupts the normal sentence structure (subject + predicate); it's in the middle of a sentence, and two commas are needed. Note that you do not need a comma in front of this clause if it is in the "natural" order (independent clause + subordinate clause): "A 14-year-old is not allowed to drive because he or she is not considered mature."

Semicolons

Knowing when a semicolon is needed is easy—there are only two basic uses:

1. **To join independent clauses** (sometimes with a conjunctive adverb such as "however"): "Jack ate no fat; [however,] Jill ate no lean." The two clauses should have some logical connection to each other. You wouldn't write this: "Jack ate no fat; Jill was from Lithuania."

2. **To divide items in a long series that have internal punctuation**: "We ate crab cakes, simmered in sauce; steak, rare to the point of being blood red; potato medallions; and asparagus, crunchy and smothered in butter." There are three internal commas in this list ("crab cakes, simmered in sauce," and so on). Without semicolons to tell the reader where each list item ends, the sentence would be unnecessarily confusing. The rule is, when there is even one internal comma in a list, semicolons are needed to separate the items clearly.

Colons

Colons have only four uses:

1.   **To introduce some sort of list or elucidation**: These colons say "Get ready because here is my explanation or catalogue of items." Examples include "The causes of nausea during fun-fair rides are the following: ice-cream cones, soft drinks, and cotton candy," or "Location, location, location: This is the mantra of the real estate agent."

     Note, however, that in most writing, and particularly in academic writing, there should be an independent clause on at least one side of the colon. Usually, the colon comes after this clause. For example, the colon before a list should follow an independent clause: "*My favourite foods are the following*: crab cakes, steak, and potatoes." But you should not use a colon after "are" in this sentence: "My favourite foods are crab cakes, steak, and potatoes." Why? "My favourite foods are" is not an independent clause.

     If you're not sure whether you have an independent clause as your introduction, use the "following" rule. Add some form of "following": "My favourite foods are *the following*: crab cakes, steak, and potatoes." If you can add this phrase, you did not have an independent clause to begin with.

2. **To introduce a quotation**: Edgar was emphatic: "I demand my rights!" Commas can also be used to introduce a quotation, of course: Helen told the storeowner, "I want my money back." Most non-academic writing, including the media and fiction writing, uses a comma to introduce quotations. The colon before a quotation is more common when what is being quoted is lengthy, as in academic writing. That said, both colons and commas can be used correctly to introduce quotations.

3. **Following the greeting in a business letter**: "Dear Ms. McInerny:"

4. **Between a title and a subtitle**: *The Art of Archery: A Master's Guide.*

Review of Commas, Semicolons, and Colons

Commas are used in the following ten cases:

1. after an introductory word, phrase, or dependent clause;
2. in formal writing, before a coordinating conjunction, although this comma is optional if the coordinate clauses are short;
3. when you have a series or list of items;
4. to introduce dialogue or a quotation;
5. to set off non-essential or "interrupting" words, phrases, or clauses;

6. when you are naming the same noun twice using different words (the appositive comma);
7. when an element at the end of the sentence offers a shift in the idea of what's gone before or is an aside that's not essential to the meaning of the main clause (end-of-sentence modifier);
8. when you have a series of modifying adjectives that could be joined by "and" and could be in any order in front of the noun they modify;
9. to separate dates, addresses, or geographical names; and
10. after the salutation and closing in personal (non-business) letters and the closing in business letters.

Semicolons are used in the following two cases:

1. to join independent clauses, either alone or with a conjunctive adverb, or
2. to divide items in a long series that have internal punctuation.

Colons are used in the following four cases:

1. to introduce a list or elucidation,
2. to introduce a quotation,
3. following the greeting in a business letter, and
4. between a title and subtitle.

Hyphens

The main reason we use hyphens is to create a compound word, that is, two or more words joined together. **Hyphenated compounds** are always joined using a hyphen (e.g., the verb "cross-examine" and the noun "daughter-in-law"). Some compound words start out with hyphens but become **closed compounds**, as in the transformation of "on-line" to "online." And some words that are joined in meaning seem to maintain their **open form** over centuries, as in "post office" or "middle class." We are concerned here with a special type of compound word—in grammar language, the compound modifier, meaning two or more adjectives or modifying words joined together with hyphens.

Hyphens between these modifiers increase clarity. Consider this sentence: "Sheila asked the salesperson for a little used car." Does she want a used car that's also very compact? Or does she want a car that hasn't been driven much? A hyphen will clear up any confusion: "Sheila asked the salesperson for a little-used car."

In compound modifiers, the *first* of the two hyphenated words modifies the *second* and not the noun directly, as in "Peter Parker was a red-suited action hero." "Red" modifies "suited," and together the two modify "action hero." Therefore, a hyphen is necessary between "red" and "suited" for clarity.

As noted in the first section of "Punctuation," you may also find before a noun two adjectives that are separated by commas: "He was an angry, bitter man." Why do we use a comma, not a hyphen, here? Well, "angry" and "bitter" *both* modify the noun "man." You could, in other words, write the sentence like this: "He was an angry *and* bitter man." The comma takes the place of the "and," and there's no hyphen.

A hyphen is not used when we combine most **adverbs** with an **adjective** or other word to modify a noun because an adverb's *job* is to modify adjectives (as well as verbs and other sentence parts), so the meaning is already clear: "His pet was a fully grown eagle." "Fully" clearly modifies "grown," not "eagle." We wouldn't say a bird is "fully eagle."

> **Worth Knowing**
> When we form a compound between some adverbs not ending in "ly" and a second modifier, it is standard to use a hyphen:
>
> It was a much-needed policy.
>
> That is the worst-paid job.

Similarly, in the sentence "Grammar offers clearly understandable guidelines for writing," "clearly" modifies "understandable"—you wouldn't say something is "clearly guidelines." If you're not sure about telling adjectives and adverbs apart, the rule of thumb is don't use a compound hyphen if the first of the modifying words ends in "ly" (most adverbs end in "ly"). Note, however, that using a hyphen in the following situation is correct: "He wrote a reader-friendly book on business communication."

The hyphen is becoming scarce today, even in academic writing. As readers, we are getting used to strings of modifiers, so it isn't strictly necessary to use hyphens to form compounds when the meaning is clear: "We deliver quality health care services." Few people would misread "little used car" to mean that the car was little, although some might. But what about: "In 2014, the pet-store owner sold 12 year old cats." Did he sell several cats that were 12 years old? In that case, the sentence should read "He sold 12-year-old cats." Or, more likely, does the writer mean this: "In 2014, he sold 12 year-old cats." Only with the hyphen is the meaning clear.

The rule: To be sure of clarity, always use a hyphen between compound adjectives.

Quotation Marks

Quotation marks are an endless source of confusion, so here's a brief primer.

Quotation marks are, obviously, used to identify quotations or parts of quotations, and sometimes to give special emphasis to certain words or phrases. Most of the time, quotation marks *follow* the punctuation: "I'm going into town," said Mark. "Can I buy you anything?" Another example: Mark told me that he was "going into town."

Quotation marks can also be used to signal that you are referring to a word or phrase as a word or phrase, that you intend a word or phrase to be read as ironic and want to distance yourself from it (sometimes called "scare quotes"), or that you are using slang: Ben told us he was "tired," but a better word is "lazy." Again, most punctuation (the period and comma in this example) will go *inside* the quotation marks. Here are more details.

Periods and commas almost always go *inside* the final quotation mark (unless you are working for an organization that uses British English or a newspaper that requires you to punctuate "scare quotes" and the like with periods and commas *outside* quotation marks).

Semicolons and colons almost always go *outside* the final quotation mark:

- According to Bill Gates, "Intellectual property has the shelf life of a banana"; it's a good thing he didn't substitute the word "apple."

Question marks, exclamation marks, and dashes go *outside* closing quotation marks unless the punctuation is part of the quoted material:

- She asked, "What's the worst that could happen if we put all our eggs into one basket?"
- Who said, "Never put all your eggs in one basket"?

If you are putting a quotation inside another quotation, then use double quotation marks for the outside quotation and single quotation marks for the inside quotation: Harriet said, "Ben told us he was 'tired,' but a better word is 'lazy.'"

If you are using a third level of internal quotation (which is rare), then go back to double quotation marks for that level (and single quotation marks for a fourth level, which is rarer still): "Harriet said, 'Ben told us he was "tired," but "lazy" is a better word.'" Note that the rules about what punctuation goes inside or outside of the quotation marks remains the same.

Double quotation marks are the default style for writing in North America. Formal British English, however, often uses single quotation marks. For a quotation within a quotation, traditional British style is the mirror image of North American style: internal quotations take two quotation marks and so on.

Canadian newspapers, magazines, and newsletters tend to use single quotation marks for quoted material in headlines, headings, and (sometimes) captions. And we suggest you do the same, although using double quotation marks is not wrong. Also, for pull quotes (see Chapter 5), you can use single quotation marks (or even no quotation marks at all).

'For pull quotes, you can use single quotation marks'

Parenthesis and Brackets

Parentheses are round, like this: ( ). **Brackets** are square [ ], although parentheses are often referred to as brackets. Parentheses and brackets are used to enclose additional and usually non-essential information ("parenthetical information," in grammar language), like an actor's aside in the theatre. The previous sentence has an example of the use of parenthesis for additional information. Here are a few other common uses:

- **presenting acronyms or abbreviations**, as in, "The World Health Organization (WHO) reported new cases of Ebola virus disease this July";
- **indicating nicknames**, e.g., "William Hayward (Mookie) Wilson was my favourite player in the 80s," although double quotation marks are often used instead; and
- **enclosing numerals that confirm spelled out numbers or that distinguish items in a list**, e.g., "This contract expires in forty-eight (48) hours" and "The important steps in choosing a good password are (1) use at least six characters, (2) mix numbers and letters and punctuation marks, (3) use both upper and lower case, and (4) be random in your choice."

Brackets are used to identify an editorial insertion into a quotation. The bracketed material sometimes inserts information provided elsewhere in the original text: "He [the airline pilot] claimed he saw an unidentified flying object (UFO) during his landing at Vancouver airport." In this sentence, the bracketed words—[the airline pilot]—give clarifying editorial information that was not part of the original sentence; the material in parentheses—(UFO)—was in the original text.

Brackets are also used to enclose parenthetical content within a parenthetical element. In other words, if you need parentheses within parentheses, you choose brackets: The airline pilot claimed he saw a UFO during his landing at Vancouver airport. (Perhaps he'd just watched the recent rerun of *Close Encounters of the Third Kind* [1977] on television.)

> **Worth Consulting**
> There is more information about using parentheses and brackets at the following websites:
>
> https://www.dailywritingtips.com/parentheses/
>
> https://www.dailywritingtips.com/when-and-how-to-use-brackets/

If an entire sentence is within parentheses, then the closing punctuation is also within the parentheses (see the *Close Encounters* example). The next sentence also offers an example: (Information that is peripheral to the main discussion is called parenthetical.)

If the parentheses enclose only part of a sentence, the punctuation goes outside the parentheses, as in: Semicolons can be used to join independent clauses (sometimes with a conjunctive adverb).

Quiz on Punctuation (answers are on page 397)

1. There are at least ten ways to use commas correctly. Name them and give an example of each.
2. What is a comma splice? Define it, give an example, and then correct the example.
3. There are two occasions when you must use a semicolon. Identify them and give an example of each.
4. There are four occasions when a colon is called for. Identify them and give an example of each.
5. Which punctuation marks are typically used inside quotation marks? Which are usually found outside quotation marks? Name four of them and give a sentence example of each. When should question marks be used outside quotation marks? Give a sentence example.
6. What is the difference between parentheses and brackets? Give a sentence example of each.

GRAMMAR ODDS AND ENDS

Much or Many? Less or Fewer? Countable and Uncountable Nouns

Some nouns are countable, e.g., "friends," and some are not, e.g., "rice." Which adjective you use to describe quantity depends on whether the noun can be counted or not.

Countable	Uncountable
Many	Much
Few	Little
Fewer	Less
Number	Amount

- **Many vs. much**: Use "many" when what you are numbering can be counted; use "much" when what you are quantifying can't be counted.
  - "I have *many* friends [countable], and they bring me *much* joy [not countable]."
- **Few vs. little**: "I have *few* friends and *little* time to enjoy the ones I have."
  - Sometimes, a variation of an uncountable noun is countable: "The *few* times I've gone to his house, he's been away." We can count the

number of times we've gone to his house, but, without some form of measurement, we can't count the *amount* of time itself.

- **Fewer vs. less**: "I have *fewer* friends than Natalie and *less* time to enjoy the ones I have."
    - Sometimes people mistake a countable noun associated with time, such as "hours," for an uncountable noun, and they write, incorrectly, "I worked less hours." The following is correct: "I have *fewer* friends than Natalie, but, because I work *fewer* hours than she does, I spend *less* time away from the ones I have."
- **Number vs. amount**: "I have a *number* of good friends, and no *amount* of pressure will make me give them up."

Quick Quiz (answer is on page 399)

Why is this slogan, once found on napkins at Starbucks, grammatically incorrect? "Less napkins, less waste, less pollution."

Tricky Grammar

Below are a number of word pairings that tend to confuse students.

- **Between vs. among**
    - Use **between** to compare *two things or qualities*. "*Between* you and me, this is an easy assignment."
    - Use **among** to compare *more than two* things or qualities. "Who *among* us is willing to cast the first stone?"
- **Simple vs. simplistic**
    - **Simple** means easy, uncomplicated. "He devised a *simple* plan, but it worked."
    - **Simplistic** means too easy, lacking all the necessary elements. "His plan was too *simplistic* to work."
    - A web-page design is "simple," not "simplistic" (unless it really is simplistic).
- **Easy vs. simple**
    - In general, use **easy** when you need an **adverb**, as in "It is *easy* to follow the instructions for this application."
    - **Easy** can be used as an **adjective**, as in "Phil was an *easy* mark." Most of the time, though, **simple** works best as an **adjective**, as in "Fang-li had a *simple* plan, but it backfired."

- **Complement vs. compliment**
  - **Complement**, used as a verb, means to go along well with or to complete something; used as a noun, it means the thing that completes or makes perfect: "George's tie *complemented* [verb] his shirt." "The battle was won by a new *complement* [noun] of troops."
  - **Compliment**, used as a verb, means to praise someone for something; used as a noun, it means a polite expression of praise or approval. "Harold *complimented* [verb] George on his tie." "George was happy with the *compliment* [noun]."
- **Principle vs. principal**
  - **Principal** means main: "the *principal* violinist," "the school *principal*," or "his *principal* and most successful idea."
  - **Principle** means a rule or truth: "a person with strong *principles*," "the main *principle* of his military success," or "the scientific *principle* of gravity."

> **Worth Considering**
> Whether to use "principal" or "principle" can get confusing. Sometimes it helps to remember that there is such a thing as "the principal principle"—the main philosophical truth.

- **Its vs. it's**
  - **It's** is a contraction of "it is"; because it's a contraction, it takes an apostrophe: "*It's* easy to make a mistake."
  - **Its** is a possessive pronoun—the possessive form of "it." Like other possessive pronouns, such as "yours" or "theirs," "its" doesn't take an apostrophe (unlike the possessives of most nouns, e.g., "dog's"): "A dog is very possessive of *its* food bowl."
- **Use vs. utilize (and the like)**
  - Avoid jargon such as **utilize** when there is a simpler word that means the same thing, e.g., **use**: "I *use* a fork for dinner."
  - **Utilize** can be used when it means being able to find a practical use for something, as in, "We couldn't find any way to *utilize* the fork as an excavating tool." But you could still use "use."

> **Worth Consulting**
> University of Victoria Professor Kim Blank's "Wordiness, Wordiness, Wordiness List" website has a comprehensive list of plain English versus jargony terms. The website is at http://web.uvic.ca/~gkblank/wordiness.html

- **Alternative vs. alternate**
  - An **alternative** is another option: "He was offered an *alternative* plan."
  - **Alternate** means to change from one to another: "He *alternated* from one position to another."
- **Practice vs. practise, and the like**
  - Although it's a grey area, where two words sound the same but one takes a "c" and the other an "s," the "c" word is usually the noun and the "s" word the verb. Examples: "practice" (noun) and "practise" (verb), "licence" (noun) and "license" (verb), and so on. Note: This distinction is not made in American English, so you can easily miss errors if your spellchecker is set to "English (US)."

CONCLUSION

Grammatically correct writing is also, in almost all cases, writing that is clear, coherent, complete, concrete and specific, courteous, and concise.

In many situations, the writer does not have to follow all the Cs—we don't expect perfect writing in an email from a friend, for example. But, in a business or professional setting, you must set for yourself the highest possible standard for your writing. Why? If for no other reason, because the quality of your writing reflects *you* as both a professional and an individual. Why would you want to be perceived as anything less than the best?

But also, as a professional, you want to do the very best work you can in everything you undertake, and that includes your writing.

To become a fine writer, at least in terms of technique, you need to have learned and practised the eight Cs to the point where they have become automatic; you no longer have to think about them. Indeed, many good writers have no *conscious* recollection of learning the eight Cs, at least by name. But they've unconsciously absorbed these principles by reading the work of writers who do practise the Cs.

For most of us, though, before the Cs become automatic, we have to learn about and then practise them. That means we need to learn at least some grammar language because grammar language allows us to *analyze* our writing and others' writing. With grammar language, we can identify the flaws and errors and then *explain* those errors to ourselves or to others who also have this language. Learning this new language is well worth the effort.

Below you will find three quizzes to test your knowledge of grammar. The answers are at the back of the book, but don't peek!

Quiz #1 on Grammar (answers are on page 399)

The sentences below contain grammar errors. Can you identify and correct them?

1. Suspecting fraud, the books were audited last month.
2. I hope you are pleased with the report, I would like to discuss it with you at your convenience.
3. Everyone deals with workplace stress in their own way.
4. Employees, who work the late shift, will receive a 10 per cent bonus.
5. The result of the tests are included in Appendix B.
6. The 909 printer is our most popular model, it offers an unequalled blend of power and versatility.
7. The truck, that ran into the ditch, had faulty brakes.

8. I read the questions carefully, therefore, I did well on the exam.
9. If you find the plastic marmot that I've lost please phone me immediately.
10. The stewardesses made sure the passengers had blankets after the flight took off.

Quiz #2 on Grammar (answers are on page 401)

Correct the grammar, spelling, and syntax errors in the following sentences. Note: *All* of these sentences were taken from daily newspapers!

1. I try and minimize my travel.
2. For example, Sunday school at the local church.
3. We'd like to thank our list of volunteers and, if in error there is an ommission of a name, we apologize as we had so many this year.
4. He said that if the federal government were serious about climate change, it would introduce a tax on carbon emissions, however, he applauded the tax on inefficient vehicles.
5. During Question Period, Mr. Dion and deputy leader Michael Ignatieff accused Mr. Harper of breaking several promises in the budget. Among them, a promise to create 250,000 day-care spaces.
6. An office romance in Abbotsford between a manager and a female subordinate that turned nasty, cost the manager his job.
7. Taking the ferry as a foot passenger results in less vehicles on the roads.
8. Along with a forgiveness of up to $2,000 on the BC provincial sales tax for hybrid cars the price premium for some hybrids has effectively disappeared.

Quiz #3 on Clauses (answers are on page 403)

The following paragraphs contain 15 subordinate or relative clauses. Identify the subordinate clauses with a single underline; mark relative clauses with a wavy underline.

Plato versus Aristotle

Philosophy in the West ultimately boils down to two Greek thinkers from the fourth century BCE: Plato and Aristotle. One of Plato's most important ideas, which he expressed using Socrates as his source, was his Theory of Forms. Forms were idealized templates for everything that we can sense and think about. For example, horses are horses because they reflect the Ideal Horse, dogs the Ideal Dog, chairs the Ideal Chair, and so on. For Plato, these Forms were not just abstract ideas; they actually existed, but beyond our senses.

Plato explains Forms with the parable of the Cave. A number of prisoners are chained in a cave. Because they are facing away from the entrance, they see on the back wall only shadows from the world outside the cave, and the prisoners believe that the shadows are Reality. However, one prisoner, who is more curious than the others, escapes from the cave, sees the reality that is creating the shadows, and returns to inform the others that what they are seeing is only an illusion. For Plato, then, when we achieve full Wisdom, we see the reality (the Forms) beyond our senses rather than mere shadows (the cave).

Aristotle, who was a student of Plato, rejected much of Plato's philosophy of Forms; he denied that the "real world" was the Forms beyond the senses. Instead, Aristotle believed that we should learn more *about* the cave through intelligent use of our senses rather than trying to transcend the senses, which was Plato's preference.

In the modern Western world, Plato's philosophy often appears as idealism: Plato's present-day followers, who are usually not aware of their debt to Plato, seek the ideal, the perfect, the permanent, the mystical. While most of Aristotle's followers today are also not aware of their link to his ideas, Aristotelians tend to be realistic and scientific, seeking that which is possible in the world now rather than an idealized Form beyond the world.

So, which philosopher do you prefer?

Chapter 4
Copy-Editing

In this chapter you will learn to

- Copy-edit text successfully.

INTRODUCTION: WHAT IS COPY-EDITING?

Anything you write needs to be copy-edited.

At the copy-editing stage, you've written your letter or news release or report or essay, and now you must make sure it's perfect in terms of spelling, grammar, word choices, logical order, and so on. Copy-editing is an absolutely crucial step in the writing process that doesn't, sometimes, get the recognition it deserves.

We normally think of copy editors as working for newspapers, magazines, and book publishers, but copy-editing is much more widespread than this. In general, you are a copy editor whenever you correct your own work, whenever you correct others' work (as part of peer editing or during a team assignment), and, of course, whenever you correct writing in the world of the professions and business.

The copy editor's aim is to ensure that any document going out to the world is, in terms of the writing, as perfect as humanly possible.

Here are some of the copy editor's duties:

- Make corrections to grammar, spelling, word order, punctuation, etc.
- Ensure text meets a publication's style guidelines or consistently follows the particular editorial style chosen. (Are all dates or all measurements presented using the same format? Is the same method of citation used throughout?)

- Write or check headings and subheadings. (Is the level assigned to each heading or subheading logical?)
- Sometimes, design and lay out pages.
- Check content and structure. (Are paragraph breaks reasonable? Is there redundant or misplaced text? Are ideas presented in a logical order?)
- Write or check photo captions (called cutlines in journalism) and the placement of photos and graphics. (Do illustrations and tables support the text? Is the artwork suitable for printing or reproducing on the web?)
- Check for legal problems such as libel and slander, violation of copyright, and the like.
- Check for completeness and accuracy. (Are all questions answered? Is anything missing? Are the facts right? Are proper names accurate? Are quotations correct?)
- Cut text to fit a predetermined length.
- Edit web-based publications. And a lot more....

What sort of problems are you looking for as a copy editor? Spelling is an obvious one, of course. Is it "recieve" or "receive"? Spellcheck will usually catch this kind of error.

Spellcheck won't work when a word is spelled correctly but it's the wrong word. For example, some people think "wrought iron" is spelled "rod iron." "Wrought" sounds like "rod," and wrought iron is often used to make iron rods in, say, iron fences. But the correct word is "wrought." Is the right term "cheery-picking" or "cherry-picking"? Unfortunately, your word processor's spellcheck won't catch errors like these.

It's easy, in the rush of writing, to leave words out ("It's no fun reading text with words that missing"), put words out of order ("words of out order") or type a word such as "now" when you really mean "not," so you end up with "We should now panic" when you meant the opposite. Or you might leave out the "not" entirely—spellcheck won't notice it's been missed—as the printers of the "Wicked Bible" did (see box).

It's been said that the price of liberty is constant vigilance. The same is true of perfect copy-editing.

If copy editors miss words out of order and don't catch missing words, the mind tends to fill in what the eye doesn't see, and the error will end up on the page or website.

So the copy editor cannot afford to be asleep at the switch. In fact, a copy editor's most important attribute, apart from a knowledge of perfect grammar and spelling and much more, is constant mindfulness of the task at hand.

Sometimes a writer has used the wrong word: "principle" (an ethical rule) rather than "principal" (main), "compliment"

Interesting Factoid
One of the most famous copy-editing errors of all time produced what has been called the "Adulterous Bible" or the "Wicked Bible," published in 1631. In that Bible, the seventh commandment left out the crucial word "not," resulting in the decree: "Thou shalt commit adultery." The printers were fined £300 (a princely sum in those days) and most of the copies were recalled and destroyed. The few copies that still exist are worth a fortune to collectors.

(flattery) rather than "complement" (go along well with), "redact" (delete text) rather than "reduce," and so on. The copy editor needs to know which one is the right word. And if she doesn't know, or isn't sure, she has the dictionary or her organization's style guide on her desk within easy reach.

The copy editor is also looking for errors in fact and logic. For example, a copy editor was handling a story on the then new sports stadium in Toronto; it was called SkyDome at the time, but we now know it as the Rogers Centre. One of the figures in the story was "$5 billion." Given that the stadium's total construction cost wasn't that much, the number had to be "$5 million," and the editor made the correction after checking with the reporter.

It's easy to miss this type of error because many news stories do involve billions of dollars. If the editor isn't alert and fully informed about the background of the story she's editing, a factual or logical error can easily slip through.

The copy editor needs to read in a special way, with an eye not just for errors in what's on the page or screen—spelling, grammar, logical errors, factual errors, and more—but also alert to what *isn't there*. Is a vital piece of information missing? If so, the copy editor's task is to get that information.

The copy editor needs to be alert for possible legal or ethical problems. For example, if a document produced by you or someone else in your office is potentially libellous, or violates copyright, your organization could end up in a lawsuit. If a copy editor believes there is a legal problem with a piece of writing, he needs to check with someone who knows, such as the permissions editor or the company lawyer. If he can't get legal advice, the copy editor should revise the possibly problematic material or delete it.

Finally, in addition to an encyclopedic knowledge about English grammar and usage, the copy editor reads widely on every conceivable topic. She is an avid collector of facts and information who knows a bit about most things, and quite a bit about many things.

For example, she will know the years when World Wars I and II began and ended, roughly how many died in those wars (civilian and military), when governments began and ended, and much, much, much more. The veteran copy editor vacuums up information and becomes a factual reference for other editors. In short, the copy editor is filled with curiosity about almost every topic you can think of.

How Errors Creep into the Language

It is increasingly common to read or hear comments such as "There is many theories about the origins of humanity" or "There were less people at the festival than last year."

The first example is wrong because the verb "is" is singular while "theories," the real subject of the sentence (the noun the pronoun "there" stands in for), is plural.

This is called, in grammar language, an error in subject-verb number agreement (SVNA). The second sentence is wrong because, as discussed in the chapter on grammar, "people" is a countable noun and takes "fewer." Uncountable nouns, such as "water," take "less": "There is less water in the reservoir this year." No literate person would say "There is fewer water in the reservoir this year." It's just as wrong, grammatically, to say "There were less people at the festival."

Average readers or listeners hearing these grammatically incorrect sentences may not consciously know there's anything wrong. But if they are literate at all, they will have a vague feeling that something isn't quite right. Your job as a copy editor is to make sure that this vague feeling of unease doesn't arise. You do this by ensuring that your text is well-written in terms of the eight Cs and free of factual, legal, and logical errors.

The copy editor is the last line of defence against bad writing and the decline of the English language. Given that we are moving into a "post-literate" culture in which more and more people entertain themselves with visual and aural media rather than print, holding the line on correct written English is a formidable task, but someone has to do it. That someone is the copy editor.

USING SPELLCHECK

You've read the copy you are editing carefully and thoroughly. What you'll likely do next is run the word processor's spelling checker. You will almost certainly discover a spelling mistake or two (or ten) that you missed on your first eyeball reading!

Unfortunately, spellcheck won't catch every error. Suppose you've got a sentence that reads "Its time for action on drunk driving." Spellcheck won't tell you that "its" should be "it's" (the contraction of "it is") because "its" is correct as the possessive of "it" and could definitely come before the noun "time," as in "its time has come." So spellcheck is just a backup to your own careful reading of the text.

Incidentally, a grammar checker might catch the "its/it's" distinction, but there are many other errors that the grammar checker will miss, so you can't fully trust a grammar checker, either.

After spellchecking and checking grammar, therefore, you must *read the text again*. Every piece of text should get at least three reads, one with your eyes, one with spellcheck, and then a final check, again, with the eyes.

Aiming for 100 per cent correctness in your copy-editing has two major advantages for you:

Copy Tip
It is almost impossible to copy-edit and proofread your own writing with 100 per cent effectiveness—you will be so familiar with what you mean to write that your eye will simply skim over errors. If possible, have someone else copy-edit your professional writing before it goes beyond your desk.

- First, the writing that goes into the world is accurate. That's good for the image of the company or organization you work for and therefore good for you. An organization that can't get its written communication right could, logically, be suspected of not getting its product or service right either.
- The second advantage is personal: readers (including your managers) will notice if you make a lot of errors. That puts in jeopardy your long-term job future or at least your reputation within the company and with the public. On the other hand, by being scrupulous in your editing, you will become known to your managers and the public for accuracy and attention to detail.

Both goals are worth striving for.

OTHER COPY-EDITING TASKS

As a copy editor in the professions or business, you may be asked to do more than just edit copy. You might be designing and laying out pages, which in practice usually means using a computer-layout template. You might be inserting text onto the page and then micro-editing to make the text fit the page length. You might have to write headings or headlines and subheadings or subheadlines.

Often a design specialist will create the layout of the page, and you just have to insert the text, headings, and pictures; in other cases, you may be making layout decisions on your own. If that is the case, you'll be trained in layout using your company's page-design software.

Photographs and graphics are an important part of many documents, and, as a copy editor, you could be choosing art for the page you are laying out, cropping the art to a certain size, and writing captions (cutlines) for it.

In all these jobs, you will need training on the graphic-design software that does these tasks. One recommendation: take good notes as you are being taught. The procedures for handling layout and graphics in professional-level design software such as Adobe InDesign or QuarkXPress can be very complex.

COPY-EDITING SYMBOLS

Today, the vast majority of writing is done on computers. But before computers, text was produced by handwriting or on a typewriter. The typed or hand-written text would go to an editor for copy-editing and then on to a printer or compositor who would put the text into print format.

It wasn't easy to correct text produced by a typewriter or by hand. Sometimes, to get a perfect version, you had to retype the whole document, or at least the whole page.

To make the process easier, symbols were developed so those typesetting a document would know what changes the copy editors wanted. These symbols are similar to the ones professors use to mark essays and reports, so you've seen them before. The most common copy-editing and proofreading symbols are shown in Figure 4.1.

Worth Knowing
A complete list of copy-editing symbols can be found online with the search term "copy-editing marks" or "copy-editing symbols."

(delete symbol)	**Delete**	According to Bill Bryson, "Language is more fashion than science, and matters of usage, spelling, and pronunciation tend to to wander around like hemlines."
(sp circled)	**Spell out word**	In Scotland, 12 highlanders and a bagpipe make a rebellion.
(caret symbol)	**Change letter**	Condense soap, not books!
(triple underline)	**Change to capital letter**	"Status quo" is latin for "the mess we're in."
(lc symbol)	**Change to lower-case letter**	Eschew Obfuscation.
(transpose symbol)	**Transpose letters or words**	A waist is a thing terrible to mind.
(insert caret)	**Insert (letter, word, phrase, or punctuation)**	Hindsight is an exact science.
(close space symbol)	**Close space**	Write a wise saying and your name will live for ever.
(add space symbol)	**Add space**	Would you let someone lookover your writing?
(paragraph symbol)	**Start new paragraph**	"Did you sleep well?" he asked me. "No," I replied, "I made a few errors."
(Stet)	**Ignore suggested revision and keep original text.**	Hard writing makes easy reading. Handwriting

Figure 4.1 Common Copy-Editing Symbols

Chances are, because most editing is now done on computer rather than paper, you won't be using these symbols much unless you need to mark student papers or proofread or correct the page proofs of a book or article. However, knowledge of the editing symbols is still part of any copy editor's basic tool kit.

Does computerization mean a copy editor's task is easier than it was in the days of paper and pencil, scissors and glue (the computer commands "cut" and "paste" are based on what copy editors once did to paper copy)? Not necessarily.

Because we live in an information-rich age, checking facts and determining that no copyrighted material has been used without proper permission are two of the copy editor's jobs that have become much more complicated. (Think of the number of answers you'd get if you did an online search to determine how many French soldiers were killed in World War II. Or just imagine trying to track down who actually owns the rights to a photograph that has been reproduced, without proper attribution, on a hundred or more websites.) Even making sure that proper names are spelled consistently and according to a reputed authority is tough. For example, there are many correct ways to spell the Russian name Alexei, including Aleksei, Aleksey, Alexey, and Alexi. Imagine maintaining consistency in the spelling of proper names on an NHL blog!

As already noted, the software used for professional publication, such as QuarkXPress or Adobe InDesign, is highly complex and can take days or weeks to master. Therefore, if you are using these tools in your job, you will be trained. That said, having previous experience with these programs is an asset when you apply for a job that requires you to use them.

Overall, paper and pencil editing was easier for a copy editor to learn, but the old way was not nearly as efficient in terms of getting text into print.

USING A WORD PROCESSOR FOR COPY-EDITING

Most word-processing programs have a function that lets you copy-edit text, share the text with others for further editing, collectively produce a final edited version, and so on. In Word, this function is called "Track Changes."

Once "Track Changes" or a similar feature is turned on, every change you (or anyone) makes in a text is tracked. How it is tracked depends on how you set the word processor's preferences. In Word, all added words and punctuation appear in coloured type. Words and punctuation that you've deleted will be either highlighted in colour and crossed out with a line or set off to the side margin in a "bubble" and marked as deleted. (See Figure 4.2.)

You can opt to have all the changes appear on your text as you edit, or you can hide the corrections and just see what the corrected text looks like. This corrected version is often easier to read, but it may hide further errors! You can also insert

Several editors can work on the same document. If several editors are working on the same documentthis is the case, each editor can have their his or her own colour so everyone knows which editor changed what part of the documentwho changed what. The Which colour is is assigned to which editor is usually chosen automatically by the word-processing program.

If several editors are working on the same document, each editor can have his or her own colour so everyone knows who changed what. Which colour is assigned to which editor is usually chosen automatically by the word-processing program.

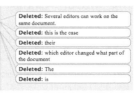

Deleted: Several editors can work on the same document.	
Deleted: this is the case	
Deleted: their	
Deleted: which editor changed what part of the document	
Deleted: The	
Deleted: is	

Figure 4.2 Two Preferences for Showing Tracked Changes in Word

comments in the text for others to read and add to, if they wish. In Word, you do this using the "Comments" function.

If several editors are working on the same document, each can have his or her own colour so everyone knows who changed what. The colour assigned to each editor is usually chosen automatically by the word-processing program, but you can change your colour manually in the program's preferences. Features such as Word's "Track Changes" are very handy editing tools for individuals or groups.

Using Editing Features

Let's say you've been given the following text to edit:

> There are two menus on the home page, one that goes across the top of the screen and then another that goes across the screen but is half way down the page. When you roll the mouse over each item of the menu it creates a pull down menu for even more options of web pages to view. The menus are full of different options in which to navigate through the website.

This paragraph is very wordy. Here's what an electronic edit of the paragraph might look like:

> There are two menus on = the The home page has two menus, one that goes across the top of the screen and then another that goes across the screen but is half-way down the page. Rolling When you roll the mouse over a each item of the menu reveals it creates a pull-down menu with for even more options of web pages to view. The menus are full of different options in which to navigate through the website.

As you can see, a text full of tracked changes is a riot of coloured and crossed-out lines and can be hard to read. However, again, most word-processing programs allow you to set your tracking preferences. In Word, you can choose to see the corrected or "Final" text without all the changes:

The home page has two menus, one across the top of the screen and another halfway down the page. Rolling the mouse over a menu reveals a pull-down menu with more options.

You can also choose to see the original text without any changes ("Original"), the original text with the changes ("Original Showing Markup"), and the final text with the changes ("Final Showing Markup").

When you are finished your part of the editing, you can send the edited text to the writer or to another editor to make his or her additions, which will be shown in a different colour.

When you or a professional copy editor are ready to put the copy into final form, these tracked changes will be either accepted or rejected. In Word, one portion of the "Review" toolbar will take you to a "Next" or "Previous" tracked change and allow you to "Accept" or "Reject" the change. Then you go to the next one, and so on. You can also "Accept All Changes in Document" or "Reject All Changes in Document," although doing this is risky because you might not want to keep all the changes.

"Track Changes" Tip
When you are doing the final edit of copy that has been through many tracked changes, it's useful to review the text using both views: with editing marks and comments showing and without.

CONCLUSION

The English language can be tricky, and the eyes are easily fooled when it comes to copy-editing text. Among the most common problems in copy-editing are the following:

- factual errors ($5 billion or $5 million?),
- speling erors,

- words of out order,
- "not" when you mean "now" and vice-versa (or other pairings such as "an" and "and"),
- words that missing,
- general grammar issues (comma splices, problems with agreement), and
- wrong word ("refudiate" instead of "repudiate" or "principle" instead of "principal").

To avoid these problems, the copy editor needs to be an expert on English grammar and spelling, knowledgeable on a wide range of topics, a logical thinker, and, above all, constantly mindful.

Copy-Editing Exercise

Your mission is to copy-edit the text below. There are at least 22 errors, including misspellings, words out of order, words missing, and so on. The answers are on page 404, but don't peek until you've done the exercise.

Copy-editing is one of most the important jobs in professional writing. You could think of the copy editor as a hunter, hidden in the foliage, waiting for their pray—a spelling mistake, a grammatical or punctuation error, a problem in wording—to appear. Then, he or she pounce and—lo!—the error no is more it is just as satisfying to take an immoderate spew of verbaige and, with a few streaks of the keyboard, create instead a measured flow of words. The copy editor may also redact five poorly chosen words to two or three, do we really have to say "in regard to" when we mean "about". But the copy editor be must also carefull. Too much editing may distract from the meaning the writer is not trying to get across and even introduce new errors. Finally the copy editor performs what can only be called a noble role in the perservation of proper English. Writers, even good ones, are constantly trying to change language by braking the rules of grammar and by concieving new spellings or even entirely new words (words like "neologism" which means "the practice of creating new words"). Copy editors are the line last of defence against error and these barbaric practices. In other words, copy editors are the last bastion of civiliized discourse. May that bastion stand forever!

Part II
Document Design

In Part II you will learn

- How to create attractive documents that are reader-friendly,
- How to write professional-looking memos, emails, and letters, and
- How to write business letters and memos in "full-block" style.

Chapter 5
Basic Document Design

In this chapter you will learn how to

- Produce documents that are reader friendly and attractive,
- Understand the fundamentals of modular layout,
- Use bullets and numbers properly in lists, and
- Use headings and graphics effectively.

INTRODUCTION: THE IMPORTANCE OF GOOD DOCUMENT DESIGN

As with your writing, the documents that present your writing to the world, whether in print or on computer, are a reflection of you and your professionalism. In this chapter, we will look at good document design through the use of lists, headings, white space, graphics, pictures, and more.

Grey Areas in Document Design

In document design, there are numerous grey areas—accepted conventions rather than grammatical rights and wrongs. Among the grey areas for document design are the following:

In Lists

- *Do lists require an introductory sentence?* Yes, almost always. Lists should not just appear out of the blue; they need to be introduced by at least a phrase or a sentence.
- *Are colons needed to introduce a list?* Ideally, if the sentence that introduces a list is a full sentence (subject, verb, object, and complete idea), the introductory sentence should end with a colon. If the introduction is only a partial sentence,

a colon is not necessary and sometimes grammatically incorrect. In practice, most readers won't know the difference, and many writers ignore conventions of grammar and punctuation when using lists. This issue will be discussed in more detail below.

- *Should there be punctuation at the end of each item on a list?* A bullet or number in a list can act as punctuation. If you choose this style, you don't need punctuation at the end of any list item, even the last one. But we suggest that you punctuate lists as you would sentences and end a list that forms a sentence with a period or other appropriate punctuation. In practice, most readers neither know nor care if list items end with punctuation or not. Pick one style, though, and then be consistent.
- *Do lists always end with a period or other appropriate punctuation?* Again, the answer depends on whom you ask. Check to see whether your company or organization has a preference, and go with that. But here is our answer: Yes. Always. Why is explained below.

In Headings

- *Use a sans-serif font for headings?* Sans-serif fonts, such as Arial and Calibri, usually look more attractive as headings than serif fonts, such as Times New Roman and Cambria, especially if the body text is in serif. There is more on serif and sans-serif fonts below.

MODULAR DESIGN

In this section of the book, we will look at various ways of designing a document to look good using lists, headings, graphics, and other elements. In some cases, such as business letters, the layout is fixed: you will always use "full-block" formatting for letters and the body of memos, for example. The details of formatting letters are in Chapter 6.

But what about documents such as brochures, flyers, reports, web pages, and the like? What kind of overall design strategy should you follow for more complex kinds of layouts?

The answer, in one word, is "modular." Modules are short "chunks" of text or graphics that the reader can take in with a quick glance before going on to the next "chunk." In other words, rather than giving the reader a long, grey column or page of text, modular layout breaks the text and pictures into smaller bits that the reader can, as it were, easily "swallow" without a lot of reading or viewing effort.

Figure 5.1 Potato Chips—Can You Eat Just One?

You could think of modular design as potato chips versus a full-course meal. A large meal can be daunting, especially if you're not particularly hungry. But potato chips, for most people, are different. It's hard to eat only one potato chip. First, you have one. Then two. Then just one more. And before you know it, you've finished the bag.

This is the approach you want to take in designing documents. You give the reader a bite-size chunk of information—one potato chip, as it were. It can be an arresting headline, a short paragraph of fascinating text, an intriguing photograph or graphic. Then you lead the reader's eye to another bite-size chunk of information. And another. Until the reader has, almost without any conscious effort, read the whole document!

By contrast, in the past when newspaper readers took up their daily paper, they were faced with an intimidating wall of grey type. For example, Figure 5.2 shows the first page of *The Times* of London from 1788.

Figure 5.2 Front Page of *The Times* of London, December 4, 1788

The text is broken up by vertical column lines, the stories are separated by horizontal lines, and each story begins with a drop capital. But there are no large headlines, no photographs, and just two small ship graphics representing the shipping news. That's a lot of grey type! And yet, readers of the day were used to a page of grey and waded in, undaunted.

Figure 5.3 Modular Layout for a Present-Day Newspaper

Over time, reading tastes and abilities have changed, and readers now want a less demanding look to their news and other documents. The preferred design style today follows more of a "potato-chip" approach—a modular approach. For example, Figure 5.3 shows a model for feature newspaper pages.

Notice that the information isn't presented as a field of grey type but in short, modular, easy-to-read chunks of information, with plenty of graphic art.

Similarly, the driver's insurance-renewal letters from the Insurance Corp. of BC (ICBC) look like Figure 5.4:

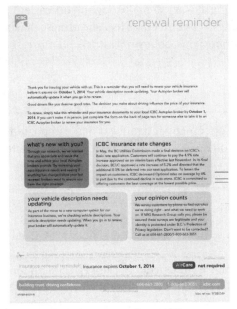

Figure 5.4 ICBC Insurance Renewal Form
Reprinted with the permission of ICBC.

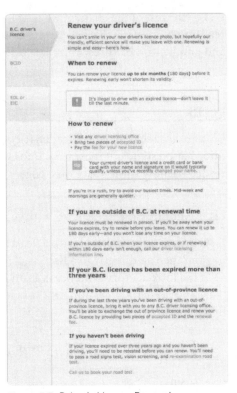

Figure 5.5 Driver's Licence Renewal Information—Online Format

Source: Insurance Corporation of British Columbia (ICBC), http://www.icbc.com/driver-licensing/getting-licensed/Pages/Renew-your-licence-or-ID.aspx. Reprinted with the permission of ICBC.

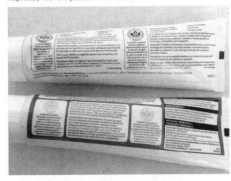

Figure 5.6 Toothpaste Tubes with the Older Style on Top and the Newer, More Modular Style on the Bottom

Note that the information is broken up into modular, boxed chunks, with each module in a different colour (you will see the colours as different shades of grey). The design makes for easy, step-by-step reading.

Figure 5.5 shows the Driver's Licence Renewal Information. Note, again, the short "chunks" of information, the boxes, the lists, and the colours, all aiming to make this page very easy to read.

Finally, here are two toothpaste tubes (Figure 5.6). The top tube is an earlier way of presenting toothpaste information; it's partly modular. The bottom tube is newer and has a completely modular look.

For the rest of the chapter, we'll be looking at ways to make documents easier to read and more attractive based on a modular layout that uses lists, headings, charts and graphs, and pictures, and that varies font styles, column widths, and more.

LISTS

Lists are an essential part of reader-friendly document design. Lists make important information stand out more than information buried in a paragraph, and lists create reader-friendly white space on a page.

Lists Should Be Introduced with a Sentence

Lists should be introduced with at least one sentence—you should not have a heading and then go directly to a list.

If the introductory sentence is a full sentence (independent clause), then, in formal (and academic) grammatical usage, the sentence should end with a colon, as in the following:

While in Japan, we ate the following foods:

- sushi,
- rice, and
- tempura.

If the introductory sentence is not a full sentence, then punctuation at the end of the introduction is not necessary:

While in Japan we ate

- sushi,
- rice, and
- tempura.

That said, the "introductory colon" rule is freely broken in business and professional writing; no one will think less of you if you break it. However, following the introductory colon rule means you can identify an independent clause, and that is a useful skill for someone trying to master grammar.

If you aren't sure whether your introductory sentence is a full sentence, you can use the "following" rule. That is, add "the following" to create a full sentence, as in "In Japan we ate *the following* foods: sushi, rice, and tempura." The introductory sentences become independent clauses because they include some form of "the following."

> **The "following" rule:**
> One way to avoid errors in introducing lists is to use "the following" in one form or another, as in the first Japanese food example. Adding "the following" creates a full sentence.

Lists Should Be Attractive

Lists look best when the second and subsequent lines are flush with the start of the first line.

Here's a list that doesn't follow this rule:

1. This is the first line of a long list that will carry over into the second and maybe even the third line.
2. This is the second line of a long list that will carry over into the second and maybe even the third line.
3. This is the third line of a long list that will carry over into the second and maybe even the third line.

This list is much easier to read if the lines after the first line in each list item are flush with the start of that item:

1. This is the first line of a long list that will carry over into the second and maybe even the third line.
2. This is the second line of a long list that will carry over into the second and maybe even the third line.
3. This is the third line of a long list that will carry over into the second and maybe even the third line.

Most word-processing programs have a bullet and numbering feature that automates this formatting process.

Also, there should be a space between the introductory sentence and the list and between the last item of the list and the next paragraph. This additional white space highlights the list even more.

> **Worth Knowing**
> To set the list off, you must put a space or partial space between the sentence introducing the list and the list itself and another space at the end of the list.

Bullets or Numbers?

Use bulleted lists when the elements of the discussion don't fall into any particular order, as in the ingredients for a recipe or the parts for a build-it-yourself desk.

This Ikea desk package contains the following:

- 12 #4 screws,
- 12 #4 bolted screws,
- 1 Phillips screwdriver, and
- everything else necessary to build your desk.

Use numbered lists when the order of the elements is important, as in actually preparing the food from the recipe or in assembling the desk.

To assemble this desk, do the following:

1. Unpack the numbered wooden panels.
2. Lay out the screws and bolts.
3. Attach wooden panel A to wooden panel B using the #4 screws.
4. Attach wooden panel C to panel D using the #4 screws....

Parallelism

Whenever possible, all *items in a list must be parallel in grammatical structure*. That is, all list items must begin with the same grammatical element: a noun, a verb, an adjective, a participle, or whatever you choose. In the Ikea desk package example, each item in the contents list begins with a noun (and adjective); each item in the numbered list begins with a verb that begins a complete imperative sentence (a command). For details on parallelism in lists, see Chapter 2, "6. Coherent."

List Punctuation

How are list items punctuated? Commas at the end of each item? Semicolons? No punctuation at all?

Punctuation at the end of list items is a grey area, and, definitely, you should check with your workplace to see whether it has any guidelines for writers that you should follow. For a start, bullets and numbers in a list are themselves punctuation; you don't *need* punctuation at the end of list items, and some style guides recommend stripping all punctuation (even end punctuation) from certain lists. We don't agree.

Worth Remembering
Ending list items with punctuation is reader friendly, especially if lists are long and carry over to second pages.

Here is what we recommend.

Use a period or appropriate end punctuation to finish a list. There are two reasons.

1. A period shows the list is finished. If a list carries over to another page and there's no period at the bottom of the first page, the reader knows the list isn't finished. In other words, ending a list with a period or other appropriate punctuation is reader friendly.
2. A list must be introduced by a full or partial sentence, so the list is therefore part of that sentence. A period (or other appropriate punctuation) is needed to end the sentence properly.

Note that if the list items are *full sentences*, they take the same punctuation as sentences and begin with capital letters. Here is an example:

When thinking about the purchase of a new laptop computer, consider the following features:

- Does the computer have sufficient internal memory?
- Is the hard drive large enough?
- Will the computer be light enough to carry easily?

In this case, each list item is a full sentence, begins with a capitalized word, and takes a question mark. If the full-sentence list items were not questions, then you'd end each list item with a period. Note, as well, that this list is *parallel*: all list items begin with a verb or an auxiliary verb (e.g., "does"). In general, you only need to capitalize the start of a list item if the list item is a full sentence.

The Japanese food example we saw previously had to use commas at the end of each item because the list included "and" in the second-last list item:

While in Japan, we ate the following foods:

- sushi,
- rice, and
- tempura.

The "and" is not necessary but, if you include it, you do need commas. That said, the commas are, strictly speaking, optional. The list could be formatted this way:

While in Japan, we ate the following foods:

- sushi
- rice
- tempura.

But be consistent!

Semicolons are also often used at the end of list items. Again, punctuation at the end of list items is optional. However, semicolons might be appropriate (and necessary for easy reading) if the list items are long and have internal punctuation. Similarly, in a non-list sentence with several items and internal commas, semicolons are used to divide the items (see Chapter 3 on semicolon use). Here's an example of a list with internal punctuation:

When you use crayons,

- be sure to use vivid colours, which will attract the most attention;
- don't press too hard on the crayon, which might break it;
- don't cross the lines when you are colouring.

Note the comma after the introductory subordinate clause. Remember, if in doubt about how to punctuate your list, you can't go wrong if you follow the conventions of punctuating regular prose:

When you use crayons, be sure to use vivid colours, which will attract the most attention; don't press too hard on the crayon, which might break it; don't cross the lines when you are colouring.

List Review

When you use lists, we recommend the following (unless you've been given other guidelines to follow):

- Introduce your list with a sentence, either full or partial.
- Put a space between the introductory sentence and the list and between the end of the list and the next paragraph. This space highlights the list and creates white space.
- End your list with a period or other appropriate punctuation.
- Be consistent in how you punctuate list items. If you are using punctuation at the end of list items, then do that in all lists in your document. If you aren't using punctuation at the end of list items, then stick to that style.
- Make all list items parallel in grammatical structure, whenever possible (sometimes it isn't).
- Use appropriate punctuation if each list item is a full sentence (such as the sentences in this list, which are full sentences).

Exercise on Lists

Each of the lists below has one or two errors. Identify what's wrong and make the correction. The answers are on page 405.

1. The most important things in life are:

   • Happiness
   • Having good friends
   • Making a good income

2. When you assemble a desk, be sure to do the following
   • Make sure all parts are in the box;
   • Use the correct tools; and
   • Keep your temper

3. My favourite movies are:

   • My Friend Flicka
   • Terminator 2
   • Mamma Mia

HEADINGS

Headings are signposts that guide the reader through your document. They show the reader the key points you are making, where those points can be found in the structure of your argument, and where the discussion is going. In other words, headings are reader friendly. There are several ways you can give your headings maximum impact while enhancing reader friendliness.

Most word-processing programs offer pre-packaged heading styles in their "Styles" menu. For example, Word offers "Heading 1," "Heading 2," and so on. Using these styles has many advantages, which we will discuss below in more detail.

For now, though, it's worth noting that if you use your word processor's pre-packaged heading styles, you can change all the text in your document styled as, say, "Heading 1"—including type of font, font size, colour, and spacing above and below—simply by modifying the elements of that heading in the "Styles" menu. All the "Heading 1" headings will change if you modify that style; you don't have to change each individual heading. Particularly for a very long document, like a formal report, using pre-packaged styles can be a major time saver.

Also, if you use the supplied heading styles, you can automatically generate a table of contents for your document. Your word processor's help menu will show you how to do this.

Heading Fonts and Sizes

Which font should you use for headings? There are two basic styles of font: serif and sans serif. Serif fonts include Times New Roman, Cambria, and Palatino. The text in this book is Minion.

A "serif," by the way, is the little icicle that hangs from the ends of letter crossbars and at the feet of letter uprights. "Sans-serif" fonts ("*sans*" in French means "without") don't have the icicles. Here's an example of each:

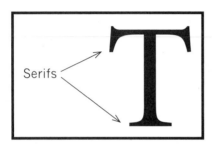 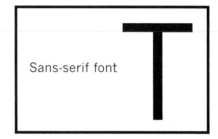

Each type of font has advantages and disadvantages. The serif fonts such as Times New Roman are easier to read in long sentences and paragraphs of text—this one, for example—than are sans-serif fonts: the serifs "guide" the eye from one letter to the next. Also, serif font letters vary in width, so they "fit" together, which also offers an easy pathway for the eye by compressing type.

On the other hand, the letters of sans-serif fonts are a bit wider than serif fonts and they don't "fit" together as serif fonts do. As a result, sans-serif fonts are "sticky" on the eyes; each letter and word stands out more than it would in a serif font. Because sans-serif fonts attract the eye and because they are different from a serif font, which is often selected for the body of a document, sans-serif fonts are excellent for headings. They easily act as signposts for the reader of your document. In short, sans-serif headings are, again, reader friendly.

As body text, however, sans-serif fonts like this one are ideal for documents in which every word is important, such as recipes or instructions for defusing a bomb, or for text with short paragraphs. And, because they are "sticky" to the eyes, sans-serif fonts appear larger than serif fonts: they give you more bang for the font size compared to serif fonts. For example, this paragraph is in

9.5-point Arial. The paragraphs above and below are in 10.5-point Minion. Yet, both paragraphs, at least at a quick glance, appear to be the same font size.

Here are two headings. Which one is the larger font size?

This is a heading in sans serif

This is a heading in serif

To most readers, the top heading is more eye-catching and obviously larger. However, both headings are 20 point; the second, in serif font, just appears to be smaller. This is because sans-serif letters are wider than serif letters and have a slightly taller x-height than serif fonts (see Figure 5.7 for an explanation of x-height).

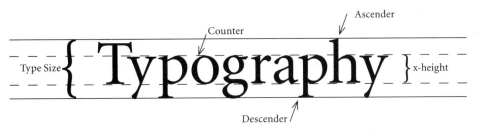

Figure 5.7 x-height explained

What size should your headings be? This book uses 10.5-point Minion as its body text style, with 10.5-point News Gothic as its first level of heading style ("Heading 1" style in Word). The same sans-serif font but in increasingly smaller sizes is used for second- and third-level headings. If the heading is too large, it will overwhelm the text; too small and it won't stand out as a heading. You should experiment with different heading sizes until you find the right balance.

Worth Knowing
Headings often look good in colour, especially if the document uses that colour elsewhere.

Serif fonts frequently used for body text include Times, Times New Roman, Palatino, and Cambria. Frequently used sans-serif fonts, for both body text and headlines, include Arial, Calibri, Verdana, Helvetica, and Geneva.

Because there are literally thousands of font choices in both serif and sans serif, it's possible to use, say, a serif font as a heading that works beautifully with a serif body style, and a document designer will have serif-font headings in her toolkit. However, for the beginning page designer, the safe choice for headings is a sans-serif font such as Arial or Calibri.

Placing Your Headings

Headings look best if they have a bit more space above them than below them. The extra space on top separates the heading from the previous section, while less space below the heading ties it to the text that follows. The result looks like this:

This is a heading

This paragraph of text illustrates the desirability of putting more space above a heading than below it. It has 12 points between the heading and the previous paragraph, and 3 points between the heading and this paragraph. Six points below the heading would also be attractive.

Most word processors offer a couple of ways of creating space above and below a heading.

One way is to use the "Style" menu to modify the spacing before and after for each heading size. If you select a 12-point space before headings and a 6-point space after, your headings will be nicely spaced between the ending paragraph of the previous section and the first paragraph of the new section.

A second option is to change the space above and below the heading manually for each heading. Most word-processing programs have a "Paragraph format" setting that allows you to set the "Spacing" before and after a paragraph. Even though it's

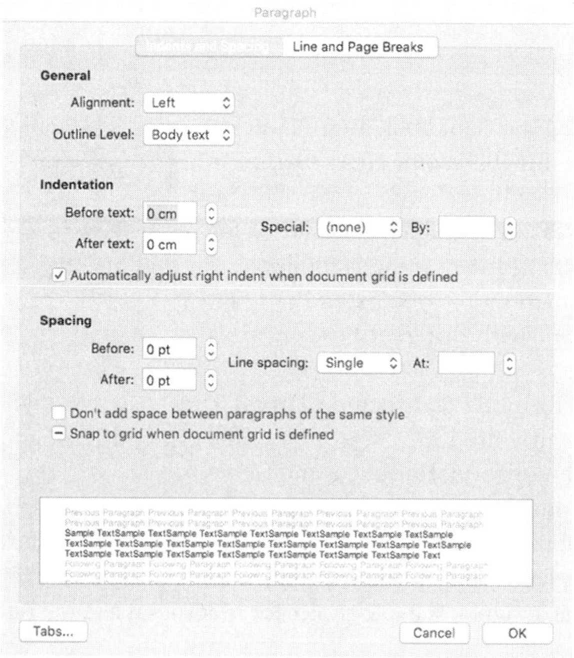

Figure 5.8 Paragraph Formatting Menu for Microsoft Word

only a line or two, a heading is considered to be a paragraph. (Figure 5.8 shows the "Paragraph" format options for Microsoft Word.)

However, individual, manual changes are cumbersome and time consuming and should be reserved for special situations. Overall, it's much easier to use a "Styles" menu to make this kind of adjustment for headings (and paragraphs) throughout the document.

One more caution: never leave a heading all by itself at the bottom of a page. Always have at least two lines of text under the heading. If that's not possible, move the heading to the next page.

Other Uses for Sans-Serif Fonts

Sans-serif fonts don't just look good as headings. If your document body is in a serif font such as Times New Roman, the text in tables usually looks good in a contrasting, sans-serif font. Like headings, tables aim to be "sticky" on the eye, and the different font style, not to mention the box holding the table, helps create variety on a page.

Sans-serif fonts also work well for photograph and picture captions, captions under graphs and charts, and for additional boxed text (see right for an example). In journalism and publishing, these text boxes are sometimes called "pull quotes." Note that sans-serif fonts can be a point or two smaller than serif fonts but will appear the same size as the serif font used for body text.

> This is an example of a pull quote in Arial 10-point font.

Headings Review

When using headings, follow these guidelines:

- Have slightly more space above a heading than below it.
- Always have at least two lines of text under a heading (and on the same page as the heading).
- Choose a heading style that stands out from the body text. If the body text is a serif font, that usually means the heading text will be sans serif.
- Consider using colour in headings.
- Use the heading styles provided by your word processor to "automate" your use of headings and to ensure they are all the same. Using heading styles will also allow you to create an automatic table of contents.

GRAPHICS

Few sights are more daunting than an entire page of unrelieved print, even with a heading at the top of it. Therefore, an important part of document design is finding ways to break up this sea of grey text—to make your publication more approachable and reader friendly.

As we've seen, headings and lists make text more reader friendly. Even more important for a good-looking print document or web page are graphic elements such as

- charts, tables, and graphs;
- photographs and pictures;
- boxes and lines;
- pull quotes;
- drop capitals; and
- variations in column widths and number of columns.

Properly used, graphic elements make the text not only more readable but also more dynamic.

Charts, Graphs, and Tables

Charts, graphs, and tables are a great way of presenting a lot of information in a format that is easier to read than a paragraph of text. For example, suppose you are presenting the sales figures for four of the regions in your company. You can write the following:

In 2014, Ontario had sales of $300,000, Quebec had sales of $432,000, the Maritimes had sales of $250,000, while sales in the West were $275,000.

Or, for better readability, you can put these figures into a table, as follows:

Region	Sales
Ontario	$300,000
Quebec	$432,000
Maritimes	$250,000
West	$275,000
Total	$1,257,000

Table 5.1 Tibia Investments—Regional Sales Figures for 2014
Source: *Canadian Business Report*, May 15, 2014.

With a table, the reader can see the provincial and total sales at a glance, which doesn't happen if this information is buried in a text paragraph. As a bonus, a table breaks up a grey expanse of text.

There is an even better way to present numbers, especially if you don't have to show the actual amounts or are working with percentages: make the table into a chart. Charts not only look good on the page, in part because they use colours or differently shaded areas, but they are better than tables at presenting comparisons at a glance.

To create a graph, you first enter the figures into your spreadsheet program and then use the software's automatic chart-creation feature to make the chart. Next, you copy and paste the chart into the document.

For example, using the figures from the table above, we end up with the following chart:

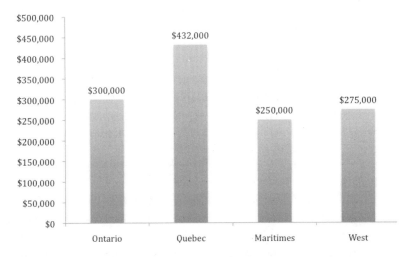

Figure 5.9 Tibia Investments—Regional Sales Figures for 2014
Source: *Canadian Business Report*, July 15, 2014.

Notice that we can see, in an instant, that Quebec had the highest sales figures and the Maritimes the lowest. And, as an added bonus, a page with a chart looks more attractive. The drawback is that, when you use some software programs, the actual values—for example, that Quebec sales were $432,000—may not be presented. In recent versions of Excel, though, you can choose to have value amounts displayed within your charts (they are at the top of the columns in Figure 5.9). If the actual figures are

Graphics Tip
When presenting numbers, if the actual figures are important, use a table. If the comparison is important, use a chart.

important and cannot be displayed within your chart, then use a table. If the comparison is important, use a chart.

If you use a chart and cannot present actual values, what do you do with the table? In reports and similar documents, you can put the table in an appendix at the end. Readers who want the actual figures can look there.

Of course, you can't just throw a graph or table into your document on a whim—there has to be a purpose for it being there. Here are a few more guidelines for using graphics:

- *All graphs, charts, pictures, and tables must be identified in some way, usually by a numbered title or caption*: Figure 1, Table 1, Picture 1, Chart 1, and so on.
    - Normally, the title of a table will be on top of the table, while the caption for a graph, chart, photograph, or other illustration will be below. (These illustrations are often called "figures.") If you right-click on a graph, your word processor may offer you the option of creating a caption.
    - *Captions and titles must have a few words identifying what the graphic or table is about*:
        - Figure 8: Gross and net sales for Manitoba, 2013
        - Portrait of the artist as a young man, December 1956. (*Cartoon by Louis Taylor. Used with permission.*)
- *All graphs, charts, pictures, tables, and data published elsewhere (digitally or otherwise) should have a source note*, e.g., "Data Source: Statistics Canada, Labour Force Survey, CANSIM, 2014" or see the "source" notes.
    - The source for a table will usually be placed directly under the table and labelled "Source."
    - For a figure, chart, or other illustration, the credit or source line sometimes appears in the lower right corner underneath the caption, often in a smaller font size than the caption (see Figure 5.9). Sometimes, credit lines for illustrations go in parentheses immediately after the title or caption (see the "Portrait of the artist" example above).
- *Tables and graphics must be referred to in the text of the document*, e.g., (see Figure 5), (see Table 3), or "as the adjacent photograph shows."
- *Don't separate a sentence with a graphic.* The full sentence must go before or after the graphic or, better still, around the graphic as a text wrap.
- *Don't, unless absolutely unavoidable, break a table between two pages.* Use a separate page for that table and its accompanying text (i.e., its title and any notes, including its source note).
- *Keep graphics and text together.* That is, don't, unless it's unavoidable, refer in your text—e.g., (see Figure 4.8)—to a graphic that is on another page.
- *If your graphic takes up more than half the page, consider giving it a page to itself.* In this case, of course, your text will be referring to a graphic on another page. This works best if the graphic and text are on facing pages.

- *Use pie charts and bar graphs to show the relationships between elements,* as we do in Figure 5.9.
- *Use line graphs when you want to display a trend,* say the price of oil over several decades or a company's sales over two months (see Figure 5.10). The crooked line represents the weekly sales; the straight line, the trend (which, in this case, is slightly down, even though Week 8 sales were up).

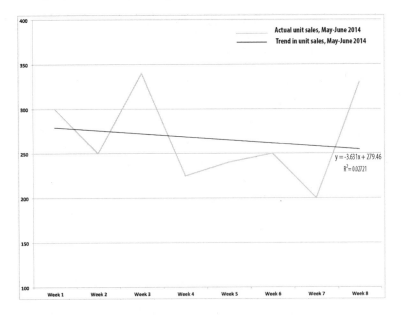

Figure 5.10 Tibia Investments—Unit Sales for May–June 2014

Boxes and Pictures

Boxed text and boxed graphics are easy ways to make your document more attractive. The box can contain additional textual material, called a sidebar. (The boxes labelled "Worth Knowing" and the like in this book are examples.)

Another technique for document design is using pull quotes: taking important points out of the text and putting them in a box.

Pull quotes can be from the text itself, or they can highlight material that is quoted in the text. In the latter case, it's best to put quotation marks around the quoted text. If you are just quoting from the document text itself, the quotation marks are not necessary.

If you're quoting from an authority (as in the quotation from sixteenth-century poet John Donne), then quotation marks can

> **'No man is an island'**
> —John Donne

> Pull quotes can be taken from the text itself. In that case, you don't need quotation marks because you are quoting yourself.

tempor, ipsum vitae vestibulum porttitor, tellus odio tempus nulla, bibendum vestibulum turpis arcu sed justo. Vivamus ac lacus at eros euismod pellentesque. Etiam lacinia. Praesent id augue sit amet quam ultrices lacinia. Nam sodales eros ac est.

Pellentesque euismod. Ut egestas vulputate orci. Praesent pede enim, ornare ut, porttitor sit amet, tristique eget, lacus. Donec felis. Maecenas ornare quam a risus. Pellentesque vitae mauris. In hac habitasse platea dictumst. Suspendisse ante leo, porta

amet metus. Pellentesque malesuada aliquam erat. Ut et tellus ac enim vestibulum egestas. Fusce hendrerit, tellus sit amet mattis fermentum, neque neque volutpat ligula, quis

> **"**
> **Pull quotes can look like this.**

sodales leo enim at justo. Duis elementum tortor faucibus ligula.

In vestibulum dolor vitae tellus. Vestibulum dapibus lacus. Nam

> **Or pull quotes can look like this.**

nunc. Etiam sollicitudin sagittis ipsum. Nullam volutpat tellus. Donec ac arcu. In non ante dapibus urna imperdiet sollicitudin. Morbi non lacus. Maecenas vel quam vitae ligula gravida interdum.

Sed enim nisl, ultrices eu, porttitor in, dictum a, nunc. Class aptent taciti sociosqu ad litora torquent per conubia nostra, per inceptos hymenaeos. Aliquam quam ante, viverra vitae, ultrices in, blandit dictum, felis. Vestibulum scelerisque neque ut purus. Etiam sollicitudin tincidunt nisl. Morbi eleifend viverra tortor. Pellentesque congue. Proin

Figure 5.11 Examples of Pull Quotes

be used. Note that in magazine and newspaper design, single quotation marks are often used in boxes and headlines. These days, however, pull quotes are indicated using various methods. See a few of these in Figure 5.11.

> Boxes can have shading, as this example shows.

Several styles of pull quotes are shown in the previous page and this one. You don't need a period at the end of a short quotation; you would include a question mark or exclamation point. The text for a pull quote is usually different in style and size from the body text. In this book, for example, boxed material is in 7.5-point News Gothic.

> This pull quote has no box line. This technique creates white space.

Another attractive option for boxes is to use colour, either for the box lines, the text, or both. Or the boxes themselves can be in colour with white text. Shading the boxes can also be effective. Or, instead of using a full box, you can have lines on top of and below the boxed text or even to one side of the boxed text, as in the second example in Figure 5.11. In fact, you don't have to put a box around the pull quote at all, as you can see on the previous page; this technique creates white space.

Finally, in document design, pictures, drawings, cartoons, and photographs enliven a piece of text, if they are appropriate and relevant. Remember that pictures, figures, charts, and the like almost always need captions to identify them, and, again, they need to be pointed to in the text, e.g., (see Picture 12) or (see following picture) or (see Figure 5).

Columns

You can vary column widths and use more than one column to make your document more attractive. Most documents on letter-size 8½-by-11-inch paper look fine with one column, left justified. Left justified means the text on the right margin is not straight; this is also called ragged right. Fully justified text has both left and right margins straight; fully justified is how the text in most books (including this one) is printed.

However, using word-processing software to fully justify text on a letter-size page creates irregular gaps between the words. The spacing between words is more regular with a dedicated page-layout program such as QuarkXPress or Adobe InDesign.

If, using a standard word-processing program, you want to put fully justified text on 8½-by-11 pages, reducing the column width will make the space between words smaller and therefore more attractive. Shrinking the column will also produce white space on the right or left margin of the page into which you can put text or graphics. You can also leave the margin column blank. For example, this paragraph is fully justified, with a narrower column width than the rest of the chapter.

You can put useful text or pictures in the margin.

Another option is to divide the text into more than one column. A word of warning, though: with two or more columns, you will want to make your text size smaller because columns are designed to make smaller text readable.

Here's an example of a narrow column in a 12-point font, with full justification. The words seem oddly spaced and not that attractive. Sentences seem choppy and are not easy to read.

> Another option is to divide the text into more than one column, fully justified. A warning, though: if you do so, you will want to make your text size smaller because narrow columns were designed to make smaller text readable.

Here's what the column looks like in a smaller font size, 10 point:

> Another option is to divide the text into more than one column, fully justified. A warning, though: if you do so, you will want to make your text size smaller because narrow columns were designed to make smaller text readable.

In the end, you should adopt whichever column strategy gives you the most attractive and readable page.

Drop Capitals

Drop capitals at the start of chapters or sections can also make your pages more attractive. This paragraph begins with a drop capital.

Many word-processing programs will "Insert" a drop capital and let you adjust the font style, size, and depth (two lines, three lines, etc.). In general, the larger the heading for the chapter or section, the larger the number of lines the drop cap should take. So, the "Heading 1" style in Word might take a four-line drop cap, "Heading 2" a three-line drop cap, and so on. It never hurts to experiment with different options to see what looks best.

One last word on graphics: don't overuse them. A hodgepodge of graphics doesn't look nearly as attractive as a clean page that uses graphics and other document-design techniques with restraint. As noted in the previous paragraph and elsewhere, you should experiment with different strategies and then pick the one that is the most attractive.

Graphics Review

When using graphics, follow these guidelines:

- Use tables, graphs, charts, and pictures to present information more dramatically and efficiently.
- Identify graphics with a descriptive caption or title (e.g., "Figure 1: Canada's performance on main factors of competitiveness, 2011" or "A lookout point over the Okanagan Valley in British Columbia, 1929"). A figure or table number alone is not enough.
- Always point to the graphic in the text (e.g., "see Figure 1" or "as the picture of the lookout over the Okanagan Valley shows").
- Use boxes to break up text.
- Try to present information in a modular ("chunk" or "potato chip") format.
- Play with column widths and more than one column to see if you can make a grey page more attractive.
- Use colours (with good taste, of course).
- Be restrained in your use of graphical elements.

Graphics Example

Let's pretend we have some text, say a page's worth (see Figure 5.12). The page looks like this (the text is the grey):

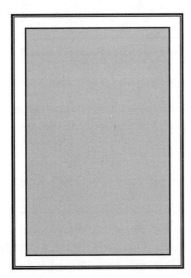

Figure 5.12 A "Grey" Page

Now imagine we have two pages to work with—let's say they're news magazine pages, and the text is about how coffee prices are being affected by droughts in Kenya. How could we make this text more attractive? For this exercise we won't worry about the actual text; we're just concerned with the layout of the page.

Well, for a start, we could give the text a headline and some subheadings, perhaps using colour. We could put the text into two or even three columns (let's go with two, for simplicity). We could add pictures, graphs, a pull quote, perhaps a sidebar box and smaller boxes.

So, what might we end up with? Perhaps something like this:

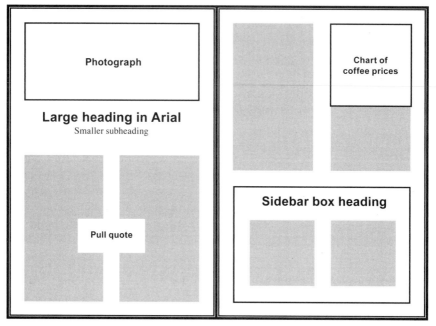

Figure 5.13 A Two-Page Magazine Spread

Note how a photograph, a chart, a pull quote, the two-column layout, some white space, and a sidebar box divide what could be a lot of grey information into easy-to-read, modular segments.

SUMMING UP

Well-written, attractively presented documents are reader friendly. Nobody wants to look at a page filled with grey text if it's avoidable. That's where document design comes in. By using lists, headings, graphics, boxes, pictures, and colour; varying column width, text size, and much more; and using a "modular" approach, you can make any page look attractive.

Keep in mind that attractive document design tells the audience something about *you*. By following the rules of document design, your message and your personal image will always be a positive one.

Chapter 6 discusses how to design professional-looking memos, emails, and letters.

Chapter 6
Formatting for Correspondence

In this chapter you will learn to write, in proper professional format,

- A memo,
- An email, and
- A letter.

INTRODUCTION

Even if you never produce any other form of document design in your professional career, you will be writing letters, emails, and memos. In this chapter, we will look at the proper formatting for these forms of communication.

Grey Areas

As with most forms of professional and business writing, letters, memos, and emails don't follow cut-and-dried rules. Here are some of the possible grey areas in correspondence document design:

- *Full-block letter format for business and professional correspondence?* Yes. Always.
- *Subject line before or after the salutation ("Dear Sir:")?* After the salutation makes sense. First we say hello to someone; then we state our business.
- *Subject line is written "Subject:" or "Re:"?* "Subject:" looks more professional. "Re:" is more commonly found in legal writing.

Worth Visiting
A website that can be found using the search terms "McMurrey Chapter 1: Business Correspondence" has good additional information on block-letter format and variations on this format, as well as on the content of business letters.

- *JT/kl or JT:kl (that is, slash or colon between the two sets of initials) when some-one else has typed out the correspondence?* As you wish, but be consistent. More on this below.

There are many other grey areas in technical and business communication, but this list will give you an idea of how to aim for consistency in formatting and style. Let's start with memos, keeping in mind that most of the formatting of memos is the same for emails. We'll discuss writing emails in more detail in Chapter 7.

MEMOS AND EMAILS

Memos are internal documents. That is, they are sent within an organization, usually between individuals who know each other and each other's business titles. Memos can be exchanged between equals or between an employee and his or her manager or boss. Memos are usually short and to the point. Any additional information can be sent as an attachment (to an email) or enclosure (if it's a paper memo).

You are already familiar with the basic format of a memo from using email, although the order of the headings (To, From, etc.) may be slightly different in the email template. Indeed, most memos these days are sent in electronic, email format, with the paper copy (if any) mostly serving as a permanent physical record for the files.

A professional memo will begin with a company letterhead, then the following headings:

To: George Smith, Parts Manager [use title only if necessary]
From: Michelle Jones, Financial Comptroller [use title only if necessary]
Date: January 23, 2019 [or Jan. 23, 2019 or 23 January 2019]
Subject: Purchase orders for accounts department

The subject line can be as shown in the example, mostly lower case with only the first word and proper nouns such as the names of countries capitalized. Or it can be in "headline style," with capital letters for all the major words (as you would format a book title), or you can use all capitals. All three styles are correct, but be consistent. Note that there is no period at the end of the subject line.

Emails and memos may have two other parts in their headers:

cc: [carbon copy]
bcc: [blind carbon copy]

Carbon copy (cc) refers to the now almost-obsolete technology of using carbon paper to make copies of typewritten documents. The "cc" means that you are copy-ing your memo to individuals other than the main recipient to keep them in the information loop. For example, a memo from the finance department to a manager might also go as a "cc" to the company president. In a print memo, the "cc" can be part of the header (placed right after the subject line), or, more traditionally, it goes at the bottom of the document. (If a more traditional style is used in print memos, the "cc" is in lower case.) Email programs usually give you the opportunity to "cc" individuals right after the "To" heading, as shown below.

Blind carbon copy (bcc) means you are sending a copy of the memo to someone else, but keeping both the main recipient and any others who were copied "blind" to this—they will not know you are sending the memo to the "bcc'd" party. The "bcc" designation will not appear on the original or cc'd memos; only the bcc'd person will know that he or she has received this memo without the other recipients' knowledge.

You might use a blind copy in the case of, say, an employment dispute in which you want to keep the company president informed of the negotiations but not inform the employee and managers that the president is in the loop.

"Bcc" in most email programs works in a similar way. Recipients who have been "bcc'd" are not able to see others who have received blind copies. For this reason, the "bcc" function is useful for organizations that want to keep the email addresses of their members confidential.

The text for the memo goes next. The writing style of a memo is usually informal, unless it is going to someone much higher up the chain of command. In that case, a more formal tone is probably both warranted and wise. In general, the sender and receiver of a memo are on familiar terms, so formality often isn't necessary.

Memo writers frequently summarize information in bulleted or numbered lists for conciseness and easy readability. The first line of a paragraph in a memo is *not indented*, and paragraphs are separated by a space.

Unlike letters, memos are not required to end with "Yours truly" or "Yours sincerely." A memo traditionally ends with a courteous sentence stating the action you would like readers to take but not a formal closing (the sender is already shown in the heading). Today, an informal first name ("Michelle") or a full name and title, depending on the context, could end an emailed memo.

At the bottom of a memo that has been typed by someone (say, Ellen Foster) other than the individual the memo is from (say, Michelle Jones), use the form MJ/ef or MJ:ef. These are called "reference initials." This convention is used so the actual typist can be identified if necessary. Either a slash or a colon is acceptable between the initials; as always, be consistent. The sender's initials are in capital letters; the typist's initials are lower case.

The memo may also contain additional material in the form of enclosures or attachments. To ensure that these are not overlooked, note them after any reference initials. There are various ways to do this:

Enclosures: Purchase order receipt form
               Report on ordering marmot figurines, January 20, 2019
               Memo from Dylan Jones, January 14, 2019
Enclosures: 3

You don't need a period at the end of the enclosure line.

Overall, then, a memo will look something like this:

Tibia Investments Corp.

To: George Smith, Parts Manager
From: Michelle Jones, Financial Comptroller
Date: January 23, 2019
Subject: Purchase orders for accounts department

Our department has revised the purchase order forms to reflect the changes suggested by your report of January 20.

Thank you for responding so promptly after Dylan Jones made us aware that we needed to redesign these forms to improve customer service and inventory control.

I've distributed the redesigned marmot figurine purchase orders to all departments, and we will begin using the new forms immediately.

Michelle

MJ/ef

Enclosure: Copy of new purchase order form

cc: Dylan Jones, Account Manager

In general, the rules for formatting and writing an email are quite similar. Headers are a bit different, and the tone of an email is usually more casual. Also, emails typically have greetings and closings. An email about the same topic might look like this:

To: George Smith <gsmith@tibia.com>
From: Michelle Jones <mjones@tibia.com>
Cc: Dylan Jones <djones@tibia.com>
Date: January 23, 2019
Subject: Redesigned purchase orders (marmot figurines)

George,

Thanks so much for helping us redesign the marmot figurine purchase orders. It was useful to have your report so soon after Dylan recognized that the old forms had to change to improve customer service and inventory control.

This is just to let you know that I've sent the marmot figurine purchase orders to Accounting. I've attached a copy of the form.

Cheers!

Michelle

Tibia Investments
Attachment: Copy of purchase orders

Currently, the line between letters and memos has become blurred because so much business correspondence takes place through email, which uses a memo format. You will definitely, for example, be required to email a business "memo" to someone outside your organization. In this case, you might have a greeting (depending on how well you know the individual you are corresponding with), you will have a closing ("Sincerely," or "Cheers,"), and the name and address of your company or organization (an email stand-in for a memo's letterhead) goes after this closing.

Memo Exercise

Take the following information and, using proper formatting and spacing, create the first and closing parts of 1) a formal memo on letterhead and 2) an emailed memo. You do not need to worry about the body of the email. You'll find the answers in the Appendix (page 407).

- The correspondence was sent by Penelope Anderson, the general manager of Terrapin Marmot Figurines, Ltd., on 24/1/19.
- The company's address is 2334 South Ripley Road, Terrapin, British Columbia, V8Q 2P5.
- The correspondence was sent to Bill Cleary, the company's financial manager, with a copy to company president Natalie Henstrick.
- The correspondence is about the possibility that Terrapin Marmot may invest in Rockcliffe Investment's family of mutual funds.
- The memo was typed by Anderson's secretary, Leslie King; the email was typed by Penelope Anderson.
- There is an enclosure (memo) or attachment (email) of financial figures for the fall quarter.

LETTERS

Letters in the business and professional world generally go to people *outside* your organization; memos are reserved for people *inside* your organization. Emails can go to either.

There are two basic types of letters: personal letters and business letters. They have different formatting.

How you write a personal letter is up to you; Aunt Emily doesn't care if you get the return address style exactly right. However, a well-formatted business letter is as important as, say, wearing a well-tailored outfit to a crucial meeting. A business letter with perfect formatting says you are a person who cares about the details, and much of your reputation and success in business and professional life depends on getting the details right.

At the top of the next page is a common style for a personal letter:

334 Peachtree Dr.,
Ruralania, BC, Q4R 3R5

January 23, 2019

Dear Aunt Emily and Uncle Hank,

　　How are you? We are fine here on the farm. The hens are laying and the pigs are farrowing and the cows are calving, which is good.
　　I just wanted to thank you both for the Nintendo player. I've played several games already and am really enjoying it.
　　Hope you are both well.

Your nephew,

Mikey

The return address and date are on the right third of the page, as are the closing and signature. The first line of each paragraph is indented and there is no space between paragraphs. The address has a comma at the end of the line, as does the greeting ("Dear Aunt Emily and Uncle Hank,"). There is no letterhead.

When it comes to business letters there are variations in style depending on the authority you consult. However, a properly formatted business letter, in the format called "full block," will look something like the following:

Tibia Investments Corp.

Letterhead

3994 Carmody Road
Terrapin, BC V9Y 2P4

Return address: The sender's name does *not* appear in the return address.

Leave one or two spaces before the **date**.

You can leave 2–4 spaces between the date and the inside address, if space is needed to centre the letter.

January 23, 2019

Michael Carruthers
President
Terrapin Marmot Figurines Ltd.
2334 South Ripley Road
Terrapin, BC V8Q 2P5

Inside address: This has the name, title, and company name of the person being written to, as well as the address.

Dear Mr. Carruthers:

Greeting: Follow this with a colon.

Subject: Order for figurines as staff picnic souvenirs

Subject line: Wording should be informative.

I am writing to inquire about purchasing plastic marmot figurines for our staff picnic in June.

In most years we have about 45 staff attending the picnic, plus their families and friends, for a total of about 100 guests. Therefore, we would like to buy 100 marmot figurines. Many of our staff members and their friends are committed to wildlife conservation, and they would treasure these marmot figurines as souvenirs.

I would be grateful if you could send us an estimated cost, including shipping and handling, for 100 figurines.

Yours sincerely,

Madeline Preston

Madeline Preston
General Manager

Courteous closing: Ends in a comma, unlike the greeting.

Handwritten signature

Sender's name and title

MP/jf

Reference initials: The sender's name is in capital letters, the typist's name in lower-case letters, separated by a slash or colon.

Enclosure: Order for marmot figurines

Enclosure: Describes the enclosure, if there is one.

Looking at the example business letter, we see that it is different from the personal letter in a number of ways.

General Pointers on Block Letter Format

- All parts of the business letter start on the *left margin.*
- All parts are *single spaced.*
- Paragraphs are *not indented* on the first line.
- Paragraphs are separated by a space.
- In the opening, the return address, date, inside address, and subject line *do not have punctuation at the end of each line.* However, the greeting (Dear Mr. Carruthers:) ends with a *colon.*
- In the closing, the sender's printed name and title (General Manager) *do not have punctuation at the end of each line.* The courteous closing (Yours sincerely,) ends with a *comma.*

Letterhead

- All business correspondence has a letterhead with the company or institution name and sometimes the company's address and contact information. A personal letterhead may have the sender's name and title.
- If the sender's address is in the letterhead, *there is no need for a return address.*

If there is no letterhead,

- *Do not* put the sender's title and company name in the return address. The return address contains only the address, city, province or state, and postal or zip code.
- The sender's title and company name will go *under* his or her name in the closing, as shown in the example.

Return address

- If the letterhead does not have the sender's address, then a return address is needed, as shown in the example.
- *If there is no letterhead,* put the sender's name, the sender's title, and the company name *under the signature at the bottom of the letter. Do not put the sender's name, title, or company name in the return address.*
- *Spell out Street, Road, Avenue, Lane, etc.* That said, whether to use street abbreviations or not is a grey area.
- The return address *does not have punctuation at the end of each line.*
- The format for city, province, etc. is this: Terrapin, BC V9Y 2P4.
    - There is a comma after the city name.

- Use the two-letter Canada Post or US Postal Service designation for provinces and states, *without periods*, e.g., BC, ON, NS, SK, NY, NJ. *Repeat: do not put periods between the letters.*
- Leave *two (repeat, two) spaces* between the province's initials and the postal code: Terrapin, BC V7Y 2P3. Again, this is a grey area. The two spaces create a clear separation between the province's abbreviation and the Canadian postal code.

Provincial abbreviations

	Post office abbreviations	Traditional abbreviations
Newfoundland and Labrador	NL	Nfld. or N.L.
Prince Edward Island	PE	P.E.I.
Nova Scotia	NS	N.S.
New Brunswick	NB	N.B.
Quebec	QC	Que.
Ontario	ON	Ont.
Manitoba	MB	Man.
Saskatchewan	SK	Sask.
Alberta	AB	Alta.
British Columbia	BC	B.C.
Northwest Territories	NT	N.W.T.
Yukon	YT	Y.T.
Nunavut	NU	Nvt.

The Date

- The date should be one or two spaces below the return address or letterhead.
- The date should be written out in full: January 23, 2019. Do not write the date as 23/1/19 (Canadian style) or 1/23/19 (American style) because, in many cases, the recipient will not be sure which national style the sender is using. What, for example, is this date: 3/5/19? It could be March 5, 2019 (US), or May 3, 2019 (Canada).
- Though most elements of a business letter have one space between them, there can be *up to four spaces between the date and the inside address.* This extra spacing can be used to centre the text on the page so that the top and bottom margins are about equal.

Inside Address

- The inside address gives the recipient's name (Michael Carruthers), without honorifics (e.g., Mr., Ms., Dr.).
- In the next line, put the recipient's position or title (President).
- In the next line, put the recipient's company name exactly as it appears on the corporate letterhead (Terrapin Marmot Figurines Ltd.).
- In the next line or lines, you place the recipient's full address, as shown in the example. Again, don't abbreviate street, avenue, road, or other such place designations.
- There is *no punctuation at the end of any of these lines.*

The Greeting or Salutation

- Use the recipient's last name and either Mr., Ms., Miss, or Mrs. (use Miss or Mrs. only if that is how the recipient wishes to be addressed). Follow the last name with a colon (e.g., Dear Mr. Carruthers:).
- If the gender of the recipient is not clear, use the first name instead of the honorific (e.g., Dear Leslie Jones:).
- If you don't know the name of the recipient, use his or her title (e.g., Dear General Manager: or Dear Sir: or Dear Madam:). Still, it's much better to find out the recipient's name.

> **Worth Knowing**
> The greeting in a business letter ends with a colon. Always.

- *Do not use* the phrase "To whom it may concern" or a similarly generic one if you can avoid it.
- At the end of the greeting in a business letter, use a *colon*. Always.
    - Dear Ms. Elphinstone:
    - Dear Dr. Farnia:

The Subject Line

- The subject line is a very useful (but sometimes optional) addition to full-block business letters. Its use is generally limited to letters in which only one subject is covered.
- The subject line says as concisely as possible what the letter is about. It is, in effect, a heading and should be informative. In the case of the example letter, a subject line such as "Subject: Future purchases" is too vague.
- This line can begin with "Subject" or, sometimes, "Re"; however, the "Re" form is more common in legal correspondence. There is no punctuation at the end of the line:
    - Subject: Proposed redesign of marmot figurine order forms
    - Re: Power of Attorney Designation, Lachlan MacPherson
- The subject line can use normal capitalization:
    - Subject: Order for figurines as staff picnic souvenirs

- Or the subject line can be capitalized like a book title:
  Subject: Order for Figurines as Staff Picnic Souvenirs
- Or, less attractive but still correct, this line can be all capitals:
  SUBJECT: ORDER FOR FIGURINES AS STAFF PICNIC SOUVENIRS
- An underlined or bolded subject line is also correct:
  <u>Subject: Order for figurines as staff picnic souvenirs</u>
- As always, the rule is to be consistent in your formatting.
- The subject line *does not*, repeat, *does not* end with punctuation.

The Text

- Paragraphs are usually a serif font body type, such as Times New Roman, for readability. Choice of font is a grey area.
- The first line of paragraphs is *not indented.*
- Paragraphs have a space between them.
- Paragraphs are usually short (5–7 lines), and the text is concisely written.
- Paragraphs are *left justified* (that is, they are ragged right, not fully justified).
- Body text size is 10–12 point, no more, no less, with 12 as the preferred size.
- Single space body text, or, at the most, use 1.5-line spacing. Do not double space this text.

> **Worth Remembering**
> If your letter is more than one page long, the closing section (Yours sincerely, etc.) never appears all by itself on the last page. There must be at least two lines of text on top of the closing.

The Closing

- "Yours sincerely," or "Sincerely yours," are the most common courteous closings in a business letter. "Yours truly," is also acceptable. The courteous closing has punctuation at the end, *a comma.*
- Leave four or five spaces for a handwritten signature, if the letter is being sent on paper. If you wish, use a "handwriting" font such as Lucida Handwriting or Brush Script as the "signature" for an electronic letter.
- Under the signature put the sender's name, then the sender's title on the next line, then the sender's company on the next line if this information isn't in the letterhead. (Note that *all* professional organizations have a letterhead!)
- *Do not*—repeat, do not!—*put the closing all by itself on the final page of your letter.* You must have at least *two lines* of text above the closing if your letter goes to additional pages. To get two lines onto the second page, you can expand your letter by adding a space or two or three under the date. Or you can create a page break before your last paragraph, or a break at the end of a sentence in the last paragraph to create a separate paragraph for page 2.

Reference Initials

- If you didn't type the letter yourself, use reference initials (e.g., MP/jf or MP:jf). These indicate that the letter was typed out by someone, such as a secretary, other than the sender.
- The sender's initials are in *capital letters*; the typist's initials are in *lower-case letters.*
- You can use a *slash* or a *colon* between the pairs of letters; be consistent.
- This convention is necessary so the actual typist can be identified—in case there is, for example, a mistake in the letter.

Enclosure

- "Enclosure" means there is additional material with the letter, lest that material be missed by the recipient in opening the letter.
- "Enclosure" can also, less formally, be written "Encl." or "Enc." However, you are always safe if you write the word out in full. Note that a *colon* comes after whatever designation you use and before your description of the material enclosed:

  Enclosure:

  Encl.:

  Enclosures:

- The enclosure line must be meaningful: "Order for marmot figurines"; putting the number of enclosures as opposed to a description of them is also conventional, but we don't recommend this practice (e.g., Encls.: 2).
- The enclosure line does not have punctuation at the end.

Below are examples of the top of a business letter based on two other options: letterhead with address (Figure 6.1) and no letterhead (Figure 6.2). A letterhead without an address is shown in the previous business-letter example.

Tibia Investments
3994 Carmody Road
Terrapin, BC V9Y 2P4
Every home should have a Tibia

January 23, 2019

Figure 6.1 The Top of a Business Letter with a Letterhead and Full Address in the Letterhead

Figure 6.2 shows how the sender's information and the return address are handled in a letter with no letterhead. The sender's name, title, and company name go after the closing, *not in the return address.* That said, almost all business letters have a letterhead.

3994 Carmody Road
Terrapin, BC　V9Y 2P4

January 23, 2019

[This figure shows the return address and closing of a business letter *with no letterhead*. The return address is above the date, but the sender's name, title, and company name go after the closing, *not in the return address*.]

Yours sincerely,

Madeline Preston

Madeline Preston
General Manager
Tibia Investments

Figure 6.2 The Top and Closing of a Business Letter with No Letterhead

If There Is More Than One Page

Ideally, a business letter takes only one page—time is money, after all. Page 1, by the way, is *not numbered*.

However, if the letter goes into page 2 or more, here is the header format for the second and subsequent pages:

Recipient's name   Page #
Date

The page 2 (or more) header looks like this:

Michael Carruthers   2
January 23, 2019

There must be at least *two lines of text* before the courteous closing.

Page numbers can also go at the bottom of the page, in the footer, usually centred. Note, again, that *you must include at least two lines of text* on the last page of a letter with multiple pages; the last page cannot contain just the closing ("Yours sincerely," etc.).

Letter Exercise

Take the following information and, using proper *block-letter* style formatting and spacing, create the first and closing parts of a business letter. You do not need to write the body of the letter. Use spacing appropriate for a business letter.

- The letter was sent on company letterhead by Penelope Anderson, the general manager of Terrapin Marmot Figurines, Ltd.
- The company's address is 43 Oak Valley Road, Terrapin, British Columbia, V8Q 2P5.
- The letter was sent on Jan. 23, 2019, to Delwan Kuthrapalli, the president of Rockcliffe Investments Limited, at 223 Earnshaw Place, Toronto, Ontario, postal code M4P 2R2.
- The letter is about the possibility that Terrapin Marmot may invest in Rockcliffe Investment's family of mutual funds.
- The letter was typed by Anderson's secretary, Leslie King.
- Terrapin Marmot's 2018 annual report has been included as an enclosure.

The answer is on page 408 at the end of the book. Don't peek until you've tried the exercise!

Correspondence Review

When formatting letters and memos, keep the following in mind:

- Letters go to people outside your organization.
- Memos go to people inside your organization.
- Business letters are written in full-block style (non-indented paragraphs, space between paragraphs).
- The body of memos also follows full-block style.
- Business correspondence is always concise and to the point.

Part III
Correspondence

In Part III, we will look at writing several kinds of correspondence:

Chapter 7
Emails and Memos

In this chapter you will learn to

- Write a proper email,
- Write a proper memo, and
- Write a proper fax or scan.

INTRODUCTION

In your professional career you will be writing emails, memos, and letters. This is true even in professions that you'd think would be remote from the writing sphere, such as engineering or the sciences. Yet an engineering company executive notes, "Engineers tell us that they spend 20 to 40 per cent of their work time writing memos, letters, email, reports, and proposals."

Good business and professional communication is as important to your reputation and success as your ability to design a strong bridge, plan an experiment, or negotiate a business deal. In Chapters 5 and 6, we looked at designing reader-friendly documents, including emails, memos, and letters. We also presented the conventional formats for these documents. In this chapter, we'll look at the writing you put into your well-designed and properly formatted emails and memos. Although faxes aren't used much any more, we'll briefly look at the format for sending faxes, as well as at the more modern methods of scanning documents.

EMAILS AND MEMOS

Just as emails and memos are similar in formatting, so emails and memos follow many of the same guidelines for content—an email is, in effect, an electronically sent memo—so we'll consider them together in this chapter. As noted in Chapter 6, memos usually go to people within your own organization; emails can go to anyone. Memos are, at least traditionally, on paper; emails are electronic memos.

The purpose of the memo or email, in a professional or business context, is to *make information clear* as concisely as possible. For example, suppose a business team is working on a project. A memo paper trail, or an email electronic trail, means every team member is clear about what he or she is supposed to do as part of the project and when it is supposed to be done.

If a team member is not clear, he can always go back and read the relevant memo or email. Other members of the team can also check a past memo or email to see who was assigned what task, what that task involved, and when it was to be finished. If someone has dropped the ball, the proof is there in the memo or email.

Or let's say a company vice-president has sent the president a memo urging a particular course of action, and the president sends back a memo approving that action. Assuming the memos are both clearly written, there should be no doubt about what the vice-president is supposed to do, and no doubt that the CEO approved her actions. If there is a question, anyone can go back and check the memo or email chain.

In other words, in a business and professional context, memos and emails are extremely useful tools.

Let's start with emails; memos will follow.

EMAILS

Emails are amazing. Thanks to the miracle of electronic communication, at the touch of a computer key an email can go anywhere in the world in seconds at virtually no cost. A reply can come back in seconds or minutes from the other side of the planet. The biggest problem with emails is that, because they are sent out electronically via the Internet, in theory anyone can read them. Emails are not private in the way that a paper memo is.

In 2005, the CEO of Seattle's Boeing Company, a multinational aircraft corporation, was fired after emails revealed rather intimate details of an extramarital affair with a fellow company executive. The emails were intercepted by an anonymous source and sent to the company.

The CEO wasn't fired for violating company policy on office romances as such. He was fired because the graphic nature of the emails called his character, and therefore decision-making ability, into question. His actions also reflected

You can read more about the Boeing case by using the search terms "Boeing executive," "fired," and "emails."

badly on the company's reputation. Boeing gets many sensitive and top-secret contracts from both the American and foreign governments; a reputation for strong ethics is considered one of the company's selling points.

Indeed, almost every week the media reveals stories of embarrassing emails made public on the Internet: a woman criticizing her boss on Facebook, another accusing an ex-lover of being less than adequate in bed—the list goes on. None of these electronic postings was meant to be made public, but they were, in part because co-workers made them public, in part because even very secure firewalls can be cracked by hackers.

The lesson to be drawn from this for the professional writer is not "Don't have extramarital affairs or slag other people on the Internet," although this is good advice. The lesson is this: Once your email or other electronic posting has gone into the Internet ether, it *can*, and sometimes will, be made public—it may even go viral.

There is another important lesson to be drawn from the Boeing case: Don't use company email for private, and especially *very* private, matters. Many companies have IT employees whose job includes monitoring company email and Internet for inappropriate use, such as downloading porn, playing games online, overly personal messages, and so on. News stories about the misuse of company Internet resources also appear with some regularity, often with a firing or public humiliation at the end.

In other words, never, ever, ever send anything out by email that you wouldn't want the whole world to read. And never, ever, ever send anything out by company email that is overly intimate. On the other hand, most companies don't mind if you make one or two personal emails or phone calls a day while at work, like asking the spouse to pick up milk on the way home from work.

An important characteristic of email is that it doesn't leave a physical paper trail. For example, suppose a government team is collaborating on creating policy. Because the policy isn't finalized and could be quite sensitive, the team might not have put their deliberations on paper quite yet, but there could be a lot of email discussion. (As we've seen, most email isn't safe from prying eyes, but let's assume in this case that the team trusts the government's firewall.)

The problem is that, in the interests of government transparency, many countries have freedom of information laws (FOI laws) that allow the public to ask for correspondence, in paper or electronic form.

A few years ago, with FOI in mind, the British Columbia government asked its civil servants to start filing paper copies of all email messages. Undoubtedly, many civil servants complied with this order. And, equally undoubtedly,

> **Good Advice**
> Never, ever, ever write an email in anger and then, because it feels so good, push the Send button. Wait 24 hours. Then, if you still think it's worth the possible fallout, hit Send. Better still, don't.

some civil servants stopped putting sensitive discussions into email or memo form and instead held meetings in person or via the phone.

General rule: If you've got thoughts or information you don't want the world to know, don't put those thoughts in an email!

Writing Emails: Dos and Don'ts

Emails aren't supposed to be long; they are intended to be short, electronic memos that can be read on one computer screen, without scrolling. If you want to email a long message, you have two options: send it on paper, or send the lengthy part as a file attachment with a short covering explanation in the email text window.

In a professional setting, emails are all about transferring information quickly and efficiently. The speedy part goes without question, thanks to the Internet. Efficient isn't as easy to achieve. The French essayist Blaise Pascal once wrote to a friend declaring, "I would have written a shorter letter, but I did not have the time."[1] It takes time, effort, and thought to make your email messages as concise as possible.

An efficient email is one that presents its information using the seven Cs—that is, clearly, concisely, coherently, concretely, constructively, and so on. The eighth C, correct grammar, spelling, and usage, always goes without saying. An email also considers the needs of its audience (it is courteous and complete). The guidelines for creating an efficient email are as follows (most of these guidelines apply to memos as well):

- *Keep it short*: The recipient of your email could get dozens if not hundreds of emails in a day. So, ideally, for easy scanning by the reader, make your email no longer than a computer screen. If you've got extra information, put it in an attachment for the recipient to read at his or her leisure.
- *Make subject lines informative*: "This is me!" or "Important!" are not informative and may get you relegated to the "Junk" or "Spam" section of your email recipient's mailbox. If it's you, say who it is ("Email from Bill Sykes"), and say why it's important ("Bill Sykes on designing a new computer tablet for Japanese client").
- *Use short paragraphs*: Aim for no more than, say, six to eight lines for each paragraph, divided by a space as in a business letter. Short paragraphs are easier on the eyes than long paragraphs. As in a business letter, the first lines of paragraphs are not indented.
- *Use lists whenever possible*: Lists are much easier to read and understand in emails (and everywhere else) than a paragraph.
- *Make sure the email contains all relevant information (is complete)*: Don't force your recipient to ask for more information you could easily have supplied in the first email.
- *Avoid emoticons and other cutesy email symbols and abbreviations*: Save these for casual, private emails to your friends. Better still, don't use them at all.
- *Use upper and lower case*: Don't send emails in all capitals or all lower-case letters, which are harder to read than conventional upper and lower case.

---

1   Blaise Pascal, "Letter XVI," *Les Provinciales, ou les lettres écrites par Louis de Montalte* (Lyon: Amable Leroy, 1807), 269. The actual quotation is "*Je n'ai fait celle-ci plus longue que parce que je n'ai pas eu le loisir de la faire plus courte.*" A rough and more literal translation: "I only have made this [letter] longer because I have not had the leisure to make it shorter."

- *Make sure your email address is respectable*: The address "bigfoot_cutie@hotmail" isn't going to impress professional colleagues or potential customers.
- *Avoid chain-letter sorts of correspondence, such as email jokes, cartoons, or inspirational messages*: Save these for your friends. Better still, don't.
- *Keep the "e-trail" short*: When you get past your message and about three earlier messages, start a new chain.
- *Use a salutation*: Unlike formal memos, emails normally have an informal personal greeting to start the body of the text: "Hi Bob," "Bob," "Hello Bob," or "Dear Bob," will all work. Note that the greeting for an email doesn't require a colon.
- *Use a closing*: Unlike formal memos, emails normally have some sort of closing at the end: "Regards," "Cheers," "Best wishes," "Looking forward to our meeting," and so on.

MEMOS

Memos are sent within your organization. As we saw in Chapter 6 on document design, memos are usually on company letterhead, and they begin with some combination of the following elements, usually in this order:

To:
From:
Date:
Subject:

The overall guidelines for memos are similar to emails, with the following additions:

- Because the memo is going to someone within the same institution, it's not necessary to put the title of the sender or recipient ("To: Bill Smyth, financial vice-president" can be "To: Bill Smyth"). Both parties will usually know the title information already. If the person's title is relevant for some reason, then, of course, include it.
- As with emails, make sure the subject line has enough information to signal clearly what the memo is about. Remember your audience: the recipient may get dozens of memos a day. Help him or her keep track of the relative importance of what's coming in by making subject lines informative.
- Formal memos (unlike emails) usually do not have a greeting and closing. They tend to end with a politely worded request for action.
- The content of a memo often takes the following form:
  - Purpose (why are you writing?)
  - Summary (what is the content of this memo, in one sentence?)

TERRAPIN INDUSTRIES

Memo

To: Jenny Partridge, Office Manager
From: William Chang, Chief Financial Officer
CC: Helen Petri, CEO
Date: July 22, 2018

Subject: Printing costs need to come down

I have noticed that office printing costs have risen 32 per cent in the past year. We need to do something about this. **[Introduction concisely sums up the point of the memo]**

> Main purpose for writing

After talking with office personnel, I believe the increase in printing costs is due to two factors: **[Provides concrete and specific details in a reader-friendly list format]**

- The new Hesperon printer/copier uses 25 per cent more toner than we were led to expect by the manufacture's specifications. Given past experience in copying and printing, we expected to use four toner cartridges a month, at $120 a cartridge, for a total of $480 a month or $5,760 a year. In fact, we are using five cartridges a month at a cost of $600 a month, or $7,200 a year, an increase of $1,440 a year.

> Summary of main points

- The Hesperon printer requires high-quality, 30-pound laser paper, costing $36 per 500 sheets, as opposed to the cheaper, multi-purpose paper, costing $24/500 sheets, that we used with our previous printer. Considering that we run through 4,500 sheets of paper each month, the cost of paper has risen from $216 a month to $324 a month, an increase of 50 per cent, or $1,296 a year.

The total increase in printing costs for the year is $2,736, which is $2,000 above the budgeted yearly increase for printing.

> Details in reader-friendly format

I would like your department to consider two options to reduce printing costs: **[Presents action items]**

- Return the Hesperon printer to the manufacturer for a refund (it is still within the year-long trial period) and purchase a printer that is less expensive, although perhaps not as powerful.

> Action items

- If we keep the Hesperon, create more stringent controls on staff use of the printer, if this is feasible, so that we are using 30 per cent less toner and paper.

I'd be grateful if you'd do a cost analysis of the two options and get back to me by next Wednesday on the option your department would prefer. **[Courteous closing with timeline for action]**

Figure 7.1 Sample Memo from a Microsoft Word Template

- Discussion (what are the key points?)
- Conclusions, actions, recommendations (what should happen next?).
- Unlike emails, memos can be any length, from one page to three pages. A memo may be the starting page of a ten-page informal report, such as a progress report (see Chapter 17 on informal reports).
- In the case of multi-page, printed memos, use the same conventions as you would for a block letter for the second and subsequent pages. That is, in the upper left corner, put the recipient's full name and, under that, the date, with the page num-

ber in the upper right corner or at the bottom centred or some variation of this.

- In terms of writing, the same rules apply as for emails or any other professional correspondence: Keep the message clear, concise, coherent, concrete, constructive, and complete (not to mention courteous and correct). Keep in mind, as always, that your written correspondence reflects *you*: if your writing is sloppy or rude, the recipient will assume you are too.
- As we saw in the section of Chapter 6 about designing letters, make your memos reader friendly by using headings, lists, tables, and charts to present complex information.

Other than that, follow the same guidelines as you would for emails, but recognize that memos are a more formal and long-lived form of correspondence. The formality of your word choice and sentence structure will depend upon your audience and purpose, but memos will likely be less casual than an email and more casual than a letter. The key thing is to always, always, keep the reader in mind. Ask yourself this: What can I do to make reading and responding to the memo easier?

Figure 7.1 shows a sample memo created using an online template from Microsoft Word.

FAXES AND SCANS

Faxing is on the decline—it's now easier and cheaper to scan a document and send it as an email attachment, and the fax machine has largely been replaced by the computer and scanner. However, some knowledge of the conventions of faxing is still useful.

Until recently, the main advantage of faxes over emails was that faxes qualified as legal copies of documents. You could sign and fax a contract in Vancouver and have it accepted as legally binding in New York, thereby avoiding several days of delay for postal or courier service, not to mention the expense. Today, however, a scanned and signed email attachment is increasingly considered the legal equivalent of a signed fax, although the covering email itself is not considered a legal document.

Faxes are also handy for sending documents with graphics and text, such as, say, house plans, although, again, a computer or printer's scanner can do the same job.

In general, faxes follow the formatting and writing conventions of email and memos. One difference is that a fax requires a cover sheet to introduce the document being faxed.

The cover sheet information will include the date of sending, to whom the document is being addressed (To:) and from whom (From:), and a subject line to introduce what the fax is about.

The cover page must state the number of pages being faxed; this is important in case all the pages aren't sent. The cover letter may end with a handwritten signature and the phone number and email address of the sender. Some word-processing programs offer templates for fax cover pages (and for many other documents as well). For example, Figure 7.2 shows the top of a fax cover page template from Microsoft Word:

TERRAPIN INDUSTRIES

Fax

Date: July 22, 2018

Fax: 555-555-3109
Attention: Jenny Partridge, Office Manager
Office location: 2nd floor, #288

From: William Chang, CFO
Office Location: 3rd floor, #244
Phone number: 555-555-2287

Total pages including cover: 4

Urgent ☐   For Review ☐   Please Comment ☐   Please Reply ☐

Comments:
Discusses increased paper and printer costs with new printer

229 First Avenue, Terrapin, BC V7Y 3R6 Phone: 555-555-2233   Fax: 555-555-3100
Website: www.terrapinindustres.com

Figure 7.2 Sample Fax Cover Page from a Microsoft Word Template

As with all correspondence, a properly formatted, well-written fax says something about you.

Chapter 8
Letters: Good News, Neutral, and Bad News

In this chapter you will learn how to

- Write an effective good-news or neutral letter and
- Write an effective bad-news letter.

INTRODUCTION

In your career, you will almost certainly be writing letters. Lots of them. In Chapters 8 and 9, we will discuss several types of letters you might send or receive as part of your professional or business correspondence. These types of letters include the following:

- neutral letters, such as a request for a product or information;
- good-news letters, in which you reply positively to a person's request or offer something to the recipient;
- bad-news letters, which convey news that the recipient may not want to hear, such as refusing a request for a purchase refund;
- persuasive letters, in which you try to persuade someone to do something he or she may or may not want to do, such as purchasing a product, giving to a charity, speaking at your company banquet, or paying a bill (although the debt-collection letter is halfway between a bad-news and persuasive letter); and
- cover letters, as part of a job search.

In this chapter and the next, we will look at each of these types of letters in turn except for cover letters, which we will discuss in Chapter 10. And, as always, we will assume that all of the elements of the eight Cs of good professional writing—clarity, conciseness, completeness, correctness, etc.—are being followed.

GOOD-NEWS AND NEUTRAL LETTERS

A good-news letter is just that—it has good news for the receiver. It's the kind of letter you *want* to send or receive because the recipient will be glad to get it. And, fortunately, it's an easy type of letter to write. There are basically three parts to a good-news letter:

- Put the good news in the first paragraph.
- Give the particulars next.
- End on a friendly note.

Why is the good news in the first paragraph? Because you want to be sure the recipient gets that good news. He or she may receive lots of letters, read the first paragraph or even just the subject line, and then discard the letter. If your good-news message isn't loud and clear in the subject line and first paragraph, the recipient may miss it.

Let's say, for example, that Mrs. Elvira Spadler has written your company complaining that her toaster, which she bought only three weeks earlier, doesn't work. She is asking for a new toaster or a refund. Since the toaster has a year's warranty, you can meet the customer's request and send out a good-news letter telling her so. The text of the letter (without the full opening and closing) might look like this:

Dear Mrs. Spadler:

Subject: Agreeing to your request for a replacement or refund for defective toaster

Consolidated Toasters is happy to replace your defective toaster with a new toaster. [**Gives the good news**]

To get your new toaster, simply take your bill of sale and the defective toaster to the dealer from whom you bought it. The dealer will give you a new toaster on the spot. [**Provides details**]

Nothing is more important to this company than the satisfaction of our customers. If there is anything else we can do for you, please do not hesitate to ask. [**Closes on a friendly and constructive note**]

Yours sincerely,

Val Vicini

Val Vicini
Customer Service Representative

In the section on bad-news letters, we'll look at how you deal with a similar request that you can't agree to (the product may be beyond its warranty date, for example).

What other types of good-news letters might you send or receive? How about this one (again, without the full opening and closing elements):

Dear Mr. Dexter:

Subject: You have won a trip to Tahiti!

Congratulations! You have just won an all-expense-paid trip to Tahiti! [**Gives the good news**]

Recently, while making a purchase at one of our furniture stores, you put your business card into our Vacation in Tahiti contest box in order to become eligible for our vacation draw. We are pleased to tell you that you are one of five Grand Prize Winners. All you need to do is fill in the enclosed form, send it to us at the above address, and you are on your way to one of the most beautiful islands in the world. [**Gives the details**]

We look forward to seeing you on the beach! [**Closes on a friendly and constructive note**]

Yours sincerely,

Paul James

Paul James
Customer Service Representative

Granted, a letter like this might be a scam (if you get an email like this from Nigeria, for example, you should be suspicious), but, if the letter is legitimate, it's certainly good news!

If the news is neutral, the same order applies: give the neutral news first, then the details, and close on a courteous note. An example here might be a letter from your local cable company announcing a new arrangement of the channels.

You may not care one way or the other where your favourite channel is on the line up as long as you can still find it, so the news is neutral to you. Nonetheless, it's important that the cable company tell you immediately what it's doing. If the letter gives you a long preamble you might get impatient, toss the letter, and then be less than neutral when you discover you've taped *Hannah Montana* instead of *Game of Thrones*.

Another type of neutral letter involves placing an order (which is a good-news letter for the seller!) or making a routine request for action.

In both cases, what you want should be clearly stated in the first paragraph. Follow with enough details so the receiver is absolutely clear about what you want, when you want it, and how you want it sent (if you are ordering a product rather than seeking some sort of action).

> **Worth Remembering**
> A letter that makes a request must make it as easy as possible for the recipient to meet the request by giving all the necessary details.

For example, suppose you are ordering a part for your oven. Because you've done some advance research on the Internet, you know exactly what part you need. The first paragraph of your letter (or email) should say something like this: "I would like to place an order for a stovetop element, Part # 443-T, for a Kelco Model 34 stove."

Then give the details of where you want the stove part sent, include your cheque or credit-card number if necessary, provide any additional contact information, and you are done. If you don't give enough details, such as the part number, the company will have to get back to you, which is a hassle for them as well as you.

A routine request for information might go something like this: "Please send me information on stovetop element replacement parts for the Kelco Model 34 stove."

If you need any more information, you can put it in a list. If you need the item by a particular time, say what the deadline is.

Good-News and Neutral Letter Review

When writing a good-news or neutral letter

- Give the news or make the request in the first paragraph of the letter;
- Follow up with details of what the recipient has to do; and
- Close on a friendly, courteous note.

BAD-NEWS LETTERS

Sometimes, as much as you'd like to avoid it, you have to give someone bad news because you can't do what she wants. In that case, the person will probably be annoyed at not having her request met. For example, if she has bought one of your products or services, asks for a refund, and doesn't get it, she may vow never to buy anything from your company again.

It's said to be about 30 times more expensive to find a new customer than to keep a current one.[1] So if you have to say "no," you want to do it in a way that's the least likely to irritate the customer (so you don't lose her business) and the most likely to leave her seeing the "no" from *your* point of view, as reasonable under the circumstances.

---

1   Laura Hansen and Karen Curtis, "Keep the Customer Satisfied," *Marketing Tools*, January 6, 2000, p. 44.

Fortunately, there are ways of writing your letter that will increase your chances of keeping that customer's good will while still turning down her request. It's called the "bad-news letter format," and it has five parts:

1. Start with a statement that the recipient is likely to agree with (this is called a "nod" or "buffer" or "common ground"). At this point, you are not saying "yes" or "no," you are just establishing contact and trying to create a rapport.
2. State clearly what the customer is asking for, such as a refund for a defective toaster.
3. Give enough details so the recipient will understand why you can't do what he or she wants, but *without saying an outright "no."* In other words, your "no" is implicit, not explicit. However, do not fall back on "company policy"—that's not a reason, it's an excuse. Any company policy must state reasons, so give those reasons. Stay positive and don't use unnecessarily negative language (avoid "we are sorry," "unfortunately," and the like).
4. Offer an alternative, a "sweetener," if possible.
5. End your letter on a constructive, friendly, and courteous note. Don't apologize. If your refusal is legitimate, you have nothing to apologize for. And don't refer back to your refusal ("sorry we couldn't help you" and the like); that's making the "no" explicit.

In the real world, you can't always follow this structure exactly. There are some situations when you have no choice but to say "no" directly. In other situations, saying a direct "no" won't damage your relationship with the other person. However, if you think about it, you've used the "bad news," indirect way of saying "no" many times in your life.

Suppose Joni is a high-school student who's been asked to go to a party hosted by Alex, a classmate she doesn't particularly like. What's her response? Is it a direct, "No, I don't want to go to your party"? Probably not. Why not? Because she doesn't want to hurt her classmate's feelings—after all, being invited is a compliment. Also, she'd prefer not to have bad feelings between them when the two meet later in class or the hall.

The solution? Create a "buffer": "Sorry, Alex, I'm busy that night." She might even create a "nod": "Going to the party would be a lot of fun [the nod], but I'm working that night [the implied refusal]."

On the other hand, if Joni really *is* busy that night, but would like to go to a future party, she'll say something like this: "Sorry, Alex, but I'm busy that night. Maybe next time?"

As another example, suppose you are the owner of a small software company and also friends with the head of a charitable organization in your community. That charity has asked your company for a cash donation that your company can't afford right now.

In this case, writing to a friend or acquaintance, you can be more direct in your refusal: "Sorry, Phil, but business is bad this year, and we can't afford to help you right now." You could offer an alternative—"Perhaps next year?"—or offer something else (a sample of your product or service, perhaps, that could be auctioned off). In this case, there is probably no risk of losing your friend's good will (and friendship) in the future, so your "no" can be more explicit.

The bad-news letter gets tricky, however, when it comes to a customer, say, whose goodwill you could easily lose. In that case, you may want to follow the bad-news format as closely as possible. Below is a case study on just such a situation.

Case Study: Euphonia Headphones Refund Request

Suppose you work for a company, Euphonia Inc., that makes a range of high-quality headphones for computers and tablets. Your headphones have a "best buy" guarantee—if a customer sees the same product in another store at a lower price, you will refund the difference in price.

You get a letter from Terry Statin stating that he has a pair of Euphonia TB230 headphones that he bought for $80 at The Source. However, he saw a pair of Euphonia headphones at Wal-Mart selling for only $60. He wants a $20 refund under the "best buy" guarantee. Furthermore, you can tell by the tone of the letter that Mr. Statin is not feeling happy about your company at the moment. He thinks he's been ripped off.

The problem is that while Mr. Statin bought his Euphonia TB230 headphones for $80, the headphones he saw in Wal-Mart were an older model, the TB130. The TB230 headphones are more expensive because they have a richer dynamic range than the TB130 model, with greater fidelity in the treble register. The TB230 headphones are also 25 per cent more compact than the TB130s and are ergonomically designed to fit more comfortably on listeners' ears.

How can you refuse Mr. Statin's request while keeping his good will as a customer?

First, you want to find a "nod" to start your letter, something you can both agree on. What might that be, in this case? Well, what do you know about Mr. Statin, the audience for your letter?

For one thing, if he's willing to spend $80 for a pair of headphones, Mr. Statin probably cares a lot about good sound quality when he listens to music, so perhaps that could be your lead paragraph:

Few pleasures in life are more satisfying than hearing good music through top-quality headphones. It's as if the musicians are playing in the same room.

If you've assessed your audience correctly, Mr. Statin will mentally "nod" at that comment; yes, that's true, he'll think. There's nothing like good-quality sound. Right at the start you've shown him that you and he are on the same wavelength, that you "get" where he's coming from.

However, you'll lose that good will if the next paragraph says something like, "However, we can't meet your request because the headphones you saw at Wal-Mart were an older model, the TB130, and therefore cheaper." You are in effect saying Mr. Statin is a bit thick for not recognizing the difference. And you're giving him a flat-out "no," which nobody likes to hear. Is there a better way of conveying the same information?

Yes, there is. Give Mr. Statin the detailed reasons why you can't meet his request, and do it in such a way that he will come to *see for himself* that your response is reasonable. Then you don't have to come out and say "no" directly. Instead, you convey the "no" indirectly; the refusal is implicit rather than explicit. So, you might write something like this:

> The Euphonia headphones you saw in Wal-Mart for $60 were one of our older models, the TB130. The headphones you bought at The Source for $80 are our newest and much improved model, the TB230. The TB230 headphones are more expensive because they offer a richer dynamic range than do our earlier models, with greater fidelity in the treble register. The TB230 headphones are also 25 per cent more compact than the TB130s and are ergonomically designed to fit more comfortably on the ears.

If you've done this right, Mr. Statin will figure out *for himself* that the TB230 headphones are more expensive because they are of higher quality and that he, therefore, shouldn't expect a best-buy refund. He may even congratulate himself on having bought the better product. There's no need for you to say, outright, "Therefore we can't grant your request." The "no" is implicit in the facts.

That said, in some situations you may be able to offer a "sweetener" or alternative. In Mr. Statin's case, you could write something like this:

> We want you to be completely satisfied with your Euphonia headphones. If you wish to send us your Euphonia TB230 headphones, we will gladly ship you a pair of TB130 headphones along with a $20 refund.

Chances are, because Mr. Statin likes great sound, he won't take you up on this offer.

Finally, you need to end your letter on a friendly, courteous, constructive note, with something like the following:

Our company builds some of the finest audio products in the world, and, whether you choose the TB230 model or the TB130, we know you will enjoy years of listening pleasure with your Euphonia headphones.

If you present the bad news properly, Mr. Statin will be happy with your explanation, with his new headphones, and with your company the next time he's thinking of buying an audio product.

Putting it all together, your bad-news letter[2] (without the full opening and closing elements) might look like this:

Dear Mr. Statin:

Subject: Request for a refund on Euphonia headphones

Few pleasures in life are more satisfying than hearing good music through top-quality headphones. It's as if the musicians are playing in the same room. [**The nod**]

You have requested a "best buy" refund after seeing Euphonia headphones for a lower price in Wal-Mart. [**What's been asked for**]

The Euphonia headphones you saw in Wal-Mart for $60 were an older model, the TB130. The headphones you bought at The Source for $80 are our latest and much improved model, the TB230. The TB230 headphones are more expensive because they offer a richer dynamic range than do earlier models, with greater fidelity in the treble register. The TB230 headphones are also 25 per cent more compact than the TB130s and are ergonomically designed to fit more comfortably on the ears. [**Giving facts for an "implicit" refusal**]

We want you to be completely satisfied with your Euphonia headphones. If you wish to send us your TB230 headphones, we will gladly ship you a pair of TB130 headphones along with a $20 refund. [**The "sweetener"**]

Our company builds some of the finest audio products in the world, and, whether you choose the TB230 model or the TB130, we know you will enjoy years of listening pleasure with your Euphonia headphones. [**Courteous closing**]

Yours sincerely,

Leslie Crosby

---

2 Adapted from Mary Ellen Duffey, Kathleen Rhodes, and Patricia Rogin, *Business Communication: Process & Product*, 3rd Canadian edition (Toronto: Nelson Thomson Learning, 2001), 318.

There are a number of elements to notice in this letter. For a start, when designing the nod, you must recognize that it's not what *you* think that matters; it's what the *recipient* thinks. Suppose you write the nod this way:

We both agree that few pleasures in life are more satisfying than hearing good music through top-quality headphones.

In this case, you are not making a statement—that listening to great sound is a wonderful experience—and encouraging Mr. Statin to "nod" at it; you are *telling* him what he thinks—and demanding that he nod at the fact that *you both agree* on this. But why should he care what *you* think? What's important in this situation is what *he* thinks! And why shouldn't he be angry at your presuming to tell him his own mind?

Or, if your sentence begins "Most people think that hearing good music through top-quality headphones is one of life's finest experiences," you are asking him to care about what most people think. But, again, it's what *he* thinks that counts. Put yourself into Mr. Statin's head and identify what *he* might think and feel. Make this into a general statement—not "I think" or "You must agree" but "Such and such is so"—and make this statement relevant to your message. Then you've got your nod.

Also, in the second paragraph, you must mention what Mr. Statin has requested. This step may seem obvious, but if you want to avoid an outright "no," it's tempting not to mention what he was originally asking for because you don't want to remind him of it. However, if you leave out what's been asked for, it's not clear what you're writing about, and the letter may make no sense.

Finally, a piece of advice on approaching the bad-news letter, or any correspondence, really: Whenever possible, don't say what you *can't do*, always say what you *can do*. This is the element of the eight Cs called constructive. Be positive rather than negative in your bad-news letters and in all your correspondence. For example, don't use words like "however" or "unfortunately" in your bad-news letter because these words point back to what you *aren't* doing. Whenever possible, stick to what you *are* doing.

Governments use this positive approach all the time in their correspondence with citizens (who are also voters).

For example, suppose a constituent writes his provincial member of the legislature about, say, changing the province's drunk-driving laws to make them tougher. Instead of setting the level of intoxication while driving at .08, this writer wants the level to be .04. The law would, therefore, be twice as strict with drinking drivers.

Worth Remembering
Whenever possible, don't say what you *can't* do, say what you *can* do.

However, the politician knows it's unlikely the law will be changed in this direction—many politicians themselves enjoy a glass of wine or two with dinner, and they're satisfied with the limit as it is. So the politician could write the constituent and say, "No, sorry, we're not going to do that." If the politician does this, however, it's likely the constituent will feel slighted, get angry or annoyed, and vote for another candidate at the next election. So what does our politician do?

What he or she writes is a bad-news letter or email that says what the government *is* doing, not what the government can't do or won't do.

He begins with a declaration about how important it is to keep the roads free of drunk drivers (the nod). He states what the writer has asked for: tougher laws on drunk driving.

And then, without directly saying no, he tells the writer about some of the steps the government is already taking to reduce and prevent drunk driving. As a "sweetener," he may offer to send information on the government's efforts to prevent drunk driving, and he will close with thanks to the writer for taking the time to write on this very important issue.

Of course, politicians generally don't write these letters or emails themselves. They get hundreds of letters and emails a month and could never reply to all of them personally. Therefore, they have a staff of writers to respond to correspondence from constituents. But, when there's bad news for the citizen-voter, the politician's letter will generally follow some form of the bad-news formula, stating what the government is doing and ignoring, as much as possible, that the government isn't going to do what the writer has requested.

Below is another example of a government response to a citizen seeking speedier trials for young offenders (without the full opening and closing elements):

Dear_____:

I am writing in response to your recent letter regarding speedier trials for young offenders and more efficient access to legal aid. I agree that delay, especially in youth cases, is a serious issue.

The problem is that, more than any other group, young people need expert legal help to deal with the complex rules and proceedings of criminal court. Also, legal counsels have a professional obligation to act in the best interests of their clients, and it's up to each lawyer to determine what this means for any particular young offender.

The Ministry of the Attorney General has taken steps to speed up the criminal court process. These measures include increasing diversion and Crown counsel review of backlogged cases. We are also expanding disclosure court, where the Crown trial date is set. These efforts have reduced the number of outstanding cases.

> I should add that we are watching Alberta's legal aid project with great interest and are exploring similar options in conjunction with the Legal Services Society.
>
> Thank you for writing.
>
> Yours sincerely,

In other words, the letter says "no." But rather than stating "no" directly, it describes other actions the government has taken to help youthful offenders. And, as you can see, the government's letter doesn't begin with the "nod" but with what the citizen had written about; the nod comes in the second sentence of the first paragraph, but it breaks the bad-news formula for the "nod" by using "I." Still, the letter follows the overall bad-news letter format in that it doesn't say "no" directly.

Here's a letter from a car company with "bad news"—a recall due to a product safety defect:

> Dear XXXX Owner:
>
> This notice is being sent to you in accordance with the requirements of the *Canada Motor Vehicle Safety Act.* XXXX [the car manufacturer] has determined that a defect that relates to motor vehicle safety may exist in certain 2006–2014 model year hatchbacks, certain 2007–2010 model year sedans, and certain 2008–2010 hybrids. Our records indicate that you currently own a vehicle that is involved in this campaign.
>
> We are now in the process of preparing the campaign remedy parts and will notify you again when they become available for your vehicle. Until that time, we are sending you this notice to provide you with important information regarding this campaign and the steps you can take at this time.

This letter doesn't start with a "nod"—the language is more legalese. But car owners need to know from the start that there is a problem with their vehicle, so they will read on to the "good news"—a fix for the problem, which is in the second paragraph. They also must be able to assess how urgent the problem is for them.

In other words, there's no one, fixed way to deliver bad news. The start-with-the-nod format offered here works in many situations but not all. And writing a successful bad-news letter is never easy. However, your chances of success are greater if you begin using the "nod" format in these types of letters. Once you've written several bad-news letters following the format, you will know when it's safe to move away from it.

Bad-News Letter Review

Follow these steps when writing a bad-news letter:

- Find something the recipient will agree with (the "nod," the "buffer," or common ground).
- State what the customer or client asked for.
- Give *concrete and specific details* showing why you can't do what the recipient is asking but without saying a direct "no."
- Avoid negative language such as "unfortunately" or "however" that points back to what you aren't doing.
- Make an apology and/or expression of regret a part of your letter whenever such an approach is clearly called for.
- Offer a sweetener or alternative if possible.
- Close on a courteous, friendly, constructive note.

Bad-News Letter Exercises

1. On the next page is a real letter from Air Canada to a customer whose luggage was lost for a week. The customer requested money to cover expenses that arose because his luggage had been lost. Those expenses included an electric razor, some new clothing, a new suitcase, and even $100 for a new power cord for his portable computer (he'd taken the computer into the airplane cabin but had packed the power cord in the suitcase). Although the luggage was eventually found and returned a week later, the passenger was out of pocket for about $400 and asked the airline to cover this expense.

   Air Canada's reply is a combination good-news/bad-news letter. The good news is that the airline offered $240.99 in compensation for expenses. The bad news is the customer won't get $160 of his claim.

   How well does this letter reflect the good-news and bad-news formats discussed in this chapter? Is the good news given immediately? Is there a nod to introduce the bad news? Are the reasons for the refusal of the $160 so clearly explained that the customer will be willing to accept the refusal without ill will? Is there an overt "no" or an implicit "no"? Rewrite the letter to do a better job. (Note: There are a few minor errors in grammar in the letter too. Can you spot them?)

A sample letter rewritten according to the good-news and bad-news letter formats is on page 410, as is a portion of the original letter with the minor grammatical errors noted and corrected. But don't peek until you finish your own work!

Baggage Claims
Air Canada Centre 1116
PO Box 8000, Station Airport
Dorval, Quebec H4Y 1C3
Fax: (514) 422-2900 1-(800) 237-3563
Without Prejudice

AIR CANADA ✹

August 28, 2007

Mr. ████████

████████

Dear Mr. ████ :

Thank you for your correspondence. We were sorry to learn that your luggage was not available for you in London on July 12th. Please accept our sincere apologies.

We recognize the inconvenience which may result from delayed baggage and every effort is made to ensure that our passengers' baggage travels with them. Unfortunately, this cannot be guaranteed as there are too many variables involved. Airline Tariff regulations therefore preclude liability for consequential claims if baggage is delayed.

As a gesture of goodwill, if a passenger is away from home and his or her baggage is delayed more than 24 hours, Air Canada will contribute towards the cost of interim clothing and toiletry purchases, to a maximum of $100.00 USD, when substantiated with original purchase receipts. This policy is common to all STAR Alliance partners as well as our Connector carriers. I am pleased to enclose our cheque for $240.99 CAD ($112.56 GBP) in connection with your claim.

Once again, we offer our sincere apologies for the inconvenience you may have experienced. We trust that all your future travels with Air Canada will be completely satisfactory.

Sincerely,

[signature]

████████
Baggage Claims Specialist

2. Write a properly worded and formatted bad-news *memo* (as this is an internal document) based on the following scenario:

   In January of 2014, the employees of the Cosmos Street branch of the Terrapin Insurance Corp. asked the manager for a "casual day" on Fridays to raise money for local charities. On casual day, in return for a $2 donation to a charity chosen by the staff, employees can wear jeans, and men do not have to wear a dress shirt and tie.

   After some discussion, the manager agreed. Casual day was instituted as of January 25, and it has been very popular with all the staff.

   Now, ten months later, the company is finding that some customers are commenting and even complaining that the employees look untidy, even scruffy. The manager has noticed that, on hot days, some of the employees, male and female, are coming to work in shorts and T-shirts or tank tops; sometimes their jeans are (fashionably) ripped or even dirty. Sandals with bare feet have also become a commonplace on casual day among some of the men. Occasionally, an employee will wear casual-day clothing on a non-casual day.

   The manager is worried, with some reason, that casual day is hurting the company's image with the public. He could, of course, remind staff of the original guidelines for casual day, and he did so, informally, in July. However, although there was an improvement for a few weeks, the standards again became too relaxed.

   Therefore, the manager has decided that casual day has not worked out and will have to be cancelled. He hopes that the employees can find another way to contribute to charitable causes that will not affect the insurance company's image. Your mission is to write the bad-news memo to the staff.

3. You, the owner of a computer store, have been asked to donate a desktop computer to a telethon supporting a charity helping refugees in Somalia. However, business has been tough for you lately. Making up whatever details you need, write a bad-news letter explaining to the charity why you can't donate what it is asking for at this time.

4. You are a Terrapin, BC, city councillor who has received a letter from a constituent complaining about the potholes on Maple Street and demanding that something be done about them soon. The writer even mentions an accident between a van and a car that occurred when the car swerved to avoid a large pothole on Maple. The driver of the car was sent to hospital with a broken arm and facial lacerations; the van driver was shaken up but not injured. The writer wants the pothole problem

fixed ASAP. The problem is that the city doesn't have the budget to repair every single pothole in its jurisdiction all at once, so road repairs are done based on a schedule. Maple Street isn't due for repairs for at least another six months. Making up whatever details you need, write a bad-news letter to the constituent explaining why the potholes aren't going to be fixed in the near future. Hint: Say what you are doing to keep the roads safe, not what you can't do.

Chapter 9
Persuasive Letters

In this chapter you will learn to

- Understand the three rhetorical techniques of logos, pathos, and ethos and
- Write an effective persuasive letter.

INTRODUCTION

The persuasive letter is more difficult to write well than the bad-news letter. In this case, you are not refusing someone something. You are asking the recipient to do something that may benefit you, perhaps, but not necessarily the recipient, at least not directly. And yet we get persuasive letters and emails all the time seeking money for a charity or for a political party, requesting volunteers for a community organization, and so on. And, ultimately, all advertising is a persuasive appeal.

A persuasive appeal aims at three possible outcomes: it wants to change the *actions*, the *thoughts*, or the *feelings* of the person being persuaded. You want your subject to behave differently, based on your persuasive appeal, or think differently, or feel differently. Sometimes you want all three.

So what is it that makes a persuasive appeal successful or not? In this chapter we suggest two approaches:

1. the three rhetorical techniques of *logos*, *pathos*, and *ethos* and
2. a persuasive format called AIDA (attention, interest, desire, and action).

THREE RHETORICAL TECHNIQUES

Another word for persuasion is rhetoric; in fact, the ancient Greek word for persuasive oratory was "*rhētorikē*." The Greeks studied the art of rhetoric very seriously because, in the popular assemblies of Athens and other Greek city-states, a citizen's prestige was, in part, measured by his ability to persuade fellow citizens on a course of action (women did not take part in Greek citizen assemblies). The Greeks identified three kinds of persuasive appeals:

- *logos*, the appeal to reason, including the use of facts;
- *pathos*, the appeal to emotion; and
- *ethos*, the appeal to authority.

In fact, we use these three techniques of rhetoric all the time without, perhaps, being aware of it. For example, have you ever tried to persuade a friend to come to a movie with you when he doesn't want to go? What do you do? You try to persuade him to come along. How?

You can use *logos*, the appeal to reason: The movie stars Liam Neeson, and Neeson's movies are almost always exciting.

You can appeal to *pathos*, the emotions: If you don't come to the movie with us, you're going to lose us as friends, and you'll have a lonely evening.

You can appeal to *ethos*, authority: The local newspaper reviewer has given the movie a five-star review, and the reviewer is almost always spot on. And, hey! It's a Liam Neeson movie!

Or suppose you want your parents to let you use the car for a date in the evening. You just got your driver's licence and your parents think it's too soon to be going out in the car at night. What do you do?

> **This website discusses the three rhetorical techniques:** http://w.web.umkc.edu/williamsgh/dialogues/225.rhetorical.appeals.html
>
> **This website lists all the logical fallacies:** http://www.nizkor.org/features/fallacies

You try various forms of persuasion. You might try a logical appeal: you have always been responsible and careful with your parents' possessions, so you'll be responsible with the car, too. And you'll be home at 10, sharp.

You might try an emotional appeal: if you don't get the car tonight, your social life will be over, and you'll be miserable. Do your parents really want to make you miserable?

You might try *ethos*, the appeal to authority: you aced the Young Drivers' course. If Young Drivers' thinks you're good enough to drive, well, aren't they the experts?

In other words, we use these three techniques of persuasion all the time, even if we aren't consciously aware of them. We are also being persuaded by these three techniques all the time without, perhaps, being aware of it. The advertising industry is based entirely on the ability to use appeals to reason, emotion, and authority to sell products and services.

Of course, these three rhetorical techniques can also support persuasive arguments that aren't valid. The Nigerian bank account email scam uses all three appeals in an attempt to get you to give money to someone you've never heard of. The "sender" claims to be a senior official in the government or the manager of a bank or a senior official's widow. That's *ethos*, the appeal to authority. This person is in a jam and needs your help—the emotional appeal (*pathos*). The "logical" side (*logos*) is why you should be involved in this scheme to help get the sender's money out of the country—you stand to make a good deal of money as your "commission." It's all a scam, and often in abominable English, but the email uses the three techniques of persuasive rhetoric.

Rhetoric also contains logical fallacies—arguments that seem to make sense but don't. For example, as noted above in the Nigerian scam example, the appeal to authority can be misused. Just because an authority says something, does that make it automatically true? Of course not. The "black-and-white" fallacy suggests you have to be on one side or the other, with no middle ground, as in telling your parents "If you don't give me the car tonight, I'll know you don't love me." And so on. You can find more information about the logical fallacies at the search terms in the "Worth Consulting" box.

> **Worth Consulting**
> Purdue University's Online Writing Lab (OWL) has a good description of the various logical fallacies. Use the search terms "Purdue," "OWL," and "logical fallacies."

Note also that there is a difference between **argument** and **persuasion**. Argument is based primarily on *logos*, the rational case based on facts (or what are presented as facts).

It's possible to win an argument—say, over whether the Montreal Canadiens or the Vancouver Canucks had the better hockey team in the 2013–14 season. You can win the argument by proving with statistics that Montreal had the better team that season. But winning the argument doesn't mean your Vancouver opponent will then be *persuaded* to switch and become a loyal Montreal fan.

In other words, persuasion is much more than just an appeal to reason. To truly persuade, you need to change the other person's *emotions* as well as his or her mind, and that's where *pathos* and *ethos* come in.

Case Study: Selling a Car

A British Columbia car salesman was extremely successful and used to give talks on the secret of his success to other auto-sales people around the province. He attributed that success to a five-step technique:

1. Meet and greet the car customer. Find common ground.
2. Present the product.
3. Demonstrate the product (through a test drive).
4. Write the offer.
5. Close the sale.

As part of Step 1, meet and greet and get common ground, he asked his customers what they wanted. What size car? How many passengers? How much horsepower? What accessories? And how much did they wish to pay?

Once he'd heard the customers' needs, he'd go to Step 2: suggest a car that would meet those needs at the right price and discuss its features, e.g., engine size, type of seats, number of passengers, luggage space, and safety features.

If the customers were still interested, Step 3 was a test drive. Finally, in Step 4, he'd write an offer, and, in Step 5, he'd close the sale based on the knowledge that the car he'd shown his customers was exactly what they were looking for. "If this is exactly the car you want," he would tell his customers, "why would you bother going to another car dealer?" Usually, this final argument closed the deal.

In this case, the car salesman used all three rhetorical techniques. He used *logos* when he presented the car's features: for X and Y reasons, this car meets your needs. He used *pathos* when the customer took the test drive: being behind the wheel, in the driver's seat, experiencing the power of the engine, enjoying the luxurious leather seats—this car *feels* good! I *want* it! The salesman had *ethos*, authority, in the sense that he was an authority, or hoped to be seen by his customers as an authority, on cars.

But he also used the technique called AIDA, which we'll discuss now.

AIDA (ATTENTION, INTEREST, DESIRE, ACTION)

AIDA is another, complementary way of approaching the persuasive letter. It is similar to the successful car salesman's persuasive rules and also incorporates the Greeks' three modes of persuasion. "AIDA" stands for

1. attention,
2. interest,
3. desire, and
4. action.

Here's how it works:

1. First you get the attention of the person you are trying to persuade.
2. Then you develop interest in whatever you are offering. But interest alone isn't enough. Most of us would be *interested* in owning, say, a Porsche sports car; whether we're willing to shell out $80,000 for one is another matter.
3. Therefore, the next step is breaking through the customer's resistance and making him or her really *want* this product or service. This is stimulating desire.
4. Finally, if the interest and desire are there, you need to get the person you're trying to persuade to take action, that is, actually buy what you are selling.

In terms of selling cars, the salesman got his customers' *attention* (meet and greet, finding common ground), then gave them details about the car (*interest*), and then took them for a test drive (there's nothing like being behind the wheel to stimulate *desire*). Finally, he gave them the opportunity for *action* by presenting them with a sales contract on the spot, no delays.

Let's go over these four persuasive elements in more detail.

1. Attention

Every time you pick up a magazine or newspaper, or turn on the television or radio, or go online, you are confronted by advertisements seeking—nay, clamouring!—for your attention. What techniques do they use to get that attention?

Invariably, the ads begin with an image or sound that is exciting, alarming, shocking, unusual, unexpected, or intriguing. If that doesn't catch your attention, what will?

A good persuasive writer catches (or tries to catch) the reader's attention with words rather than pictures or sounds, and this is true for almost any type of document, from a persuasive letter to a newspaper article to an editorial or column to an advertising pitch. If the writer doesn't capture the reader's attention, the writer has failed.

How do you do it? How do you get the reader's or viewer's or listener's attention? You find an arresting quotation, an amazing fact, a surprising statistic, a thought-provoking question, a stimulating statement, a fascinating story, an interesting or astonishing image.

You might start with a compliment ("We are sending this special offer to you as one of our most favoured customers") or offer a bargain ("Don't miss our Boxing Day sale!"). You might challenge the reader ("Do you have what it takes to join today's army?"). You might offer a shocking statistic ("Thirty per cent of children in our community go to bed hungry!"). Whatever approach you choose to get attention, it shouldn't be dull.

For attention to work, though, you need to know your audience. What, specifically, will work with this particular person or group of people? Obviously, an appeal to join the army will fall flat if sent to a seniors' home.

Most of the time, the attention item is also an interest item, but it's your most striking interest item. We'll discuss interest in more detail in the next section. To determine your attention item, you ask yourself this: Is there an interest detail that would make your reader think "Yikes!" or "Wow!"? That's the detail you can use to capture attention.

> **Worth Remembering**
> When it comes to getting attention, aim for a "yikes!" or "wow!" if you can.

As a general rule, when it comes to getting attention, aim for a "yikes!" or "wow!" reaction from the reader if you can. If you can get the reader to think "Yikes!" after reading the first paragraph of your appeal, you will almost certainly have gained his or her attention.

2. Interest

Stirring interest is basically appealing to *logos*, to reason, and perhaps to *ethos*, expert opinion. The interest section of your pitch gives the reader enough detailed information so that she will want to find out more—in other words, so she will become interested.

You create interest with concrete and specific details, with facts and figures, about your proposal. To inspire interest, you describe, concretely and specifically, why you are making this persuasive appeal. If you represent a charity, for example, you give details about the problem your charity is facing and how you are planning to solve that problem. If you are selling a product, you give details about the product, what it is and what it does.

Note: you must give the interest details *before* you make your appeal. The interest details are why you are making the persuasive appeal in the first place, so it makes sense that these details go before the appeal. If you make the appeal before you've given the reasons for it, your subject might reject the appeal out of hand.

Most people are fascinated (which is another word for "interested") by details, especially if they are concrete and specific enough to create a *mental picture* of the product or service or benefit you are offering.

And that's the key to interest: you must use concrete and specific detail to create a mental picture that is almost as vivid as the reality it describes. Most people love a story, so your interest details could also be thought of as a story, like ones that begin with "Once upon a time…" (only you take out the "once upon a time" part).

The interest story usually begins with the ultimate cause of, say, the social problem your charity attempts to solve or the source of the urgent need that your product or service will meet—the "big bang" as it were. Interest is often a story, of sorts, and stories usually begin at the beginning. Because of X (the "big bang"), Y happened. Because of Y, Z happened—and so on through the chain of cause and effect, from earliest cause (the "big bang") to the most recent effect.

Interest details may include the benefits of the action you propose, but in a more abstract way than the benefits listed in the desire section of your pitch. For example, suppose you are trying to persuade a local business to let your business use some of its parking spaces for your customers. Obviously, one benefit would be the rent you are offering—let's say it's $300 a month for four spaces, or $3,600 a year. And, by the way, make sure you include the yearly figure—it's larger than the monthly rent and therefore more tempting.

Note, however, that, to encourage *desire*, you refer to the monetary benefit in a different, more concrete and specific way—perhaps mentioning how the business could use that money to buy more stock or beautify the storefront. *Interest* is created by the offer of the rental money itself, *logos*; *desire* is based more on how the money could be used, which is more *pathos*. Putting this another way: to offer someone money will definitely arouse interest, but getting money all by itself isn't the goal (for most people, anyway). The reason we want money is for what it will allow us to buy. So, desire points to what the person can use that money for.

And, again, your attention grabber or "yikes" moment is usually your most striking interest detail.

We'll see how to develop interest details in the example of seeking funding for a homeless shelter.

3. Desire

It's not enough just to interest someone with your appeal. Who wouldn't be interested in, say, taking a trip to Hawaii? But, if they're so interested, why aren't they in Hawaii right now?

In fact, each of us has only so much time, money, and energy to spend, no matter how "interested" we might be in helping the homeless, owning a Porsche, or vacationing every winter in Hawaii. So, the desire portion of an AIDA letter has to create not just intellectual interest but a strong desire (emotion, *pathos*) for the product or service you are promoting. Sure, most people want to help the homeless, but are they willing to donate $100 to the cause? That's where desire comes in.

The desire part of the appeal has to take the recipient from "Gosh, that's interesting" to "I've gotta have (or do) that!" To get your reader from interest to desire, the appeal has to break down the recipient's natural resistance to spending time, money, and energy.

Desire is created in two basic ways:

- by stressing the benefits, practical and perhaps emotional, of what you propose and
- by answering the recipient's possible objections.

Often, citing benefits and answering objections is the same thing.

In terms of answering objections, your potential customer might say, "But we can't afford a Hawaiian vacation right now." You might reply, "We offer an attractive, low-interest payment option that will only cost you $50 a month."

Your customer might say, "We can't afford a new furnace right now." You, the salesperson, might point to cost savings ("This high-efficiency furnace will pay for itself in 30 months in saved gas bills") or offer guarantees ("Your money back if you aren't completely satisfied").

As you can see, showing the buyer that the furnace is cost effective both offers a benefit (a monetary saving) and answers the buyer's objections (a furnace isn't affordable right now). Answering objections while creating desire often uses the *logos* kind of approach—it gives logical reasons why the person *can* do what you want him or her to do.

Benefits attract your customer more along the lines of *pathos*, the emotional appeal. "You will feel a strong sense of satisfaction by helping the homeless." Some charities for children promise that "your" child will write back to you, thanking you for your help—a heart-warming idea. "You'll be the first one on your block to own a backyard swimming pool"—this appeals to the desire for status and prestige, which is ultimately more emotional than rational.

Finally, in the desire section, you might offer testimonials by others who've used the product or service, including celebrities. If Angelina Jolie endorses your product, it must be good! You might mention awards the product has received. You might note that nine out of ten dentists recommend your toothpaste.

In these cases, you are using *ethos* to overcome buyer resistance and make your sale. And keep in mind, "sale," in this case, means persuading the other person about anything, not just a product. It could be a charitable donation, it could be voting for a particular political party, it could be joining a demonstration against (or for) a particular government policy, or a million other possibilities.

If you've successfully created desire, then the last step is to get your recipient to fulfil that desire by taking action.

4. Action

The end of your persuasive appeal is no time to be wishy-washy: you've got to tell the recipient *exactly* what he or she needs to do to fulfil the desire you've (hopefully) created. To do this, you must give concrete and specific details on **what** that person needs to do next, **how** she needs to do it, and **when** she needs to take action. In particular, if possible (and it usually is), you should give a *date* by which Action must take place and a plausible *reason* for that date.

Your action spur might include incentives to act:

- "Purchase this toaster before Oct. 30 and receive a free kitchen knife set."
- "We hope this matter is resolved at November 3rd's city council meeting."
- "Due to high demand, this video will be available only until March 21."
- "If we don't act before the end of summer, pollution will kill the lake."
- "We need your donation by December 15, so we can buy food for our annual Christmas dinner for the homeless."

In the action section of your persuasive appeal, you want to create *a sense of urgency* by planting in the recipient's mind an actual date by which action must be taken. The reality is, if the receiver of your persuasive appeal doesn't act immediately, or very soon, your appeal will likely go into the trash (electronic or real) and never be seen again.

You want to make the action as *easy* to do as possible: for example, you might provide a self-addressed, stamped envelope and an online address for donations, or mention times and places where protesters against some government policy can meet, or, following the car salesman's example, write up a one-time offer immediately after the test drive.

Finally, you want to end with a courteous closing sentence or two that thanks the recipient (if that is appropriate) and looks forward to continued good relations.

Table 9.1 summarizes some of the ways AIDA can be used to make your persuasive appeals more effective.

Gain Attention with	Build Interest with	Stimulate Desire/ Reduce Resistance with	Motivate Action with
Interesting anecdote		Emotional appeals (*pathos*)	
Problem summary	Rational appeals (logos)	Counter-arguments to anticipated objections	Description of specific request
Thought-provoking statement	Expert opinion (ethos)	Indirect benefits (e.g., status)	Guarantees
Reader benefit	Facts, figures	Guarantees	Convenient follow-through (make action easy to take)
Compliment	Specific details of product	Performance statistics	Incentives
Startling fact	Direct benefits to reader (e.g., $300 for talk)	Samples of product	Deadlines
Stimulating question	List of proposal's value or benefits	List of awards or results of polls	Limited-time offers
Testimonial	Examples	Testimonials (*ethos*)	
Current happening		Cost savings	
Offer (of a bargain, for example)			

Table 9.1 Using AIDA in Persuasive Appeals

Adapted from Mary Ellen Guffey, Kathleen Rhodes, and Patricia Rogin, *Business Communication: Process and Product* (Scarborough: Nelson, 2001), 268, 271.

PERSUASIVE COMMUNICATION ETHICS

With great power comes great responsibility! The tools used in business and professional communication, like AIDA, are often powerful and, like any tool, they can be used for good or ill. Hammers are great for banging in nails, but hammers can also do a lot of damage in the wrong hands. So, how can you assure yourself and those you communicate with that you are on the side of the good? This question takes us into the realm of business and professional ethics.

All reputable organizations believe, or at least they tell their clients and communities, that they are ethical. These ethics are often summarized in the organization's "mission statement."

For example, Starbucks' mission statement begins: "To inspire and nurture the human spirit—one person, one cup and one neighbourhood at a time." Surely inspiring the human spirit is a rather large task for a cup of coffee! But a latté is often a lot more than a latté. When people meet to chat or to plan a strategy or just to create friendly ties, it's often over cups of coffee. The Starbucks mission statement recognizes that coffee isn't just a hot, delicious beverage; it's also a bonding agent.

Here's the mission statement for Levi Strauss & Co., the world's top-selling company for jeans:

> The mission of Levi Strauss & Co. is to sustain responsible commercial success as a global marketing company of branded apparel. We must balance goals of superior profitability and return on investment, leadership market positions, and superior products and service. We will conduct our business ethically and demonstrate leadership in satisfying our responsibilities to our communities and to society. Our work environment will be safe and productive and characterized by fair treatment, teamwork, open communications, personal accountability and opportunities for growth and development.

That's quite a mouthful! Yes, like all companies, Levi Strauss wants and needs to make a profit or it won't survive. But, like most companies, it wants to make that profit "ethically," while "satisfying our responsibilities to our communities and to society."

Google, perhaps, put its ethical goals most directly with its former corporate mission, "Don't be evil." In 2015 the company changed its mission statement to "Employees... should do the right thing—follow the law, act honourably, and treat each other with respect." But given that Google is one of the world's largest businesses, you have to think its first motto was chosen with some care before the company switched to a blander version (do the right thing, follow the law, act honourably, treat people with respect, which could just as easily be the mission statement for the Boy Scouts).

So, how do you ensure that, when it comes to written communication, you and/

or your organization behave as ethically as possible? You can start by following a few simple ethical principles.

Let's start with the obvious: while ethical behaviour is also legal behaviour, you can obey the letter of the law and still not be fully ethical. For example, most tax systems have "loopholes," ways of skirting the tax regulations without breaking them. A politician or businessperson may not be breaking the law by charging all of his or her meals to the government or company expense account; it's possible the law or company guidelines aren't clear on this. But the politician's or businessperson's "legal" behaviour would be considered unethical by most of us.

You are already familiar with communication ethics as part of your university or college experience. All universities and colleges have guidelines explaining academic integrity and the penalties for failing to follow the guidelines in your written and spoken work. For example, one university describes academic integrity as "commit-ment to the values of honesty, trust, fairness, respect, and responsibility."

So, as part of academic integrity, researchers, instructors, and students are expected first and foremost to be ruthlessly honest in reporting their research and in academic publications and essays. Professors who falsify their research findings can be, and sometimes are, fired; at the very least, they are considered a disgrace within the academic community. Similarly, business and professional communica-tors have an obligation to be *truthful* in what they communicate. Half-truths will not do; communicators must be as honest as possible.

Out of *honesty* is built *trust*: we trust the words of someone we know or believe to be honest. Honesty demands *fairness*, a willingness to look at all sides of an issue to come to the best conclusion. *Respect* for others, and for others' points of view, is part of fairness. Finally, ethical people recognize that they are *responsible* for their words and behaviour; they don't hide behind excuses or evasions. Their word is their bond.

Complete, one-hundred-per cent ethical behaviour isn't always easy in a busi-ness and professional context. One person's "honesty" might appear to be another person's lie. And an ethical dilemma is rarely black and white.

For example, suppose you are an advertising firm running a taste test of a new soft drink. You ask tasters to try your beverage and that of a competitor and report on their experience. Some might love the drink: "It's delicious!" Others might hate it: "It tasted like mud!" Which conclusion are you, the advertiser, going to report? Obviously, the positive comments, given that you are trying to promote your product to the public.

Have you been untruthful? Not really; some tasters enjoyed your product. You just aren't mentioning the (perhaps majority of!) tasters who didn't. Filmmakers practise this selective quoting all the time in their advertising: the positive review gets quoted ("A smash hit!"); the negative reviews are ignored or the words are twisted to make them positive (the original review said: "I wanted to *smash* my head against the wall and *hit* something during this dreadful movie...."). Unethical? Hmmm....

Other situations are more clear-cut. Suppose you are working for a tobacco or pharmaceutical company. It's well-established that tobacco products can cause lung and other cancers and that some pharmaceutical drugs can have unpleasant and sometimes dangerous side-effects. In these cases, you clearly have an obligation to inform potential buyers of these potential hazards. Indeed, anything less than complete honesty in these situations is unethical, which most pharmaceutical companies, for example, fully recognize: often their television advertising includes a long list of possible side-effects for their product.

One of the most powerful ways to avoid unethical behaviour, in business and professional communication and elsewhere, is to ask yourself: would I be happy with family and friends knowing what I'd done? Or would I be ashamed? If you are fine with everyone knowing what you wrote or did, then your actions are probably ethical. If you are ashamed, you have probably behaved unethically, and perhaps illegally as well.

So, to summarize, the principles that an ethical business and professional communicator must observe include the following:

- You must be **honest** in your business and professional communication. If you can't tell the whole truth (remember those misleading movie reviews!), then at least you have an obligation not to tell outright lies. Similarly, if your product has potentially negative side-effects, you must say so.
- As part of being honest, you must **stay within the law** and avoid promoting illegal activity. For example, if you are working for a company that sells black-market cigarettes or other illegal and/or harmful products, then you have not behaved ethically. If a product is legal but potentially harmful, like cigarettes or alcohol, then you might want to examine your reasons for being with that company, but technically your behaviour is not unethical.
- As part of being honest, you must **give credit** to others if you borrow their ideas—in the academic world, this means avoiding plagiarism, in the business and professional world, not stealing others' ideas and claiming them as your own, copyright infringement, and the like.
- You must be **fair** in your communication. Situations are rarely black and white, so you need to consider all sides of an issue, not just your preferred side. For example, those who communicate on behalf of politicians should be particularly careful that opposing parties and their positions are treated fairly.
- You must show **respect** both toward those you are communicating to and toward those about whom you are communicating.
- You must be **responsible** in your communication; if you have made a mistake, libeled someone, or caused harm in your communication, you must own up to it. In other words, a responsible communicator has a duty to accept the truth, even if that truth hurts, say, an organization's profitability or reputation.

Case Study: Appeal for a Homeless Shelter

Let's say you're trying to raise money for a homeless shelter in your city or town. How could you use AIDA to make your appeal as persuasive as possible?

Attention: What startling fact—"yikes!"—might jolt your readership into a greater awareness of the problem of homelessness in your city? How about this: "The homeless population of Terrapin has increased 50 per cent in the past year. Our city had 800 homeless people in 2018, but today almost 1,200 people are now without basic shelter." In this case, you are using a statistic to show the size of the problem and, you hope, to get the reader's attention by creating a "yikes!" response. A startling picture might also grab attention.

Interest: In this section, you will give facts and figures about the homeless problem in Terrapin.

You might start by telling the story of how this unfortunate situation arose: what is the cause of this increase in homelessness (the "big bang")? A downturn in the economy? A sudden increase in housing prices? You might offer one or two case histories of people who've been made homeless because of job loss or mental illness or just bad luck. Keep in mind at all times that you are telling a story: "Once upon a time...." And then leave out the "once upon a time" opening.

After you've given details about the problem and how it arose, you need to offer your detailed solution. Here is where you prepare the ground for your appeal. Your solution might be $10 a month from each donor to help finance one room in a shelter or to feed one person for the day. Or you might want a single donor, such as a government ministry or a company, to give a one-time, large donation for a specific problem. Note, however, that you must not make the appeal—tell what you want—until you've given all the reasons behind the appeal.

Desire: In the desire section you show the recipients how doing what you ask, meeting your persuasive request for funds, will benefit *them*. In this case, detailing benefits may be difficult because you are asking people who aren't homeless to give money to help people who are homeless. What's the benefit for the giver who already has a home? In the desire section, you may use *pathos*, the emotional appeal, combined with *logos* and *ethos*.

For example, you might mention how good it feels to help others in need. But this particular desire approach, appealing to the donors' unselfish instincts, must be subtly worded; ideally, donors are supposed to give without expectation of reward or return. In more general terms, though, most of us don't want to see others suffer, and it does feel good to give. You can, subtly, remind your potential donors of that fact. You might also mention how much better off the city would be if people weren't forced to live on the streets. If you are a registered charity or non-profit, you can also offer a charitable-donation tax receipt. You need to put yourself in your potential donors' shoes and imagine what would make you want to give.

As part of creating desire, you want to answer donors' possible objections. You might assure donors that their money will be used wisely: 80 cents of every dollar given to your appeal will go to the homeless and only 20 cents to administration. You could list possible objections that donors might have. Why might potential donors say "no" to helping the homeless? They might say, "It's the government's problem, not mine" or "I can't afford to help" or "There are already helping agencies that 'these people' aren't using." Your desire section will rank these objections, and answer the ones you think your audience most likely has.

As *ethos*, you might have testimonials from people who've used the shelter in the past or from community leaders and other citizens who support the shelter. You might offer incentives for giving: e.g., a plaque with the donor's name on the homeless shelter's wall of honour, a mention in the local newspaper, a donors' dinner, and, as noted above, a charitable-donation tax benefit.

Action: In this section, you create a spur to action. "Your donations are needed by November 1, so we can prepare our shelter for the winter rush." "If you donate by October 30, we can purchase five new beds at a reduced price."

Again, you must make it very *easy* to act: include a self-addressed stamped envelope or an online address for donations; mention stores downtown where donations are accepted; give the date, place, and time for a rally against homelessness; and so on.

Below is the persuasive letter you might write to several wealthy community business leaders soliciting donations for a homeless shelter.

Terrapin Homeless Volunteer Committee
3551 Alder Street
Terrapin, BC V7R 2X7

September 21, 2019

Harriet Rousseau
President
Rousseau Industries
874 Cornwall Avenue
Terrapin, BC V7E 3R5

Dear Ms. Rousseau: [Note the colon, indicating business-letter format.]

Subject: New homeless shelter desperately needed in our city

[Attention/"yikes!"] In the past year, the number of people living on the streets of Terrapin has gone from 800 to 1,200, an increase of 50 per cent. As a result, Terrapin's only homeless shelter, HomePlace, has been overwhelmed.

[Interest details] The crisis began in 2018 when, faced with a $20 million deficit, the Terrapin city council cut spending by 10 per cent, which forced the layoff of 600 government workers. [This is the "big bang"] These layoffs have had a major trickle-down effect on the local economy. For example, many of these laid-off city workers have, in turn, had to let go people working for them—housekeepers, child-care providers, gardeners, and others. Many of those laid off have no other source of income, have lost their homes, and are now forced to live on the street.

[Interest details] Currently, Terrapin is desperately short of shelters for the homeless. HomePlace can take in only 220 people each night, and, with the huge increase in homelessness, it has been overwhelmed. Our city desperately needs a second shelter.

[Interest details] We can buy the old Terrapin Gazette building on Alder Street for $250,000. An additional $250,000 for basic renovations and repairs, using mostly volunteer labour, would give Terrapin a shelter that could take in more than 200 a night—a doubling of our city's capacity. Therefore, we are asking the citizens and businesses of Terrapin to help us help the homeless by giving a one-time donation of $1,000, or as much as you can, or a pledge of $25 a month. With enough donations, we can begin work on the new shelter by the end of October.

[Desire] We know we are asking a lot of you, our city's business leaders. But the rewards are significant. You will be helping some of our neediest, most vulnerable residents regain control of their lives. You can be sure that every dollar you give will be put to good use—we are all volunteers and the Gazette building will be restored using volunteers. The name of every donor will appear on a "Wall of Honour" when the shelter is finished, and the shelter will be named after the citizen or company that is most generous. And, finally, we are a registered charity so donors will receive a tax-deduction receipt.

[Action] Please give before October 1 so we can purchase the Gazette building by the end of October and finish repairs before winter sets in, when the plight of the homeless will become truly desperate. We have enclosed a stamped, self-addressed envelope for your convenience. You can also donate through our website, www.terrapinhomeless.com, using your credit card or PayPal. Donations can also be accepted at most downtown businesses.

[Courteous closing] On behalf of the homeless of Terrapin, we thank you for your support.

Yours sincerely,

Alicia Kronstadt

Alicia Kronstadt
Chief fund-raiser

Conclusion

Think of the AIDA process as a four-stage rocket. Your attention grabber is the blast-off, the ignition of the rockets. That's the "yikes!" moment. Interest carries the rocket higher. Desire takes it higher still. Action puts your persuasive appeal into orbit. But each stage has to go off in order, or your appeal is likely to fail. Therefore, it's important to know the difference between, in particular, interest and desire, since these are the easiest to confuse.

In general, the interest appeal gives *details* and is centred on *logos* and often, to some degree, on *ethos* (an expert's opinion, for example); the desire section focuses more on the *benefits*—often emotional benefits (*pathos*)—for the recipient and others. That said, one person's interest might be another person's desire. For one person, safer streets might be an interesting goal but not something vital; for another person, safer streets are a passionate ambition. The persuasive document has to be tailored to each particular audience.

> Use the search terms "changing minds" and "AIDA" for a website with more details on AIDA.

And keep in mind that AIDA doesn't apply just to persuasive letters, including, crucially, job-application cover letters, which we'll discuss in Chapter 10. AIDA works for advertising and oral presentations as well. In fact, AIDA applies in almost every situation in life where persuasion is called for!

How often in the day do you try to persuade friends or colleagues or your family to do something, say, going to a particular movie or concert, attending a lecture, lending you the car or a sweater, or giving to a charity? The AIDA approach will increase your chances of success in all these situations and many more.

Persuasive Letter Review

When writing a persuasive letter,

- get attention,
- create interest,
- stimulate desire, and
- spur action.

Exercise

Write an AIDA appeal based on one of the following scenarios. Make up any details you need to make your appeal as persuasive as possible.

1. You want former Liberal Party leader Michael Ignatieff to speak to your community group. You know Ignatieff has written and spoken extensively on human rights, but you also know he is a very busy man. How, using AIDA, could you persuade this in-demand speaker to come to your city?
2. You are a store owner in downtown Terrapin. You have noticed that your business has fallen 20 per cent since the city began a new, tougher approach to controlling parking in the downtown core. If business falls any more, you could be out of business. Write a persuasive AIDA letter to the city council explaining why the city should relax its parking regulations.
3. You are running a telethon to benefit a children's charity. Using AIDA, write an appeal to a local business seeking donations to the telethon. Be specific about what charity you are writing for and the company to which you are writing.
4. You live on Maple Street, which is riddled with potholes to the point that drivers and pedestrians are now at risk. In fact, within the past week, a van and a car collided after the car driver swerved to avoid a large pothole. The driver of the car, Sam Parsons, suffered a broken arm and facial cuts; the driver of the van wasn't hurt but was shaken up. The car was a write-off. Using concrete and specific details and the AIDA format, write a letter to your local city councillor asking him or her to fix the potholes on your street ASAP, before further accidents and perhaps even a death occur. (You may remember this scenario from the bad-news exercises; this is the persuasive side of the pothole issue.)

Part IV
Writing for a Job

In Part IV you will learn

- How to write an effective cover letter (Chapter 10) and
- How to write an effective résumé (Chapter 11).

Chapter 10
Cover Letters

In this chapter you will learn to

• Write an effective job-application cover letter.

INTRODUCTION

The cover letter and résumé are probably the most important documents you will ever write, at least in the early stages of your career. A strong cover letter and well-written résumé can mean the difference between getting your dream job or just something that pays the bills. The cover letter and résumé can literally change your life! Let's begin with the cover letter. Résumés are discussed in Chapter 11.

The cover letter on paper is not the only way to apply for a job these days. Many job applications are now made online or as emails. But whether on paper or online, the same basic principles apply.

It should go without saying, but needs to be said, that before you send your cover letter and résumé, you should research the company or organization you are seeking to join. What product or service does it sell or provide? Are you interested in this line of work? Did the company have record profits this year or is it on the verge of bankruptcy? And, if the latter, will you be jumping onto this ship when others may be jumping off?

Most of this background information can be learned from a simple Internet search of the company name or, if the information isn't available online, through a visit to your public or university library.

It's also useful to know something about the personnel in this company. What is the name of the CEO? What is the name of the personnel or human relations manager to whom you are sending your materials? It's better not to send in a job application addressed to "To whom it may concern" or "Personnel Manager" or "Dear Sir or Madam." Find the names you need either online or by phoning the company and asking. Use that name, both in your letter and in your phone calls or other communications ("I wrote to Personnel Manager Meredith Lewis on March 3. I am checking to be sure she got my letter.").

This chapter is about the written portion of your job search, not the other elements of job hunting such as making "cold calls," giving a strong personal interview, and dressing for success. Research on these other areas will help you enormously in finding a job, and there is a vast amount of material online about successful job-search strategies. However, a strong cover letter and résumé are a key part of this strategy.

THE COVER LETTER

When an employer puts out an employee-wanted ad, she may get hundreds, perhaps even thousands, of applications. For example, in 2007, a new Toyota car-manufacturing plant in Woodstock, Ontario, got 40,000 applications for 2,000 jobs. Sifting through job applications is a lot of work, and the boss or personnel manager will be looking for ways to streamline the process. One simple way is to automatically toss out cover letters and résumés that have obvious spelling, grammar, logic, and formatting errors.

In most cases, the employer will assume that the writer of a letter with lots of errors either isn't highly literate or is careless and therefore probably not a good candidate for the job, especially if that job requires writing (as most reasonably well-paying jobs do these days).

This assumption may be unfair and untrue. But it's further evidence that the quality of your writing reflects on *you*, your education, and your character. As one employer put it, "The guy couldn't find Argentina on the map. If I want a high school dropout, I'll take one without a college degree."[1]

So to make the best possible first impression on a future employer (keeping in mind that you only get one chance to make a good first impression), you need to have mastered the business and professional writing skills presented in this book: the eight Cs, including correct grammar, spelling, and wording; plain English (which is a variant of the Cs); and attractive, correct formatting.

> "If I want a high school dropout, I'll take one without a college degree."

Once letters with obvious errors are culled, the employer will be left with perhaps dozens of well-written cover letters and résumés. It's at this point that your cover letter needs to shine, or you, too, could end up in the discard pile. What can you do to increase your chances of making the winner's circle?

---

1   George Jonas, "High-Tech Gadgetry No Replacement for the Three Rs," CanWest publications, May 5, 2005, http://www.georgejonas.ca/recent_writing.cfm?id=309.

Formatting the Cover Letter

The cover letter is a business document. That means it should be written in block business-letter format (see Chapter 6 on "Formatting for Correspondence"). Show the employer that you know proper business-letter format and you've already got a head start over applicants without this knowledge.

The cover letter, ideally, should be no more than a page long, including opening and closing elements. The font is normally serif (e.g., Times New Roman) because that is easier to read than sans-serif fonts (e.g., Arial). Point size should be no smaller than 10 and no larger than 12. Twelve point is the best because it is easy to read, but you may have to go to 11 or 10 point to get all your information on one page.

Like any other business document, your cover letter must be reader friendly. Therefore, your sentences and paragraphs should be short and punchy rather than long and rambling. Your writing should be concise, filled with details rather than abstractions, and absolutely clear about what the employer wants to hear. If you can put your skills in a bulleted list, by all means do so. Remember, the employer may be reading hundreds of application letters and an unrelieved sea of grey print is daunting.

Above all, keep this in mind: The cover letter isn't about *you*; it's about what you can do for the *employer*. Write a "you"-centred letter rather than "me"-centred one, even though you are trying to sell your skills. Your skills are only useful if they are useful to the employer—that's the point you need to make in your letter: *you* have the skills the *boss* is looking for.

Writing the Cover Letter

One page doesn't leave much space to make a good impression. That's why you need to recognize that a cover letter is a *persuasive* document; it's a variant of the persuasive letter that we discussed in Chapter 9.

Therefore, the cover letter will benefit from the AIDA approach: get the employer's *attention* with an arresting first paragraph; build the employer's *interest* with facts, figures, statistics, and details about your skills; create *desire* in the employer to learn more about you and your skills; and, finally, stimulate *action* by the employer, getting him or her to interview you or hire you as soon as possible. Let's look at each of these in turn.

1. Attention
In the first paragraph of a cover letter, unlike in the persuasive letter, getting attention can be difficult because most application cover letters begin about the same way: "I would like to apply for the marketing manager position advertised in *The Globe and Mail* on May 3, 2019."

The first paragraph needs to indicate the job you're applying for and where you saw the advertisement. Indeed, if you get too fancy or cutesy in this paragraph, you might turn an employer off. That said, the employer is looking for workers and is holding your letter in her hand, so you've automatically got some attention.

You might get more attention if, in your first paragraph, you can show some prior connection with the company, e.g., "Joanna Kelsey, a friend of mine who works in your accounting department, told me that your company is looking for a junior accounting clerk, and I would like to apply for this position."

It's often not what you know but whom you know that gets you the job, so if you have a personal connection, exploit it to get attention! If the employer feels comfortable hiring someone based on a quick phone call to Joanna Kelsey, rather than on scrutinizing dozens of applications, then your chances of success are much better.

2. Interest

In the AIDA pattern of persuasion, facts, figures, concrete details, and statistics build the reader's, viewer's, or listener's interest in whatever you are promoting. The interest section of your cover letter should appeal primarily to *logos*, the intellect, and to some extent *ethos* (perhaps you know someone in the company), rather than to *pathos*, the emotions.

This section describes, with concrete and specific detail, your skills, experience, and knowledge, thereby building the employer's interest in you. But what skills, experience, and knowledge is the boss looking for? The answer lies in the ad that attracted you in the first place.

That ad will almost always list in detail what the employer is looking for, such as proficiency with Microsoft Word and QuarkX-Press, familiarity with a spreadsheet program such as Excel, knowledge of Sanskrit and Punjabi, strong communication and leadership skills, and at least five years experience running dog teams in Alaska.

For example, the following online job advertisement asks that the ideal candidate have

> A retired Canadian Forces paratrooper was describing the difficulties in finding a job in the civilian world with his skill set. "Basically," he said, "I jump out of planes and kill people. There's not much portability in these skills."

- successfully completed a recognized two-year technical diploma or a university degree program in computer science/information technology;
- a minimum of seven years related IT experience;
- a minimum of four years project management experience;
- superior interpersonal and leadership skills;
- strong verbal and written English communication skills;
- the ability to work under pressure with multiple priorities;
- the ability to work in a team environment;
- the ability to perform successfully under limited supervision;

- strong problem-solving, analytical, and decision-making abilities;
- fully proficient use of MS Office, MS Outlook, MS Visio, MS Project, and other office tools; and
- a background in IT, including systems development lifecycle, methodologies, estimating, etc.

Whew! How many people have got *this* combination of skills and experience? But your potential employer is only going to be *interested* if you can show you've got these skills, or most of them, or skills that are very similar.

So, for example, in replying to the advertisement above, you may want to cite your work or volunteer experience (volunteer experience can sometimes count) with working in a team environment ("Camp counselling leader" or "Scout troop leader"), times you've worked independently without supervision, and so on.

As you list your experience, skills, and qualifications, be *concrete and specific*. If you were a manager at a Burger King restaurant, then describe (briefly) how many people you managed and what you actually did as a manager. If you are familiar with computer programs, list them by name. If you've operated heavy machinery or driven a truck, describe what you operated or drove, the type of driver's licence you have, and other specific information. When trying to create interest, use concrete and specific detail to give the employer a *mental picture* of what you've done and, therefore, a mental picture of you and your qualifications.

Incidentally, you may not have every single one of the skills the employer is looking for—the IT ad has a very long list! But that doesn't mean you shouldn't apply for the job. It's possible that nobody who sees the ad has all of those skills. If you have most of the requirements, tell the employer that you are either studying to get the missing skills now or will get them in the near future.

> *Pathos, logos,* and *ethos* as persuasive elements are discussed in detail in Chapter 9 on writing persuasive letters.

The cover letter is, ideally, only a page long. Therefore, in the interest section, you have space to mention only the jobs and skills that are most relevant to the position. The cover letter is a summary of your experience; your résumé will list all of your relevant work, education, and life experience. We will discuss résumés in the next chapter.

Finally, you might be tempted, in the interest paragraphs, to demonstrate what a great person you are and what a great employee you'd be. However, that part of your letter properly belongs in the next section, the one stimulating *desire*. First you've got to develop the employer's interest in your skills, experience, and qualifications. Then you can sell yourself as the perfect employee.

3. Desire

In most cases, you won't be the only applicant who's got the skills, or a majority of the skills, the ad calls for. How do you make the employer pick *you* out of the dozen or so top candidates? Here's where you try to build *desire*.

If the interest section focuses on *logos* (reason, facts, the details of your previous experience and education) and perhaps *ethos* (maybe you've worked with a major figure in the company's field), the desire section focuses more on *pathos*—making an emotional connection and showing yourself as a human being who, incidentally, would be a great fit with the employer's mission and other employees. If interest paragraphs tell what you've *done*, desire paragraphs show who you *are*. The desire section is also about overcoming the employer's natural resistance to hiring you, just as a car salesman has to overcome a customer's natural resistance to spending $30,000 even if the customer is interested in the vehicle.

Often, an employer's advertisement will state the personal qualities the firm is looking for in an employee, such as "detail oriented," "works well with others," or "enthusiastic and committed to quality." In the desire paragraphs, you show that you've got the personal qualities the employer is looking for and reveal how much you want to work for *this* company, that it's been a childhood dream to build widgets.

> **Worth Knowing**
> It is crucial that your cover letter be truthful—if you claim skills or accomplishments that you don't have, sooner or later, you will be caught out. Put yourself in the best possible light, but tell the truth.

That is, you state that you are enthusiastic and want to work hard, as shown by your experience in the interest section. The desire paragraphs are all about you presenting yourself as a person, not just a set of job skills and experience (although you have those, too). And, keep in mind that how well you write and format the cover letter also tells the employer more about you as a person than you may realize.

For example, the 1970s *Mary Tyler Moore Show* was about a young woman, played by Mary Tyler Moore, who gets a job in a television news department despite having no news or TV experience. Given her lack of experience, she asks her employer, gruff news director Lou Grant, why she got the job.

He explains that, during her interview, he noticed that she was desperately trying to hide a small run in her stocking. He figured an applicant who was that concerned about getting this small detail right would get the details right in the job, too, and he hired her.

This example is, of course, fictional, but the principle applies in the real world. Get the small details right in your application cover letter and résumé and you tell the employer you'll probably get the details right on the job, too.

4. Action

It's not easy to get an employer to take action. After all, once you've submitted your application, what the employer does next is in his or her hands. Well, maybe not. You don't want to be seen as a pest, but it doesn't hurt to get in touch, by email or phone, a few days after you've submitted your application to ask how the process is going.

For example, you might email Personnel Manager Meredith Lewis to say, "I wrote to you on March 3. I am checking to be sure you got my letter." Again, Lewis might think you're being a pest. Or she might think you're really keen about the job—keener than applicants who didn't get in touch.

If it doesn't seem too pushy, you might also include in the action section of your cover letter a sentence or two such as this: "Perhaps we could schedule an interview in the next week, at your convenience. I am available at any time." If the employer doesn't want to interview you, that's her prerogative. But sometimes a little push like this may actually make her life easier—if you clearly stand out in terms of keenness, perhaps she doesn't have to interview 30 other candidates.

Anything that pushes the employer toward action in your direction is a good thing, as long as it's done tactfully.

Cover Letter Example

Take a look at the example cover letter. How well does it fit the AIDA persuasive pattern?

Mike Gregorius
35 Clearview Road
Prince George, BC V0J 2P5

March 22, 2016

Colin Bannister
General Manager
British Columbia Forest Service,
Wildfire Management Branch
PO BOX 9502 STN PROV GOVT
Terrapin, BC V8W 9C1

Dear Mr. Bannister:

Subject: Application for Fire Crew Member position

This letter highlights my interest in wildfire fighting and my abilities relating to the British Columbia Wildfire Management Branch's position of Fire Crew Member.

I have worked outdoors all my life, performing a variety of wilderness work that includes seeding steep, rocky, decommissioned logging roads near Nelson, B.C., and carrying heavy loads of dirt for machine compacting while landscaping in Kamloops, B.C.

I have worked for Wilkerson Forest Management's firefighting service and received the S100 and S185 training, so I am knowledgeable in basic fire-line procedures. I completed my OFA Level 3, learning first-aid techniques to keep fire crew members safe and to provide effective care for injured workers. This knowledge will allow me to take control and lead in intense, dangerous situations. Geography 110, which I completed at the University of Northern British Columbia, increased my knowledge of energy flows through B.C. forests and ecosystems as well as of human and resource interactions.

To prepare for the physically demanding tasks of wildfire fighting, I maintain a high level of fitness through regular exercise with tailored gym routines, I referee competitive ice hockey, and I practise Bikram yoga.

My strong work ethic and ability to lead, but also my willingness to follow commands, will make me an effective and committed member of B.C.'s wildfire-management team.

I can be reached at the email address and phone number below. My résumé is enclosed. I am available to come for an interview at any time, at your convenience. I look forward to hearing from you.

Yours sincerely,

Mike Gregorius

Mike Gregorius
mgregorius@netconnect.com
(250) 555-3451

Enclosed: Résumé

How did Mike Gregorius do?

- To get *attention* he states his interest in wilderness firefighting and his knowledge of the field by applying for the available position.
- To build *interest*, paragraphs 3, 4, and 5 present, in concrete and specific detail, what Mike has done and is doing that would prepare him for fire-crew work.
- Paragraph 6 tries to create *desire* by mentioning Mike's personal qualities, with his work history as evidence that he does, in fact, possess these qualities.
- To get *action*, in paragraph 7 Mike makes it as easy as possible for the employer to get in touch with him to arrange an interview.

In other words, this letter follows the principles of AIDA.

Now take a look at this letter, which is applying for a government job in the health field (it does not have the opening and closing elements). How well does it follow the AIDA formula?

Dear Ms. Elphinstone:

Subject: Application for Wellness Coordinator

It is important to have reliable and productive employees in the workplace. Many positions call for a significant amount of trust and dedication in workers. I display these attributes and am applying for the position of Workplace Wellness Coordinator.

My experience working with the public has developed my skills in workplace relations. I have worked in a number of public areas and can work well with a wide range of personalities. Previous jobs have taught me to work on my own with minimal supervision when needed. I am eager to learn in the workplace and put all my effort into my assignments and tasks.

Enclosed you will find my résumé. Thank you for taking the time to consider me for this position. I hope to hear from you for an interview.

Yours sincerely,

Jessica Bradshaw

Jessica Bradshaw

Most of this letter focuses on creating desire; it's a list of the job applicant's personal qualities intermixed with some very generalized details about her work experience. Jessica doesn't give any concrete and specific work detail to back up her claims of being "reliable and productive" and so on. There's nothing here to *show* a potential employer that this person meets the requirements of the job. In other words, it's unlikely that this cover letter will get Jessica the job she wants.

CONCLUSION

Remember, your cover letter makes your first impression with the employer. Your potential boss isn't just looking for a set of skills; she's also interested in *you* as a person who would fit well into her organization. And the person she's looking for is one who cares about the small details, who tries to get it right each and every time, just as she does in her business.

An impeccably formatted and well-written cover letter is a strong signal to the employer that you are the intelligent, conscientious, detail-oriented person she is looking for.

So, as you write your cover letter, keep AIDA in mind.

You can find more information about writing cover letters, including sample cover letters, at the following websites:
http://jobsearch.about.com/od/coverlettersamples

http://www.youth.gc.ca/eng/topics/jobs/cover.shtml

- First, get attention.
- Then, to create interest, give *concrete and specific* details about your work experience, qualifications, and skills.
- Wait until the desire section to present yourself as a hard worker who communicates well, likes working with people, is detail oriented, and so on. In the desire paragraph or paragraphs, you sum up the personal qualities that allowed you to work well at the jobs you listed in the interest section.
- Then, if you can, try to get action—ask for a meeting, say you'll phone back in a week, show that you are eager and ready for an interview or to work at a moment's notice.

Worth Considering
Here's a tip that will improve your life in every way: You've heard the expression "if it's worth doing, it's worth doing well." It's also true that, even if it isn't worth doing, it's still worth doing well.

Employers have a sixth sense for potential employees who always strive to do their best—in sports-interview jargon, the people who give "one hundred and ten per cent" in everything they do. Employers also have a sixth sense for job-seekers who are sloppy and uncaring in most areas of their lives.

If you strive to do your very best in every part of your life, no matter how menial or trivial, employers will recognize this quality, and you'll increase your chances of getting the job of your dreams.

And, to repeat, always keep in mind that the cover letter isn't about *you*. It's about what you can do for the employer, period. If the employer doesn't see how you will fit into her organization, then your cover letter and résumé will not have succeeded.

In Chapter 11, we'll look at writing the perfect résumé.

Exercise

Find an advertisement for a job that appeals to you from a newspaper or online.

Analyze the ad.

- List the specific skills and qualities the employer is looking for. Do you have these skills?
- Make a second list detailing all your education, experience, skills, and qualities that might be relevant.
- Match the two lists and rank items. Which are the strongest and weakest points in your favour? Which are the most important skills and qualities to the employer?

Write the letter.

- Make a point-form outline of your cover letter. Which skills, qualities, and knowledge will you highlight?
- Write a one-page cover letter, using the AIDA pattern, applying for the job, making up the details you need to make your letter persuasive.

Revise the letter.

- Exchange this letter with a fellow student who has also done the exercise and apply the same critical analysis to that letter.
- Finally, when you get your peer-edited letter back, rewrite it based on the comments from your fellow student that you think are justified.

Chapter 11
Résumés

INTRODUCTION

If a potential employer likes your cover letter, then he or she will move on to your résumé or CV (*curriculum vitae*).

A résumé gives more details about the skills and accomplishments you mentioned in your cover letter. It is usually no longer than two pages, in bulleted form, and very concise.

A CV is a specialized type of résumé used mostly for academic and scientific research positions and grant applications. It is a complete summary of your educational and academic backgrounds as well as your teaching and research experience, publications, presentations, awards, honours, and affiliations. Unlike the résumé, which is usually a maximum of two pages, the CV can be several, even many, pages long depending on how extensive your credentials are.

Before writing your résumé, study the job announcement carefully, looking at the key words and seeing how many you can match with your skills. If there's a good match, then make a list of your work experience, including

• dates you've worked,
• names and addresses of the companies you've worked for,

- your primary duties on your various jobs,
- special projects you've worked on,
- equipment and software you've used,
- problems you've solved or challenges you've faced, and
- savings you've made for the company.

Dos and Don'ts for Résumés

Do
- Keep the résumé to two pages.
- Use lists and white space for reader friendliness.
- Make sure your lists are parallel.
- Use 12-point body font and 14-point headings.
- Use sans-serif fonts such as Arial for headings, even if your body type is also sans serif (sans-serif fonts are "sticky" on the eye).
- State your career goal or objective at the beginning.
- Proofread your résumé with extreme care to avoid even the smallest grammatical, spelling, wording, or factual error.

Don't
- Include high school experience unless it's very relevant.
- Say whether you are male or female, unless the job is seeking someone in a specific gender category.
- Say whether you are married or single.
- Say your religious affiliation.
- Say what ethnic or racial group you belong to, unless you are applying for a job seeking a person in a specific ethnic or racial category.
- Include personal details that aren't relevant to the position you are applying for.

In your résumé, mention specific product names, industry standard names (such as health and safety training), and detailed statistics (such as the number of employees you've managed, calls handled per day, or products assembled per week). Don't say "familiar with software": give an accurate picture (type of software, level of expertise, and so on).

Then make a list of your relevant experience and include the following:

- **Education**: List the dates you attended school; your degrees, diplomas and certificates, courses and projects, and GPA (if applicable); the topics or subjects you've studied; and the awards and honours you've received.
- **Paid and unpaid work**: Merge paid and unpaid work if the unpaid work is relevant—give the same details you would for paid work.

- **Other related experience**: Mention skills and hobbies that relate to the job or "round you out," especially if you can point to an achievement such as a junior hockey championship and the like.

Then you need to decide the headings at the start of your résumé. Here are some common choices:

- **Letterhead**: At the top of the résumé, put your name, address, phone number, email address, and web-page URL (if you have a web page).
- **Objectives**: Include this element if you have a specific and realistic objective or objectives related to the job.
- **Summary of experience/Career summary**: A career summary section can show how your work experience has made you suitable for the position. Include your best and most relevant qualifications.
- **Fitness for the job**: List personal (relevant) qualities you've developed that make you the ideal candidate, such as leadership ability.

> **Worth Knowing**
>
> Most résumés, and especially the chronological ones, require the following information, in roughly this order:
>
> 1. **Personal details** (name, address, contact numbers, etc.)
> 2. **Job objective/Career summary** (optional, but very common)
> 3. **Education and qualifications**
> 4. **Career history/Work experience**
> 5. **Training** (courses you have taken, etc.)
> 6. **Personal activities and interests** (that might have a positive effect on your work performance)
> 7. **References** (usually available on request rather than listed).
>
> From *Employment360.com*, www.employment360.com/resume-layout.html

The top of the first page of your résumé might look something like the one below:

Mike Gregorius

35 Clearview Road   555-555-3451
Prince George, BC V0J 2P5   Email: mgregorius@netconnect.com

OBJECTIVE

To find a career opportunity within the British Columbia Wildfire Management Branch as a Fire Crew Member.

CAREER SUMMARY

- Worked for Wilkerson Forest Management firefighting service.
- Received S100 and S185 training on basic fire-line procedures.
- Performed a variety of wilderness work, including reforestation and landscaping.
- Completed OFA Level 3 first-aid training.
- Completed basic small-business accounting training.
- Completed three of four years toward a BSc in exercise, health, and fitness.
- Maintained a high level of physical fitness.

The career summary could also have broken down Mike's accomplishments under headings such as "Leadership and Management Skills," "Communication Skills," "Physical Fitness," and so on. Bulleted lists are often appropriate in these sections. Be sure, however, that your lists are parallel; that is, each item in a list must begin with the same type of grammatical unit: noun, verb, participle (e.g., an "-ing" verbal), etc.

Note that, legally, you do not have to state the following on your résumé or in your cover letter:

- whether you are male or female (unless it's a condition of employment),
- whether you're married or single,
- what religious affiliation you have, or
- what ethnic or racial group you belong to (unless it's a condition of employment).

You are now ready to write the rest of your résumé. There are three basic résumé styles: reverse chronological, functional, and combined (chronological and functional). In the next sections, we'll look at each type, along with the electronic, scannable résumé.

REVERSE CHRONOLOGICAL RÉSUMÉ

This is the most common type of résumé, and it's a good choice when you have a fair amount of job experience. In the reverse chronological résumé, you list your employment history, training, and education starting with the *most recent* relevant jobs, training and education (hence, a *reverse* chronological résumé; a chronological résumé would start with your *first* job).

Do you begin with your work experience or your education? That depends on which puts you in the best light. If you have been to highly prestigious schools, such as McGill, but are still a bit light on actual work experience, then you might want to list your educational attainments first. If you have a strong employment history but are a bit lacking on the education front, you might start with your work experience and put your "Education" heading further down.

In general, the main headings for a chronological résumé are

- Objective,
- Summary of qualifications,
- Education (education might go after work experience),
- Work experience,
- Community service/Volunteer work (if relevant),
- Hobbies/Interests (if relevant), and
- References (if required).

That said, most résumés begin with your education in reverse chronological order, followed by your jobs in reverse chronological order. For an example, see Mike Gregorius's chronological résumé (Figure 11.1).

Mike Gregorius

35 Clearview Road	555-555-3451
Prince George, BC V0J 2P5	Email: mgregorius@netconnect.com

OBJECTIVE

To find a career opportunity within the British Columbia Wildfire Management Branch as a Fire Crew Member.

CAREER SUMMARY

- Worked for Wilkerson Forest Management firefighting service.
- Received S100 and S185 training on basic fire-line procedures.
- Performed a variety of wilderness work, including reforestation and landscaping.
- Completed OFA Level 3 first-aid training.
- Completed basic small-business accounting training.
- Completed three of four years toward a BSc in exercise, health, and fitness.
- Maintained a high level of physical fitness.

EDUCATION

2011 – Present	UNIVERSITY OF NORTHERN B.C., Prince George, B.C. **3rd year, Bachelor of Science (Exercise Science, Health and Fitness)**
2010 – 2011	KWANTLEN COLLEGE, Richmond, B.C. **Diploma in Small-Business Accounting**

WORK EXPERIENCE

Dec 2013 – Present (part time)	SPORTTECH, Prince George, B.C. **Assistant Sales Manager** • Managed (part time) a staff of six in selling equipment for skiing, hockey, golf, and other popular sports. • Took inventory of stock weekly along with sales manager. • Managed sales receipts and returns.
May 2013 – Aug 2013 (summer job)	WILKERSON FOREST MANAGEMENT, Fraser Lake, B.C. **Firefighting Intern** • Learned basics of forest-fire fighting and forest management. • Fought several small brushfires. • Helped keep company accounts.

Figure 11.1 Reverse Chronological Résumé from Mike Gregorius

| May 2012 – Aug 2012 (summer job) | FOREST RESTORATION SERVICE, Ltd., Kamloops, B.C. **Tree Planter and Reseeder** |

- Planted seeds for reforestation on steep, decommissioned logging roads.
- Supervised a team of four tree planters on a day-to-day basis.

| May 2011 – Aug 2011 (summer job) | EVERGREEN LANDSCAPING, Ltd., Vernon, B.C. **Landscaping Assistant** |

- Operated dirt-compacting machine as part of landscaping business.

| May 2010 – Aug 2010 (summer job) | WHISTLER BLACKCOMB SKI RESORT, Whistler, B.C. **Assistant Sports Director** |

- Helped provide sporting opportunities for summer guests.
- Took guests on mountain hikes, bicycle tours, and all-terrain-vehicle expeditions.
- Helped maintain accounts and records for resort's summer sports office.
- Named employee of the month three times.

| Sep 2009 – May 2011 (part time fall–winter) | PUBLIC LIBRARY, Prince George, B.C. **Desk Clerk** |

- Worked at check-out desk.
- Shelved books.

VOLUNTEER POSITIONS / COMMUNITY SERVICE

| 2009 – present | PRINCE GEORGE FIRE SERVICE, Prince George, B.C. **Junior volunteer** |

| May 2007 – Feb 2008 | HELPING HANDS HOMELESS SHELTER, Prince George, B.C. **Volunteer in soup kitchen** |

| 2006 – 2008 (fall and winter) | PRINCE GEORGE EAGLES JUNIOR HOCKEY **Team captain** |

| 2006 – 2007 (July – August) | FRASER LAKE YMCA CAMP, Fraser Lake, B.C. **Camp counsellor** |

REFERENCES

References are available upon request.

As you list your jobs, give concrete and specific details about what you've done, the number of people you've managed, the tasks you've performed, the equipment or software you've worked with, and so on. Don't be vague. In general, unless you are just starting to look for work, don't include your high-school jobs. And you don't need to list every job you've ever had, just the ones that are relevant to the position you are applying for.

> **Worth Noting**
> Résumé lists start with verbs or words created from verbs, such as participles, because you want to create a sense of *action* in your résumé—it's a catalogue of what you've *done*.

In preparing lists, make sure they are parallel in grammatical structure. That is, if you are writing about your responsibilities, use either *participles* or *verbs* but not both in the same list. For example, a list using gerunds, participles ending in "ing" that are frequently used as nouns, would look like this:

My duties included

- writing letters,
- editing brochures and promotional material, and
- creating trade-show schedules.

A list using verbs would look like this:

As part of my duties, I

- wrote letters,
- edited brochures and promotional material, and
- created trade-show schedules.

A chronological résumé may include headings on interests and activities, but you should list no more than six items, e.g., bridge, skiing, playing guitar, hockey. Be truthful in describing these activities because, if you get to the interview stage, the interviewer may well bring your interests up to "break the ice." If she begins to talk about how much she, too, likes playing bridge and your idea of good bridge is not drawing to an inside straight, your career with this company is probably over before it began.

The chronological résumé has a drawback: it may reveal embarrassing gaps in your work history. You don't need to dwell on these gaps (that is, just don't refer to them), but be honest if asked about them.

> **Worth Knowing**
> Many websites offer cover-letter and résumé template designs, such as the Microsoft Office website at https://templates.office.com/en-us/Resumes-and-Cover-Letters

And, while we're on the topic of honesty—you must be scrupulously honest in your résumé. You want to show yourself in the best possible light, but a padded or dishonest résumé will eventually be found out and you will be in trouble.

The final sentence of a chronological résumé (and most résumés) will state that references are available on request, unless the company has explicitly asked for references. Obviously, you should have set up your references in advance, in case they are required.

Most word-processing programs offer built-in templates for résumés, cover letters, and many other types of documents in many different styles and designs. And you can find many templates for résumés and cover letters online.

FUNCTIONAL RÉSUMÉ

The functional résumé has the same information as a chronological résumé but rather than a series of employment dates, it is arranged under skills and abilities, e.g., project management, communication skills, and leadership skills.

In most job searches, you will use the reverse chronological résumé or the combined (chronological and functional) résumé, discussed below. However, the functional résumé is useful if you don't yet have a lot of job experience because you can include non-employment experience in each category. In other words, a functional résumé highlights your skills rather than your (perhaps spotty or almost non-existent) work history. It's a good format for someone entering the workforce right out of high school or after raising a family.

> **Worth Reading**
> A good discussion of the merits of chronological versus functional résumés can be found at www. Employment360. com/functional-vs-chronological-resumes.html

For example, under "Leadership skills" you might put your time as president of the college student council, or captain of your high-school hockey team, or editor of your high-school yearbook. You probably weren't paid for any of these tasks, but all required leadership skills.

In general, the main headings for a functional résumé are

- Objective,
- Accomplishments,
- Capabilities,
- Employment History,
- Education, and
- References.

If Mike Gregorius were to use a functional résumé when seeking a job in the fire service, the "accomplishments" and "capabilities" part of this résumé might look like the portion reproduced here (note that the list items are all verbs and that these are not full grammatical sentences).

Leadership/teamwork skills

- Managed staff of six at sports equipment store.
- Was assistant sports director for summer activities at Whistler, B.C., resort.
- Was employee of the month three times at Whistler resort.
- Managed team of four tree planters for a summer.
- Captained junior hockey team for two seasons.
- Was counsellor at YMCA summer camp for two summers.

Firefighting experience

- Was firefighting intern with Wilkerson Forest Management.
- Received S100 and S185 training on basic fire-line procedures.
- Completed OFA Level 3 first-aid training.

Outdoor experience

- Spent summer as a tree planter.
- Worked as landscaping assistant.
- Was camp counsellor at YMCA camp.
- Was outdoor summer sports assistant director at Whistler, B.C., resort.

Accounting skills

- Earned diploma in small-business accounting from Kwantlen College.
- Managed sales accounts and returns for sporting-goods store.
- Helped keep company books for forest-management company.
- Helped maintain accounts and records for summer sports office.

Portion of a Functional Résumé that Lists Skills and Experience Relevant to Job

Next, Mike would list the various companies he's worked for (his employment history), his educational qualifications, and his relevant volunteer experiences. See Figure 11.2 for Mike's complete functional résumé.

Various websites provide templates and samples of functional résumés. See, in particular, the section on functional résumés from the JobStar website (http://jobstar.org/tools/resume/res-func.php). This is one of many styles of functional résumé templates that can be found online.

MIKE GREGORIUS

35 Clearview Road   555-555-3451
Prince George, BC V0J 2P5   Email: mgregorius@netconnect.com

OBJECTIVE: To find a career opportunity within the British Columbia Wildfire Management Branch as a Fire Crew Member

SUMMARY OF QUALIFICATIONS

- Trained in forest firefighting and basic fire-line procedures
- Experienced in wilderness work, including reforestation and landscaping
- Experienced with working in a complex, fast-moving environment
- Works well with others
- Trained in first aid
- Maintains a high level of physical fitness
- Completing third year of BSc in exercise, health, and fitness
- Trained in small-business accounting and therefore detail-oriented.

RELEVANT SKILLS AND EXPERIENCE

Leadership/teamwork skills

- Managed staff of six at sports equipment store
- Was assistant sports director for summer activities at Whistler, B.C., resort
- Was employee of the month three times at Whistler resort
- Managed team of four tree planters for a summer
- Captained junior hockey team for two seasons
- Was counsellor at YMCA summer camp for two summers.

Firefighting experience

- Was firefighting intern with Wilkerson Forest Management
- Received S100 and S185 training on basic fire-line procedures
- Completed OFA Level 3 first-aid training.

Outdoor experience

- Spent summer as a tree planter
- Worked as landscaping assistant
- Was camp counsellor at YMCA camp
- Was outdoor summer sports assistant director at Whistler, B.C., resort.

Accounting experience

- Earned diploma in small-business accounting from Kwantlen College
- Managed sales accounts and returns for sporting-goods store
- Helped keep company books for forest-management company
- Helped maintain accounts and records for summer sports office.

Figure 11.2 Functional Résumé from Mike Gregorius

EMPLOYMENT HISTORY

- **Sporttech**—Prince George, B.C.
  Assistant sales manager, 2013–present
- **Wilkerson Forest Management**—Fraser Lake, B.C.
  Firefighting intern
- **Forest Restoration Service**—Kamloops, B.C.
  Tree planting supervisor, May–September 2012
- **Evergreen Landscaping**—Vernon, B.C.
  Landscaping assistant, May–August 2011
- **Whistler Blackcomb Ski Resort**—Whistler, B.C.
  Assistant sports director, May–August 2010

EDUCATION

- **University of Northern British Columbia**, Prince George, B.C.
  Third year, Bachelor of Science, specializing in Exercise Science, Health and Fitness, 2011–Present
- **Kwantlen College**, Richmond, B.C.
  Diploma in Small-Business Accounting. September–April, 2010–2011

VOLUNTEER POSITIONS / COMMUNITY SERVICE

- **Prince George Fire Service**, Prince George, B.C.
  Junior volunteer, 2009–present
- **Prince George Eagles Junior Hockey,** Prince George, B.C.
  Team captain, 2006–2008
- **Helping Hands Homeless Shelter**, Prince George, B.C.
  Soup kitchen volunteer, 2007–2008
- **Fraser Lake YMCA Camp,** Fraser Lake, B.C.
  Camp counsellor, 2006–2007

REFERENCES: References are available upon request.

COMBINED CHRONOLOGICAL AND FUNCTIONAL RÉSUMÉ

While the functional résumé lists your abilities, it may not easily incorporate where you learned or applied these abilities, i.e., for whom you actually worked. That information is in a separate section. The combined résumé solves this problem by including, usually in reverse chronological order, where you worked under each set of skills.

For an example, see Mike Gregorius's combined (chronological and functional) résumé (Figure 11.3).

Mike Gregorius

35 Clearview Road   555-555-3451
Prince George, BC V0J 2P5   Email: mgregorius@netconnect.com

OBJECTIVE

To find a career opportunity within the British Columbia Wildfire
Management Branch as a Fire Crew Member.

CAREER SUMMARY

- Worked for Wilkerson Forest Management firefighting service.
- Received S100 and S185 training on basic fire-line procedures.
- Performed a variety of wilderness work, including reforestation and landscaping.
- Completed OFA Level 3 first-aid training.
- Completed basic small-business accounting training.
- Completed three of four years toward a BSc in exercise, health, and fitness.
- Maintained a high level of physical fitness.

Leadership/teamwork skills

Dec 2013– Present   SPORTTECH, Prince George, B.C.
(part time)   **Assistant Sales Manager**
- Managed (part time) a staff of six in selling equipment for skiing, hockey, golf, and other popular sports.
- Took inventory of stock weekly along with sales manager.

May 2012 – Aug 2012   FOREST RESTORATION SERVICE, Ltd., Kamloops, B.C.
(summer job)   **Tree Planting Supervisor**
- Worked with others to plant seeds for reforestation on steep, decommissioned logging roads.
- Supervised a team of four tree planters and seeders.

May 2010 – Aug 2010   WHISTLER BLACKCOMB SKI RESORT, Whistler, B.C.
(summer job)   **Assistant Sports Director**
- Helped provide sporting opportunities for summer guests at Whistler Blackcomb Ski Resort.
- Took guests on mountain hikes, bicycle tours, and all-terrain-vehicle expeditions.
- Worked with others to help maintain accounts and records for resort's summer sports office.

2006 – 2008   PRINCE GEORGE EAGLES JUNIOR HOCKEY
(fall and winter)   **Team Captain (2007–2008 seasons)**

May 2007 – Feb 2008   HELPING HANDS HOMELESS SHELTER, Prince George, B.C.
                             Soup Kitchen Volunteer
- Helped feed 120 homeless men and women three times a week for seven months.

Figure 11.3 Combined Chronological and Functional Résumé from Mike Gregorius

2006 – 2007   FRASER LAKE YMCA CAMP, Fraser Lake, B.C.
(July – August)   **Camp Counsellor**
                        • Supervised recreational and sport activities for 9- to 12-year-
                          olds.

Outdoor experience

May 2013 – Aug 2013 WILKERSON FOREST MANAGEMENT, B.C., Fraser Lake, B.C.
(summer job)   **Firefighting Intern**
                        • Learned basics of forest-fire fighting and forest management.
                        • Fought several small brushfires.

May 2012 – Aug 2012 FOREST RESTORATION SERVICE, Ltd., Kamloops, B.C.
(summer job)   **Tree Planter**
                        • Planted seeds for reforestation on steep, decommissioned
                          logging roads.
                        • Provided daily on-site supervision to team of four tree planters.

May 2011 – Aug 2011 EVERGREEN LANDSCAPING, Ltd., Vernon, B.C.
(summer job)   **Landscaping Assistant**
                        • Operated dirt-compacting machine as part of landscaping
                          business.

May 2010 – Aug 2010 WHISTLER BLACKCOMB SKI RESORT, Whistler, B.C.
(summer job)   **Assistant Sports Director**
                        • Helped provide sporting opportunities for summer guests at
                          Whistler Blackcomb Ski Resort.
                        • Took guests on mountain hikes, bicycle tours, and all-terrain-
                          vehicle expeditions.

2006 – 2007   FRASER LAKE YMCA CAMP, Fraser Lake, B.C.
(July – August)   **Camp Counsellor**

Accounting skills

2010–2011   KWANTLEN COLLEGE, Richmond, B.C.
                        Diploma in Small-Business Accounting

Dec 2013 – Present   SPORTTECH, Prince George, B.C.
(part time)   **Assistant Sales Manager**
                        • Managed sales receipts and returns.

May 2013 – Aug 2013 WILKERSON FOREST MANAGEMENT, B.C., Fraser Lake, B.C.
(summer job)   **Firefighting Intern**
                        • Helped keep company accounts.

May 2010 – Aug 2010 WHISTLER BLACKCOMB SKI RESORT, Whistler, B.C.
(summer job)   **Assistant Sports Director**
                        • Helped maintain accounts and records for resort's summer
                          sports office.

EDUCATION

2011 – Present	UNIVERSITY OF NORTHERN BRITISH COLUMBIA, Prince George, B.C. **Third year, Bachelor of Science (Exercise Science, Health, and Fitness)**
2010 – 2011	KWANTLEN COLLEGE, Richmond, B.C. **Diploma in Small-Business Accounting**

VOLUNTEER POSITIONS / COMMUNITY SERVICE

2009 – present	PRINCE GEORGE FIRE SERVICE, Prince George, B.C. **Junior volunteer**
2006 – 2008 (fall and winter)	PRINCE GEORGE EAGLES JUNIOR HOCKEY **Team captain**
May 2007 – Feb 2008	HELPING HANDS HOMELESS SHELTER, Prince George, B.C. **Soup-kitchen volunteer**
2006 – 2007 (July – August)	FRASER LAKE YMCA CAMP, Fraser Lake, B.C. **Camp counsellor**

REFERENCES

References are available upon request.

The combined résumé is a good choice if you are aiming for a change of career. For example, Mike Gregorius is applying for a job as a forest firefighter. But he also has training, skills, and experience as an accountant or bookkeeper. If he were already a firefighter now trying for a job in accounting, he would put his accounting skills first and find another category in place of "Outdoor experience."

In general, the categories in a combined chronological and functional résumé are the following:

- Objective,
- Summary,
- Accomplishments (by category),
- Experience (names of companies),
- Education, and
- References.

Templates and samples of various résumé forms, including the combined chronological and functional résumé, are available from the websites of most university career centres. See, in particular, Western University's Student Success Centre (http://uwo.ca/careers/get_a_job/resumes_cvs__letters/resumes/index.html).

ELECTRONIC OR SCANNABLE RÉSUMÉ

For an electronic or scannable résumé, a potential employer uses software to electronically scan for key words and phrases in your résumé. If those key words aren't there, you won't get the job interview. Therefore, as you read the employer's job advertisement, make sure those key words and phrases are in your résumé!

For the employer, this type of résumé is a major time-saver (so it saves money too). If a particular job has attracted 3,000 résumés, scanning for key words can rapidly reduce this large figure to a more manageable number for the actual human being who has to read the résumés that passed the scan.

One section of your scannable résumé, right under contact information, can be "Keywords"—a list of the key words and phrases from the job advertisement that apply to you. These keywords could include the following (from the IT advertisement in the cover letter section):

- Superior interpersonal and leadership skills.
- Strong verbal and written English communication skills.
- Ability to work under pressure with multiple priorities.
- Ability to work in a team environment.

An employer who wants an electronic résumé will also specify the criteria for the résumé. So make sure you follow these guidelines to the letter. In the absence of any company-specific rules, consult the following checklist.

> **Worth Knowing**
> The following websites have useful information about scannable résumés:
>
> http://www.quintcareers.com/scannable_resume_sample.html
>
> https://owl.purdue.edu/owl/job_search_writing/resumes_and_vitas/scannable_resumes_presentation.html
>
> https://careercenter.missouristate.edu/students/Electronic Scannable Resumes.htm

Checklist for Producing an Effective Scannable Résumé

Content
- Your name and address should appear at the top of each page of the résumé on its own line. Use standard address format below your name, and list each phone number on its own line. (Don't put parentheses around area codes.)
- Use well-known major headings (e.g., Education, Work History).
- Provide a keyword or qualifications summary after your contact information. Use the "buzzwords" common in your profession, the ones that appear in relevant job descriptions.

- Throughout the résumé, use more nouns than action words, e.g., "project management" or "project manager" instead of "managed projects." You want to describe your skills using the search terms employers will be looking for (electronically).
- Use only those abbreviations that are common in your field. Write the names of software applications and programming languages that you have used as these appear in professional literature: e.g., Java, Adobe Dreamweaver, C++, Microsoft Word.

Format

- Use boldface and/or all capital letters for section headings, but avoid both in the rest of the résumé.
- Use a standard, serif font, e.g., Courier, Times New Roman, Palatino, or a common, easy-to-read sans-serif font, e.g., Arial, Lucida Sans, Univers. (Some companies require the use of sans-serif fonts because they scan better.)
- Use a font size of 10 to 12 points for regular text; many organizations prefer 11-point typeface. A 14-point font size is fine for headings or your name at the top of the page.
- Avoid lines, boxes, tables, and borders.
- Do not use special characters, graphics, bullets, dashes, italics, highlighting, shading, shadows, or underlining.
- Avoid punctuation as much as possible; use white space between words instead. Some optical character recognition (OCR) programs do not recognize a word with a comma or period after it, although this software scans with more accuracy in recent years.

Printing and Sending

- Print your résumé and cover letter on plain white paper. Scanning accuracy is affected by coloured paper.
- Print on one side only; do not submit a two-sided résumé.
- Provide a copy with good print quality; for example, send a printout from a laser printer or a high-quality photocopy. Many companies do not scan faxed résumés, so, if you must use email, create a high-quality PDF to send.
- Mail the résumé flat and in a protected envelope, to avoid folds and creases. Do not use staples, and do not attach business cards, transcripts, or other documents. (If you need to keep pages together, use a paperclip.)

In other words, everything about the electronic or scannable résumé is plain, simple, and functional. Fortunately, if you get past the scanning stage to an interview, you can bring and submit your more readable, beautifully formatted résumé.

For an example, see what Mike Gregorius's chronological résumé might look like if it were formatted as a scannable résumé (Figure 11.4).

MIKE GREGORIUS
35 Clearview Road
Prince George, BC V0J 2P5
Phone: 555-555-3451
Email: mgregorius@netconnect.com

OBJECTIVE

To find a career opportunity within the British Columbia Wildfire Management Branch as a Fire
Crew Member

KEYWORDS

-Outdoor skills
-Firefighting skills
-Accounting skills
-First aid training
-Physical fitness

CAREER SUMMARY

-Worked for Wilkerson Forest Management firefighting service
-Received S100 and S185 training on basic fire-line procedures
-Performed a variety of wilderness work, including reforestation and landscaping
-Completed OFA Level 3 first-aid training
-Completed basic small-business accounting training
-Maintained a high level of physical fitness

EDUCATION

2011–Present
University of Northern British Columbia, Prince George, B.C.
-3rd year, Bachelor of Science (Exercise Science, Health, and Fitness)

2010–2011
Kwantlen College, Richmond, B.C.
-Diploma in Small-Business Accounting

WORK EXPERIENCE

Dec 2013–Present (part time)
Sporttech, Prince George, B.C.
Assistant Sales Manager
-Managed (part time) a staff of six in selling equipment for skiing, hockey, golf, and other
popular sports
-Took inventory of stock weekly along with sales manager
-Managed sales receipts and returns

Figure 11.4 Scannable Chronological Résumé from Mike Gregorius

May 2013–Aug 2013 (summer job)
Wilkerson Forest Management, Fraser Lake, B.C.
Firefighting Intern
-Learned basics of forest-fire fighting and forest management
-Fought several small brushfires
-Helped keep company accounts

May 2012–Aug 2012 (summer job)
Forest Restoration Service, Kamloops, B.C.
Tree planter and reseeder
-Planted seeds for reforestation on steep, decommissioned logging roads
-Supervised a team of four tree planters on a day-to-day basis

May 2011–Aug 2011 (summer job)
Evergreen Landscaping, Vernon, B.C.
Landscaping Assistant
-Operated dirt-compacting machine as part of landscaping business

May 2010–Aug 2010 (summer job)
Whistler Blackcomb Ski Resort, Whistler, B.C.
Assistant Sports Director
-Helped provide sporting opportunities for summer guests
-Took guests on mountain hikes, bicycle tours, and all-terrain-vehicle expeditions
-Helped maintain accounts and records for resort's summer sports office
-Named employee of the month three times

Sep 2009–May 2011 (part time fall–winter)
Public Library, Prince George, B.C.
Desk Clerk
-Worked at check-out desk
-Shelved books

VOLUNTEER POSITIONS/COMMUNITY SERVICE

2009–present
Prince George Fire Service, Prince George, B.C.
Junior volunteer

2006–2008 (fall and winter)
Prince George Eagles junior hockey team
Team captain

May 2007–Feb 2008
Helping Hands Homeless Shelter, Prince George, B.C.
Volunteer in soup kitchen

2006–2007 (July–Aug)
Fraser Lake YMCA Camp, Fraser Lake, B.C.
Camp counsellor

REFERENCES

References are available upon request

CONCLUSION

As noted, you're not on your own when preparing a cover letter and résumé—there are many websites offering advice on both. Often, sites provide templates for you to follow. But a template won't help you in making sure the information you put into the template is well written and persuasive. That's up to you!

Exercises

1. Bring your résumé to class and exchange it with another student's résumé. Analyze the other résumé based on what we've learned in this chapter. How well does it meet the requirements for a strong résumé?
2. Revise your résumé based on the suggestions from the other student.
3. Rewrite your résumé using the three formats: chronological, functional, and combined.

Part V
Promotional Materials

Promotion is the lifeblood of business and many of the professions. If the public doesn't know about you, whether you are a company selling a product or a professional selling a service, how will they know what you are offering? If you have a cause you want to advance, say, saving the rainforest, the same problem applies: you need to get your message out, and that means promotion.

In this part, we focus on three ways of getting publicity: news releases, brochures, and web pages. There are many others, from advertising to hand-out flyers to newsletters to company matchbook covers.

In all cases, the effectiveness of your promotion depends heavily on how well you write your material as you present your case to the world. Grammar and spelling problems and factual errors damage your credibility and therefore the credibility of whatever it is you are promoting.

Strong promotion also means being aware of the three forms of persuasion—*logos*, *pathos*, and *ethos*—and knowing which form to emphasize depending on your audience and what you hope to achieve. Finally, good promotion depends on AIDA: getting **attention**, creating **interest**, stimulating **desire**, getting **action**.

Promotion is more than just an attractive face! Good public promotion takes a lot of hard work and attention to detail, including writing detail, behind the scenes.

In Part V, we will look at news releases (Chapter 12), brochures (Chapter 13), and promotion online through websites and social media (Chapter 14).

Chapter 12
News Releases

In this chapter you will learn how to

• Write a successful news release.

INTRODUCTION

Getting public attention for a product or service is a never-ending problem in professional and business communication, and this is true whether you work for private industry, government, or a non-governmental, non-profit organization. No matter how good your product or service, it's never easy to get your message out to the public.

In this chapter, we'll look at how to design a news release that will get your product or service noticed by the media and, hopefully, the public. In Chapter 13, we'll discuss how to design an attractive and effective brochure to promote your product or service. In Chapter 14, we'll look, briefly, at using the Internet and social media to get your message across.

NEWS RELEASES

Even if you never set foot in a newspaper or broadcast newsroom, if you have a professional career, chances are you will end up writing for the media. How? By putting out a news release for your organization. And here you face a problem.

With a news release you are writing for two audiences. One audience, obviously, is the public you want to reach with the news of your amazing new product or service. You hope people will be intrigued and want to buy or try what you're offering.

Worth Remembering
"Who is my audience?" is the very first question you should ask yourself whenever you sit down to write anything, whether it's a letter, a news release, or an academic essay.

To be successful, though, you must *know* your audience. There's no point in sending a news release about, say, an amazing new ski wax to a newspaper in Florida—most readers in Miami won't be interested in what you are selling. A news release to publishers in Whistler will have a much better chance of generating interest and sales.

In fact, "Who is my audience?" is the very first question you should ask yourself whenever you sit down to write anything, whether it's a letter, a résumé, a news release, a brochure, a report, a web page, or an academic essay.

The second audience is actually a much tougher sell and that's the editor of the newspaper, broadcaster, or web page who decides whether to publish your news release.

Editors are jealous of the space in their news columns or the time in their broadcasts; they feel they never have enough column inches or hours. And they wonder: if you want to publicize a product or service, why can't you just buy an advertisement?

So your news release had better be well written—*very* well written—for two reasons. One is that a well-written, well-formatted news release gives your company and its product credibility with the editor. The second reason is that editors are notoriously picky about grammar and good writing in general. In fact, editors are professional nitpickers: it's their job to find grammar errors and factual mistakes. They're very good at it, so you must be very sure your release is both factually accurate and grammatically correct.

Even if it's written in perfect news-release style, the chances are low that your news release will be published unedited and intact. A senior editor who receives a news release he likes will take one of two courses of action.

One, he could send your release to a subeditor for copy-editing, where changes will be made to conform to that news outlet's style; your release may also be shortened to fit the news space or broadcast time available. A page-long release may even end up as one paragraph.

Second, if the editor thinks your news release really is newsworthy, he might pass it on to a reporter who, in turn, will get in touch with you for more details. This is good!

Fortunately, there are ways to increase the chances that your news release is published, rather than ending up in the circular file under the editor's desk, or in the editor's computer "Trash."

News Releases Must Be about News

For a start, to be successful, your news release had better deliver real news and not just an announcement that your bakery has issued a new line of cookies. That's why it's called a *news* release! News is information that is new and, in the editor's eyes, potentially of interest to readers or listeners.

If the news release is on a safety problem, such as a warning about a popular toy with small parts that could choke a child, the chances of getting your release published are pretty good.

If you've developed a product that actually cures male-pattern baldness, your news release has a very good chance. If you are promoting a charitable event, your chances are good. If you've got a new perfume endorsed by a mega-celebrity like Angelina Jolie (or, for that matter, anything endorsed by Angelina Jolie), your chances are excellent.

If your company is announcing its annual profits, the business section of the paper or news website might well be interested. If your city's NHL franchise has just signed a major player for $3.5 million, the sports editor will almost certainly bite. You might even make the front page.

But if you just want press or online space or broadcast time to advertise a new line of skin products, you might be better to buy an ad.

News Releases Are AIDA Documents

In Chapter 9, we discussed using the AIDA formula—attention, interest, desire, and action—for persuasive letters. AIDA is just as useful in creating news releases, brochures, and websites. Promotion and publicity are, after all, ways of *persuading* people to buy your product or service or ideas or anything, really.

So, in your news releases (and brochures and web pages), using AIDA will increase the chances of persuading your audiences—the editor and the public—that what you are offering is worth having. Here's how AIDA works in a news release. We'll discuss brochures and web pages later.

Attention
The first paragraph of your news release has to get attention. If it doesn't, who's going to read the rest of it? So, how do you get attention in the first paragraph of a news release?

The first step toward getting the attention of the reader is the news release's headline, which may or may not be the headline that finally appears in the news outlet's version. The headline should be punchy, and include a verb: "Cure for male-pattern baldness announced" should get readership among balding males, which is this particular product's main audience. A headline is not a label, such as "Cure for male-pattern baldness." The headline must have a verb to denote action. See the "General pointers" section for more on headlines.

If your product or service is as newsworthy as you think it is, then just describe it; there's no need to embellish. For example, let's say your company, Bald-No-More, is promoting a genuine cure for male-pattern baldness. That's amazing, and millions of men will be interested! But you have to be careful how you present this amazing discovery because, although a news release is a promotional document, it isn't written in promotional language. A news release has to be written in newspaper language.

Newspaper language is, ideally, objective in tone. The reporter's job isn't to promote a product or service but to describe it in an unbiased fashion. Similarly, your news release should be written in wording that doesn't appear to be self-interested or promotional—you present only the facts about the product. It's as if your news release were being written not by someone from your company who's keen to promote the product but by a neutral reporter. Basically, news style states the facts; promotional style makes claims ("revolutionary," "exciting," "amazing").

The traditional lead paragraph for a news story answers most (rarely all, or the paragraph would be too long) of the following six questions: who, where, what, when, why, and how? As we discussed in Chapter 2 under the heading "Complete," these questions are sometimes called the "five Ws plus an H":

- **Who** is the news story about?
- **What** happened?
- **Where** did the news happen?
- **When** did it happen?
- **Why** did it happen?
- **How** did it happen?

Your first paragraph should answer most of these questions.

Here's how the announcement for a baldness cure might look as promotional language:

> Bald-No-More, an innovative hair-care company that operates out of Terrapin, B.C., is very excited to announce a revolutionary new product that cures male-pattern baldness.

The words "excited," "innovative," and "revolutionary" here make this paragraph promotional rather than newspaper language.

In newspaper language, the first paragraph should read something like the following:

> A clinically tested cure for male-pattern baldness was announced yesterday by Bald-No-More, a hair-products company that operates out of Terrapin, B.C.

Worth Knowing
If you're not sure what newspaper language is, read a newspaper or news website. If you are looking for examples of news releases, they are everywhere. A good place to look is the "Communications," or "Media," or "News" links on any corporate, university, or government website. There you will find the news releases that the organization has put out over a period of time. After a few readings, you'll have a pretty good idea of what your news release should look like and read like.

Worth Knowing
A news release is about news, and you want to deliver that news quickly.
Here is a template for the ideal first sentence:

A [product/service/object] that [whatever it does] was announced [when] by [name of organization].

Here are a few sample first sentences:

- A program that provides hot breakfasts to schoolchildren was announced yesterday by provincial Children's Affairs Minister Charlene Ashcroft.
- A pen that electronically improves a writer's penmanship was announced yesterday by U-Pen-It Corp.
- A car that can travel 500 kilometres on a single litre of gasoline was announced yesterday by Gofar Motors Inc.
- A collar that uses GPS technology to keep track of pets was announced yesterday by PetFind, Ltd.

Note two things about the two different versions of the first paragraph. One is that "innovative," "excited," and "revolutionary"—all promotional words—are gone from the second version; what's left is "just the facts" (amazing enough, if true!).

And, second, the news-language version starts with details about the product, not the company name. Why? Readers are usually more interested in the product than the company that produced the product. Who cares about Bald-No-More, Inc., as a company? It's the product that counts.

This rule can be broken if the product is being announced by a really well-known company such as Apple, Microsoft, Google, or General Motors. Here, the fame and power of the company itself makes anything it announces newsworthy.

One final point: The first paragraph of a news release is not, repeat, not, a "tease" that tries to hook the reader by withholding information. A tease might read like this:

> Bald-No-More, an innovative hair-care company that operates out of Terrapin B.C., is very excited to announce a revolutionary new product.

Note that this paragraph doesn't say what the revolutionary new product actually *is*; you are forcing readers to go further. In other words, it's a trick. That might work in advertising, but it doesn't work in a news release. Be upfront with your customers in the first paragraph.

Interest

Now that you've got the editor's (and, you hope, readers') attention, it's time to develop interest. As we saw in Chapter 9, you develop interest by producing facts, statistics, a story, data, and so on, with concrete and specific details. So the next two, three, or four paragraphs of your news release will be factual—with one exception.

The exception is the second or third paragraph of the release. The second or third paragraph is almost always a quotation from someone involved in promoting or producing the product or service—a company president or manager, a government minister, or some other official spokesperson.

Why a quotation after the first paragraph? News stories are ultimately about *people*, not products; products only exist to please people. So your news release needs a human voice making the announcement, but quoted objectively, as if he or she had been interviewed by a reporter.

Here's how the second paragraph of the baldness cure release might read:

Worth Remembering
Most readers are more interested in the *product* than the company producing the product, so start your news release with the product, not the company name (unless the company is, itself, a major selling point, e.g., Apple or Google).

Worth Consulting
This website has an excellent summary of how to write a news release:

http://web.uvic.ca/~sdoyle/E302/Notes/PressReleaseNotes.html

"Most men would rather not be bald," said company president Clark Bissonette. "With Bald-No-More, every man can have a luxuriant head of hair without hairpieces or implants."

The quotation paragraph, in a news release, may try to evoke either desire or interest. In this case, Mr. Bissonette is presenting the desire side of this product—the desire of many bald men to have a full head of hair—because a quotation *can* use promotional language. A quotation is the company speaking directly to the reader. But Bissonette could equally have presented an interest-evoking detail:

"Our product is made from a hitherto-unknown plant found deep in the Brazilian rainforest," said company president Clark Bissonette. "The plant was discovered by biologist Claude Elphonse during an expedition to the Amazon headwaters."

This is a factual, interest detail about the product.

Note that the start of the quotation goes *before* the speaker's name. Why? Most readers don't care about *who* made the announcement; they want to know more about the product or service. That said, if the speaker is well known or influential, such as former Microsoft chairman Bill Gates or the prime minister of Canada, you can start with that person's name:

Microsoft founder Bill Gates said, in making the announcement, "Our new operating system is both faster and less expensive for computer users."

Your quotations should be short—20 to 30 words—in short sentences. If there are two sentences, the speaker's name and title should follow the first sentence of the quotation. News releases generally use commas rather than colons with quotations to create a casual, informal dialogue form.

The next two or three paragraphs should give interest-generating details about the product or service, written objectively as if by a reporter. You may sometimes quote a company spokesperson in the interest section, but here the quotations, whether direct (with quotation marks) or indirect (without quotation marks), are factual details. The interest section of our sample news release might read as follows:

The hair-restoring chemical comes from a hitherto-unknown plant that a company biologist found in a remote part of the Amazon rain forest, said company vice-president Michelle Groves. [This paragraph would be used if the Bissonette quotation in the second paragraph was to generate desire rather than interest.]

In testing, the company added several other chemical ingredients, such as magnesium sulphate and a mild form of carbolic acid, to the plant extract.

"When it is applied to the scalp of bald or balding men," said Ms. Groves, "the result was renewed hair growth with no harmful or unpleasant side effects."

The product is available in two strengths: Ultra, for men with complete baldness, and Minimal, for men with only partial baldness. Each treatment will cost $30, and three treatments are required. Ms. Groves said the company guarantees that the new hair will be permanent.

All of the above are interest details, facts about the product, including the cost. Note that it's not necessary to say "she said" or "Ms. Groves said" for every sentence or paragraph if it's clear who is providing the information.

Desire

A news release is normally no more than a page long, whether you are submitting the release as a printed document or electronically. If there is additional important information, it should be put in an attachment. So far, our sample news release is about five paragraphs long, so we only have room for two or three more short paragraphs. The next paragraph or two should be about creating desire.

In the desire paragraphs of a news release, as in this section of a persuasive letter, you want to present the benefits and advantages of the product or service to the buyer, and you also aim to overcome possible objections. For example, you might include a testimonial quotation from a satisfied user or have a company official emphasize, again, that this product is perfectly safe, with no harmful side effects. This section of our sample news release might read as follows:

"For the first time in years I go out on dates with complete confidence," said architect Mike Hartley, who helped test the product. "Women love to run their fingers through my new head of hair."

"I was amazed at how easy the treatment was," added Dan Hepworth, an accountant. "There was a bit of tickling as the hair grew, but my scalp felt great afterwards."

This promotional language is acceptable because the release is quoting someone.

Action

In the action section, if possible, you want to give an action date and a reason for taking action by that date, just as you did in this section of a persuasive letter. But not all news releases have or need an action part; that depends on the product. For example, a government minister might announce a new policy through a news release and try to interest voters in what the government is doing, thereby stimulating a desire to keep this government in office. But there's no need for a spur to action; the election might be a long time away.

Bald-No-More

March 23, 2019—FOR IMMEDIATE RELEASE

Cure for baldness announced

TERRAPIN, B.C.—A clinically tested cure for male-pattern baldness was announced yesterday by hair-products company Bald-No-More.

"Most men would rather not be bald," said company president Clark Bissonette in making the announcement. "With Bald-No-More, every man can have a luxuriant head of hair without hairpieces or implants."

The hair-restoring chemical comes from a hitherto-unknown plant that a company biologist found in a remote part of the Amazon rain forest, added company vice-president Michelle Groves.

In testing, the company added several other chemical ingredients, including magnesium sulphate and a mild form of carbolic acid, to the plant extract. "When it is applied to the scalp of bald or balding men," said Ms. Groves, "the result is renewed hair growth with no harmful or unpleasant side effects."

The product is available in two strengths: Ultra, for men with complete baldness, and Minimal, for men with only partial baldness. Each treatment costs $30 and three treatments are required. Ms. Groves said the company guarantees that the new hair will be permanent.

"For the first time in years I go out on dates with complete confidence," said architect Mike Hartley, who helped test the product. "Women love to run their fingers through my new head of hair."

"I was amazed at how easy the treatment was," added Dan Hepworth, an accountant. "There was a bit of tickling as the hair grew, but my scalp felt great afterwards."

Bald-No-More is offering its hair-restoring treatment at 10 per cent off for the first 100 customers at its Terrapin clinic, 32 Partridge Ave.

-30-

For further information, please contact Michelle Groves
at 555-555-4444, email mgroves@netmail.com

Figure 12.1 Sample News Release

In the case of our baldness product, the company may offer an inducement to purchase the product now rather than later, such as a 10 per cent discount for those who buy the new product in the next week. The action paragraph might read something like this, again in neutral newspaper language:

Bald-No-More is offering its hair-restoring treatment at 10 per cent off for the first 100 customers at its Terrapin clinic, 32 Partridge Ave.

Because this states a fact, it's not necessary to write "the company said."

In Figure 12.1, we've put all these sections of a news release together into one document.

General Pointers about the News Release

Here are some other general pointers to help you write the perfect news release. This list might seem long, but a news release is like, say, a space station. The space station has millions of parts, most of which are essential. If one part fails, the entire station may be jeopardized. Similarly, every part of the news release is important.

- Use the company logo at the top of your news release, if you have a logo (and you should).
- Have a short, punchy, intriguing, and memorable headline at the top of your release, one that's just like a newspaper headline. Note that headlines have verbs in them; they are not labels. This is a label: "Hair-growing product." This is a headline: "Hair-growing product announced."
- Make your headline stand out from the text in the main part of the release, just as a newspaper headline does. You can combine various strategies to do this, such as making the headline larger (14 or 16 point) than the body text, using boldfaced text, or selecting an eye-catching font such as Arial.
- Include, at the top of the release, the date when the news can be released. Usually the release will say "For Immediate Release," but the news may be delayed: "For release July 8, 2014" or "Not for release until July 8, 2014."
- Begin the first paragraph with a capitalized city name followed by a dash (e.g., VANCOUVER—). This is called the dateline. If the city is well known, say, Toronto or New York or London, the city name is enough. If the city isn't well known or has the same name as a major city (such as Paris, Ontario), then add the abbreviation for the province or state (TERRAPIN, B.C.— or PARIS, Ont.— or VICTORIA, Tex.—). Note that the province or state abbreviations here are the traditional abbreviations (Ont., Man., Nfld., B.C.), not the two-letter postal version (ON, MB, NL, BC).[1]

---

1 In fact, you might notice that these abbreviations (e.g., B.C. or BC) are handled differently in the regular text of this book than they are in exercises and examples. The reason is that the "no-periods" style (BC or US or UK) is common for publishers while the "with-periods" style (B.C. or U.S. or U.K.) is more common in business and newspaper writing.

- Use an 11- or 12-point font, serif or sans serif, for the body of your news release. For news releases, a serif font such as Times New Roman is more common than a sans-serif font such as Arial, but both are acceptable. Your headline may, as noted above, be a different font to be more eye-catching.
- Put all the key information in the first paragraph (in newspaper language it's called "Don't bury the lead"). The first paragraph should get attention but it is not a "tease."
- Remember that a description of the product almost always comes before the name of the company that produced the product, and the first quotation sentence almost always comes before the name of the speaker. The exception is when either the company or speaker is very well known.
- The first paragraph almost always has a time element: "announced yesterday," "said Monday," or "said on July 3." If the date occurs in the same year as publication, you don't need to include the year.
- The second paragraph expands the main idea, usually with a quotation from an authority. The authority's quotation should be no later than the second or third paragraph.
- Some news outlets use honorifics (Mr., Ms., Dr., etc.) on second reference to a source; some don't, so adjust your news release to the style of the outlet. On first reference, your speaker is given his or her full name and title—"company president Claude Bissonette." On second reference, use "Mr. [or Dr. or Prof.] Bissonette" if the outlet uses honorifics, or just "Bissonette" if it doesn't.
- Make quotation paragraphs short: 30 words or so.
- Quote a second person later in the release if that person offers a different, interesting, but supportive point of view.
- Be sure your release is in just-the-facts newspaper language, not gee-whiz promotional language. That means pruning adjectives such as "amazing" and "revolutionary" and avoiding words that speak directly to the reader (e.g., you, we, your, or our). This rule doesn't apply to quotations.
- Keep the release to the equivalent of one 8½- by-11-inch page (250–300 words). Put any additional but important information in an attached, separate sheet.
- End with "-30-" ("I'm done, now"; this is an old telegraphic signal) centred at the end of the release.
- Under the "-30-" signal, include a contact person, with phone number, email, and address, so the editor can get in touch.
- Rewrite, rewrite, rewrite. Proofread, proofread, proofread. Don't let a single grammar or spelling or factual error, or just dull writing, kill your chances of getting your news release taken seriously!

Finally, despite all this work, be prepared for the editor to rewrite your news release or cut it to two paragraphs. It's often a thankless business, writing news releases, but someone has to do it.

Exercise

Writing a News Release

In the world of work, how do you end up writing a news release in the first place? Likely, the situation is this: your boss has handed you several pages of information and told you to write a news release about it. Below is an example of the background information (or draft news release) you might have received. Take this raw material and write the news release. The release that eventually got written is on page 411, but don't peek until you've tried the rewrite on your own.

At the end of this exercise are questions to test your knowledge of writing news releases.

Original Draft News Release (Version 1)

EverQuest University

FOR IMMEDIATE RELEASE

EverQuest University Announces MBA Guarantee

EverQuest University is pleased to announce the introduction of the MBA Graduation Guarantee. It encourages undergraduates and executives to advance their skills and knowledge of business. The guarantee expresses confidence in EQU learning approaches. It is designed to encourage qualified, enthusiastic, and highly motivated candidates to invest in themselves at EQU. This is the first guarantee of its kind in Canada.

EverQuest University (EQU) believes that all students are active partners in learning and that we share jointly the responsibility for learning. As an equal partner, EQU is committed to providing environments that enable student success. Based on this commitment, EQU provides a graduation guarantee for any student accepted into the MBA Program. This guarantee is based on two principles:

1. EQU believes that all successful applicants are committed to self-improvement in order to gain an edge in the real business world.

2. EQU is confident in the curriculum and delivery systems available to students and is committed to provide the resources necessary to ensure graduation for every successful applicant.

The guarantee encourages success. Students need only be highly motivated to achieve their education goals. In fact the university is adamant that any applicant that meets the entrance requirements and follows the EQU Graduation Guarantee Contract will graduate. Simply put, if a qualified applicant agrees to and actively engages in the EQU learning model by committing his or her time and knowledge to the MBA program, EQU will guarantee graduation.

Flexible curriculum designs allow candidates to choose from one of three MBA offerings:

1. One year Online (includes a three-week residency) MBA for University Commerce and Business graduates;
2. Two year Online (includes a three-week residency each year) MBA for non-business graduates;
3. One year face-to-face intensive MBA.

A partnership in learning

EQU supports a learning-centred model wherein students become active partners in the university process. The EQU model engages students at the beginning of the learning process to ensure that each is prepared, ready and able to fully and actively participate. The guarantee sets out the university and student responsibilities to the learning model and when accepted, provides the pathway to graduation.

Follow-Up Questions and Exercises (answers on page 411)

1. What are the *key differences* between the two versions of this news release, i.e., 1) the original draft and 2) the one in the answer key? Is version #2 more effective than version #1? If so, what makes it more effective? If it is not effective, why not?
2. Pretend that you are a company offering a product or service—it can be any product or service, from a bakery to a line of clothing to picnic outings on Mars. Let your imagination run wild! Write a news release announcing this product or service. Feel free to make up any details you need to make your news release convincing.

Chapter 13
Brochures

In this chapter you will learn to

• Write and design a successful brochure.

INTRODUCTION

Brochures are an inexpensive way of getting your message out to the world, whether you are running a pizzeria, offering bear-watching vacations in the BC rainforest, soliciting for a charity, or campaigning for a political party. And, although brochures are difficult to do well, they aren't difficult to do—most word-processing programs have brochure templates that you can download and alter to your taste.

BROCHURES ARE AIDA DOCUMENTS

You won't be surprised to hear that the brochure is an AIDA document. That is, you must gain the reader's attention, then build interest, then stimulate desire, then get action (if you can). Because it follows an AIDA format, a brochure also uses the three forms of rhetorical persuasion: *logos*, *pathos*, and *ethos*—reason, emotion, and appeal to authority. So, let's see how you might put together a brochure using the AIDA principles and the three forms of rhetorical persuasion.

Attention

Most brochures appear in a two- or three-fold arrangement. Let's focus on the two-fold type of brochure because that's the easiest and most common. It's an 8½-by-11-inch piece of paper in "landscape" mode (i.e., sideways) with two folds to make six panels, three on the front and three on the back. Figure 13.1 shows one way (although not the only way) to distribute AIDA appeals among the six panels:

5th panel: **Desire**. Testimonials from customers. Biographies of company founders. Possibly your mission statement.	6th panel (the back): **Action**. Contact details. Map. Coupons or special offers.	Front panel: **Attention**. Company logo Striking graphic. Company name. Slogan. City, if appropriate. Says exactly what the company is offering.
2nd panel: **Interest**. Concrete and specific details about your product or service, supported by dynamic layout and graphics.	3rd panel: **Interest**. More details about your product and service, including price if appropriate.	4th panel: **Interest** and/or **Desire**. How good your customer will feel after using your product or service. The benefits. Answering any possible objections.

Figure 13.1 Brochure Divided into AIDA Panels

You get attention with the front panel. It's the panel a potential customer sees first and it may have to compete with the fronts of dozens of other brochures. For example, airports, bus stations, train stations, tourist information offices, and many other places often have a large rack of brochures all aiming to catch the attention of passers-by. That means your front panel has to be striking enough to stand out in the crowd. How do you do that? The front panel has four (sometimes five) elements:

1. the name and logo of your company,
2. a heading that describes *exactly* what your company is offering,
3. a striking graphic or picture,
4. possibly a catchy slogan ("The Best in the West!"), and
5. the city, town, or region where the company is located, if location is relevant.

If you are an international company, say, Starbucks, then the location of your coffee shop may not be needed (there's a Starbucks on every street corner, after all). If you are a downtown bakery or a tourist office, then you need to include your city on the front panel, usually at the bottom. Readers can get your street address on the back panel.

Who is your audience for a brochure? Obviously, the audience is anyone interested in your product. But you need to look a bit deeper than that.

Suppose you are a day spa in Vancouver, BC, and you put your brochures on the ferries that travel between Vancouver and Victoria. Your audience is travellers coming *from* Victoria *to* Vancouver, not people going to Victoria from Vancouver. That's why the city name is necessary on the front panel. How else will your audience know whether you are in the city they are travelling to and decide to make your spa part of their visit?

You want your front panel to create some *excitement*—it's competing with dozens of other brochures also trying to get attention; a boring front panel will get lost in the crowd. So you need a striking, colourful graphic or picture. A picture is worth a thousand words, after all. Therefore, the picture has to vividly present what your product or service is, while the text makes it crystal clear what you are offering.

Look at the front panel in Figure 13.2, from a student brochure project. The panel is attractive and even striking, but it doesn't say directly and clearly, either with the pictures or text, what makes this product special—every car ad promises luxury, performance, and adventure!

What makes this (imaginary) car special, even unique, is that it converts to a boat or submarine—it can travel across and even under water! But the panel doesn't clearly say that, so it fails to attract the audience for this kind of car—the person who needs to cross water in, say, his or her daily commute to work.

Figure 13.2 Front Panel for a Car Brochure, but There's Information Missing

Figure 13.3 is an example of a front panel that has all the necessary information.

Interest

The second, third, and fourth panels (we'll call them the "inside" panels; see Figure 13.1) are on the opposite side of the page from the front panel and two back panels (the "outside" panels). Most people, when they pick up a brochure, look first at the front panel, then turn to the inside panels. These three inside panels, although separated by folds, can also create a large, three-panel canvas on which you can develop interest and, perhaps on the fourth panel, desire.

To generate interest, you can again use the newspaper formula of the five Ws and an H: what, who, where, when, why, and how. First, on the second panel, we need to say *what* the product is (in one example, a submersible car). The "what" offers concrete and specific detail so the reader will have a clear *mental picture* of what the product or service is or does. "What" is the introduction to the product.

Next you need to describe the product in more detail:

Figure 13.3 Front Panel of Brochure for Underwater Hotel

- more **what** details,
- **who** makes the product or offers the service,
- **how** the product or service works, and
- **why** this is a product or service worth having.

At the end of the interest section, once you've described the product or service, you may want to say how much your product or service costs. Hopefully, by this point, you will have described the product or service so appealingly that cost will not be a problem and you can go on to stimulating desire.

Not all brochures state the price. For one thing, the price for that product or service may fluctuate. If your brochure is for a fish market, for example, with ever-changing prices, the best you can do is say the fish are "market price." Also, the price may be quite high (as a luxury car's price would be, for example) so that "if you have to ask the price, you can't afford it." In that case, the price isn't necessary.

For smaller items, or for a budget-conscious audience (and that's most of us), you will probably want to state what your product or service will cost as the last part of the interest section. Or, if the price is very attractive, such as a sale or discounted price, it could be mentioned in the desire section. Whether the price information creates interest or desire is a grey area.

In these "inside" panels, you will use some of the techniques we discussed in Chapter 5 on document design: a modular ("potato chip") layout; pictures and graphs; short, easy-to-read paragraphs; bulleted or numbered lists; and attractive headings that stand out because they are larger than the body text and in a different colour.

In general (not always), the inside page is more attractive if it doesn't break into three vertical columns at the folds. You avoid a boxy, vertical look by having pictures, headings, graphics, and text that cross the folds. The aim is to create an inner-page design that ties the three panels together into an attractive, integrated whole. How do you do this? The brochure templates available through most word-processing programs and online will do much of this design work for you.

One path to thematic unity is to use a consistent colour palette so that the same two, three, or four colours appear on all the panels. For example, the text may be white against a dark blue background with gold headings, and there may be a picture with a lot of blue (light or dark) or gold in it.

Figure 13.4 Inner Panels of a Brochure for an (Imaginary) Underwater Hotel

The colour should be, if possible, tied to a characteristic of your product or service. For example, if you were promoting a seaside hotel, then a blue theme would be appropriate. You might have a graphic that "swoops" across the top and/or bottom of the three panels, tying them together. Figure 13.4 shows the brochure for an (imaginary) underwater hotel that ties the three panels together in a dynamic fashion.

Other points to notice about the brochure example: paragraphs are short, headings stand out, a blue theme (which you can't appreciate in the greyscale reproduction here) complements the idea of an underwater hotel, the pictures are attractive and striking, and a bulleted list makes the material easy to read.

Desire

After you've developed interest in your product or service, you need to create desire—the feeling that goes beyond, "That's really interesting!" to "Yes, I really want that!" Where you start the desire portion of your brochure—panel 4? panel 5?—depends on many factors, but, in most cases, your desire appeal will begin on panel 4, the last panel of the three inside folds.

In the interest section, you described the product or service in detail, including cost if appropriate. The desire panel is where you state the benefits of your product or service, why it is worth the money, and answer any possible objections.

> **Worth Remembering**
> "You aren't selling a product, you are selling a feeling."
> —Tony Robbins

Above all, you must convince potential customers that your product or service will make them *feel* good. As Tony Robbins, a motivational speaking guru, has stated, "You aren't selling a product, you are selling a feeling." This is absolutely true!

Another motivational speaker, Patrick Schwerdtfeger, agrees:

> If you really want to grow your business, you need to focus your marketing efforts on the customer experience, not your product's features.... You sell the emotions your customers experience when they use your product.[1]

"A once in a lifetime experience!"
-Paul Michaels, Hotel Critic

"We've never felt this relaxed & revitalized!"
-Dick & Jane Walters, Newlyweds

Ψ

Founders Kara Schneider, Jane Wilson and Edith List devoted 16 years to perfecting the technologies that allowed them to create the oasis that is Poseidon's Underwater Resort.

Figure 13.5 The Fifth or "Desire" Panel of a Brochure for an (Imaginary) Underwater Hotel

---

1   Available at the website of Patrick Schwerdtfeger, http://www.patrickschwerdtfeger.com/category/speaker-2/page/22/.

The desire section, in other words, is where you highlight not just the benefits but also the good *feeling* your customers will enjoy when they buy your product or service.

One element of creating desire can be using testimonials from people who've already enjoyed your product or service. If they are famous people, like actor George Clooney, so much the better since you've added *ethos*! Testimonials often work well on panel 5, but short testimonial statements may also appear as pull quotes in panels 2, 3, or 4 as well.

Another useful strategy for creating desire is introducing the founders of your company, with photos, to establish a "human" connection. And, of course, in the desire portion you will answer any potential objections. Is the product safe? Can I afford it? And so on.

Action

Not every brochure needs an action spur. If your brochure is promoting an idea, for example, such as recycling, you're trying to get your audience to "buy" your idea, but there's no specific deadline. If you are selling a product or service, you'd like your customers to buy as soon as possible, so you might include on your brochure, say, a coupon for 10 per cent off or a special deal for the first 100 customers.

As part of AIDA, a logical place for the action section of your brochure is panel 6, the "back" panel of the brochure. Here you can put any special offers, along with your contact details (address, email address, web-page address, phone number, and so on) and a map pinpointing your office or store, if that's appropriate.

Note that this isn't a "dead" panel—it's got to be as attractive as the rest of your brochure.

CONCLUSION

A brochure is a persuasive document. An effective brochure will combine all of the elements that we've discussed: strong document design, strong and correct writing, AIDA, plus the three forms of persuasive rhetoric: *logos, pathos,* and *ethos.*

Which of the three rhetorical techniques or which combination of the three techniques your brochure will use depends entirely on your audience. Is your brochure's

Book your vacation before January 1ˢᵗ, 2014, and receive an exclusive opportunity to stay in our executive Poseidon suite at a 35% discounted rate.

Contact Information

1835 Barrier Reef Ave
Sydney, Australia NSW 2150

www.poseidonresorts.com

Figure 13.6 The Sixth or "Back" Panel of a Brochure Promoting an (Imaginary) Underwater Hotel Hopes to Inspire Action by Making a Special Offer and Giving Contact Information

audience most likely to respond to an AIDA appeal based in logic and reason (*logos*)? Or would your best bet be to insert quite a bit of emotional appeal (*pathos*)? Or is *ethos*, the appeal to authority (through a celebrity endorsement, for example), the way to go?

For example, let's say you are promoting vacations in Greece. If your audience is university students and professors, you might emphasize that your vacation includes talks and tours that illuminate the history and philosophy of ancient Greece. This is the *logos* approach. If your audience is just looking for fun in the sun, then *pathos* is the way to go—gorgeous beaches, the hot sun, warm waters for swimming. *Ethos* might include a glowing comment by a famous person on how much he or she enjoyed the holiday you are offering.

Ultimately, when it comes to a persuasive appeal, the proof is in the pudding. Did your brochure or news release change your audience's *actions* as you'd hoped (for example, did they buy your product or service)? Did the audience's *feelings* change as you'd hoped? Did the audience's *thinking* change as you'd hoped? If so, then your persuasive brochure was a success.

Exercises

1. Bring to class three or four brochures on a variety of topics. Form into teams of two or three, each team with five brochures. Analyze the five brochures based on AIDA, attractiveness, dynamism, effectiveness, and use of *logos*, *pathos*, and *ethos*. Rank them from best (1) to worst (5). Then have a member of each group explain to the class what three qualities of the best brochure made it the most effective, and what three qualities of the worst brochure made it the least effective.

2. You and one or two other students have created a company that offers a new, totally imaginary product or service. Imaginary means it's something never seen before, like vacations to Alpha Centauri or a perpetual-motion machine. Let your imagination go wild! Using the brochure-making capabilities of your word-processing program, or one of the many brochure templates found online, create an attractive, informative, and dynamic brochure using AIDA, the three rhetorical techniques, and everything you've learned about document design to promote your product or service. As part of the exercise, write a one-page news release, also using AIDA and the other techniques we've studied for an effective news release, announcing your new product or service to the world.

Chapter 14
Promotion on the Web

In this chapter you will learn how to

- Write and design a successful web or social-media promotion.

INTRODUCTION

Promotion on the web is a bit outside the scope of this book—indeed, a full discussion of this topic would fill several books—but a few brief comments are in order.

Over the past two decades, websites have become an essential promotion and information tool for all organizations, public and private, profit and non-profit, large and small. Even curbside food trucks now have their own websites! A website is an organization's persuasive window on the world, so the site had better be good.

Ultimately, websites are electronic brochures. Therefore, you should approach creating a persuasive website in the same way you'd approach designing a persuasive brochure. That means that, once again, reader-friendly document design; strong, correct writing; AIDA or some variation of AIDA; and the three rhetorical techniques of *logos*, *pathos*, and *ethos* come into play:

- The home page of the website (the equivalent of a brochure's front panel) needs an appearance and information that attracts attention.
- The pages of the website must contain useful, well-presented details about whatever product, service, or idea the parent organization is promoting. These elements create interest.

- The website, if it is selling a product or service, needs to stimulate desire by listing the benefits of the product or service and meeting any possible objections.
- Finally, the website needs to promote action, if appropriate. That is, if the site is selling a product or service, it has to be *easy* for the potential customer to buy or access that product or service.

Basically, website visitors fall into two categories. Some are seeking specific information or a particular product or a software download or update. That's their goal, and if the website's search feature doesn't make finding what they want easy, these visitors will quickly take their business to another site.

A second category of visitors is just browsing, literally. They're curious about what's on your site, happy to move from link to link as long as they find content that interests them. When they lose interest, they, too, move on.

So to keep viewers (who may also be customers or future customers), your website has to make finding specific information easy but also provide a pleasant experience for those just browsing. Ultimately, again, finding this balance comes down to being reader friendly, writing well, and using AIDA. Get browsers' attention, keep their interest, create desire for your product or service or idea (if that's what the site is about), and get action if you can.

CREATING A WEBSITE

Most organizations hire professional designers to create their online presence. Fortunately, just as word-processing programs offer ready-made templates for brochures and many other documents, the Internet offers myriad professionally designed website templates so that, even if your organization can't afford a web designer, you can still establish an attractive and effective web presence.

The simplest—and cheapest—way for a web newbie to get a presence on the Internet is through a blogging site such as WordPress, Blogger, or Instagram. These sites offer attractive web templates (or "themes") that make it fairly easy to put information up on the site, within the constraints of the template you choose, of course (see Figure 14.1). Most of these blogging sites are free, but some of the templates created for these sites must be purchased or leased. Also, you may have to pay a small fee to customize a theme to your taste, add features, and so on. But then, presto! Within minutes, at very little cost, your message is on the web!

The disadvantage, of course, is that if getting a presence on the web is relatively easy for you, it's easy for millions of other people, too. Thus, it's all-important that your message stand out from the crowd.

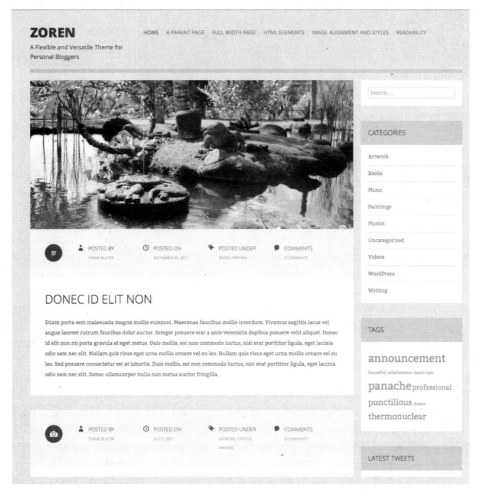

Figure 14.1 A WordPress Website "Theme." You Just Have to Add Content

SOCIAL MEDIA

The arrival of social media, and particularly Facebook and Twitter, added another wrinkle to creating an online presence. Just as all organizations need websites, now all organizations also need to be on Facebook and Twitter. And this means that virtually all organizations—even very small businesses—now ask patrons to "Like Us" on social media, and they post regularly on their social-media sites. Clearly, most organizations now consider social media an important part of their persuasive message.

Social media differs from the traditional corporate website in that social media is "social." The corporate website is just that—corporate. It's an information resource

Figure 14.2 Wendy's Facebook Page Offers a Movie Caption Contest

about a company or organization or service. It may reflect the company's corporate image and sell products or services, but it's also somewhat impersonal.

Social·media is all about personal! Social-media projects your or your company's *personal passion* for whatever it is you are selling or offering or suggesting. In other words, social media relies as much on *pathos* and *ethos* as *logos*.

When you log into your Facebook or Twitter site, for example, you can follow what your "friends" are saying and doing (often in great detail, and sometimes in too-great detail!). You can share material, say, jokes and photos and videos, and comment on other people's material. It's (mostly) a friendly interchange.

The nature of social media means that corporate social-media accounts also have to be, above all, friendly. It's as if the company is just another pal cracking jokes, telling stories, and generally being fun to hang out with (see Figure 14.2).

Here's where the promotional power of social media kicks in. But first, a story.

A king wanted to reward a wise man who had invented the game of chess. "What can I give you?" the king asked the sage. The sage pointed to the chessboard. "All I want," he said, "is a grain of wheat on the first square of the board, two grains of wheat on the second square, four grains on the third square, and so on for all 64 squares." The king was delighted! The sage's invention would cost him only a few grains of wheat.

The king discovered that one grain of wheat doubled on 64 chess squares equalled more grains of wheat than he had in the whole kingdom. Here is a calculation to give you an idea of how many grains the sage would receive: the 32nd square would need to hold 4.2 billion grains. And that's only halfway. The final answer is $2^{64} - 1$, which is about 461 *billion* metric tons or a mound of wheat as large as Mount Everest.[1] The king had discovered the power of geometrical progression.

So how does this story apply to social-media marketing? Suppose you have 15 Face-

---

1 "Wheat and Chessboard Problem," Wikipedia, http://en.wikipedia.org/wiki/Wheat_and_chessboard_problem.

book friends and each of them has 15 Facebook friends and each of those friends has 15 friends. And suppose you put something on your Facebook site that all 15 friends like and pass on to their 15 friends, and then on to their friends. Now do the math: 15x15x15 = 3,375. In three jumps, 15 Facebook friends have become several thousand.

If a company can make fans of 15 Facebook users and these 15 recommend the company to their 15 friends and so on, the company can reach not just thousands of users but millions, at minimal cost, because Facebook communication creates a geometric progression, like doubling the grains on the chessboard.

Now consider that the average Facebook user has 130 friends.[2] Multiply 130 by 130 by 130 a few times, and you can see the power of social marketing and why companies want in! A company won't get 130 out of 130 "likes," shares, or comments, of course. But even if ten of the 130 friends "share" a corporate page, and ten of their friends share the page, the number of contacts quickly builds up. The same geometric progression applies to Twitter and other social-media sites.

However, social-media users won't "like" or "share" or comment on a corporate page that appears to just want their money. That's where the passion comes in.

Let's say you are trying to market a self-published book through Facebook or other social media, as well as a web page. Obviously, you want to sell the book. But what you need to emphasize on your book's Facebook page is not the book itself but your *passion* for the topic of the book. If the readers pick up your passion for the subject, a few might decide to learn more about this subject that so clearly fascinates you and buy your book.

> **Worth Remembering**
> It's the soft sell, not the hard sell, that is persuasive with social-media users.

This "friendly" approach to marketing doesn't just apply in Facebook and Twitter. Look at the back of the cereal box in Figure 14.3. It reads: "We're so happy our paths have crossed," as if the buyer and the cereal were friends meeting.

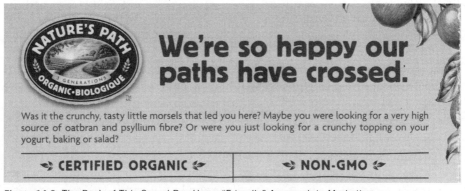

Figure 14.3 The Back of This Cereal Box Has a "Friendly" Approach to Marketing

---

2   According to the website Big Think, the average number of Facebook friends per user is 338. "Do you have too many Facebook friends?" at https://bigthink.com/praxis/do-you-have-too-many-facebook-friends.

In general, then, on its social-media sites, and elsewhere if it can, a company does not want to appear solely profit oriented; what it's promoting is, again, the company's passion for this product, not because it makes money but because the product is healthy or natural or pure—and therefore good for you.

You may recall the statement by marketing guru Tony Robbins from Chapter 13 on brochures: "You aren't selling a product, you are selling a feeling." What social-media marketing sites sell above all is a *feeling*—a good feeling—about the product or service or idea.

Yes, the product or service may be created for profit, but it's also a product or service that is created for the company's "friends." And that's the image you want to project on your organization's social-media sites and in general: the company or organization as a buddy. Maybe even one of the family!

And so, a Facebook site for, say, a fast-food company will promote its latest burger or salad. But it will also offer contests and recipes, tempting pictures of its meals, maybe a short comment about a particularly helpful server. It's as if the company were chatting over the backyard fence with a friend, not trying to create a customer.

The corporate website is still vital to a company's or organization's success. But when it comes to social media, it's the soft sell, not the hard sell, that promotes the organization's image and goals.

Internet Security

Given Facebook's troubles with fake election news generated by foreign governments, and also its troubles in general with the privacy and data security of Facebook users, this is a good place to briefly discuss security on the Internet. Of course, Facebook isn't the only social-media platform with security and data problems, but it is the most prominent.

If you are a business or professional communicator who uses Facebook or any other social-media platform to get out your message, you must protect yourself and/ or your organization against hacking and theft of personal and financial information, not to mention embarrassing leaks of comments you never intended to be public. How? The following tips are well-known, but too rarely followed.

- **Encrypt your data.** Encrypting used to be quite complicated; today, protecting your hard drive is a fairly easy process. If you really care about the privacy of your data, encrypt it with a strong password.
- **Make your passwords hard to crack.** Don't use words that can be guessed from your social-media accounts. For example, a birthday date is an easy password to remember, but also very easy for hackers to figure out if your birthday has been celebrated on Facebook or elsewhere. If you really enjoy the *Star Wars*

films, and have written so publicly, then "Star Wars" isn't the best answer for the security question "What's your favourite movie?"

- **Don't use the same password or passwords for several accounts.** Once the hacker has the password for one account, your other accounts are an open book. Using different passwords for different accounts will make the hacker's work harder.
- **Change your passwords often, or at least from time to time.** Changing passwords is an incredible hassle, especially when you have passwords that you can easily remember (like your cat's name) for accounts you use a lot. Here's where a password manager like 1Password or Dashlane comes in handy: these programs can not only create hard-to-crack passwords, but they make it easy to change the password whenever you wish. What you lose, however, is the ability to easily remember your key passwords (unless you're lucky enough to have a photographic memory!).
- **Don't write anything on social media (or anywhere on the Internet) that you wouldn't want the public to read.** The stories of indiscreet but supposedly private email or social-media comments being revealed to the world are legion and can result in embarrassment, public ostracism, and even firing. If you want to be absolutely sure some inflammatory social-media comment won't be made public, don't put it on the Internet!
- **Don't post material on social media that can come back to haunt you.** For example, potential employers can search your Facebook site. The wild photos from your Mexican vacation may be fun to share with friends, but an employer might think you're a bit too wild for his or her company. And once that wild evening is on the Internet, it's pretty much there forever. Count to ten before posting potentially damaging material!
- **Be aware of your social-media security settings.** You can set your audience in most social-media platforms to private, public, semi-public, just close friends, and so on. To make this work, you need to be aware of the people or sites you "Friend" or "Like." When people ask to join your network, don't just click "Yes." Do some research so you know who they are and whether you really want them getting your information.
- **Get anti-virus and/or firewall software and keep it up to date.** This is especially important if you are a company with data on customers and clients—these details are gold for a hacker. But if you do get a virus, you'll be glad you followed the next tip.
- **Back up your data somewhere in the Cloud and on a separate hard drive.** If somebody does hack your computer, you may have to reformat your entire hard drive and re-download all your data (files and applications). That means you also need your data in places that can't be easily hacked.

The Internet is the greatest tool ever invented for sharing information and promoting products, services, and ideas. Unfortunately, it can also be a jungle, with predators lurking at every turn. While Internet security can never be one hundred per cent, a few precautions can make life online a lot safer, for you and your organization.

Exercise

In the exercises in the sections on news releases and brochures, you were asked to create an imaginary product or service and then promote it through a news release and brochure. Now, create a promotional website homepage for the same product or service using a blogging site "theme" from, say, WordPress or Blogger. Or create a Facebook page. As with the previous exercises, make up any details you need so your website or Facebook page is as persuasive as possible.

Part VI
Oral Presentations

You will almost certainly be giving talks in your professional career. In this part, we'll look at talks from two perspectives: individual presentations (Chapter 15) and group presentations (Chapter 16).

Chapter 15
Individual Oral Presentations

In this chapter you will learn to

- Give a persuasive individual oral presentation.

INTRODUCTION

How important is it to be able to give a good oral presentation in a professional and business context? As one professional has written, "People live and die on presentations. It's as important as being able to turn on your computer." In fact, "showing you can make a good presentation is essential these days to climbing the corporate ladder and getting the attention of senior management."

In a 2005 episode of his reality TV series *The Apprentice*, billionaire and, as of 2018, US President Donald Trump describes one candidate for a job in his multinational company: "Frank may know real estate, but he gives a lousy presentation." Frank, by the way, didn't get the job. The candidate who did give a good presentation got the job.

Just as you need to be able to write well in a professional and business setting, so you also need to be able to speak well, to present what you've written in a spoken format. In this part of the book, we'll look at how you can do that most effectively, as an individual (this chapter) and as part of a group (Chapter 16). You will likely be doing both individual and group talks in your professional career.

INDIVIDUAL PRESENTATIONS

It's been said that most people would rather die than give a talk in front of an audience. In other words, they'd rather be in the coffin at their funeral than speak at their funeral! In fact, if you follow a few simple rules, giving a good talk is no more difficult than creating good writing.

A strong talk involves three simple principles:

- preparation,
- content, and
- delivery.

Let's look at each of these in turn.

Preparation

It's an all-too-common occurrence: the speaker is trying to give a talk but the electronic equipment isn't working. Either the computer won't play the PowerPoint slides or the slide or video projector has died or the microphone is dead—or something. This mess is usually the result of poor preparation. In terms of human, rather than technological, error, poor preparation means the speaker may lose track of what she's saying in mid-talk, say, and have to shuffle her notes until she finds her place again.

Solid preparation for your talk can reduce the chances of these embarrassing gaffes happening to you. Here's how.

Know Your Audience

To whom are you speaking? Is it a school parents' group or a group of NASA engineers? The type of talk you give, including the level of language you use (e.g., plain language vs. technical jargon) will depend on your audience.

Among other audience issues that involve preparation are the following:

- Will you be speaking in the morning or after lunch? If the latter, your audience might be sleepy after a big meal and need some waking up.
- Are the audience chairs comfortable or hard? If the chairs are hard, you might want to keep the talk shorter (the mind can only absorb what the rear can bear).

Know Your Venue

Never go into a speaking situation "cold" if you can avoid it. Check out the room before your talk—preferably the day before your talk, so you've got time to make a fix, if necessary. Other matters to consider are the following:

- Is the room large or small? If large, you'll want to make sure the microphone works and that the text on your PowerPoint slides is large enough to read from the back of the room.
- Is the audiovisual equipment working?
- Does the AV equipment work with your computer, if you're using one?
- Is there an electrical outlet near where you are speaking, or do you need to bring an extension cord?
- Is there a built-in screen, or do you have to bring your own?
- Is there a blackboard or flip chart if you need it?
- Do the windows have blinds or drapes so you can keep sunlight out if you have to?
- Is there a lectern? Is there a table for your materials, if needed?

Know Your Purpose

Why you are making the talk will determine the types of visual aids (or not) that you use and the style of your talk. Are you delivering an academic lecture? Then your style, language, and visual aids may be a bit formal. Is it a sales presentation? Then your style, language, and visual aids will need to be polished, authoritative, and enthusiastic. Giving an inspirational talk? Then your style, language, and visual aids must be exciting and, well, inspiring.

In general, the reasons you might be giving a talk probably come down to these five:

- to entertain (comedian),
- to instruct (teacher, expert),
- to inform (public service advocate),
- to inspire (religious teacher), and
- to persuade (selling a product or idea).

Again, your purpose will determine the type of talk you give, how you prepare for it, and the style in which you deliver it.

Know Your Material

A talk read from extensive, sentence-long notes is rarely exciting or persuasive. Most audiences prefer a talk that appears "natural," "spontaneous," and "off the cuff," even if the speaker knows every word in advance. Indeed, one of the secrets of a strong talk is that it appears unrehearsed and unprepared, as if the person had just turned up in your living room for a chat.

And think about it: You go over to a friend's place for a visit. Do you prepare in advance in detail what you are going to talk about when you get there? Do you make sentence-long notes about the discussion you intend to have? If you did, the conversation would be very stilted. Instead, you follow the conversational topic wherever it goes and respond spontaneously.

This is what you are aiming for in a good talk, and particularly in a talk aimed at persuasion: you want to appear relaxed, at ease, confident, and "natural."

Why? Well, if you are trying to persuade an audience, that audience needs to believe that you are authoritative, that you know your topic inside and out, and that you are utterly convinced about what you are saying. If that's the case, you don't need to constantly refer to notes, any more than you refer to notes during a friendly conversation.

In this type of "natural" talk, you might take a quick glance at your notes or the PowerPoint slides, just to make sure you are on track, but otherwise you want to just ... talk. Or at least, make your talk appear as if you are just speaking off the cuff.

How do you achieve this apparently effortless, "natural" style? Partly, of course, by knowing your stuff. But you also do it by relying on *minimal* notes and trusting that you do, in fact, know your stuff.

Therefore, in preparing your talk, by all means work out what you want to say in detail. You may even write an essay on the topic or prepare a detailed outline. But, *do not memorize your talk word for word*. If you memorize and lose your place, your talk will stumble until you remember what you wanted to say and get back on track. You may even have to return to something you said earlier and retrace your steps. This fumbling around is not very convincing, particularly in a professional or business setting, because you look less than competent.

That said, be sure to practise your talk a few times, particularly if you have a time limit. In general, if you have a specific time, prepare what seems to you *too little* material. You'll be surprised at how the time flies by and suddenly you've gone over the allotted time limit.

Why is this? If you take the relaxed, "natural" approach, your talk will likely be *longer* than you had expected. To be sure of staying within your time, aim for less material, not more.

One useful technique: Record your talk; then listen to it. Is your delivery too fast for your audience to follow easily? Too slow, so the audience gets bored? Is the talk within the allotted time? A recording will give you this information.

When it comes time to go to the podium, make your notes minimal—a few words, perhaps a word or two for each part of the topic. Similarly, don't fill your PowerPoint slides with text: a few brief, bulleted notes will do.

When you're speaking, you can refer to your notes or the slides from time to time—just a brief glance to be sure you are on

---

1   John Clive, *Macaulay: The Shaping of the Historian* (New York: Knopf, 1973), 160.

These websites have additional information on giving good talks:

http://www.phys.unsw.edu.au/~jw/talks.html

http://www.trentu.ca/academicskills/resources/essays.php#presentations

Worth Remembering
One of the most celebrated British orators of the nineteenth century, Thomas B. Macaulay (1800–59), recommended that speakers never put into writing words that are intended to be spoken. Macaulay felt that the written word, when spoken, loses "the vivacity essential for effective oratory." Instead, Macaulay used to rehearse his speeches in his head, "relying on his memory to serve him in the course of actual delivery." He also practised his speeches in front of his family.[1]

track—but then turn your attention back to the audience and continue speaking. You could call this the "riffing" approach to public speaking—you know what you are going to say in advance, but you choose the words in the moment. You "riff" off the notes, like a musician at a jam session.

Incidentally, the longer the talk, the more likely the speaker is to rely on notes; a short talk—say, two to ten minutes—should not need notes, although the speaker may use overhead or PowerPoint slides as notes. A formal academic lecture is often a sentence-based presentation, but, even then, successful academic lecturers somehow make their talks seem "spontaneous," "natural," and conversational.

It's scary at first, speaking almost without notes or even completely without notes, but, in most cases, you'll rise to the occasion and your riffed talk will be much more "natural" and therefore more engaging for your audience and therefore more successful than a scripted talk.

And as you give more and more talks on the same or a similar topic, you'll find it's easier and easier to just "stand and deliver"—because you know your topic so well and because you are confident that you won't lose your way. And if you do get lost, you can usually "riff" your way back on track. One final advantage of the "riffing" approach is that you aren't tied to notes on a podium or on slides—you can move around the speaking platform.

Know Your Visual Aids

The kind of visual aids you use will depend on the type of talk you are giving and the facilities available. If it's a talk out of doors in daylight or in a sunlit room without drapes or blinds, presentation slides may not be clearly visible; you're better with a flip chart or blackboard or nothing but your voice. For some talks, you may not want any props or aids at all. It all depends on what you want to accomplish.

If you are using PowerPoint, Keynote, or some other presentation program, keep in mind a few points:

- Use a "clicker" to advance the slides rather than having to go to the computer for every slide change. Or have someone else change the slides off to the side.
- Don't fill your slides with text. Four bulleted points per slide should be the maximum (fewer points is better), with no more than eight lines of text per slide in total.
- Use a list format (bulleted or numbered) for the text on your slides. This is the default for presentation software because lists are easy to read.
- Make sure your slides are uniform—don't use different slide styles for the same talk.
- Similarly, use the same type of transition between slides. Don't create a crazy quilt of transitional flourishes.
- While the templates that presentation programs such as PowerPoint and Keynote offer are often quite beautiful, the slide designs may also be a distraction.

Consider keeping your slides simple. Sometimes, the most effective slides are simple black text on a white background because the audience isn't distracted by the flashiness of the template design.

- Make sure the slide text is readable—for example, green letters on a yellow background are not readable. And keep in mind that some of your audience may be colour-blind. That means, say, that red on black text will appear black to them.
- Do not read from your slides—that's as bad as reading from your notes. Slides should have notes, not full sentences that you will be tempted to read from.
- Have a backup plan. This is crucial because computers and projectors have (far too often!) been known to fail. If your slides don't work, do you have a Plan B? If nothing else, make sure you print out your slides so you can still "riff" off them on the podium. You can also have hand-outs prepared for your audience. That way, if disaster strikes, you'll have something to work from. You may also be very glad to have a flip-chart stand or blackboard nearby. Never give an important talk without preparing for a computer, projector, software, or electrical failure! On the plus side, audiences are sympathetic when something goes wrong—they want your talk to succeed!—and very impressed when you recover from disaster thanks to a Plan B.
- Control what the audience sees. Don't get too far ahead of yourself when it comes to presentation slides or other visual aids. That is, if the slide shows what you will be talking about next, the audience will be anticipating that and, perhaps, not listening to what you are saying now. The slide should deal with what you are talking about now, not 30 seconds from now. That means the information on the slide has to be minimal. If you are using a flip chart or overhead projector, cover the part you're not talking about at the time.

Content

US civil rights campaigner Martin Luther King, widely regarded as one of the greatest American orators in recent history (see Figure 15.1), described how he constructed his talks in this way: "First I tell them what I'm going to tell them. Then I tell them. Then I tell them what I told them." In other words, his talk had an introduction, a middle, and a conclusion or summation. So should your talks.

Exit surveys after talks show that most people in your audience, if you're lucky, will remember *three* of the points you made during the talk. Three! Three is about the limit of what an average audience member can remember from a talk.

So a key question to ask yourself when it comes to the content of your talk is this: What

Figure 15.1 Martin Luther King Jr. in Washington, DC, 1963

three points do I most want my audience to remember? Write them down. You may have other points, too, but these are the three that you want to stick in your listeners' minds when the talk is over, so build your talk around those three points.

Before you deliver your talk, you need to ask, and answer, three key questions:

- What do you want your audience to *remember*?
- How do you want your audience to *feel* at the end?
- What do you want your audience to *do*?

Pay attention the next time you are listening to a really good speaker. He or she will probably make three points and hammer them in. He or she will try to evoke feelings in you: sadness, anger, a resolution to do better. And he or she will often leave you with a plan of action: sign a petition, canvass the neighbourhood, write your MP, start eating more healthily.

Like an essay, a talk is an *argument*. It has a *thesis*, a point that could be argued for or against. A talk that doesn't argue for or against a point of view is wishy-washy, and usually boring. And this is true whether the audience is for you or against you. Most of us like a good argument, even if we don't agree with the arguer (see the section on argument versus persuasion in Chapter 9)! So, make sure your talk has a thesis, a definite point you want to get across, a definite position you want to argue and that others might want to argue against.

As noted above, a talk has three parts: an introduction, the body, and a conclusion.

In the introduction, you introduce yourself and your topic, and you identify your audience. A typical introduction might go something like this:

> Good evening, members of the Victoria Garden Club [**identify the audience**]. My name is John Plantworthy [**identify yourself**], and I'd like to thank you for inviting me to speak to you this evening on the topic of "Orchids of the Brazilian rainforest" [**introduce the topic**].

An appropriate joke or story is a great way to begin a talk—everyone loves a story or a joke. Another great technique is asking a question to see what your audience already knows: "How many of you have been to the Amazon?" If nobody at the Garden Club has been to the Amazon, then you may have to include more background. If everybody has been to the Amazon, then you need less background. A starting question like this will allow you to tailor your talk to the audience.

Sample 30 minute talk

- ❖ Set the stage (5-10 minutes)
  - ▪ Tell the audience what the main issues are
  - ▪ Lay out your problem/issue
  - ▪ Describe why it's important!
- ❖ What happened (10-15 minutes)
  - ▪ How was the problem resolved
  - ▪ Only need the key ideas here
  - ▪ Don't necessarily need chronological order
- ❖ Summarize (5 minutes)
- ❖ Questions?

Figure 15.2 A Plan for a Longer Talk

Source: Juan Meza, "Giving good talks isn't as hard as it looks," Power-Point presentation available as a pdf from Lawrence Berkeley National Laboratory, https://www.juancmeza.com/s/giving-good-talks-isnt-as-hard-as-it-looks.pdf. Reprinted with the permission of Juan Meza, Dean, School of National Sciences, University of California, Merced.

As part of the introduction for a longer talk, you should briefly summarize what you are going to tell your audience. This means identifying the problem or issue you are speaking about, explaining the main issues, and stating why this topic is important. If the topic isn't important in some way, why bother giving a talk about it?

The body of your talk is where you give your data and make your case, and this section should be clearly structured, like an essay. You can construct this structure by using an outline, just as you might before beginning to write an essay. Most word-processing programs have an "outline" view that will allow you to create an outline easily. But, again, don't read your talk or follow the outline slavishly. "Riff"!

The conclusion of your talk should be signalled. That is, as you are coming to the end, let your audience know that you are coming to the end: "And, in conclusion...." or "My final point is...." Then you summarize what you've said (tell them what you've told them).

Finally, you close with something along the lines of "Thank you very much for allowing me to speak to you this evening. Are there any questions?"

AIDA in Talks

In Chapter 9 on correspondence, we discussed the AIDA format for persuasive letters, as well as the three persuasive techniques: *logos, pathos,* and *ethos.* You should use the AIDA format and the three rhetorical techniques in your talks as well.

That is, at the start of your talk, you try to get attention with a startling fact, a story, a provocative question, a serious problem (or perhaps a not-so-serious problem, if it's a light-hearted talk)—ideally, you want a "yikes" or "wow" of some kind. You may also begin to provoke desire in your introduction, such as the desire to help sick children with money for research, to live a healthier life, to read and comprehend more quickly, or to learn more about curing cancer. How you begin depends, of course, on the type of talk you are giving.

Then, as the talk goes on, you build interest by giving concrete and specific facts, data, and details about the problem or topic (*logos,* primarily, but often *ethos* as you quote expert opinion). Before you make your appeal, in other words, you need to make your case.

Then you create desire by stating the benefits of what you are proposing and answering possible objections. Here's where you make your appeal, which will often include an appeal to the emotions (*pathos*) or authority (*ethos*).

Finally, in your conclusion, if it's appropriate, you try to stimulate action—get your audience *to do* something as a result of your talk: write to their MP, eat more fruits and vegetables, volunteer for a seniors' home, and so on. In other cases, rather than getting direct action, you may be trying to change your audience's thoughts and feelings.

If you consciously structure your persuasive talk (and most talks are persuasive in some way or another) around the AIDA format, incorporating the three rhetorical techniques of *logos*, *pathos*, and *ethos*, you will give a strong, engaging, and persuasive talk.

Handling Questions

Most talks and presentations take questions at the end, but you may decide to answer questions during the talk as well—you can set this up by telling your audience to feel free to ask questions at any time. Here are a few pointers for handling questions:

- Anticipate and practise the questions you are likely to get. Preparing answers in advance is especially important in a professional context; you don't want to be caught flat-footed while the boss or a client is looking on.
- Repeat the question. You repeat the question to be sure, first, that you heard it correctly and, second, to be sure that the rest of the audience also heard it. Repeating the question is especially important in a large room, such as an auditorium or theatre.
- As you answer the question, do not pin the questioner with your gaze. Instead, allow your eyes to wander over the whole audience as you reply, and then come back to the questioner from time to time and then at the end. It's uncomfortable to have a speaker stare at you and you alone while he answers your question.
- Ask if you have answered the question ("Did I answer your question?").
- If you don't know the answer to the question, say so, with a promise to get the answer in the near future. Don't try to fake an answer.
- Signal an end to questions: "I have time for one more question."

Then, once again, thank your audience.

Delivery

You're well prepared. You've got strong content. Now it's time to deliver your talk. Are you nervous? Most beginning speakers are; even veteran speakers sometimes get butterflies in the stomach before a talk. However, as you get more experience in delivering talks, the butterflies before a talk will gradually diminish and, over time, may disappear entirely.

Here are ways you can reduce before-talk nerves:

- Stay outwardly calm. Take some deep breaths. Don't rush—remind yourself there's plenty of time.
- Remind yourself that what you have to say is worth saying. That will take some of the self-consciousness out of the experience. The talk isn't about *you*, it's about the issue.

- Take time to set up your material and survey your audience before speaking. A few moments of silence before you begin builds up anticipation and gives you time to breathe and recollect your thoughts.

But if, despite your best efforts, you still feel your palms sweating and a stomach that's doing somersaults, take heart from this fact: If you just start talking, most of your audience won't have the faintest idea that you are nervous! And, after about 15 seconds, as you get into the rhythm of your talk, the nerves go away. It's like jumping off a cliff into water or parachuting out of a plane: once you've gotten the courage to jump, you are so caught up in the experience that nerves stop being an issue.

What else should concern you in the delivery of your talk?

Avoid, Like, You Know, Verbal Distractions

Few experiences are worse than a speaker who, every couple of sentences, says "um" or "ah" or "you know?" or "like" or one of the many other possible verbal distractions. These verbal tics drive audiences crazy and are completely unnecessary.

A speaker says "um," "ah," and the like as a space filler to buy time while thinking of the next thing to say. There is a better space filler: silence.

Don't say anything as you pause to reflect on your next words. Most conversations have pauses, if for no other reason than to take a breath. We are so used to conversational pauses that we don't even notice them. Why not pauses in a talk, then? In fact, audiences not only expect pauses, they welcome them as a chance to absorb the material and keep up with the speaker's argument.

How do you get rid of verbal distractions? If you are someone who often uses the verbal space fillers such as "um," then you need to start being more aware of your "ums" in daily conversation and begin to prune them.

Like any bad habit, verbal distractions take some time to break. But, after a relatively short time—usually just a few days, simply by being aware that you are about to say "um" and then not saying it, you will get the verbal space fillers out of your speech. The result is fluent speech: speech that seems to flow uninterrupted by anything but the occasional pause for thought.

There are several other verbal distractions you need to guard against. One is the "up" tone: the speaker ends each sentence as if it's a question rather than a statement. The up tone sounds like this: "My name is Dawn Phillips? And I'll be speaking to you about child and youth care in custody?" The questioning up tone makes the speaker seem uncertain, so, if you have this tendency,

Worth Remembering
Caroline Kennedy, the daughter of former US president John F. Kennedy, was interviewed by *The New York Times* as a possible appointment to the Senate. In the interview, Kennedy reportedly said "you know" more than 140 times.

You can read the transcript of the interview, complete with all the verbal distractions, by using the search terms "Caroline Kennedy" and "you know."

The point? Kennedy's verbal distractions probably cost her the Senate job!

curb it in exactly the same way as you prune "ums"—pay attention to your speech patterns and don't indulge this verbal distraction.

Another is the "down" tone, where the speaker swallows the end of each sentence. This is sometimes called "vocal fry" because the down tone often sounds like sizzling bacon deep in the throat. As with the "up" tone, the "down" tone can be improved with practice.

Finally—and this list doesn't include all the verbal distractions by a long shot—some speakers have a habit of joining all their sentences with "and": "And then I wrote to the prime minister and told him he needed to change the law and he sent me a letter back and...." Better: "I wrote to the prime minister and told him he needed to change the law. He sent me a letter back that said...."

> **Worth Viewing**
> YouTube has many examples of vocal fry when you use the search term "vocal fry."

Avoid Physical Distractions

Physical distractions are behaviours that distract your audience and detract from your message. They can include chewing gum, moving aimlessly around the stage, tossing a pencil up and down, jangly jewellery, scratching your nose, playing with your hair, funny hats, bizarre hairstyles—the possibilities are legion.

What do you want to do instead? It's okay to move around the stage while speaking—in fact, it's a great way of creating energy for your talk—but your movements must appear purposeful, not aimless. You should avoid pacing or wandering. If you aren't moving, then be steady, as if planted at the podium or on the stage. Don't rock back and forth or side to side. This doesn't mean being stiff and rigid, but you do want to convey an image of solidity and what the Romans called "gravitas"—gravity, seriousness, authority.

Your body language conveys all kinds of messages. If you cross your arms, you are shutting your audience out (the crossed arms are a symbolic "fence"). If you put your hands on your hips or wag your finger at the audience, you appear to be nagging. If you face away from your audience, appearing reluctant to look at your listeners, you seem unsure of yourself.

And never, ever, unless absolutely unavoidable, turn your back on the audience. Even if you are writing on a blackboard or flip chart, try to do it sideways so you are still partly facing the audience.

In a formal talk, you can, occasionally, put one hand in your pocket, but it's better not to. Two hands in your pockets makes it seem that you are hiding something. Shifting from one foot to another makes you seem insecure.

On the other hand, facing your audience squarely says, "I'm being direct with you." Having your hands in the open in front of you says the same thing.

What do you do with your hands during a talk? You can clasp them in front of you about waist height, or put your hands on the podium, or use your hands and arms for gestures, but make sure the gestures are not too grandiose or, again, you will distract your audience. On the other hand (there's almost always an "other hand"), if the auditorium is large, you may have to exaggerate your hand and body gestures, so the people at the back get the non-verbal message.

What you wear for your talk also conveys a visual message. In a professional context, you want to be well dressed and well groomed. That means at least a shirt and tie for a male plus a haircut, and some sort of business suit for a female. Being poorly dressed—wearing fashionably ripped jeans or a tank top or baseball cap— usually counts as a distraction, albeit a non-verbal one.

To repeat: In general, in giving a talk, you want to give a physical impression of steadiness and seriousness—that Roman gravitas—to send a message of authority and reliability.

Make Lots of Eye Contact

Eye contact lets you engage with the audience and the audience with you. If you are making lots of eye con-tact, you can assess the audience reactions and level of interest and make adjustments. Are you talking too fast? Too slowly? Is your wording too complex? Are people interested, bored, comfortable? But, more important, eye contact implies that you are as *inter-ested* in your audience as you are interested in deliver-ing your message (see Figure 15.3).

Figure 15.3 The Eyes Are the Windows on the Soul—and on the Audience

Ultimately, communication isn't just about getting the message across; it's also very much about getting the message across *to fellow human beings*. A speaker who seems aloof and uninterested in her audience, who is constantly looking at her notes or the slides or the far wall—at anything but the people in the audience—isn't making this all-important people contact. Chances are, her audience, deprived of human contact, will get bored and restless, and the talk will be a failure.

How much eye contact should you make during your talk? As much as possible: 100 per cent if possible or at least 90 per cent! The very best speakers don't use notes; they stand up and just talk to the audience, as if they were talking to friends in their living room. But, as noted in the section on answering questions, speakers should never "pin" one or two audience members with their gaze. Instead, speakers should constantly scan the faces in the audience, making brief periods of eye contact with an individual then moving on to the next person.

Don't Rush; Slow Down

If there's one quality that separates a good talk from a poor one, apart from pres-ence or absence of verbal and non-verbal distractions, it's pacing. We've all been at talks where the speaker raced through his notes as if he couldn't wait to be finished and go home. Chances are, we were glad when he was finished, too. If the speaker isn't interested in what he's saying, doesn't want to linger, why should we be interested?

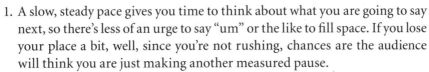

A "natural" style of speaking, on the other hand, is unhurried. The speaker has all the time in the world. He's in no rush. Indeed, he's fascinated by the material he's delivering; he'd like the talk to last longer, if possible.

So, here's one of the most useful pieces of advice you will ever receive about giving talks: Don't rush. Slow down. What does this do for you?

1. A slow, steady pace gives you time to think about what you are going to say next, so there's less of an urge to say "um" or the like to fill space. If you lose your place a bit, well, since you're not rushing, chances are the audience will think you are just making another measured pause.
2. A slow, steady pace gives your audience time to keep up with your ideas. Chances are you're far more familiar with the material than your audience; the slower pace allows your listeners to absorb what you're saying and stay with you as you make your points one after the other.
3. A slow, steady pace is how we normally speak—most of the time we're not rushing to say what we want to say and get it over with. We're interested in communicating for its own sake.
4. As noted, a slow, steady pace conveys an aura of authority and that you are interested in the topic—you're not trying to get the talk over with, and you're serious about it.

Two words: Don't rush. Again: Don't rush. And two different words: Slow down. If you follow just this one rule for public speaking, your talks will eventually take on the relaxed, "natural" pace that really good speakers employ. If you think you're speaking too slowly, you're probably just right.

Vary Your Tone, Project Your Voice

When we speak to people in normal conversation, we naturally vary our tone. If the topic is exciting or we're angry, the voice rises. If we're conveying a secret or we're sad, the volume gets softer.

In real life, we don't speak like robots; why would we speak like robots when giving a talk? So part of a "natural" delivery is variation in tone—the opposite of the "monotone" (one tone), from which we get the word "monotony."

How do we cultivate this variation in tone?

- Speak at a natural pace (i.e., not too fast).
- Don't memorize the talk or read from notes; doing either makes the speech sound as if it's being read, and the result is almost always "monotone."
- Be enthusiastic about the topic. If we're not enthusiastic about the topic, why bother speaking on it? Communicate that enthusiasm in your voice and gestures. Audiences will pick up your passion and be not only informed but entertained and engaged.

Enthusiasm, by the way, is what can make a talk on a "dull" topic suddenly seem fascinating. If the speaker is fascinated by Brazilian orchids, he's got a reason for that (dozens of reasons, likely). As an audience member, even if you couldn't care less about orchids, the fact that someone else lives and breathes orchids is bound to pique your interest. Pretty soon, you're on the edge of your seat. The speaker has conveyed enthusiasm; you've picked it up. Now the talk is no longer "dull."

Keep in mind that a talk is also a show, like acting in a play. All the great speakers have a great sense of "showmanship." It's up to you to put on an Oscar-winning performance!

And, finally, make sure everyone can hear you, especially if you're in a large auditorium or the acoustics are poor. Project your voice. If you're not sure whether you're being heard, ask: "Can everybody hear me?" If some can't, raise the volume.

But also keep in mind that one of the tricks of the speaking trade is *lowering* your voice when you've got something important to say. The audience will strain to hear, which is exactly the heightened attention you want for an important point.

Have Fun!

Really, this is a repeat of the point on enthusiasm. If you enjoy speaking, your audience will enjoy hearing you as well. It's like a party: as soon as one person gets into the spirit of it, others will, too, and, suddenly, you've got yourself a bash. On the other hand, if a partygoer starts to yawn with boredom, after a while everybody else is yawning and the party becomes a dud.

So, when speaking, smile from time to time. Start your talk with a joke or a good story. Be the life of the party when you speak! If you're having fun, so will your audience.

INDIVIDUAL PRESENTATION CHECKLIST

Below is a checklist of what to look for in a well-delivered individual talk:

- ❑ You introduce yourself and your topic and identify your audience.
- ❑ You use AIDA and the three rhetorical techniques.

❑ You aim to make three points that the audience will remember after the talk.

❑ Your visual material is visible and readable by everyone.

❑ You aren't reliant on notes or slides—you "riff" your delivery.

❑ You speak at a steady pace, without rushing, so your delivery is relaxed and "natural." If the pace seems too slow to you, it's probably about right.

❑ You avoid verbal and physical distractions.

❑ You vary your tone and volume and project your voice so everyone can hear.

❑ You make plenty of eye contact.

❑ Your movements around the stage and hand gestures appear purposeful.

❑ You convey enthusiasm, energy, and "showmanship."

❑ You appear to be having fun!

❑ You signal when the talk is nearly over ("finally" or "in conclusion").

❑ You finish the talk within the time limit.

❑ You ask for questions, repeat each question, and then ask if the question was answered.

❑ You don't "pin" the questioner with your gaze.

❑ You thank the audience at the end of the talk.

Exercises

1. Annoyed because full buses continually pass you by when you're trying to get to class on time? Think the cafeteria food needs to be improved? Give a two- or three-minute talk about an issue or problem for students or anyone. Choose a topic that you feel passionate about, something you believe needs to be changed, improved, fixed, or abolished. Because the talk is only two or three minutes long, you'll need to limit your topic to one that can be discussed in a short time.

2. Give a two- or three-minute "teaching" talk about some aspect of business communication: it could be a talk on being concise, being coherent, the correct use of colons, avoiding comma splices, proper business letter format, how to write a news release, the ideal cover letter—any topic from the textbook will do.

Chapter 16
Group Presentations

In this chapter you will learn to

- Be part of a persuasive group oral presentation.

INTRODUCTION

Group presentations are common in the business and professional world, and you need to know how to do them. Although most of the pointers for individual presentations continue to apply, group presentations also present some new challenges, which we'll look at in this chapter.

PREPARATION

Your group must make several decisions before the talk:

- Should the group's appearance be coordinated?
- Should there be a group leader?
- How should the speakers be ordered?
- How will the group deal with questions?

Let's look at these in turn.

- **Look like a team?** Comedian Jerry Seinfeld has a routine in which he notes that humans who go to other planets, say, the Star Trek crew, always wear the

Figure 16.1 Team Canada before the Game with Switzerland in April 2012. Looking Like a Team!
Source: Wiki Commons, http://commons.wikimedia.org/wiki/File:Team_Canada_-_Switzerland_vs._Canada,_29th_April_2012.jpg. Photo by Fanny Schertzer.

same uniform "so we look like a team." And that's the bottom line: a group giving a talk looks more like a team if the members are wearing similar clothing, even if the similarity is just in the colours of their shirts. A dress code shows the team is working together, which enhances the team's credibility. In other words, yes, you often want to look like a team (see Figure 16.1).

- Should there be a team leader? Teams need a leader during the talk to make sure the various parts of the presentation and the individuals in the group are working together.
- How should the speakers be ordered? That's the team leader's job, but basically, each team member will have his or her specialty in terms of the content of the talk. At the same time, *each member should also be familiar with all aspects of the presentation*—somebody else may have to fill in for a team member who, for whatever reason, has missed the presentation.
- How will the team deal with questions? Normally, the presentation leader will field audience questions and hand each question to the group member best qualified to answer. Ideally, several members of the team should answer questions, not just one. As with individual talks, the team leader or responder

should repeat the question, the responder shouldn't pin the questioner with his or her gaze during the answer, and, at the end, the responder should ask if the question was answered.

- How will the team deal with audiovisual aids? If you are using PowerPoint, obviously the slide theme should be the same for all members. Slides should be visible and readable, as with individual presentations (see Chapter 15). And, as with individual talks, be sure that the room is suitable, that the electronic equipment is working, and that you have a backup if the PowerPoint or other audiovisual aids fail.

As in the individual talk, you must introduce yourselves and the presentation's context. So, at the start, the team leader should identify each of the team members by *full name*, identify the audience ("it's a pleasure to be speaking to...."), and introduce the topic.

Finally, the team needs to practise the talk beforehand until the presentation is seamless. In particular, the hand-off from one member to another should be done slowly, clearly, and enthusiastically: "And now, Clarice will speak about...." Clarice will say, "Thank you, Bill. I'll be talking about...." If the talk is more formal, then you will use first and last names.

In your rehearsals, aim to present your segments of the talk in the same style. That is, you don't want one speaker all gung-ho while the next speaker is laid-back and even sleepy. Just as your presentation team signals togetherness by wearing a sort of "uniform," you want to present your talk in as consistent (preferably "natural") a style as possible.

CONTENT

At the start of your talk, you will introduce yourself as a group and then each team member by full name. So the team leader will say something like this: "Good afternoon. We are here from XYZ Promotions, and it's a pleasure to speak to the Vancouver Olympic Committee about housing for athletes at Whistler Village. I'm Bill Watton, and our other team members are Clarice Jones and Mike Albany."

As with individual talks, a short team talk will centre on the two or three key points you want to make.

DELIVERY

As with individual talks, team members *should not* rely on extensive notes but *should* make extensive eye contact, speak slowly, and look and sound enthusiastic. A team talk is a show, so you need showmanship!

When one member is speaking, the other team members should be still and in the background, focusing their attention on the speaker or surveying the audience. They should not move except, perhaps, to work the PowerPoint or other AV equipment. Their hands should be stationary, perhaps in front of them.

Above all, those not speaking must appear *interested* in what's going on! They should not be gazing at the ceiling, shuffling their feet, fiddling with their hair. It's a team presentation, after all, and everyone—speaking or not—is part of the team, so those not speaking should keep their eyes open and alternately on the speaker and the audience.

GROUP PRESENTATION CHECKLIST

Below is a checklist of the features that make a strong group presentation:

- ❑ The group leader has presented all members by full names, introduced the topic, and identified the audience.
- ❑ The group uses AIDA and the three rhetorical techniques in the talk.
- ❑ The group has a clear idea of what it wants the audience to do, feel, and think after the talk.
- ❑ The group appears well prepared without the talk sounding memorized.
- ❑ The group is visibly a team in dress and general demeanour.
- ❑ Visual material is visible and readable by everyone.
- ❑ Group speakers aren't reliant on notes or slides—each member "riffs" (or appears to "riff") his or her portion of the talk.
- ❑ All group members speak at a steady pace, without rushing, so the delivery is relaxed and "natural." If the pace seems too slow, it's probably about right.
- ❑ The group avoids verbal and physical distractions, including distractions caused by group members who are not speaking.
- ❑ The group members vary their tone and volume and project their voices so everyone can hear.
- ❑ The group members make plenty of eye contact.
- ❑ The group members' movements around the stage are purposeful.
- ❑ The group conveys enthusiasm, energy, and "showmanship." The group appears to be having fun!
- ❑ A group member signals when the talk is nearly over ("finally" or "in conclusion").
- ❑ The group finishes the talk within the time limit.
- ❑ The group leader asks for questions, repeats the question, directs the question to one of the group members, and then asks if the question was answered. In some cases, it is the responder who asks if the question was answered.

❑ The responder doesn't "pin" the questioner with his or her gaze.
❑ Several group members answer questions, if possible.
❑ The group leader thanks the audience at the end of the talk.

Good luck and have fun!

Exercise

Get into groups of three or four, pick a topic that interests all of you (or most of you), and prepare a six- to eight-minute group talk on the topic, using all the techniques discussed in this chapter.

Part VII
Reports

Reports are common features for most businesses and professions. In this part, we'll look at informal reports (Chapter 17) and formal reports (Chapter 18). You'll find an example formal proposal report in Chapter 19 and an example analytical formal report in Chapter 20.

Chapter 17
Informal Reports

In this chapter you will learn to

- Understand the purpose of informal reports,
- Write a progress report in the correct format,
- Write a problem-solving report in the correct format,
- Write an incident report in the correct format, and
- Write a proposal report in the correct format.

INTRODUCTION

Informal reports are usually short—often two to three pages, although they can be much longer—and they are often internal to an organization, which makes them, in many cases, extended memos. If an informal report goes outside the organization, then the cover letter will follow block-letter format.

Informal reports come in two main types: informative and analytical:

1. Informative reports, as the name implies, give information. One example is the progress report, which keeps managers up to date on how a particular project is proceeding. Is it going to meet its deadline, for example? Is it on budget? What unexpected problems have come up?
2. Analytical reports analyze problems or issues and can take many forms, but among the most common are problem-solving reports, incident reports, and proposals.

Because they are usually short, informal reports rarely have a table of contents, as a formal report would. However, they may use lists, graphs, charts, tables, and pictures to make the information as easy to read as possible. Headings will usually be in a sans-serif font (such as Arial), with body text in a serif font (such as Times New Roman), but this is a matter of choice. In general, informal reports have page numbers. In other words, follow the rules for good document design found in Chapter 5.

Because they are informal, many of the conventions we will discuss in Chapter 18 for a formal report are relaxed. For example, the informal report can use contractions, can refer to "I," and can be written in a more casual tone and style than an academic paper or formal report.

Pagination for informal reports is usually the same as for letters and memos because that is often what informal reports are—extended letters and memos. That is, the page numbers are in Arabic numerals (unless it is a long informal report, which might have an introductory section in Roman numerals). The first page is usually not numbered, depending on style (the page number of the first page of a letter or memo is not printed). On the second page, at the top left, is the name of the person the report is going to with the date underneath, as shown below. The page number is either top right, as shown, or at the bottom of the page, centred.

Barbara Skorseky   2
June 13, 2018

In the next few sections we'll discuss four kinds of informal report: progress reports, problem-solving reports, incident reports, and proposal reports.

PROGRESS REPORTS

A progress report tells superiors, colleagues, or someone outside your organization how well (or badly) a particular project is proceeding. A progress report keeps everyone in the loop, as it were, but it is also an incentive to stick to the project's timeline. This type of report also provides an early-warning system for a project that is going off the rails.

If the informal report is internal, it takes a memo format; if external, a letter format. A progress report may inform the reader on how well a formal report is proceeding.

A progress report has some or all of the following elements:

- subject (in letter format; memo format has subject built in),
- reporting period,

- goals (this part may or may not be included),
- summary,
- work completed,
- work underway (or work in progress),
- problems encountered or anticipated (with analysis),
- work to be completed,
- outline, and
- conclusion.

The subject line should be informative. "Progress report" is too vague; "Progress report on Veeblefetzer account audit" is specific enough.

The reporting period is the period covered by the report (e.g., November 3, 2013–January 14, 2016).

The goals of the project may or may not be included. In some cases, the goals are already clear and don't need to be mentioned.

The summary is in effect an executive summary (a highly condensed version of the full report), although normally much shorter than the executive summary for a formal report—three or four sentences might be enough. It should still pass the "elevator test," though—in a minute or two, anyone reading the summary should be familiar with all the important elements of the full report. In other words, all key questions are answered in the summary.

Work completed: This section details what you and your team have done so far. It is a good place to put a table or graph showing what you've accomplished in relation to what needs to be done. Lists are also appropriate for these sections.

Work underway (or Work in progress): In this section, you tell what you and your team are working on right now, perhaps in a list, table, or graph, if appropriate (see Figure 17.1).

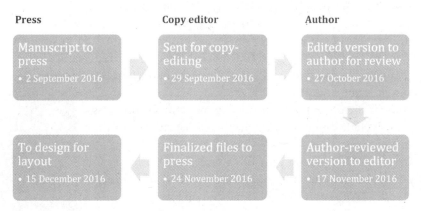

Progress report of work completed to December 15, 2016

Figure 17.1 A Progress Report Flow Chart Documenting Part of the Publishing Process

Project Timeline

Semester I

9/6/01	9/20/01	10/4/01	10/18/01	11/1/01	11/15/01	11/29/01	12/13/01	12/27/01

Begin research
Patent search
Begin modelling existing binding
Research on knee mechanics and binding mechanics
Design prototype
Model prototype
Presentation paper

Semester II

1/10/02	1/24/02	2/7/02	2/21/02	3/7/02	3/21/02	4/4/02	4/18/02	5/2/02	5/16/02

Research on knee mechanics and binding mechanics
Design specifics (dimensions, materials)
Schoofs Prize for Creativity
Functional prototype
Testing and analysis
Presentation paper

Figure 17.2 Another Type of Progress Timeline Showing Research on a New Ski Binding

Source: Adapted from timeline in the archives of the College of Engineering, University of Wisconsin-Madison, http://homepages.cae.wisc.edu/~bmedesgn/spring02/skibind/#timeline.

Problems encountered (or anticipated): If your group has met challenges or problems, tell about them here. These challenges could include an inability to get information or perhaps even conflicts among team members.

The important thing in this section is to remain *constructive*. In a professional context, problems exist only to be solved; if you can't overcome them, then perhaps you should be in another line of work. So "Problems encountered" also details how you are meeting these challenges, described in a positive way.

Work to be completed: A timeline might be appropriate in this section. The timeline would show, at a glance, where the project is compared to where it has been and will be over its expected time period. An example is given in Figure 17.2. This section might also give details about how the budget for the project is, or is not, being met.

Outline: If the project is a report of some kind, the progress report will include an outline, in numbered list format, of the full, finished report.

Conclusion: This section provides a brief final summary of what you or the team has accomplished so far and your anticipated results ("We expect to be on time and on budget").

Worth Knowing
The bar-graph timeline in Figure 17.2 is called a Gantt chart. For instructions on how to create a Gantt chart in Microsoft Excel, go to the Microsoft Office site (https://support.office.com) and enter the search term "Gantt chart."

Sample Progress Report

Below is the progress report of a project investigating the feasibility of a bridge between Vancouver Island, BC, and the mainland. Note that this progress report is in memo format and that additional pages should follow block-letter heading format.

Memo

To:	Dr. Pauline Desjardins
From:	Ryan Tisdale
Date:	March 13, 2019
Subject:	Progress update on bridge feasibility report

Project Overview

The details for our group report are as follows:

- *Purpose.* The purpose of our report is to research the possibility of a bridge to cross the Strait of Georgia between Vancouver Island and Vancouver.
- *Scope.* This report will have a broad scope as it will incorporate ocean, traffic, construction, engineering, economic, governmental, and funding data.
- *Plan.* Our report will include
  1. the pros and cons of the current ferry system,
  2. the spectrum of benefits a bridge would incorporate for the province,
  3. an investigation of the possibility of constructing such a structure with current technology and supplies, and
  4. an assessment of whether this bridge would provide improvements and better cost over the current ferry system.
- *Status.* Our report will be submitted on time, near the end of March.

Work underway or completed

This section details the work that we have accomplished as well as the work that still needs to be done towards the group report. It also indicates any problems that we encountered in research and writing.

Researching the topic
We have completed all of the field research of our project:

- Calculated tide levels and ocean currents as well as drilled for various ocean bed samples across the Strait;
- Examined the shores where the bridge is planned to make landfall, determining the stability and occupation of the property; and
- Contacted all parties that are needed for planning, funding, design, construction, and implementation.

Our research will be complete once we meet with the provincial government and construction firms.

Writing our report
We drew up a report outline roughly two weeks ago, then chose separate parts to write about among the three members of our group. The sections that I am responsible for include the currents, costs, and capacity of the ferry system; the impact of the bridge on economics; a comparison between the bridge and ferries; and the conclusion.

Plan for Completion

The following table provides our plan for the completion of our report. Also included is what has already been finished. The report will be completed by the due date of April 1.

Feb 1–7	Feb 8–15	Feb 16–28	Mar 1–20	Mar 21–26	Mar 27–31
Outline	Choosing sections	Research	Individual drafts	Putting all sections together	Writing of the final copy

PROBLEM-SOLVING REPORTS

The problem-solving report can be sparked by many issues: a breakdown in a key piece of machinery, the failure of an advertising campaign to get results, an accusation of sexual harassment in the workplace, or a contract from another institution with a problem to which your institution brings expertise. The problem-solving report may be solicited or unsolicited. The audience for the problem-solving report is whoever can implement a solution to the problem.

Like other reports, the problem-solving report is reader friendly: it uses headings, lists, graphs, tables, and other visuals for maximum clarity and to add interest. Headings are specific and detailed: not "Problem" but "Problem with Yukon pipeline sabotage." Graphics are clearly labelled.

The problem-solving report is a *persuasive* document. It is suggesting a course of action to fix the problem, not just reporting on the problem. Therefore, you should use the persuasive techniques and structure (AIDA) described in Chapter 9 on persuasive letters.

The problem-solving informal report has the following elements:

- It identifies the problem.
- It considers possible causes.
- It considers possible solutions.
- It analyzes or evaluates the solutions.
- It draws conclusions before making a recommendation.

There are two possible formats for presenting an informal or formal problem-solving report: direct and indirect. The indirect format is used when the recommendations might be controversial; therefore, your conclusions and recommendations *follow* your analysis. The parts of an indirect problem-solving informal report are

1. the summary overview,
2. an introduction,
3. the body/analysis,
4. the conclusions, and
5. the recommendations.

If the recommendations are not controversial, your report might follow the direct format in which the solutions are given *before* the analysis leading up to the solutions. A direct informal report has the following structure:

1. Identify the problem the report addresses.
2. Give your conclusions and recommendations.
3. Give the analysis and data that underlie the conclusions and recommendations.
4. End with a summary.

The summary: In short reports, you can combine the summary and the introduction. As with any summary, the reader should get the gist of the entire informal report in a few sentences, including the conclusions and recommendations.

The introduction: The introduction

- details what the problem is,
- explains why the problem concerns the reader, and
- gives the scope of the report (tells what it covers).

The introduction may also include the history of the problem or other relevant background details.

The body: This section provides a detailed discussion and analysis of the problem.

Conclusions: Using clear, concise language, this section gives concrete, specific details and examples to support the recommendations. It includes

- a brief background summary of the issue to provide context;
- recommendations, starting with the most important;
- a course of action that should be followed; and
- the benefits of the recommendations for the employer or institution.

Recommendations: Here, you provide the actual, bare-bones recommendations, usually in a list form introduced with a sentence. Each recommendation starts with an *action verb* (e.g., buy, sell, create, eliminate, order).

Sample Problem-Solving Report

Below is a sample problem-solving report. Note that this report uses the indirect pattern: it analyzes the problem before giving conclusions and recommendations.

Traffic Planning Division
City of Terrapin
2331 Pinetree Road
Terrapin, BC V9R 5T6

To: Christine Phelps, Mayor
From: Mike Richards, Traffic Planning Division
Date: October 24, 2019
Subject: Report on safer intersection at Gorge, Pine, and Highway 1

As requested by the Terrapin City Council in June, we are submitting the following
report on a proposal to reduce accidents at the intersections of Gorge Road East, Pine
Street, and Highway 1. We look forward to your comments and are happy to answer
questions on our report at the council's convenience.

Summary

The three-way meeting of Gorge Road East,
Pine Street, and Highway 1 has for several
years been Terrapin's most dangerous
intersection. In June, Terrapin City Council
asked the Traffic Division to offer options for
a safer intersection, at an affordable price, that
would also lower drivers' carbon emissions.
The Traffic Division explored three options—
replacing the "dumb" traffic signals with
computerized "smart" signals ($820,000),
reconfiguring the intersection into two streets
($3.4 million), or building a traffic circle ($2.4
million)—and recommends the traffic circle.
While not the cheapest option, a traffic circle
would increase safety at the intersection by an
estimated 45 per cent while reducing carbon
emissions by 23 per cent.

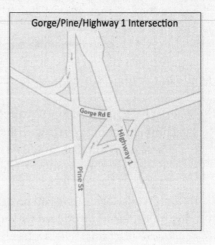

Figure 1: Intersection of Gorge Road East, Pine,
and Highway 1

Introduction

The coming together of Gorge Road East, Pine Street, and Highway 1 has, for
several years, been the city's most dangerous intersection, with an accident rate
that, over the last five years, has been three times higher than that for any other
location in Terrapin. The reason, in part, is that three roads converge at this
intersection, making driver choices more complicated.

1

In June, City Council asked the Terrapin Traffic Planning department to do a study and report on how to correct this problem. The department examined three possible solutions, while also taking into account the environmental impact of car exhaust emissions:

- installing computerized traffic signals
- reconfiguring the intersection to two roads
- building a traffic circle.

The department concluded that a traffic circle, while the second most expensive solution, would be the safest and also the most carbon-neutral in terms of reducing emissions from idling vehicles.

The City of Terrapin is growing in population at a rate of about 1.5 per cent a year, and though growth is very welcome, the increased population has brought with it an increase in vehicle traffic, which in turn has meant an increase in traffic accidents. The number of traffic accidents can, however, be reduced through proper road design.

Although Terrapin is mostly laid out on a north-south and east-west grid system, in several places the geographical terrain dictates a more complicated road layout, including three intersections where three roads converge. Two of these intersections are in outlying areas of the city and have rarely been a problem. However, the intersection of Gorge Road East, Pine Street, and Highway 1 (see Figure 1, above), has been the site of numerous accidents.

Because this intersection is part of a major commuter route into and out of Terrapin, it is extremely busy from 8 a.m. to 10 a.m. and from 4 p.m. to 6 p.m. The majority of the accidents at this intersection have occurred during high-use commuter times. Table 1 shows the frequency of accidents by time of day in 2018.

Table 1: Frequency of accidents by time of day during 2018

Time	Number of accidents	Percentage of accidents
8 a.m. to 10 a.m.	34	29%
10 a.m. to 1 p.m.	12	11%
1 p.m. to 4 p.m.	14	11%
4 p.m. to 6 p.m.	48	40%
6 p.m. to 8 a.m.	11	9%

Of the total of 119 accidents at this intersection in 2018, 69 per cent occurred during the two peak commuter times.

Although the intersection has traffic lights, they are "dumb" lights, i.e., not sensitive to the volume of traffic or the direction of traffic during the peak morning and afternoon times. As a result, many of the accidents occur when drivers, frustrated by having to wait when there appears to be no oncoming traffic, try to ease through the lights or make ill-advised right or left turns. Fortunately, there have been no fatalities so far.

2

To solve this problem, Terrapin City Council voted unanimously on June 17 to commission a study by the city's Traffic Planning Division on how to reduce accidents at this location. Specifically, council asked the department to consider three possible strategies:

- move to "smart" traffic lights;
- merge the three roads into two;
- build a traffic circle.

Council also asked the division to propose a solution that maximizes both traffic flow and the reduction of carbon emissions from idling vehicles.

Analysis

The Traffic Planning Division looked into the costs and effectiveness of the three traffic-enhancement options:

- an upgrade to a "smart," more computerized traffic-light system;
- a reconfiguration of the roads entering the intersection into two roads rather than three; and
- a traffic-circle system.

"Smart" traffic lights

As Table 2 shows, the upgrade to "smart" traffic lights is the least expensive of the three options.

Table 2: Relative benefits of the three options

Proposal	Cost	CO_2 reduction	Safety increase
"Smart" traffic lights	$820,000	5%	22%
Reconfigure intersection to two roads from three	$3.4 million	10%	"Smart" lights: 24% "Dumb" lights: 18%
Traffic circle	$2.4 million	23%	45%

However, many of the driver-impatience problems that plagued our "dumb" lights would continue with the computer-controlled, traffic-sensitive lights, as even the "smart" system would still require fairly long waits for drivers between the green lights. Also, these long waits go against the city's commitment to reducing carbon emissions from idling vehicles. We calculate a benefit of only about 5 per cent in reduced emissions from upgrading the traffic-light system.

In addition, a "smart" system of lights would require roadwork to install sensor pads in the pavement to detect the presence of vehicles, information that determines how long lights remain red or green. On the plus side, safety would be enhanced by an estimated 22 per cent. The total cost for this option would be an estimated $820,000.

3

Reduction of converging roads

Rebuilding the intersection to reduce the converging traffic to two streets from three is by far the most costly solution, at an estimated $3.4 million. As with the "smart" traffic-light solution, there is very little benefit in terms of reduced carbon emissions (10 per cent). Although safety would improve when measured against the current system, the safety benefit will be no more than 18 per cent if we keep the "dumb" lights and 24 per cent with "smart" lights. Moreover, as part of the reconstruction work, council would probably also want to add "smart" traffic lights to the new intersection, with that additional cost.

Traffic circle

Though not the least expensive option at $2.4 million, a traffic circle offers several significant benefits. Drivers no longer have to wait for a light to change, which reduces frustration and therefore accidents. Carbon emissions from idling are decreased by an estimated 23 per cent—more than twice the amount achieved with the other two options. As well, traffic-circle studies in major cities in North America and Great Britain (where circles are called "roundabouts") show that, for both large intersections and small, planners are increasingly adopting traffic circles to increase safety and reduce carbon emissions.

The drawback of a traffic circle is a temporary "learning curve" as drivers get used to the etiquette of adapting to a new traffic pattern. However, evidence from other cities indicates the adaptation problems disappear after the first month or two.

The city will also make some significant monetary savings in moving to a traffic-circle system. For one thing, traffic lights would no longer be necessary at all, with a considerable reduction in maintenance costs. And, of course, fewer accidents means a sizable saving in terms of the costs of police, fire, and ambulance call-outs.

Conclusions

The City of Terrapin is growing at a rate of about 1.5 per cent a year. With each year of growth, traffic increases. Each increase in traffic puts more pressure on the city's roads to be accident-free, efficient in terms of moving vehicles, and environmentally friendly. In recent years, one location in particular has been a problem in terms of both accidents and the creation of traffic gridlock: the three-way intersection of Gorge Road East, Pine Street, and Highway 1.

At the request of Terrapin City Council, the Terrapin Traffic Planning Division prepared a report analyzing three possible solutions to the intersection's problems: smarter traffic lights, a reconfiguration of the intersection from three roads to two, or a traffic circle. The council also asked that, apart from safety, a smoother flow of traffic during rush hours and the reduction of carbon emissions be taken into consideration.

4

Installing smart traffic lights is the least expensive solution, and these lights produce a 22 per cent increase in safety. However, their effect on carbon emissions (5 per cent) and improved traffic flow is, at best, marginal.

Rebuilding the intersection to reduce the incoming roads from three to two would be the most expensive solution, but it would have only a limited effect on traffic flow, safety (18–24 per cent), and carbon emissions (10 per cent).

Creating a traffic circle is not the least expensive solution. In the long run, however, a traffic circle is preferable to a smart traffic-light system (the least expensive option) in terms of increased traffic flow, low maintenance costs, and greatly increased safety (45 per cent). This solution also provides the greatest reduction in carbon emissions (23 per cent) given that cars no longer idle at the intersection. Therefore, we recommend that City Council choose the traffic circle option shown in Figure 2.

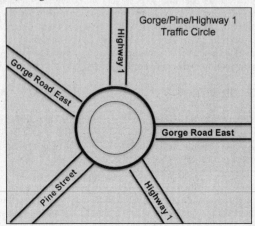

Figure 2: Proposed Gorge/Pine/Highway 1 traffic circle

Recommendation

The Traffic Planning Division recommends that the City of Terrapin adopt a traffic-circle solution for the intersection at Gorge Road East, Pine Street, and Highway 1.

5

INCIDENT REPORTS

An industrial accident in the factory or a complaint by a restaurant customer might trigger an incident report. This report aims to answer the questions *who, what, where, when, why,* and *how.* All important details must be included because the incident report may become part of a larger proceeding, such as a court case, inquiry, or coroner's inquest.

In many cases, an incident report will be written on a standardized form, like the childcare incident report form shown in Figure 17.3. In other words, most of the formatting work will be done for you.

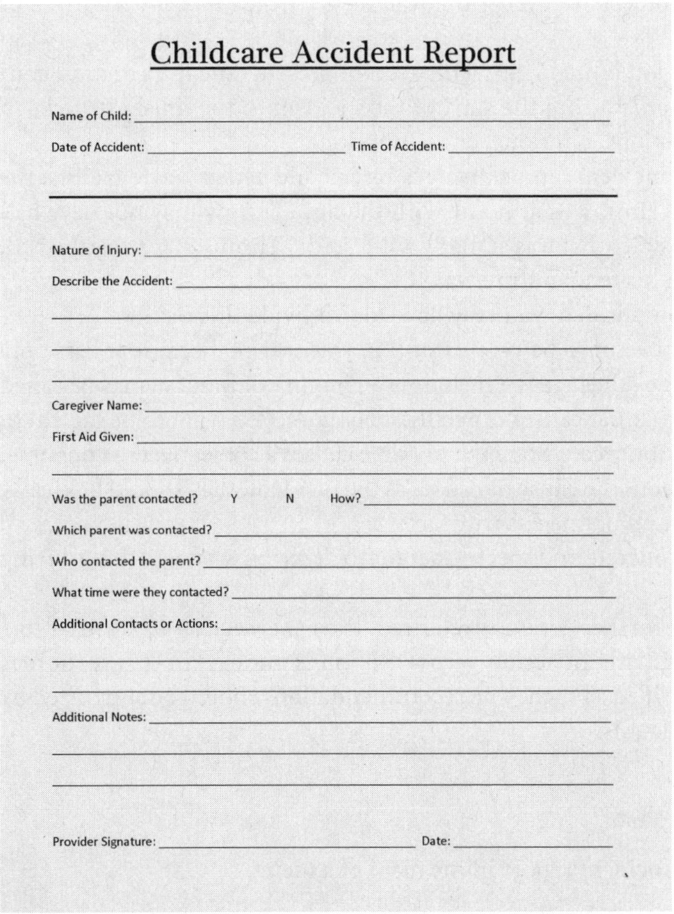

Childcare Accident Report

Name of Child: ____________________

Date of Accident: ____________ Time of Accident: ____________

Nature of Injury: ____________________

Describe the Accident: ____________________

Caregiver Name: ____________________

First Aid Given: ____________________

Was the parent contacted? Y N How? ____________

Which parent was contacted? ____________________

Who contacted the parent? ____________________

What time were they contacted? ____________________

Additional Contacts or Actions: ____________________

Additional Notes: ____________________

Provider Signature: ____________ Date: ____________

Figure 17.3 An Example of a Template for an Incident Report

Source: "Childcare Accident Report," Samplewords, http://www.samplewords.com/wp-content/uploads/2010/06/childcare-accident-report.pdf.

The basic incident report format will contain all or most of the following elements:

- subject (in letter format; memo has this already),
- summary,
- details (or description of incident),
- possible causes,
- action taken, and
- action required.

Subject: The subject should be specific. "Industrial accident" is too vague; "Arm injury on Dodge Ram production line" describes what the report is actually about.

Summary: This should have everything the reader needs to know in three or four sentences.

Details (or description of incident): This section presents the information concisely *in chronological order*, from the start of the incident to the finish. It sticks to the facts; it avoids emotions, opinions, or assumptions.

For example, if the incident report involves a sick child at a day-care facility, the report would not say "Timmy went home with the flu." Timmy may not have had flu! The report should state what was actually witnessed: "Timmy's face was flushed, he seemed listless, and his temperature was 101."

If the incident is complicated, you may have to subdivide this section.

Possible causes: You want to be very careful in this section because it lists only "possible" causes—some other agency, including an inquiry or inquest, may be called upon to determine the actual causes officially. Therefore, you want to be tactful to avoid assigning blame too freely. State the possible causes as objectively as possible. If there are opinions about the cause or causes of the incident, they should be clearly identified as opinions and not necessarily facts.

Action taken: Use concrete and specific details to describe what was done during and after the incident.

Action required: If further action is required, then this section lends itself to a list, each item starting with an action verb. Opinion is allowed in this section as long as it's clearly identified as such. The recommendations should be supported by specific and concrete details.

Sample Incident Report

Following is a sample incident report in the form of a memo.

Memo

Terrapin Heights Middle School

To: Jardine Corcoran, Superintendent
From: Kelly Trask, Principal
Date: October 25, 2018
Subject: Student injured using playground equipment
CC: Hilary Custis

Summary

On October 23, a 9-year-old Grade 4 student, Michael McDonald, fell off the monkey bars in our school playground after school hours and broke his arm. His parents could not be immediately contacted, so I drove Michael to Terrapin General Hospital Emergency. Thanks to a written authorization from Michael's parents for medical care if the parents could not be reached, the doctor put a cast on Michael's arm. Michael's father arrived shortly afterward and took him home. Apart from some bruises and cuts, and the broken arm, Michael appeared to be recovering well. It has been recommended that we upgrade our playground equipment and grounds to reduce the chances of similar accidents in the future.

Details

At 3:30 p.m. on Tuesday, October 23, teacher Hilary Custis was supervising after-school day care in the Terrapin Heights school playground when she noticed one of the students had fallen off the monkey bars and appeared to have hurt his arm. The Grade 4 student, Michael McDonald, aged 9, was lying on the ground, holding his arm and crying while several other students gathered around, obviously concerned. Hilary took Michael to the school nurse's office but the nurse had already left for the day. Hilary left Michael on the couch in the nurse's office and came to the school office to see me.

My secretary immediately telephoned and messaged Michael's parents at their home and work numbers and emails. We waited five minutes but, when we didn't get a reply, I decided to drive Michael to Terrapin General Hospital Emergency. Fortunately, the school has authorization from the parents for emergency medical treatment, and the doctor on duty, Caroline Walkham, was able to determine that Michael had a broken arm and immediately put a cast on the arm.

Michael was made comfortable on a bed in the emergency ward while we waited for word from his parents. About 5 p.m., Michael's father rushed into the hospital, very apologetic for taking so long, thanked me for taking such good care of his son, and took the boy home. Despite a few superficial cuts and bruises, in addition to the broken arm, Michael appeared to be in good spirits.

Action Taken

After the accident we took the following actions:

- The next day (i.e., earlier today), I inspected the playground and equipment with an engineer from the school district to assess the playground's safety. The engineer noted that the playground equipment at Terrapin Heights has not been upgraded since the school was built in 1987 and that the ground around the monkey bars is bare earth and gravel. He recommended an upgrade for both the equipment and the ground around it (for example, a base of wood chips or recycled rubber mulch rather than earth and gravel).

- I contacted the school district budget office about upgrading our playground equipment and the area around it. I was told there might be some money available for this.
- I telephoned Michael's parents to offer our regrets and the hope that Michael is recovering from his accident. They said he was actually quite proud of his cast and had already collected several signatures on it. He is looking forward to returning to school on October 26 and collecting more signatures from his classmates.
- I have scheduled a refresher course for all teachers and staff on the procedures to follow in case of a future accident to a student or staff member.

Action Required

As principal, I recommend the following:

- Replace the monkey bar set with a more modern "net" climbing system that is safer.
- Cover the ground around the new climbing equipment and around some of the other above-ground equipment with wood chips or rubber mulch for greater safety in the case of falls.

PROPOSAL REPORTS

Proposal reports can be informal or formal, depending on the complexity of the proposal. For example, a business-plan proposal can be dozens or even hundreds of pages long. A proposal seeking grant funding may be a page or two or quite long.

Proposals may be solicited (as when a granting agency asks for proposals) or unsolicited (you have generated the proposal yourself, perhaps to seek capital funding). Proposal reports—called briefing notes—are a big part of government decision making. A feasibility study is also a type of proposal report.

The most common proposal report, however, is written in response to a "request for proposal" or RFP. An RFP is a solicitation made by an organization or company interested in purchasing a product, service, or other asset. So the proposal report written in response to an RFP is often, in effect, a bid on a job.

As you can see, a proposal report is a *persuasive* document, so use the persuasive techniques (AIDA) discussed in Chapter 9.

The format of the proposal can be either a memo (internal) or letter (external). If the proposal is a long one, then you will want to follow a variation of the format for a formal report, i.e., letters of authorization and transmittal, table of contents, list of figures, executive summary, and so on. Formal reports are discussed in Chapter 18.

In general, a proposal will have most or all of the following elements:

- benefits, results, and feasibility of your proposed project (this section will include enough background to put the proposal in context);
- report audience—to whom the report is addressed (e.g., a funder, a decision maker);
- your method and plan;
- a tentative schedule or timeline or a summary of steps;
- your qualifications to do the proposed project;
- what the proposal will cost and resources needed;
- the graphics, pictures, tables, and sources that will be used; and
- other supporting information (e.g., bibliography, list of consultants or stakeholders).

A briefing note provides a government official, such as a cabinet minister or deputy minister, with very concise background information on a possible policy position and, often, a policy recommendation. Briefing notes follow this general style:

- issue (topic, purpose),
- background,
- current status,
- key considerations,
- options, and
- conclusions and recommendations.

Sample Proposal Reports

An example of a government briefing note follows. Note that the report uses parenthetical citation; in other words, sources are listed by author and date in parentheses, e.g., (B.C. Ministry of Health Planning, 2005). A list of references is not included because, presumably, the deputy minister would know well the most important sources of information for this portfolio.

File No.: 016789237 Date:

February 26, 2018

**BRIEFING NOTE FOR THE DEPUTY MINISTER OF EDUCATION:
AMENDMENTS TO HEALTH EDUCATION IN B.C. SCHOOLS**

SUMMARY

- From 2009–2017, the B.C. Ministry of Education has amended Physical Education and Health Sciences in B.C. schools in response to growing rates of obese and overweight children in Canada.
- To reduce the rate of obese and overweight children, Health Canada recommends children consume at least five servings of fruits and vegetables per day; however, a study by the Ministry of Education in 2015 showed none of the B.C. children surveyed consumed five servings of fruits and vegetables per day.
- Fewer than 18% of B.C. schools currently offer after-school workshops and brochures to teach both parents and children about eating and cooking more nutritiously.
- After-school parent/child workshops and information brochures will cost the Ministry of Education an extra 3% of its current budget, but this will save the province dollars in the future, as health issues related to obesity cost the province between$730 and $830 million annually.

Issue

To help prevent obesity in both children and adults, the B.C. Ministry of Education reformed Health Sciences and Physical Education studies in the provincial curricula. However, to combat the rise of obesity effectively, schools as well as parents need to participate. Thus, we propose that B.C. schools offer after-school healthy-living workshops to parents and children and distribute brochures to parents to help children make nutritious food choices inside and outside of the home.

Background

- Up to 84% of Canadian children do not get enough physical activity to maintain healthy bodies and minds (2014/15 National Population Health Survey).

- The B.C. Ministry of Education recommends 10% of instructional time in classrooms should be dedicated to physical activity (B.C. Ministry of Education, 2010).

- Over 33% of Canadian children and youth are overweight and approximately 15% are obese (B.C. Ministry of Health Planning, 2010).

- Five or more servings of fruits and vegetables per day substantially decrease the risk of obesity in children and youth (Canadian Community Health Survey, 2013).

- 59% of Canadian children and youth consume fewer than five servings of fruits and vegetables per day (CCHS, 2013).

Current Status

- The Ministry of Education now requires students from kindergarten to Grade 9 to participate in 30 minutes of physical activity each day and students from Grades 10 to 12 to complete 150 minutes of physical activity per week.

- The Health Education curriculum has also been amended to teach and encourage children to develop better eating habits and make informed, practical food choices. However, Health Education in school is not enough, and parents must encourage good nutrition at home.

- Fewer than 18% of schools have a policy or guideline in place, through workshops and brochures, to help parents promote healthy choices. However, the programs do prove to be effective where they are implemented.

Key Considerations

- To implement after-school programs and distribute brochures will cost the Ministry of Education only 3% of its current budget.

- Health issues and losses in economic productivity that are related to inactivity cost B.C. approximately between $730 and $830 million annually (GPI Atlantic, 2015).

- Economically, B.C. would save $49.4 million if physical activity and healthy eating were increased by only 10% by 2010 (B.C. Ministry of Health Planning, 2010).

- If lifestyle choices can be implemented into children's daily routines while they are still growing, developing, and forming habits, then these same children will grow up to be healthier adults who know how to make good choices about food and exercise. Schools and parents must work together to combat this growing problem, so, by offering after-school workshops and brochures, schools can help parents reaffirm healthy living practices that are taught in the classroom.

Originator's name and phone #: Carly Vickers, (555) 555-9898

Here is another example of a proposal report. This one calls for a new heating and cooling system at a hotel that will save money and energy.

Business Case – Heat Pump for Terrapin Towers Hotel

To: Dolores Alvarado, General Manager
From: Gil Patten, Operations Manager
Date: April 19, 2016
Subject: Installing heat pump system in Terrapin Towers Hotel

SUMMARY OVERVIEW

At present, Terrapin Towers Hotel is heated by natural gas (forced-air heating) and cooled by electricity (through wall-vented air-conditioners). The cost of both natural gas and electricity has increased substantially in the past year due, in part, to provincial government support for renewable, but more expensive, energy sources as part of the province's program to reduce greenhouse gas emissions. It is possible that the hotel could achieve substantial savings by switching to a centrally controlled warming/cooling system using a geothermal heat pump. A comparison between the costs of the hotel's current system and the costs of a heat-pump system shows that, although the initial outlay would be high, over five years the hotel will save up to $18,000 a year in heating and cooling costs. This report therefore recommends that Terrapin Towers Hotel switch to a geothermal heat-pump system.

INTRODUCTION AND BACKGROUND

Terrapin Towers Hotel has 36 rooms. These rooms and the hotel's common areas are currently heated by a central forced-air furnace fuelled by natural gas, while cooling comes from wall-vented, electrically powered air-conditioners in each room. This equipment is functioning well and should last for at least another five to ten years before needing to be upgraded.

However, in the past year alone, the rate for electricity has risen 8 per cent, while the natural gas rate has risen 5 per cent. Further large utility rate increases are expected in coming years as the provincial government tries to reduce fossil-fuel emissions by depending on renewable, but more expensive, energy sources as part of its overall energy mix. These rate increases are expected to cut severely into the hotel's revenue, and therefore profitability, unless changes are made.

On March 12, 2016, General Manager Dolores Alvarado asked Gil Patten, the hotel's operations manager, to report on the possibility of converting Terrapin Towers Hotel from natural gas and electricity to a geothermal heat-pump system for both heating and cooling.

RATIONALE

The rationale for proposing this change is to save on utility costs while also working toward the province's targets for reducing greenhouse gas emissions. At the same time, any changes must not sacrifice, and will preferably enhance, the comfort of the hotel's guests.

GOALS AND OBJECTIVES

1. Increased comfort of hotel guests (heat pump is quieter than in-room air-conditioners; room temperature is more easily controlled)
2. Savings of more than $18,000 a year in utility costs on both natural gas and electricity
3. Reduction in overall greenhouse gas emissions by about 3 per cent a year.

ANALYSIS

The hotel's chief operations manager, Gil Patten, and mechanical engineer Miguel Rodriguez researched heat pump costs and technology using the Internet and meetings with sales people at Caliente Heat Pumps in Terrapin. They also consulted with Terrapin Light and Power about the projected costs of natural gas and electricity in future years.

A reversible geothermal heat pump works on the principle that the ground contains warmth that can be extracted. Using a refrigerant under pressure, the pump's evaporator draws heat from the ground and pipes it into a building where a condenser releases the warm air.

And, in reverse, to produce cooling, the heat pump condenser becomes an evaporator that absorbs heat from within a building (similar to the inside of a refrigerator) and expels it outdoors or into the ground (see Figure 1).

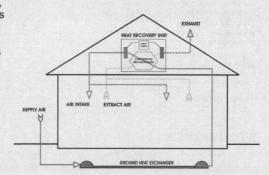

Figure 1: Heat pump operation

ADVANTAGES

The heat pump uses less power than other forms of heating and cooling because it does not actually *create* heat, like a gas-fired furnace or electrical resistance heater. Instead, it takes heat from the ground and *moves* it to where it is needed, and the reverse for cooling. This makes heat pumps three to four times more efficient in their use of electricity than electrical resistance heaters, while not using natural gas at all. Another major advantage: one heat-pump system can produce both heating and cooling. Finally, the hotel could save money by not removing the current natural-gas heating system and using it as an emergency backup, if needed.

DISADVANTAGES

A heat-pump system large enough to heat the Terrapin Towers Hotel is two to three times more expensive than installing a new electricity- and/or natural gas-fuelled heating/cooling system in the next five to ten years. However, our figures show the initial cost of the heat-pump system will be recovered in savings after only four years (see Table 1).

Table 1: Current system versus heat pump costs over 5 years

Current system	Current costs/year	Projected costs					
		Year 1	Year 2	Year 3	Year 4	Year 5	Total cost/ 5 years
Current electricity cost/year	$21,000	$22,500	$23,000	$23,500	$24,000	$24,500	$117,500
Current natural gas cost/year	$18,000	$18,500	$19,000	$19,500	$20,000	$20,500	$97,500
Total cost of utilities over 5 years	$39,000	$41,000	$42,000	$43,000	$44,000	$45,000	$215,000
Average cost/year							$43,000
Heat pump system							
Heat pump system initial cost including installation (one-time cost)							$62,000
Removal and/or de-commissioning of current system (one-time cost)							$23,000
Estimated operating costs (electricity and maintenance)/year		$7,250	$7,500	$7,750	$8,000	$8,250	$38,750
Total estimated cost of heat pump system over 5 years							$123,750
Average cost/year							$24,750
Average saving/year							$18,250

RECOMMENDATION

We recommend that Terrapin Towers Hotel switch from a combination natural-gas furnace for heating, and wall-vented, electricity-operated in-room air-conditioners for cooling, to a central geothermal heat pump system for both heating and cooling.

CONCLUSION

Informal reports perform many useful tasks in the world of the professions and business. These reports inform, often by providing background information and data on the progress of a project. They also analyze and sometimes persuade, as in incident reports, problem-solving reports, feasibility reports, and proposals.

They are, as the name implies, less formal than the formal report in their use of language (contractions and first-person forms are allowed), and, unless they are very long, they don't have the same divisions (e.g., front matter, body, and final matter) as the formal report, which will be discussed in the next chapter.

That said, each type of informal report has its own structure, as described previously. In most cases, if you are commissioned to write an informal report, you will either be familiar with your organization's format for each type of report, or you'll be given a template to follow, such as the childcare incident report template in Figure 17.3.

DISCUSSION QUESTIONS

1. What are the two basic types of informal report?
2. What are the parts of a progress report?
3. What are the parts of a problem-solving report?
4. What are the differences between the "direct" and "indirect" formats?
5. What are the parts of an incident report?
6. What are the parts of a proposal report?

Exercises

1. **Progress report exercise**: Write a progress report on a major class assignment you are currently working on. If the assignment is an essay or report, include a tentative outline of the paper.

2. **Incident report exercise**: You are the production manager for a pulp-and-paper company. Due to an employee's error, a large spill of mercury-laced water has been released into the river that runs next to your plant. Write an incident report of one to one and a half pages describing how the accidental discharge occurred, what was done, whether there were any health risks to individuals or the community, and what you recommend to avoid similar incidents in the future. For this exercise, you may make up any details you need to make the report convincing.

3. **Problem-solving report exercise**: You are the manager of a fast-food restaurant. Lately, you've noticed that the lines at the service counter have grown unacceptably long, and some customers are getting frustrated—this is a "fast-food" restaurant, after all. Write a short (one to two pages) problem-solving report outlining the problem and recommending a solution or solutions. For this exercise, you may make up any details you need to make the report convincing.

4. **Proposal exercise**: A university committee is offering several $5,000 grants for projects that will make the university more environmentally friendly. Based on some research, write a proposal of two to three pages applying for one of the grants. For this exercise, you can make up the details of your qualifications to do the proposal.

Chapter 18
Formal Reports

In this chapter you will learn to

- Write a formal report in the proper style,
- Format a formal report in the proper style,
- Create a meaningful survey, and
- Write minutes for a team meeting.

INTRODUCTION

At some point in your professional or business career, you may be called upon to write a formal report, either on your own or as part of a team. The project could be a business proposal, a company annual report, or an in-depth, problem-solving study that answers questions (e.g., should our company invest in the natural-gas industry at this time?). It could also be a report of a scientific experiment or enquiry or a technical document.

The possible topics for a formal report are almost limitless, but, ultimately, like the informal report, a formal report has one of two basic goals: to inform or to analyze.

An **informative report** can be **periodic**, such as an **annual report** that presents an organization's financial and administrative situation for the past year or fiscal year, or a **progress report** on how well a particular task is proceeding (Chapter 17 has an example of a progress report on building a bridge). An academic essay can be an informative report if it gives in-depth information about a particular topic. However, informative reports typically don't make recommendations; they just present the facts.

An **analytical report**, by definition, looks into a particular topic and will likely make recommendations based on that analysis; in other words, it may also be **persuasive**.

For example, a **problem-solving report** might look at why a company lost market share in the second quarter, or why accidents in the plant this year have increased 20 per cent over the previous year. The report would then make recommendations on how to increase market share or reduce the number of accidents.

The example report in Chapter 17 on changing a street intersection to a traffic circle is an informal problem-solving report that includes a recommendation (build the traffic circle). Chapter 20 has an example of an analytic report based on Exercise 2 at the end of this chapter: in the example report, the authors analyze and recommend two websites as models for the website of a new hotel.

A **formal proposal** is an analytical report that offers to design and/or supply a product or service, often in response to a Request for Proposal (RFP). It might also be called a **feasibility study**—a report that analyzes whether a particular course of action is doable and/or desirable. A **business proposal**, a report that seeks support and funding for a business enterprise, is a type of feasibility study. In a university context, a formal proposal might apply for funding for a research project, whether based on an RFP or not.

Chapter 17 has two examples of informal proposal reports (the government briefing note on child obesity and the report on the benefits and drawbacks of investing in heat pumps for a hotel). Chapter 19 has an example of a formal proposal report on creating a bicycle-sharing network at a university.

Unlike informal reports, which we discussed in Chapter 17, formal reports are external documents that go outside your organization. They are almost always longer than informal reports—a formal report can be dozens, hundreds, or even thousands of pages. Furthermore, the writing style is formal, and the presentation is highly structured, with many sections and subsections.

Ultimately, what makes a formal report different from an informal report is that it is formal. For example, the writing in a formal report is closer to academic writing than to business writing. The language and ideas may be more complex. The sentences may be longer and may contain more than one idea. Paragraphs may be longer than those in most of the business and professional communication we've studied so far.

In formal-report writing, you won't be using contractions (such as "won't") or as many abbreviations ("etc." becomes "and so on" or "et cetera"). It's not necessary, but you may decide to go formal when it comes to punctuation. That is, you may use a more formal, academic style of punctuation (e.g., the "Oxford" comma in lists and commas before coordinating conjunctions). We discussed this more formal style in Chapter 3.

Formal reports do not use "you" or "I." Instead, reports are written in a third-person, objective style, which may mean more use of passive constructions: "The evidence shows that investment by our company is not warranted at this time," rather than the more plain English "We do not think, based on the evidence, that the company should invest at this time." If you do want to use first person, use "we" (not "I") or the third-person pronoun "one."

Depending on the sophistication of your audience, you may be using a highly technical vocabulary and specialized terms, even jargon, if appropriate.

This doesn't mean you should abandon plain English! Plain English is the most transparent form of written communication possible. It just means that, in writing your formal report, you are going to put your clear, transparent writing into a formal tone that is closer to the one expected in an academic essay than to the tone of a, say, business letter.

FORMAL REPORT DESIGN

Reports can appear in a variety of designs, from plain vanilla with pages of grey text to highly attractive pages full of pictures and colour.

For example, at one end of the spectrum, a company's investment prospectus or annual report can be very grey. Figure 18.1 shows a page of an investment prospectus.

As you can see, the text is dense, the headings are small, and the only white space is what's needed to separate the paragraphs. This document is meant to be read strictly for its content by serious investors, not savoured for its style and appearance.

Other report pages show more design features, such as the page from a report by BC Statistics that includes extra margin space, colour, and pull quotes (see Figure 18.2).

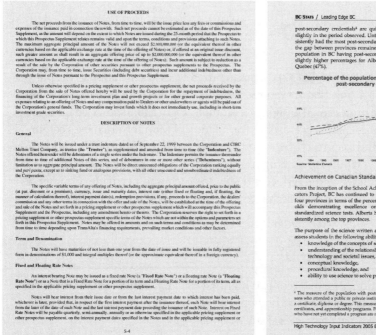

Figure 18.1 An Investment Prospectus. Really Grey!

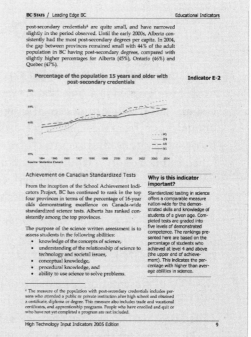

Figure 18.2 A Page from a Report by BC Stats and Leading Edge British Columbia

Source: Jade Norton and Dan Schrier, Input Indicators of the British Columbia High Technology Sector: 2005 Edition (Vancouver: BC Stats and Leading Edge British Columbia, March 2006), 9.

Flowering Dogwood Gala

Over 900 people enjoyed an enchanted evening at the 8th annual Flowering Dogwood Gala at the Virginia Mutual Conference Center in May. The event was presented by The Statin Family and raised $275,000.

Monday, May 22nd, 2017 has been reserved for the 9th annual Flowering Dogwood Gala. To reserve your tickets, please call 542-555-8223.

Book Fair

Established in 1955, the Children's Hospital Book Fair is the Foundation's longest running fundraiser, and 2016 was another successful year. St. Norman Center hosted all three sales with approximately 600,000 books raising $525,000 to support Children's Hospital programing.

Over $8-million has been raised by the Book Fair to date. Tremendous dedication and tireless effort from our volunteer team is responsible for this awe-inspiring achievement.

Radiothon

The Comm Caring Day was held on Friday, April 10th, 2016 on SQ1080 and SPIN98. The Orchid Lounge at 292 Fenwick hosted the ONBC Phone Bank. Running between 6am–6pm, the one-day event raised over $475,000. Sheryl Nettlemane inspired a Matching Program and helped raise $100,000 through her friends and family. Volunteers from various businesses including Tibia Investments, Terrapin Marmot Figurines, Oceanic Airways, Ogdenville Insurance, and ONBC generously donated their time on the front lines of the ONBC Phone Bank.

Figure 18.3 A Page from the Annual Report of the Children's Hospital Foundation of Manitoba

Source: Children's Hospital Foundation of Manitoba, Building a Stronger Tomorrow Together: Report to the Community 2012 (Winnipeg: Children's Hospital Foundation of Manitoba, 2013), 11. Reprinted with the permission of the Children's Hospital Foundation of Manitoba.

On the other hand, a report that also hopes to promote an organization to the public will be designed in a style that is even more reader friendly, with pictures, graphs, colour, and attractive professional design. For example, Figure 18.3 shows a page of an annual report from the Children's Hospital Foundation of Manitoba that uses colour, bold fonts, large headings, and pictures to attract readers and therefore public support.

How much effort you put into making your report both informative *and* attractive will depend on the audience the report is trying to reach and persuade. Chapter 5 has details on how to make a document attractive through reader-friendly design.

FORMAL REPORT FORMATTING

In terms of presentation, a formal report is highly stylized. It consists of three parts: the front or preliminary matter, the body of the report, and the back matter, also called final parts. Each part has several subsections.

The format for the three parts depends on the style used by your organization or on the style expected by the recipient of the report (usually the individual or institution that has commissioned it). The format also depends on the kind of report it is: informative, analytic, problem-solving, proposal, and so on. Report formats vary

Figure 18.4 Example of a Formal Report Cover

Source: Dan Schrier and Lillian Hallin, Profile of the British Columbia High Technology Sector: 2008 Edition (Vancouver: BC Stats, September 2008), cover.

from organization to organization, but what follows is common in the professional and business world. In the world of work, when you set out to write a formal report, you will know, or be told, what the format should be.

In terms of document design, the text of formal reports is usually in a serif font, for example, Times New Roman. The text may be flush left (ragged-right edge) or fully justified. The text may be in one column or several. Headings are usually in a sans-serif font such as Arial, but not always. The headings may be in colour. Many companies have staff or contractors whose job is to create a pleasing, professional look for the company's formal reports.

In most reports, figures, pictures, graphs, and other visuals are labelled as, for example, "Figure 1" or "Table 4," and each has a descriptive caption ("Figure 4: The rising cost of living in South Korea"). For details on document design for formal reports, see Chapter 5 and the sample formal reports in Chapters 19 and 20.

Reports may appear on high-quality paper with coloured dividers and are usually bound, sometimes spiral bound. They may have attractive covers (see Figure 18.4). And, of course, they may also appear online as web documents or PDFs.

For now, let's take a look at the parts of a formal report. First we'll look at the parts of a basic *analytical* report, followed by the parts of a basic *formal proposal* report.

Front Matter

The front matter goes before the body of the report and introduces the report's contents. The front matter has a page-numbering system that is different from the body of the report: it uses Roman numerals (iii) rather than the Arabic numerals (3) that appear in the body of the report. Depending on an organization's style, not every report has a letter or memo of authorization and transmittal. In most cases, though, the front matter consists of the following:

- Title Page (the report may also have a cover page, like the cover of a book);
- Letter or Memo of Authorization that, as the name suggests, authorizes or commissions the report;
- Letter or Memo of Transmittal, which presents the report to the person or group that authorized or commissioned it;
- Table of Contents;
- Table or List of Figures (if the report has figures; most do);
- List of Tables (if the report has tables); and
- Executive Summary (sometimes called an abstract).

Let's go through these sections one by one.

Title Page

The title page of a formal report counts as page one (in lower-case Roman numerals, "i") but *the page number is not printed.*

This page has the title of the report, who it has been written for (often worded as "Prepared for:" or "Submitted to:"), who wrote the report (often "Prepared by:" or "Submitted by:"), and the date that the report is being submitted (January 27, 2018).

The report title has all important words capitalized, like the title of a book. The title may be boldfaced or all in capital letters for dramatic effect. The main title would normally be in an 18-point font or larger, and it could be in a fancy type, such as Microsoft Word's WordArt styles. If you are doing your own design, though, remember to avoid cutesy fonts and effects; you want your formal report to be taken seriously. Report titles usually have a main title and a subtitle, divided by a colon.

The other elements of the title page will normally be in 14- or 16-point font. A plain-vanilla version of the title page for a formal report will look something like the one pictured in Figure 18.5.

A title page may also have the full address of the recipient and the full address of the preparer. It may also have the preparer's corporate logo.

The title page can also be fancier than the plain-vanilla version, with colour and graphics to make the page more attractive. The title page in Figure 18.6 uses colour and Microsoft Word's WordArt for the report title, plus a picture.

The report title page might also have the submitting company's logo or any other elements that will make the page more attractive.

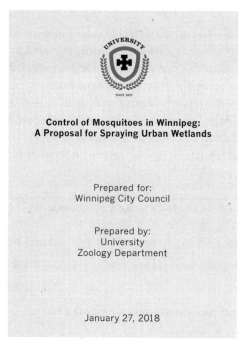

Figure 18.5 Plain Title Page for a Formal Report

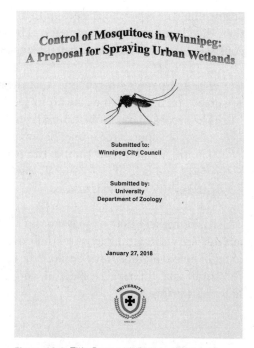

Figure 18.6 Title Page with Picture and Logo

Letter or Memo of Authorization

Next is the letter or memo of authorization—the official letter that commissioned the report, assuming the report was commissioned; some reports are generated by their author. This part of the report will be in memo format if the report was ordered from inside your organization and in letter format if ordered from outside.

The letter of authorization is page two of the report—Roman numeral "ii"—but the number may or may not appear on the page depending on the report style being used. If a page number is printed, it is usually at the bottom centre of the page.

The letter of authorization uses block-letter format (see Chapter 6 on formatting for letters). This letter normally has three parts:

- an opening paragraph with background on the reasons for commissioning the report,
- a description of the commission itself plus a date when the report should be submitted, and
- a polite closing with contact information.

A typical letter of authorization will read like the example in Figure 18.7.

Letter or Memo of Transmittal

The letter or memo of transmittal is normally page 3 (Roman numeral "iii"). It "transmits" the report to the group that commissioned it; if the group is internal, then this document will be a memo. The letter or memo of transmittal typically consists of three main points, usually one point per paragraph.

- The first paragraph explains what the report is about and announces that it is ready on or before the date promised (it is hoped).
- The second paragraph summarizes, very briefly but concretely and specifically, the report's recommendations.
- The third paragraph thanks the person or people who commissioned the report and helped in writing it, suggests further steps if necessary, and offers further information if needed.

Although there may or may not be a letter of authorization (it's possible the authors are writing the report on their own account), a formal report always has a letter or memo of transmittal because the report must have been written for *someone*. Its overall tone is formal, respectful, and helpful. Figure 18.8 provides an example letter of transmittal.

Terrapin General Hospital
Human Resources Department
5298 Westham Road
Terrapin, BC V8T 5J7

August 11, 2018

Daniel Johnson
Principal Consultant
Terrapin Medical Consultants
6711 View Street
Terrapin, BC V8T 1R8

Dear Mr. Johnson:

Subject: Evaluation of hip-replacement websites

In the last year alone, 58,714 hip-replacement surgeries were performed in Canada. This is an overall increase of 87% over the past ten years. In response, Terrapin General Hospital is increasing hip-replacement services for local residents.

As we discussed on July 5, we would like to commission your firm to evaluate and recommend the three best hip-replacement websites available on the Internet. These websites would appear in a brochure with helpful information on hip-replacement surgery for patients and families. We would like you to develop evaluation criteria that take the hip-replacement demographic (patients between 50 and 80 years old) into consideration.

We would like to have the brochure prepared and printed by November 5. To meet this deadline, we must receive your report by October 15.

We look forward to receiving your report. If you require any further information, please feel free to contact Jim Reese at 555-555-6636, ext. 224.

Yours sincerely,

Andrea Stewart

Andrea Stewart
Director of Human Resources

— ii —

Figure 18.7 Example Letter of Authorization with Page Number Printed

TERRAPIN MEDICAL CONSULTANTS
6711 View Street
Terrapin, BC V8T 1R8

October 15, 2018

Andrea Stewart
Director of Human Resources
Terrapin General Hospital
5298 Westham Road
Terrapin, BC V8T 5J7

Dear Ms. Stewart:

Subject: Hip-replacement website evaluation completed

Here is the report evaluating hip-replacement websites for the hospital's brochure that you requested in your letter of August 11.

We have recommended three websites that provide relevant information in, an organized and concise manner:

- **OrthoInfo**, published by the American Academy of Orthopaedic Surgeons;
- **Joint Replacement**, published by Hamilton Health Services in Ontario; and
- **BoneSmart**, published by The Foundation for the Advancement of Research in Medicine (FARM).

We are confident that these three sites represent useful, up-to-date resources that will be helpful for your patients.

We have enjoyed working on this report. We would like to thank Jim Reese for assisting us in developing a set of evaluation criteria relevant to the needs of your patients. If you have any questions or comments about the report, we will be happy to meet with you. I can be reached by phone at 555-555-3332, ext. 1.

Yours sincerely,

Daniel Johnson

Daniel Johnson
Principal Consultant

DJ/hk

Enclosure: Report on hip-replacement websites

— iii —

Figure 18.8 Example Letter of Transmittal

Table of Contents

Unless it is very short—say, four or five pages—a formal report almost always has a table of contents (TOC), usually right after the letter or memo of transmittal.

The TOC's page number is usually in the footer of the page, centred, and in Roman numerals (it will likely be page "iv"). The page header may have the report's title. Unless it is very short, the TOC should be given an entire page.

Many word-processing programs, including Microsoft Word, Pages, and Open Office, allow you to create a table of contents automatically, in a number of styles (e.g., modern, traditional, and simple).

To enable the automatic table of contents feature, use the program's "heading" styles for the report's headings and subheadings. Then, on a blank page, you can "insert" a table of contents with up to four levels of headings. That is, "Heading 1" will be the main heading, "Heading 2" a section heading, "Heading 3" a subsection heading, and so on. This automatic table-of-contents feature can be a huge time-saver, especially for long reports!

Note that the page number for the TOC itself is *not included* in table of contents, which makes sense. If you are on this page, you don't need to find it. Including the letter of authorization and letter of transmittal in the TOC is also optional but not uncommon.

The TOC listings can be double spaced, as in the example to the right, or single spaced. The sample TOC has three levels of headings, but it can have more. A TOC page will look something like the one featured in Figure 18.9.

> **Worth Knowing**
> To generate an automatic TOC listing for the two letters, which do not have headings, put "Letter of Authorization," and "Letter of Transmittal" in a Heading style somewhere on the letter pages but in white text. The headings will not show up in print or electronically, but will be included in an automatically created table of contents.

Table of Contents

Figure 18.9 Table of Contents with Three Levels of Headings

List of Figures and List of Tables

If you have used figures, pictures, charts or tables in your report, and you probably will, they will appear here, in the same format as the headings in the table of contents. This page is numbered.

Normally, the list (or table) of figures and list (or table) of tables each appears on its own page. However, if both are short, they can appear on the same page. You can use "table" instead of "list," but "table of tables" sounds a bit awkward.

As with the table of contents, some word-processing programs will automatically generate a list of figures. In Word, you can use the program's "Insert–Caption" feature to create figure captions, which can then be listed automatically. Once again, go to the "Insert" menu, and click on "Index and Tables" and then on "Table of Figures," instead of "Table of Contents."

> **Worth Remembering**
> Figures and tables should have descriptive captions after the figure or table number (e.g., "Figure 5: Example of Table of Contents").

As when you automatically generate a table of contents, there are several styles available in most word-processing programs for your list of figures and list of tables.

Figure 18.10 shows an example of a report page listing figures and tables.

List of Figures

Figure 1: Woman experiencing TGA........ 1
Figure 2: Cases of TGA over five years........ 1
Figure 3: Healthline logo........ 2
Figure 4: User-friendliness survey results........ 2
Figure 5: Healthline website home page........ 3
Figure 6: Mayo Clinic logo........ 4
Figure 7: Content survey results........ 4
Figure 8: Mayo clinic website homepage........ 5
Figure 9: Medscape logo........ 6
Figure 10: Visual appeal survey results........ 6
Figure 11: Medscape website home page........ 7
Figure 12: Terrapin General Hospital........ 8
Figure 13: Summary of survey results........ 8

List of Tables

Table 1: Content survey results........ 12
Table 2: Visual appeal survey results........ 12
Table 3: User-friendliness survey results........ 12

—v—

Figure 18.10 Example of a Page from a Formal Report with Both a List of Figures and a List of Tables

Executive Summary

The executive summary (sometimes called an abstract) gives the entire body of the report in a nutshell. Some highly technical reports have both an abstract and an executive summary. This "nutshell" summary may be several pages if the report is a long one. As a rule of thumb, the executive summary is about one-tenth the size of the full report.

The executive summary page or pages uses Roman numerals; in the example (Figure 18.11) the summary is on page "vi." Depending on style, some formal report formats have the executive summary before the table of contents.

> **Worth Knowing**
>
> The executive summary is expected to pass the "elevator test." Suppose you and your boss are presenting a formal report to a meeting of the board of directors. However, your boss hasn't yet read the report. If you can get on an elevator on the fifth floor of your building, give your boss the Executive Summary and, by the sixteenth floor, be sure she's got the overall gist of the report, then your summary has passed the elevator test.

Executive Summary

An increase in cases of transient global amnesia (TGA) in Terrapin, BC, has increased demand for reliable and useful information about this condition. TGA is a potentially alarming but harmless medical condition characterized by short, sudden episodes of memory loss.

The Internet offers an abundance of information on TGA, but reliable information is difficult to find among thousands of websites. Terrapin General Hospital asked Clark & Mackay Consulting to recommend three websites that provide easy-to-understand, reliable, and supportive information about TGA for a non-medically educated audience. These websites will be included as resources in a brochure on TGA for Terrapin patients.

Clark & Mackay's task was to find websites with reliable and thorough information that the hospital's target audience could easily understand. As part of the analysis, visual appeal and user-friendliness of the websites were also evaluated.

Each website was analyzed and rated using the following criteria:

- **Visual Appeal**: Useful images, colour, format, absence of distractions;
- **Content**: Simple language, credibility, easy access to contact information; and
- **User-Friendliness**: Excellent search engine, easy navigation, reliable links.

The results of our analysis, which were supported by a public survey, led us to recommend the following three websites for the Terrapin Hospital brochure:

- Mayo Clinic,
- Healthline, and
- Medscape.

We are confident that our analysis and recommendations will support the needs of the patients at Terrapin General Hospital who suffer from this condition.

— vi —

Figure 18.11 Example Executive Summary

The structure of the executive summary follows that of the body of the report. You may even use the report's major headings as subheadings within the executive summary. The text of the body and the summary can use the same wording as well. That is, you can select the most important sentences from the report and either put them into the summary as is or condense them. As a very rough guide, each paragraph of the full report would get one sentence in the executive summary.

The executive summary, then, contains a brief background of the topic, an abbreviated version of the data, and a short version of the conclusions and recommendations. We will discuss these parts of a report in more detail in the next section, on the body of a report.

Body of the Report

The body of the formal report has the following basic elements:

- introduction and, sometimes, background;
- analysis and data (including how you conducted your research, sometimes called the mode of analysis);
- conclusions; and
- recommendation or recommendations.

This structure uses the "indirect" approach we discussed in Chapter 17; that is, it lays out the argument first and then presents the conclusions and recommendations. You would use this pattern if the reader (typically someone in higher authority within your organization or the person or group for whom you wrote the report) needs to be persuaded of your conclusions. The indirect approach is the most common for formal reports.

If you are sure your conclusions and recommendations will be welcomed or are not controversial then you might use the direct approach:

- Identify the problem the report addresses.
- Give your conclusions and recommendations.
- Give the analysis and data that underlie the conclusions and recommendations.
- End with a summary of the report.

The page numbering of the body of a report is in *Arabic numerals* ("2," "45," "88," etc.). The introduction begins on page "1," and this number may or may not be shown on the page depending on the report style you are using. In the report example in Chapter 19, the first page number is shown.

Introduction and Background

As the name implies, the introduction introduces the subject matter of the report and discusses

- how and why the report came to be written (the background),
- the scope of the problem or issue it addresses,
- the methodology that the report writers chose to tackle the issue,
- why you or your firm were commissioned to do the report and the expertise you bring to the issue, and
- the report's significance.

In other words, the introduction offers all the context the reader needs to understand the data and conclusions that follow.

In longer reports, you may separate the introductory section into two, one called "Introduction" and the other "Background." The "Introduction" will discuss how and why the report was commissioned, why your firm was chosen to do the report, and the scope of the problem. The "Background" will do as its name suggests: give detailed background information that underpins the reasons for the report.

In longer reports, your discussion of methodology—how you conducted your research—may have its own section called something such as "Mode of Analysis."

Note that the introduction does *not* give the conclusions or recommendations, nor does it summarize the analysis section that follows. For now, you are just setting up the discussion.

Mode of Analysis or Methodology

Again, in longer reports, this might be a separate section following the introduction, which might also give background information. The "Mode of Analysis" section describes how you did your research. For example, if you were doing research into public attitudes toward a natural-gas pipeline from Alberta to California, you might survey residents along the route about their attitudes. You might also research natural-gas pipeline safety, markets, and so on. This section is not your analysis, but how you did the research and analysis.

If you are conducting a survey, you should explain how you did the survey: how you enlisted the survey participants, how many surveys you sent out, how many were filled out (this is often a considerably smaller number than the number you sent out), and the gist of the questions you asked.

Analysis of the Data

In this section, you present the results of your research. To explain and support your research and analysis, you will also include tables, graphs, charts, and pictures. This is probably the longest section of your report, and it will likely be divided into several (or many) subsections.

Conclusions

Although conclusions and recommendations might seem to be the same, they are not. Or, not quite.

The "Conclusions" section may be a page long or more and offers a detailed discussion of what you concluded from the research you did for the report.

It begins with a brief description of the background of the report to provide the context that led to your conclusions. Then, concretely and specifically, you offer your conclusions, based on your research.

> **Worth Remembering**
> This section is labelled "Conclusions," with an "s," meaning what you have concluded, not "Conclusion," meaning the end of the report.

The "Conclusions" section *includes* your recommendations, but each conclusion is described in greater detail here than in the "Recommendations" section that follows.

Recommendations

The "Recommendations" section is the short, snappy version of your conclusions. It provides the conclusions at a glance and is usually in a bulleted list format, introduced by a sentence, with each list item beginning with an action verb. It usually has its own page.

So, for example, if your report was on the need for better washrooms for executives in your company's office, the "Conclusions" section would give detailed information on what you've discovered. The "Recommendations" section, however, might read as follows:

We recommend that XYZ Inc. do the following:

- Buy a copy of da Vinci's *Mona Lisa* for each executive washroom.
- Install gold taps in all executive washrooms.
- Give each executive at or above the rank of vice-president his or her own private washroom.

If you have only one recommendation, you, obviously, would not use a bulleted list.

Back Matter

In the back matter of your report is the material that supported your report's analysis but isn't necessary in the body, or material that offers supplementary information. The back matter may include appendices, exhibits, endnotes, and lists of sources (often titled "Works Cited" or "References").

For example, if you did a detailed customer survey as part of the research for your report, you will, of course, present a summary of the survey research in the body of the report, often in the form of graphs and tables. However, the raw data from the survey can go as an appendix in the back matter of the report. What appears as a graph in the body of the report might appear as a table in the appendix.

The back matter can continue the Arabic numbering of the body of the report or switch back to Roman numerals, based on the style of the organization preparing or receiving the report.

Appendices

In the appendices, you will put supporting information that was too detailed to put into the body of the report, such as the raw data from a customer survey or a detailed table. The body of the report will have a summary of this data, often in the form of a graph or chart.

Each appendix, no matter how short, has its own page with a title explaining what the appendix is about (e.g., "Appendix A: Customer survey" and "Appendix B: Customer survey results"). If you don't put a title with each appendix item, readers consulting the table of contents won't know what the appendix is about.

Documentation of Sources

As with an academic essay, if you have cited or quoted some-one else's work in your report, you need to acknowledge the other person's contribution. Your citations can be in the form of footnotes or endnotes, in one of the accepted academic reference styles: e.g., Modern Language Association (MLA), American Psychological Association (APA), Chicago (*Chicago Manual of Style*), Council of Science Editors (CSE), and so on.

Footnotes, of course, will appear at the foot of the report's pages. If you use endnotes, they will appear after the appendices as part of the back matter of your report. The endnotes, even if there are only two or three, have their own separate page. If you have given full bibliographic information in your notes, a "works cited" section is not necessary. However, you might want to include a bibliography of useful sources. This section, entitled "Bibliography," would go after the appendices and after any endnotes.

> **Worth Knowing**
> You can find information about the different academic styles—APA, MLA, etc.—on many websites. Two good sources are
>
> https://owl.purdue.edu/owl/purdue_owl.html
>
> http://www.uvic.ca/library/research/citation/guides/

If you use citations in parentheses rather than notes, such as (Wilson, 2003), you will also have a section entitled "Works Cited" or "References" with a listing of all the articles, books, websites, and other sources that you mentioned (cited) in your report, just as you would for an academic essay.

Like your footnotes or endnotes, your report's parenthetical documentation should be formatted according to one standard style for both in-text citations and your references section: e.g., MLA, APA, Chicago. The key here is to pick one style and stick to it throughout the report: you must be consistent in the style of your in-text parenthetical references and your works-cited reference list.

Similarly, in a formal report, you will integrate information from your sources in the same way you include information in an academic paper: either as a *paraphrase* that uses different language or as a *quotation* that uses the same language as the source but is clearly identified by quotation marks as not your own words. Remember that statistics and facts not generally known also need to be documented. In other words, in a formal report as in an academic paper, you could be guilty of plagiarism if you don't clearly identify your sources.

FORMAL PROPOSALS

In this section we'll look at the format for a formal proposal type of report. As noted in Chapter 17, formal proposals or feasibility studies are often the response to a Request for Proposal (RFP) from an organization. The report writers analyze the data, make a proposal, and then explain why their proposal should be accepted or funded.

Formal proposals can be solicited by an organization through an RFP or unsolicited. Formal proposals can also be internal (if the RFP is directed toward those within the organization, the document of transmittal would be a memo) or external (if an RFP goes to those outside the organization, the document of transmittal would be a letter). The proposal may be indirect, so the evidence goes before the conclusions and recommendations, or direct, with the conclusions and recommendations first, followed by the evidence that supports the conclusions.

For example, suppose a university wants to make the campus more environmentally friendly. The university might issue an RFP asking campus members and/or non-members to propose ways to reach the RFP's goal: a more eco-friendly campus. Each submitted proposal would be read and assessed, and successful proposals would be approved and perhaps funded. Chapter 19 has an example of a formal proposal report that responds to a university's RFP for eco-friendly projects.

As you write your proposal, you will need to keep in mind the following issues:

- Is your proposal actually feasible with current technology (assuming you are choosing a reality-based topic)? If new technology is needed, can it be invented within a reasonable time period?
- Has your proposal been done elsewhere? What were the results (success or failure)?
- What will your proposal cost the client? Can your client afford this? Are there external budget issues that also need to be considered, such as possible government funding restrictions or grants?
- Is your proposal likely to meet with approval by the target audience?
- Are there any legal or regulatory issues to take into account?

Formal Proposal Format

The format of a formal proposal is a little different from the report structure we've looked at so far in this chapter. The division into front matter, body, and back matter (also called final parts) is usually followed, but not always, with each main section usually beginning on its own page but not always.

In the list of the parts of a formal proposal below, the main heading titles are capitalized and in blue. For a more detailed description of what is included in each section, see the discussion above on report sections for an analytical report.

Front Matter
- Title page: page 1 (actually, Roman numeral "i") but the number is not printed.
- Letter or Memo of Authorization (the RFP itself): this section may or may not appear in the proposal report depending on an organization's style. If it is included, as front matter it would be numbered "ii," in Roman numerals, with the page number printed. From here on, all page numbers are printed.
- Letter or Memo of Transmittal: this introduces your submission of the proposal. Use a memo if the issuers of the RFP are within your organization (e.g., a university grants committee). If there is a letter or memo of authorization, this would be page "iii." If there is no authorization document, then page "ii."
- Table of Contents: page "iii" or "iv," depending on whether there is an authorization document.
- List of Figures: page "iv" or "v."
- List of Tables: could be on same page as figures or a separate page if there are many tables.
- Executive Summary or Summary or Abstract: summarizes the entire report, page "vi" or "vii." In some proposal report formats, the summary goes after the letter or memo of transmittal.
- Glossary: a glossary of technical terms is optional and most often found in engineering and scientific proposals; it would be page "vii" or "viii." The Glossary may also go ahead of the Executive Summary, or even in the back matter section, depending on your organization's report style.

Body of Report
- Introduction: as this is the beginning of the body of the report, the page number is "1," in Arabic numerals, printed. As part of the Introduction you may include the following:
  - **Purpose**: why the report is being written (for example, in response to an RFP) and why this proposal will solve the problem.

- ○ **Background**: enough detail to put the report's proposal in context.
- ○ **Scope**: what the report will cover—the boundaries.
- **Project Description**: how you propose to address the topic, including
  - ○ how you will show that your project is feasible.
  - ○ the specific expected benefits.
  - ○ negative consequences of not doing as you propose.
  - ○ obstacles to your proposal, recognition of problems in achieving your goal.
  - ○ methodology: how you did your investigation; how you conducted your survey, if you have one.
- **Qualifications**: you and/or your team's qualifications/expertise to investigate this topic.
- **Resources**: what is needed to make the proposal feasible, e.g., institutional funding, access to organizational resources, a source of raw materials, and so on.
- **Projected Timeline**: a detailed timeline, probably using a Gantt chart, on how long you will need to finish the project, with timelines for each stage of the project.
- **Budget**: an itemized, detailed estimate of costs to finish the proposed project, in a table format.
- **Conclusions**: what you are proposing and why it is both feasible and desirable.
- **Recommendations**: summary of what you are proposing in bullet-list format; each list item begins with an action verb ("improve," "allow," "incorporate"). This may be included in Conclusions and therefore not as a separate section. If there is only one recommendation, then don't use bullet list format.

Back Matter (or Final Parts)

- **Appendices**: additional material, such as the questions for a survey. Appendix A would be the survey itself; Appendix B would be the data from the survey, in table format. Since this is back matter, you could switch to Roman numerals, starting with "i." However, as with the analytical report, this change of number style is optional.
- **Notes**: if the report's notes are within the body of the report, at the bottom of pages, this section is not necessary.
- **References**: works cited in one of the accepted reference formats (MLA, APA, Chicago, CSE), if you have cited resources.

Not all formal proposals or feasibility reports have this exact structure, so there is some flexibility, but most formal proposals follow this general outline.

SURVEYS

Part of a report, either informal or formal, might be a market survey or questionnaire to add empirical support to the report writers' conclusions. To elicit useful information, the questions on these surveys must be as *meaningful* and *objective* as possible.

Meaningful questions are concrete and specific and elicit concrete and specific answers. So, for example, in a survey of opinions on the marketing effectiveness of a website, is this question meaningful (i.e., concrete and specific)?

> Did you find the website reader friendly?
> Yes/No/Don't know/No opinion

This question will not make sense to someone not familiar with the idea of reader-friendliness. Better questions would be the following:

> Did you find the website's font large enough to read easily?
> Did you find the website's layout attractive?
> Did you find the website easy to navigate?
> Did you find information easy to find on this website?

Worth Consulting
The following websites have useful information on creating and conducting surveys:

https://www.qualtrics.com/blog/writing-survey-questions/

https://blog.cvent.com/events/feedback-surveys/survey-basics-types-of-surveys/

These questions will elicit more concrete and specific answers and are more meaningful and therefore more useful.

The other problem is bias in survey questions—questions that are aimed to elicit a specific answer.

For example, a phone and online survey in Victoria, BC, on public attitudes to a new sewage-treatment system began with this statement of purpose: "We are calling to ask you two quick questions because we are concerned that the CRD [Capital Regional District] sewage project will continue to flush toxic chemicals and pharmaceuticals into the ocean even after treatment."

Who would want to flush toxic chemicals into the ocean? So a question like that is aiming for the answer the surveyors want. It is a leading, biased approach.

A more objective statement might be this: "Are you concerned that, although the CRD eliminates 99 per cent of toxic chemicals and pharmaceuticals before sewage is sent into the ocean, treatment does not eliminate 100 per cent of these pollutants?"

In this case, some respondents might reasonably conclude that, because nothing in this world is perfect, 99 per cent is good enough. The second question is more objective because it is more factual and will elicit less of a knee-jerk response.

Another example of a leading question might be this: "Do you support wasteful spending by government on welfare?" Who would support *wasteful* spending on anything? Remove "wasteful" and the question becomes more objective and the responses more meaningful.

Survey questions can take many forms. They can be "yes/no" responses for relatively black-and-white questions (e.g., "Should Canada allow assisted suicide?"). That said, a yes/no option should include two other options: "don't know" and "no opinion."

These are known as "closed-ended" questions because they aim to elicit a specific answer. Another example of a closed-ended question: "Have you ever been involved in a traffic accident?"

An "open-ended" question aims for a more detailed and nuanced response, such as, "How did you feel after your accident?" "What do you think caused the accident?"

Survey questions are often asked using the Likert scale, which runs from "strongly disagree" to "strongly agree," with several gradations in between. Likert-scale surveys are often presented as statements rather than questions. Likert-scale questions are "closed-ended" because they limit the response.

For example, let's say you were doing a report on the desirability of a new natural-gas pipeline from Alberta to California, and you asked 100 randomly selected adults for their opinions on this topic. The result for a five-part Likert-scale survey might look like this:

Issue: Canada should approve a natural-gas pipeline from Alberta to California

Strongly disagree	Disagree	Neutral	Agree	Strongly agree
10	20	15	45	10

What you've created is a table, which you could put in your report. But tables are not as easy to interpret as graphs. To make a graph from this data, you would enter the numbers into a spreadsheet program such as Excel or Numbers.

Attitudes toward international pipeline					
	Strongly disagree	Disagree	Neutral	Agree	Strongly agree
Canada should approve a natural-gas pipeline from Alberta to California.	10	20	15	45	10

To turn this data into a graph (using Excel), select the cells and go to "Charts" in your spreadsheet. If you choose a column version, you will end up with a chart that looks like the one shown in Figure 18.12. (In the report, it is labelled "Figure 1.1: Attitudes toward international pipeline"; remember that you should number and add a meaningful caption to your charts and tables.)

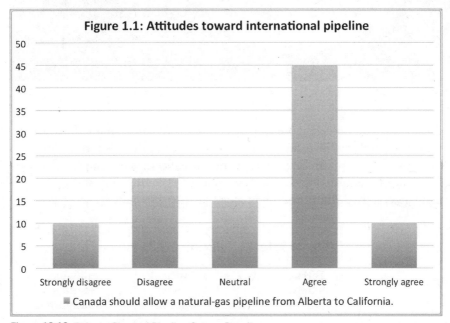

Figure 18.12 Column Chart of Pipeline Survey Results

From the graph, it's clear at a glance that more Canadians favour allowing the pipeline than are opposed.

Another possibility is a pie chart, as in Figure 18.13. Once again, at a glance it's clear that, in this imaginary survey, a majority of Canadians favour the new natural-gas pipeline.

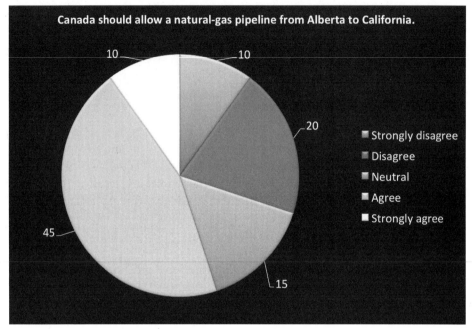

Figure 18.13 Pie Chart of Pipeline Survey Results

Let's say you want to do a more complex graph with data on more than one element, such as graphing the results of a survey comparing 100 visitors' attitudes to three (imaginary) science museums. Your specific concern is to compare the interactivity of the museum's exhibits. Your statement was: "The exhibits at this museum are highly interactive." Your data might look like this:

Table 1: Interactivity of exhibits			
	Terrapin Science Museum	Atlantic Science Museum	Midwest Science Museum
Strongly disagree	5	5	20
Disagree	5	5	40
Neutral	20	15	20
Agree	45	30	15
Strongly agree	25	45	5

Your chart would look like the one in Figure 18.14 (numbered and labelled "Figure 1.2: Interactivity of exhibits" in the report itself):

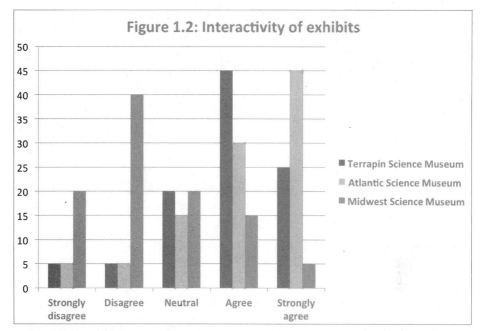

Figure 18.14 Summative Chart of the Interactivity of Exhibits at Three Science Museums

Which were the best and worst of the three museums on this criterion? Both the Terrapin Science Museum (darkest) and the Atlantic Science Museum (lightest) have many admirers, although the Atlantic Science Museum has the edge in the "strongly agree" category. Meanwhile, it's clear the Midwest Science Museum has work to do in improving the interactivity of its exhibits.

Averaging Likert Data

Even so, it's still not that easy to assess how the three science museums rank in terms of the *overall* response for each museum for this question. We can clearly see that the Midwest Science Museum fares poorly, but the other two museums appear to be neck-and-neck. The solution is to find the *Mean*, or average, for each museum's scores. Fortunately, finding the average of a Likert-scale answer is quite easy.

To find the average score for the Terrapin Science Museum, follow this formula:

1. Strongly disagree = 1 times the number of responses (5) = 5 (1x5)
2. Disagree = 2 times the number of responses (5) = 10 (2x5)
3. Neutral = 3 times the number of responses (20) = 60 (3x20)
4. Agree = 4 times the number of responses (45) = 180 (4x45)
5. Strongly agree = 5 times the number of responses = 125 (5x25)

Now add up the final figures: $5 + 10 + 60 + 180 + 125 = 380$.

Divide this total by the number of respondents (in this example, 100): 380/100 = 3.8.

The average (or mean) for the Terrapin Science Museum is 3.8 out of a possible 5.

Following the same formula, we end up with averages of 4.5 for the Atlantic Science Museum and 3.25 for the Midwest Science Museum.

To create a graph of these numbers, we input them into a spreadsheet program, as shown below:

Table 2: Average Scores for Interactivity of Exhibits

	Average score
Terrapin Science Museum	3.8
Atlantic Science Museum	4.5
Midwest Science Museum	3.25

You end up with the following graph, which shows more clearly than a Likert graph, with its five columns, how each of the museums ranks against the others on interactivity of exhibits (Figure 18.15). In this case, it's clear that the Atlantic Science Museum is the best at interactivity, the Midwest Science Museum the worst.

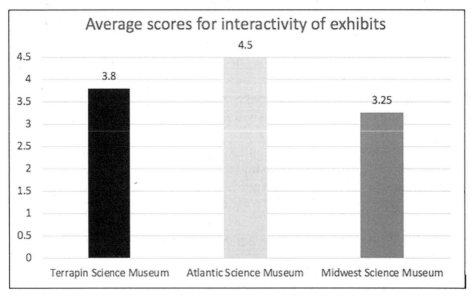

Figure 18.15 Chart Showing Average Scores for Interactivity of Exhibits at Three Science Museums

Suppose you are comparing three museums based on more than one category (say, interactivity, affordability, and completeness of exhibits) and calculated the average of each category. Can you then average these categories as well to create a total overall score for each museum? Yes, you can.

Take each museum's average score for each category, as shown in Figure 18.16, add up the three average scores for each category for each museum, and divide by the number of categories (in this case, three). You'll end up with three averaged numbers, one for each museum, which you can then put into a spreadsheet and convert to a graph that compares the three museums on their *overall* quality, based on the three criteria.

Let's say the average scores for the three criteria are as follows:

Museum	Interactivity	Affordability	Completeness	Total	Total average (/3)
Terrapin	3.8	4.2	3.1	11.1	3.7
Atlantic	4.5	2.5	4.6	11.6	3.9
Midwest	3.25	4.3	2.5	10.05	3.35

Your final comparison chart would look like this:

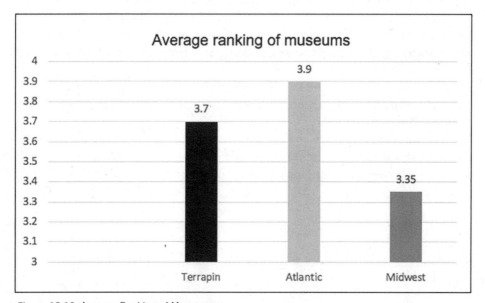

Figure 18.16 Average Ranking of Museums

Using this graph, it's clear that the Atlantic museum is considered the best museum overall by the survey sample, while the Midwest comes last.

One final point: surveys aren't perfect reflections of reality. Even though our museum survey showed that the Atlantic Museum was best of the three museums by a considerable margin, another survey with a different sample population might get a different result.

The best surveys are those that include a very large population: the larger the sample, the more likely that the survey results will be accurate, or close to accurate. National election pollsters consider a sample of 1,000–1,500 a good indicator of the national electorate's intentions. But even a large population sample might be off the mark.

For example, in the 2013 British Columbia provincial election, most BC pollsters were wrong in predicting a resounding victory for the NDP. In fact, the Liberals won by a landslide, with 49 seats to the NDP's 34. Similarly, during the 2017 mayoral election in Calgary, Alberta, surveys by polling company Mainstream Research put challenger Bill Smith consistently higher—and sometimes 9 to 17 points higher—than incumbent Naheed Nenshi. In fact, Nenshi won handily.

Because polls can fail, they include a margin of error that, typically, reads like this: "The results of this survey are accurate at a 95% confidence level [sometimes the wording is '19 times out of 20'], plus or minus 2.5 [or some other figure] percentage points."

This means that the survey is expected to be accurate within 2.5 percentage points 95 per cent of the time (i.e., 19 times out of 20). However, it's possible that a particular survey is in the errant 5 per cent and is off by more than 2.5 per cent. This is unlikely in a large survey with a 95 per cent confidence level but it's possible, which is why one should never take a poll as gospel truth. Even the best-conducted surveys can miss the mark!

In general, as we discussed in Chapter 5 on document design, when the actual numbers are important, you should use a table format. When the comparison of the numbers is important, use a graph.

Once the graphs are ready you can use them in the body of your report, both to offer data that is easy to interpret and to add colour to a page. The table on which the graph is based can go into the report as an appendix.

Exercises on Surveys and Graphs

1. You have been asked to do a survey on attitudes within your city towards an issue of importance (you choose the issue; it could be anything from parking to homelessness to basement suites). Create five concrete and specific questions, using whatever type of question you prefer (open- or closed-ended questions). Design questions to draw out the views of an imaginary sample of 100 citizens on whatever issue you select—you don't have to do an actual survey. Make up any details you need to make your scenario as realistic as possible.
2. Once you have your (imaginary) data, turn each question into a graph that illustrates the range of opinion that you found.
3. Create a graph that compares a survey population's preferences for apples, oranges, and bananas (or any three comparable objects), using a five-part Likert scale. Then produce a graph that shows the *average* score for each fruit (or whatever objects you have chosen).

MINUTES

If your career ever calls for researching and preparing a formal report, you will likely be part of a team of writers. And this means that you will be taking minutes of your meetings.

All organizations take minutes at meetings. Why? Organizations need a record of who was present at the meeting and who was absent, what was discussed, what decisions were taken, who is supposed to do what action, when, and so on. If you are part of a team that is writing a report, someone in the team will be taking minutes of all your meetings.

Minutes are, frankly, a tedious chore, but somebody has to do them. In some teams, the same person is the recording secretary for all meetings. In other teams, the recording secretary job rotates among the members.

The Agenda

A team meeting begins with an agenda, a list of what the members will discuss. The agenda is sent out to all attendees well before the meeting, so they can suggest changes or additions to what is discussed, and so they can get ready by researching the topics or preparing a presentation. An agenda might look like the one in Figure 18.17.

XYZ Corp.

FINANCE COMMITTEE MEETING
Garden Room
Monday, February 12, 2018, 5:30 PM

AGENDA

I.   Call to order

II. Approval of Agenda

III. Minutes

    a. Approval of Minutes of January 14, 2018

    b. Items Arising from Minutes (if any).

IV. Treasurer's Report

V.   Director's Report

VI. Other business

    a. Corporate reorganization for expansion

    b. Date for annual general meeting

    c. Candidates for finance committee

    d. Date of next committee meeting.

VII. New business

VIII. Adjournment

Figure 18.17 A Meeting Agenda

Minute Formats

There are many templates online for writing up minutes, but they all follow roughly this format:

- **A letterhead or heading** for the organization the group works for
- **Date and place of the meeting**
- **Time the meeting is to begin**
- **Attendance**
  - **Members present**: If a member is present but arrived late, then record the time that person arrived: "Kendra Subash (5:45)." Similarly, if a person leaves before the meeting is over, mark the time he or she left. Also, indicate who was chairing the meeting: "Sam Malkin (chair)." You could also give the titles of the other chief officers at the meeting: e.g., "Jerry Preston (treasurer)."
  - **Absent**: Those who didn't make the meeting and didn't let anyone know they were not attending.
  - **Regrets** or **Excused** (sometimes included in minutes): Members who have let the group know in advance they can't make the meeting.
- **Recording secretary** (the minute-taker's name)
- **Time the meeting began** ("Call to order"): This may not be the same time as was scheduled.
- **Approval of the agenda**: At this stage, with the approval of the group, agenda items can be added.
- **Approval of the minutes from the previous meeting**: The previous minutes should have been sent to all members several days before the meeting. This is an opportunity to fix possible errors in the previous minutes.
- **Reports from group members**, such as the treasurer's or executive director's report
- **Other business**
- **New business**
- **Adjournment**, including time of adjournment

Minutes can be in a bulleted or numbered format or in paragraphs. The example given in this chapter follows a numbered outline format.

Minutes are usually written using full, grammatically correct sentences. They can be in past tense ("Sam moved that...."), which is most common, or present tense ("Sam moves that...."). Depending on the formality of the meeting, the minutes will use full names (Sam Malkin) or first names (Sam).

Worth knowing
Meetings are run according to Robert's Rules of Order. A summary of Robert's Rules is available at http://www.robertsrules.org/

XYZ Corp.

FINANCE COMMITTEE MEETING MINUTES
Garden Room
Monday, February 12, 2018, 5:30 pm

AGENDA

I. **Call to order: 5:30 pm**
    a. **Present**: Sam Malkin (chair), Jerry Preston (treasurer), Jane Chan, Kendra Subash (5:45), Terry Singh (recording secretary)
    b. **Absent**: Petra Ouspenksy
    c. **Recording Secretary**: Terry Singh
    d. Kelly d'Sousa (company lawyer, non-voting member)

II. **Approval of Agenda**: Kendra moved, seconded by Terry. Passed unanimously.

III. **Previous Minutes**
    a. Approval of minutes of last meeting. Sam moved, seconded by Jerry. Passed unanimously.
    b. Items arising from Minutes (if any): None.

IV. **Treasurer's report** (Jerry)
    a. Jerry reported that the financials were in good shape. He distributed copies of the most recent budget,
    b. The company plans to invest $30,000 in new desktop computers.
    c. The year-end budget will be ready for the next meeting.
    d. Vote to accept treasurer's report: Sam moved, Kendra seconded. Passed (Terry abstains).

V. **Director's report (Sam)**
    a. Sam reported that the development of the Richmond location office is proceeding smoothly and that the company's discussions about a merger with TerraCorp are in the final stages.
    b. Discussions about increases in staff compensation are proceeding well. Jane moved that office staff receive a 2% pay increase. Seconded by Jerry. Jerry said the company could afford the increase. Passed (Terry and Kendra opposed).

VI. **Other business**
    a. **Corporate reorganization for expansion (Kelly)**
        i. Kelly presented the company's plans for corporate reorganization.
        ii. Sam noted that these plans are moving slowly due to slow economic growth in the 1st and 2nd quarters.

Figure 18.18 Example of Minutes in a Numbered Outline Format

iii. Jerry suggested switching banks to get a higher rate of interest on the company's liquid assets.

iv. Sam said this is a good idea.

v. Jerry moved that the liquid cash be moved to TD Bank from ScotiaBank. Seconded by Sam. No discussion. Passed (Terry abstains, Jane votes no).

b. Date for annual general meeting (Jane)

i. Jane reported that Tuesday, June 26, would be a good date for the company's AGM as a room at the convention centre is available for that date.

ii. Sam suggested the time of the meeting be moved from 5 pm to 6 pm to allow more time to attend for those working until 5. All present agreed.

iii. Kendra asked Jerry if the full budget will be available for that date. Jerry said yes.

iv. Moved by Sam that the AGM be set for Tuesday, June 26, 6 pm. Seconded by Terry. Passed unanimously.

c. Candidate for finance committee

i. Jerry suggested that Kelly be made a full member of the finance committee. He explained that negotiations surrounding the merger with TerraCorp need a lawyer, and Kelly's expertise would be a valuable asset. Sam moved that Kelly be made a member of the finance committee. Seconded by Jane. Passed unanimously.

d. Date of next committee meeting

i. Sam suggested the committee meet in one month, Monday, March 12, at 5:30 pm. He noted that the committee might have to meet every two weeks after that to prepare the budget for the AGM.

ii. Jane wondered if the next meeting should also be in two weeks. Jerry suggested the financials are in good enough shape that a month to the next meeting would not cause a problem.

iii. Sam moved that the next meeting be Monday, March 12. Seconded by Kendra. Passed unanimously.

VII.   New business

a. There was no new business.

VIII.   Adjournment

a. Sam moved that the meeting be adjourned. Passed unanimously. Meeting ended at 6:45 pm.

Minutes should be as brief as possible while still capturing all the important decisions made at the meeting and the gist of the discussion that led up to these decisions.

Most word-processing programs include built-in templates for minutes, and the Internet offers a wealth of examples of minutes in many different formats. Figure 18.18 provides an example of minutes in a numbered outline format.

Another useful way of structuring the action parts of your minutes is

- topic,
- discussion,
- decision, and
- action (what action, who is to do it, and when it should be complete).

Sometimes, the last item (action) is copied into a separate document called an action list, and this list is distributed to members as a reminder of upcoming responsibilities.

Once the minutes are written and edited, they should be distributed to all members of the group.

CONCLUSION

A formal report is formal—that is, it has a more formal style of writing (although it's still in clear, plain English) and structure than most business and professional writing. For example, a formal report doesn't use contractions (e.g., do not use "doesn't"—use "does not"). Sentences and paragraphs are shorter than in academic writing but a bit longer and more polished than in most business and professional writing.

Report formats vary somewhat with an organization's style, but a common structure is the following:[1]

1) Front matter or preliminary parts (with pages in Roman numerals)

a) **Cover page** (optional): no page number
b) **Title page**: page i, but page number is not printed
c) *Letter of Authorization* or *Memo of Authorization* (if the report was commissioned): page ii, page number printed
d) *Letter of Transmittal* or *Memo of Transmittal* (always): usually page iii, page number printed

---

1   In this list, the names of the parts of a formal report that should be headings in your report are in title case and italics.

e) **Table of Contents** (you do not need to list the TOC in the table of contents): usually page iv, with the page number printed

f) **List of Figures** and **List of Tables** (also called "Table of Figures" and "Table of Tables"): usually page v, page number printed

g) **Executive Summary**: usually page vi, page number printed.

2) Body (with pages in Arabic numerals)

a) **Introduction**: page one, usually with a printed page number ("1") depending on style

b) **Background** (for a long report): page number printed

c) **Mode of Analysis** or **Methodology**: page number printed

d) **Data and analysis**: page number printed

e) **Conclusions**: page number printed

f) **Recommendations**: page number printed.

3) Back matter (with pages in Arabic or Roman numerals depending on style)
Note: If Arabic numerals are used, continue the page numbering from the body of the report. If Roman numerals are used, start the numbering from "i."

a) **Appendices** (labelled, for example, "Appendix A"): pages numbered

b) **Notes**: pages numbered

c) **Reference list** (with parenthetical citations, use the title "Works Cited" or "References," depending on the documentation style chosen; with footnotes, a section entitled "Bibliography" is optional): pages numbered.

Not all reports have surveys, but a basic knowledge of how to create a survey can be useful in many situations. Finally, if your report is being written by a team, you will be taking minutes, so you should know how to do this.

Below is a formal report checklist, several discussion questions, and a report-writing exercise. In the next two chapters you will find examples of "A+"-worthy formal reports—a formal proposal and an analytical report—by two student teams.

FORMAL REPORT CHECKLIST

- ❑ Report has all the essential elements of a formal report (e.g., front parts, body, final parts, letter of authorization, executive summary).
- ❑ All sections are written in a consistent style (an issue if this is a team report).
- ❑ Report uses 11- to 12-point body font, with headings that are larger than the body font (14–18 point).
- ❑ Title page has an interesting title, prepared for (or submitted to) and prepared by (or submitted by) information, and the date the report was delivered in full date format (December 9, 2018).
- ❑ Headings clearly label each section in descending order of size (that is, large headings for main sections, smaller headings for subsections, etc.).
- ❑ Headings stand out from the body text because of their size, font type, and sometimes colour.
- ❑ Headings do not appear at the bottom of a page without at least two or three lines of text under them (do not "stack" headings).
- ❑ One heading does not follow another with no text in between.
- ❑ All lists are introduced with a sentence or partial sentence and are punctuated correctly (see Chapter 5 on bulleted and numbered lists).
- ❑ Pages are correctly numbered and in the appropriate style for the section (Roman or Arabic numerals).
- ❑ Conclusions are concrete and specific.
- ❑ Recommendations are concrete and specific, in bulleted list format introduced by a sentence or partial sentence, and with each list item beginning with an action verb (e.g., buy, create, take).
- ❑ All graphics, pictures, charts, and tables are pointed to in the text (e.g., see Figure 5, see Table 3).
- ❑ All graphics, pictures, charts, and tables are clearly labelled with captions (Figure 5: Waiting Room in Terrapin Hospital).
- ❑ All pages are attractive, with white space, lists, pictures, graphs, or whatever is appropriate to achieve the report's purpose and to enhance reader-friendliness.
- ❑ Writing style is more formal than that used in most business and professional communication, but prose still is plain English (follows the seven Cs).
- ❑ Paragraphs and sentences are longer than in most professional writing, but not as long as in academic writing.
- ❑ Writing does not use contractions (use "do not" rather than "don't").
- ❑ Report is carefully edited and proofread.
- ❑ Writing is grammatically perfect.

DISCUSSION QUESTIONS

1. What is the writing style of a formal report?
2. What are the three parts of a formal report?
3. What is the letter of authorization? What information does it contain?
4. What is the letter of transmittal? What information does it contain?
5. What is the executive summary?
6. What is the difference between the direct and indirect report formats?
7. What differences are there between a report's conclusions and its recommendations?
8. What sorts of information go into the appendices?

Exercise 1: A Formal Proposal Report

The Campus Committee on Sustainability (CCS) of your university or college has sent out a Request for Proposal for a report of about 12–15 pages to improve the university's eco-friendliness by reducing energy use, curbing carbon emissions, or just generally any project that would make the campus more eco-friendly.

In teams of two, three, or four, your mission is to come up with a proposal idea, research the topic to determine if it is feasible or not (it's acceptable to conclude that the project you propose is not feasible), and then write the proposal. If further research is required to ensure feasibility, then you should include that information as well.

Note that, for the purposes of this assignment, your topic may be imaginary (e.g., building a dome over the campus). However, you should write the report as if the proposal is feasible, making up whatever details you need to make your proposal seem realistic.

Your proposal should follow the structure for this type of report as explained in the section on Formal Proposals above (you'll find additional information on informal proposals in Chapter 17). You should also create an imaginary survey (that is, you don't have to do actual interviews, although you can if you wish) of not more than 5–10 questions to see whether there is a market or audience for your idea.

For example, in the sample formal proposal report in Chapter 19, the report authors have proposed a bike-sharing plan for their campus. As part of their formal proposal, the authors have created an (imaginary) survey of students to determine whether there is a demand for bike-sharing. You should use charts from this survey in the body of your report. The survey questions should be in Appendix A, the data (in table format) in Appendix B, as with the analytical report.

Exercise 2: An Analytical Report

You are a company that specializes in designing websites. In teams of three or four, write a formal report of no more than 22 pages following the report format and writing style we've discussed.

Subject of your report: you have been commissioned to analyze two or three websites based on one of the following three scenarios.

1. Give suggestions for the design of a *new* website for an organization of your choosing, based on two (if you are working in teams of three) or three (if teams of four) websites in the same line of work as the website you have been asked to design. That is, the new website will be a combination of the two or three sites, picking the best features of each. For example, you could design a website for a new junior hockey team based on the best elements of the websites of two or three other junior hockey teams.
2. Pick two or three websites (depending on the size of your team) to cite as references in a brochure for a hospital that is promoting a new procedure of your choosing (e.g., heart transplants, knee replacements, or laparoscopic surgery) and wants to offer helpful and reassuring information for potential patients.
3. Choose the winner out of two or three websites (depending on the size of your team) for an award as best website for that year in an industry of your choosing.

The maximum 22 pages will thus consist of six pages of front matter; no more than two pages of introduction and background; perhaps one page for a "Mode of Analysis" section (if brief, this could be part of the introduction); an "Analysis" section of no more than two pages for each website (two or three websites depending on the size of the team), including all graphics and pictures; one or two pages for conclusions, and one page for recommendations. So far that's about 16–18 pages: six pages for the front matter, ten to twelve pages for the body of the report (assuming three websites at two pages each), plus three or four pages for back matter (e.g., appendices).

You will analyze each website based on three major criteria of your choosing (e.g., reliable content, attractive presentation, ease of navigation).

As part of the exercise, design an imaginary survey (you don't have to actually interview anyone, although you could) with concrete and specific questions to support your analysis. You should not have more than ten questions; five or six would be adequate. Put your questions into "Appendix A" and your raw survey numbers in "Appendix B." Use the survey, in the form of tables and graphs, in the body of your report to support your conclusions.

As your subject matter, you can choose any industry: sports websites, business websites, government websites, university websites—you have a wide choice. The only limit is that the websites must be in the same industry—you can't compare museum websites with hockey websites. Other than that, you are free to make up any details you need to make your report more realistic.

Chapter 19
Formal Proposal Report Example

This chapter has an example of an analytical formal proposal report from a student project. It is based on the scenario from Exercise 1 at the end of Chapter 18.

University of Terrapin

Bike-Sharing Proposal:
Eco-Friendly Transport at Terrapin University

Prepared for:

Terrapin University Committee on Sustainability (TUCS)

Prepared by:

John Chen, Carol Bronski, and Alvin Schmidt
Engineering students

June 29, 2018

Faculty of Engineering

Memo

To: Jillian Howard, Chair, Terrapin University Committee on Sustainability
From: John Chen, Carol Bronski, and Alvin Schmidt, students, Faculty of Engineering
Date: June 29, 2018
Subject: Feasibility Report: Terrapin Student Bike-Sharing

This document is in response to a request for proposals by Terrapin University's Committee on Sustainability (TUCS) on ways to increase environmental sustainability on campus. This report contains a thorough feasibility analysis of a bike-sharing program based at Terrapin University. The proposed service will not only lessen the environmental impact of the university by reducing carbon emissions, but also provide many City of Terrapin residents as well as students with an eco-friendly, healthy, and affordable method of transportation.

From our research, we have determined that the Terrapin bike-sharing program will cost $752,600 for the first year. This total cost includes estimates for

- bike-storage facility construction (including quotes for construction permits),
- wholesale bike and helmet purchases,
- mobile application development, and·
- advertising costs.

In closing, we would like to thank the Committee for looking at our research proposal. We hope that our analysis addresses all concerns, and recommend that the Committee implement a bike-sharing program at the University of Terrapin.

Table of Contents

List of Figures

List of Tables

Executive Summary

In response to a Request for Proposals by Terrapin University's Committee on Sustainability (TUCS), this report investigates the feasibility of a bicycle-sharing and/or bicycle-rental program for Terrapin University and the surrounding City of Terrapin. We hope that the proposed program will not only reduce greenhouse-gas emissions in Terrapin but also provide a healthier, greener commuting alternative.

Through a survey of student commuters, we have discovered a significant demand for a bike-sharing service among students, with nearly 40 per cent of respondents interested in participating. To meet this initial demand, we estimate the program will require at least 1,000 bicycles at the outset. We have investigated the initial costs of the program, including

- 1,000 bicycles and helmets,
- four storage facilities, including one on-campus and three off-campus,
- a companion mobile application, and
- local advertising.

The report further discusses the results of the student survey while providing an analysis of Terrapin's current bicycle accommodations and student population density. From this data, we have confirmed the feasibility of a bike-sharing program and found the best locations for constructing storage and rental facilities.

In total, we estimate the university's initial investment to be approximately $752,600. However, with rental fees we expect this investment to be recouped within five years of the program's implementation. As the program grows, we expect revenue to increase each year, ultimately yielding a profit for the University of Terrapin, which can be invested in further sustainability projects for the university.

Introduction

In response to a Request for Proposals by Terrapin University's Committee on Sustainability (TUCS), this report aims to determine the feasibility of a university-based bicycle-sharing program that might eventually include the surrounding city. By considering student interest, costs, and environmental impact, our analysis hopes to determine if local bike-sharing would be

- useful,
- environmentally sustainable, and
- profitable for the university.

Background

In 2018, over 3,000 cars drove to Terrapin campus each day [1]. By encouraging University of Terrapin students, staff, and City of Terrapin residents to participate in bike-sharing, the university can expect to significantly lower greenhouse gas pollution in the region. According to Statistics Canada, transportation accounts for 27 per cent of all greenhouse gas emissions in this country [2]. Since greenhouse gases "are the most significant driver of observed climate change" [3], reducing these emissions must be a primary goal in increasing environmental sustainability.

A well-implemented bike-sharing program would give campus and city residents an incentive to bike for the improvement of personal health, fitness, and the environment. With fewer cars parked on campus, the considerable space now used for parking lots could be transformed into gardens, athletic facilities, and/or additional housing.

Projected Plan

Overall, there are four main components to the proposal.

First, we will need to construct at least three bike storage facilities within the City of Terrapin, plus a major storage centre on the

Figure 1: Terrapin University clock tower

Terrapin campus. We would build our satellite facilities in areas of the city where student population densities are high. This will ensure that bikes are more easily accessible to a greater number of people.

1

Second, we need to stock our storage facilities with bicycles and helmets. From our preliminary feasibility research, we can estimate the minimum number of bikes to buy from a national distributor to satisfy an initial number of customers.

Then, to maximize the awareness of our bike-sharing program, we will need to advertise. This new transportation initiative should be presented as a viable option for students and residents of Terrapin. We hope to target potential cyclists with advertisements in local newspapers and the campus newspaper *The Tortoise*, on Terrapin Transit buses, on billboards in the region, and on local websites.

Finally, our bike-sharing program would use a mobile application to connect cyclists to bikes available near them. This application will be focussed on allowing customers to

- reserve bikes,
- locate nearby storage facilities,
- unlock bikes in storage facilities, and
- review account and rental history details.

Analysis

The following section analyzes the data collected during our research. Feasibility will be determined by

- surveying the student body to gauge interest,
- analyzing Terrapin University's student population density and landscape,
- obtaining permits from city planners to construct storage facilities off campus, and
- obtaining quotes for mobile application development, bike-storage facility construction, wholesale bike and helmet purchases, and one year of advertising costs.

This research will provide insight into the expected costs of operating a bike-sharing program.

Student Survey

To determine student demand for an extensive bike-sharing program, we designed and conducted a university-wide survey of students, faculty, and staff distributed through campus email. Our survey consisted of nine questions designed to evaluate the current state of campus commuting and whether a bike-sharing program would be a desirable solution to increase campus sustainability. Copies of the survey and its results can be found in Appendices A and B, respectively.

We received 384 replies, a response rate of 35 per cent. We will discuss and analyze some of our findings below. We believe our results accurately reflect the opinions of the majority of students, faculty, and staff.

Student Transportation

To begin, we will discuss the modes of transportation students currently use to get to school. As Figure 2 shows, nearly a third of surveyed students drive to school in a car; in contrast, only nine per cent of students currently ride bicycles to school.

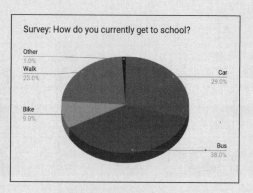

Figure 2: Student transportation methods

Although the percentage of student cyclists was low, when asked how far they live from Terrapin, over 75 per cent of students indicated that they live fewer than ten kilometres away, or within a reasonable biking distance. Clearly, more students could be biking to school, and we hope to change this with an affordable and accessible program.

3

Furthermore, asked why they do not currently bike to school, 38 per cent of respondents answered because they do not own a bicycle. This suggests that the up-front cost of a bicycle is one factor keeping many students from riding to school.

Cost and Demand

As shown in Figure 3, our survey results suggest that potential demand for a bike-sharing program is high, with nearly 40 per cent of students interested in participating in the program in some form.

In addition, Figure 4 shows that students overwhelmingly believe that a bike-sharing program would improve the environmental sustainability of the university. We believe this outlook will add to Terrapin's green image, further driving interest in the program.

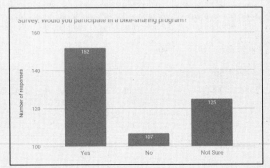

Figure 3: Expected participation rates

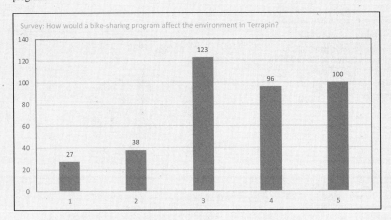

Figure 4: Student opinion on environmental effects of bike-sharing
(1 indicates no effect; 5 indicates a very positive effect).

4

Asked how much they would be willing to pay for the program, most students (32 per cent) preferred the lowest-cost option of $20 per term (see Figure 5). However, students were torn between potential payment methods. Since a sizeable proportion of respondents showed interest in a student-fee-funded program, we think including bike-sharing in student fees, with an opt-out option for non-cyclists, would best spread the cost across the student population and allow us to charge students less per term.

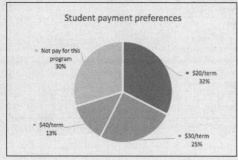

Figure 5: Student payment preferences

Another approach would give students an option between the current mandatory bus pass and proposed bike pass. This way, students satisfied with the services provided by Terrapin Transit will have another transportation option.

We also plan to offer our bike-sharing services to non-student Terrapin residents and visitors. Payment methods for non-students will differ, but we plan to make subscription plans and daily bike loans available for purchase online and at our storage facilities. Non-student participants will enjoy all of the benefits of our program, though non-student rates will be higher to help offset reduced student rates.

Revenue

Based on student interest, if an opt-out student-fee program is implemented, we expect at most 50 per cent of students to voluntarily opt out of the program. Under this assumption, we would charge $30 per term to participate, yielding a revenue of approximately $300,000 per term. Taking into account the slow summer term, we expect the first year of the program to yield $650,000 from student fees alone.

Furthermore, we expect revenue from non-student participants over the course of the first year to yield an additional $150,000. In total, then, the program is expected to generate $800,000 of revenue in its first year.

Storage and Rental Facilities

Ideally, we hope to build storage and rental facilities at three locations in the City of Terrapin: at Memorial Park, at the Midtown Mall, and the Old Town business district (see Figure 6).

5

Initial research into construction costs has yielded a price of $50,000 per facility for all labour, equipment, and supplies, or $150,000. At minimum, these satellite facilities should be 334 square metres.

Additionally, a facility would be constructed on the Terrapin campus. This storage centre would be larger (400 square metres) to accommodate broken bicycles for maintenance. The construction costs of the larger on-campus facility would be $75,000, for a total of $225,000.

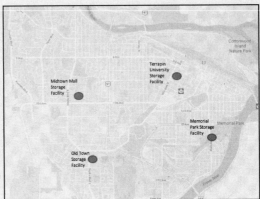

Figure 6: Map of storage facility locations

Purchasing Bikes and Helmets

To maximize our budget, we will need to bulk-purchase road bikes and helmets from a national distributor. Based on the results of our survey, we estimate that the program will require approximately 1,000 bikes to meet initial demand. This estimate assumes a 15–20 per cent student participation rate at the start of the bike-sharing program. As the program grows, we hope to provide bikes to more students and to surrounding campus-area residents.

We have discussed the costs with one company, ACS Distributing [4]. At wholesale rates of $300 per bicycle and $40 per helmet, the initial budget for populating storage facilities with equipment from ACSD would be $340,000.

Terrapin Bike Routes

Cyclist accommodation in Terrapin, as shown in Figure 7 below, is already quite advanced. Many roads (shown with dotted lines) are equipped with bicycle lanes and shoulder bikeways so that cycling is easy and safe. We can also see from Figure 7 that advanced bike routes are well-distributed around the four main regional growth centres (shaded ovals), and civic buildings, which provide people with numerous biking opportunities.

Building bike-sharing facilities in these well-populated areas and growth centres will be very convenient for Terrapin residents. By distributing bicycles in popular zones like Midtown Mall, Terrapin campus, Old Town, and Memorial Park, we can form a large cycling network for fast bicycle transportation.

One of the difficulties of cycling in Terrapin is that some routes have steep inclines. Luckily, the main arterial roads are mostly level, and only a few major streets are difficult to climb. Most roads have only occasional hills and can be climbed easily. Furthermore, one helpful function of our companion mobile application, which will be described below, will be to find the route that avoids too many steep hills.

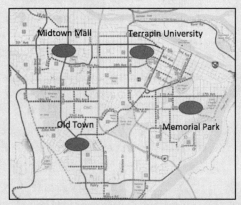

Figure 7: City of Terrapin regional growth areas (shaded ovals). [5] Dotted lines indicate streets with bicycle lanes.

Population Density Analysis

According to a survey conducted by the Terrapin Student Society [6], three major student population centres in Terrapin are the Midtown Mall area, the Old Town, and the neighbourhood bordering Memorial Park. These areas also coincide with some of the regional growth centres seen in Figure 7.

As mentioned above, to best distribute bicycles across the student population of Terrapin, we will build three off-campus bike-sharing and storage facilities near these locations. The first will be built at the Midtown Mall, the second at Old Town, and the third at Memorial Park. We have already spoken with representatives of these locations and have agreed that construction may begin once our proposal has been accepted. In total, property leasing for these locations will cost $8,000 per month.

Advertising

By raising awareness of our proposed service, we hope to promote Terrapin's commitment to an environmentally stable future. Appropriate advertisements can help to persuade residents considering alternative commuting methods. Therefore, we plan to cooperate with Lamar Advertising [8]. An initial set of quotes from Lamar indicates that advertising costs will be as follows:

- Local newspapers: $1,000/month.
- Terrapin Transit (buses and bus stops): $1,500/month.
- Memorial Highway billboards: $2,000/month.

7

Official Website

We plan to develop an official website to provide information on our bike storage locations, rental rates, and a link to our mobile application on various mobile platforms (see Figures 8 and 9).

The official website will be synchronized with the phone application. For example, customers will log into their bike-sharing account through the official website to check their account balances, transaction details, and other functions that are also available in the mobile application. We will then advertise links to our official website on local websites, such as Terrapin Gazette, City of Terrapin, Terrapin University, and Used.ca to direct more traffic to the website and raise awareness of the program.

Mobile Application Development

To develop a mobile application, we will cooperate with local start-up tech company MobiFy [7]. From initial quotes, we expect development to cost $10,000, with an additional $500 for monthly maintenance.

The mobile application should automatically update user information and provide a running count of the available bikes in storage facilities (Figures 8 and 9). Using the application, users should be able to

- locate the nearest available rental facilities,
- find the easiest routes to help avoid hills as much as possible,
- check out trip details,
- unlock bicycles by scanning QR codes or with NFC tap,
- view user account details and balance, and pay for rentals, and
- reserve bikes and helmets ahead of time.

Figure 8: Bike-sharing mobile app log-in page

Figure 9: Bike-sharing mobile app home page

MobiFy predicts a beta version of the application can be ready after two months of development.

8

Projected Budget

Table 1 outlines the initial expected costs of a bike-sharing project.

Table 1: Terrapin bike-sharing project budget for one year of services.

ITEM	TOTAL COST
Bicycles	
Purchase (1000 × $300/bicycle)	$300,000.00
Helmets	
Purchase (1000 × $40/helmet)	$40,000.00
Storage Facilities	
Construction (3 × $50,000)	$150,000.00
Construction (1 × $75,000)	$75,000.00
Property lease (12 × $8,000)	$96,000.00
Mobile Application	
Development	$10,000.00
Maintenance (12 × $500/month)	$6,000.00
Advertising (for one year)	
Terrapin Transit (12 × $1,500/month)	$18,000.00
Local newspaper (12 × $1,000/month)	$12,000.00
Memorial Hwy. billboards (12 × $2,000/month)	$24,000.00
Official website (12 × $1,800/month)	$21,600.00
	Total: $752,600.00

Conclusions

In response to a Request for Proposals from Terrapin University's Committee on Sustainability, our proposed bike-sharing program aims to provide an alternative method of travel for students and alleviate the environmental impact of greenhouse gas emissions in Terrapin. This report researches the feasibility of such a bike-sharing program through a student survey and cost analysis.

From the results of the student survey, we discovered that 41 per cent of respondents are interested in a Terrapin bike-sharing program. However, 30 per cent of respondents would not want to pay for this program, while remaining students would accept a $20 to $40 opt-in or opt-out fee per term.

Extrapolating the survey results across the student population, we expect 1,000 bikes and helmets will be needed to initially satisfy the student population. Considering that the program needs a large number of bikes, three 334-square-metre storage and rental facilities should be built in high-density student-population areas so that students can pick up and return bikes.

Figure 10: Bike-sharing stand ready for cyclists

The expected construction costs for these three centres is $150,000. Additionally, one facility should be built on campus to store extra bikes and for repairs, at a cost of $75,000.

Our research into student population distribution revealed that the three satellite facilities should be built near Midtown Mall, in Old Town, and adjacent to Memorial Park. Combined, the property lease for these three locations totals $8,000.

In addition, MobiFy, a local mobile-tech company, has provided a quote of $10,000 to develop a Terrapin bike-sharing phone application. This system will allow customers to rent and reserve bikes, view and manipulate trip details, and find nearby bike-storage facilities.

To spread awareness of this new service, Lamar Advertising provided a quote of $75,600 per year to advertise through local newspapers, Terrapin Transit buses and bus stops, Memorial Highway billboards, and local websites.

Finally, a Terrapin bike-sharing and rental service that sticks to the projected budget can be expected to be profitable after five years. Conservatively, we predict that the program will generate $300,000 after its first year. This estimate accounts for a 50 per cent student opt-out rate.

Recommendations

We recommend the following to the Committee:

- implement the proposed bike-sharing program as a cost-effective solution for better environmental sustainability
- construct four storage and rental facilities in Terrapin
- develop a companion mobile application that provides information such as user account information and the availability of nearby bicycles
- advertise this program in local media to introduce the system to students and residents.

Appendix A: Survey

This survey will ask you to consider your methods of travel in the City of Terrapin. Additionally, you will be asked to provide feedback about a Terrapin University-run bike-sharing program. Your answers will help to improve this program for the benefit of University of Terrapin students as well as faculty, staff, and residents of Terrapin.

EXPECTED TIME TO COMPLETE: 5–10 minutes

Q1: How far from Terrapin do you live?
  ○ Less than 2 km   ○ 2–5 km   ○ 5–10 km   ○ More than 10 km

Q2: How do you currently get to school?
  ○ Car   ○ Bus   ○ Bike   ○ Walk   ○ Other

Q3: Why don't you bike to school?
  ○ I do
  ○ I don't have a bike
  ○ Driving is more convenient
  ○ Busing is more convenient
  ○ Walking is more convenient
  ○ I live too far away

Q4: How would you rate Terrapin's bus system?
  ○ Very good   ○ Good   ○ Satisfactory   ○ Poor

Q5: What is your opinion of cycling accommodations in Terrapin?
  ○ Very good   ○ Good   ○ Satisfactory   ○ Poor

Q6: How do you think a bike-sharing program will affect the environment in Terrapin?
  (very positive)   ○ 5   ○ 4   ○ 3   ○ 2   ○ 1   (no effect)

Q7: Would you participate in a bike-sharing program?
  ○ Yes   ○ No   ○ Not sure

Q8: What is the most you would be willing to pay for such a program?
  ○ $20/term   ○ $30/term   ○ $40/term   ○ I would not pay for this program

Q9: If bike-sharing was available at University of Terrapin, how would you like it to be paid for? (If you answered Q8)
  ○ Included in student fees [opt-in]
  ○ Included in student fees [opt-out] (similar to the bus pass program, but not mandatory)
  ○ Separate from student fees (purchase a bike pass online or at school)

Appendix B: Survey Results

The number of people surveyed: 384

Q1.

Distance from Terrapin	Less than 2 km	2–5 km	5–10 km	More than 10 km
Quantity	153	106	76	49

Q2.

Transportation methods	Car	Bus	Bike	Walk	Other
Quantity	111	146	35	88	4

Q3.

Why don't you bike?	I do	Don't have bike	Driving is convenient	Busing is convenient	Living close so that walking is easier	Living too far away
Quantity	35	146	38	54	33	78

Q4.

Bus system rating	Very Good	Good	Satisfactory	Poor
Quantity	77	162	105	40

Q5.

Terrapin cycling accommodations	Very Good	Good	Satisfactory	Poor
Quantity	134	153	60	37

Q6.

Environmental impact	5 (very positive)	4	3	2	1 (no effect)
Quantity	100	96	123	38	27

13

Q7.

Participation rate	Yes	No	Not sure
Quantity	152	107	125

Q8.

Cost	$20 per term	$30 per term	$40 per term	Not pay for this program
Quantity	124	97	49	114

Q9.

Payment methods	Included in student fees [opt-in]	Included in student fees [opt-out]	Separate from student fees
Quantity	103	82	75

References

[1]   Bunt & Associates, "2016 Campus Traffic Survey University of Terrapin," Jan. 10, 2017. Available at: https://www.Terrapin.ca/sustainability/assets/docs/reports/campus-traffic-survey-2016.pdf [Accessed: June 19, 2018].

[2]   Statistics Canada, "Greenhouse Gas Emissions from Private Vehicles in Canada," April 2017. Available at: https://www150.statcan.gc.ca/n1/pub/16-001-m/2010012/part-partie1-eng.htm [Accessed: May 29, 2018].

[3]   Statistics Canada, "Climate Change Indicators: Greenhouse Gases," June 2016. Available at: https://www.epa.gov/climate-indicators/greenhouse-gases [Accessed: May 29, 2018].

[4]   ACS Distributing, "Bike Sales." Available at: http://acsdistributing.com/ [Accessed: June 22, 2018].

[5]   Jessie Abraham, "Terrapin Bike-Share Program Planning and Design," Nov. 30, 2017. Available at: http://www.terrapinbike.com/assets/Departments/Sustainability/Documents/441%20Bike%20Share%20Program%20Report.pdf [Accessed: June 1, 2018].

[6]   Terrapin Student Society, "Major Student Population Centres." Available at: http://www.utss.ca/student/survey [Accessed: June 28, 2018].

[7]   MobiFy. "Mobile Application Development." Available at: https://www.mobify.com/platform/progressive-web-apps/ [Accessed: June 26, 2018].

[8]   Lamar Advertising, "Start Your Advertising Campaign," Oct. 2016. Available at: http://www.lamar.com/BCCinternational/ [Accessed: June 26, 2018].

Chapter 20
Formal Report Example

This chapter has an example of an analytical formal report from a student project based on the scenario from Exercise 2 at the end of Chapter 18.

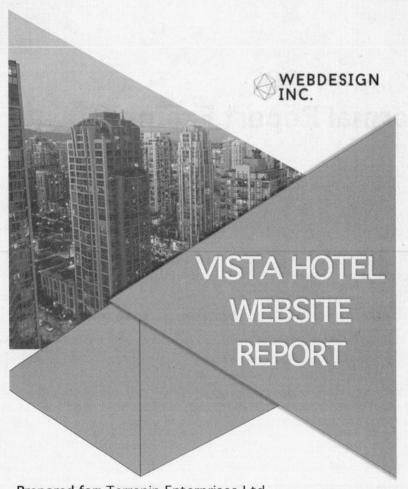

WEBDESIGN INC.

VISTA HOTEL WEBSITE REPORT

Prepared for: Terrapin Enterprises Ltd.

Prepared by: Web Design Inc.   June 30, 2018

Terrapin Enterprises

8476 Pineapple Street
Terrapin, BC V8P 2G8

April 15, 2018

Bruce Wayne
President
Web Design Inc.
4398 Yonge Street
Toronto, ON M9R 1Y4

Dear Mr. Wayne:

Subject: Hotel website report commission

Because of the success of our restaurant, the Silver Fork, Terrapin Enterprises Ltd. has decided
to open a neighbouring upscale hotel, The Vista. We would like to develop a user-friendly and
eye-catching website for our guests. The website would include pictures of rooms and amenities,
booking options, deals, and general information about the hotel.

We are asking your firm to analyze two existing hotel websites to guide the creation of The Vista
Hotel's site. The two hotels analyzed should range from midscale to upscale. In addition to the
analysis, we would like recommendations on specific features to include in our website.

We would like to create the website by November 1, 2018, one month before our grand opening.
To ensure we have time to construct the website and implement your recommendations, we
would like to receive your report by June 30, 2018.

We look forward to receiving your analysis. If you have any questions, please contact our
marketing director Mark Baron at mark.baron@vista.com.

Yours sincerely,

Tom Phillips

Tom Phillips
President

TP/jr

WEBDESIGN
INC

4398 Yonge Street
Toronto, ON M9R 1Y4

June 28, 2018

Tom Phillips
President
Terrapin Enterprises Ltd.
8476 Pineapple Street
Terrapin, BC V8P 2G8

Dear Mr. Phillips:

Subject: Hotel website report completed

We are pleased to present the hotel website report that you requested in your letter of April 15. The report analyzes the webpages of the Aurora Hotels and Grand Rialto Hotels and provides recommendations to help develop The Vista Hotel website.

We chose to analyze the two websites based on their visual appeal, strong content, and ease of navigation. Based on our analysis and results of a public survey, we have recommended that The Vista Hotel's website incorporate the following:

- visual appeal elements from both the Aurora and Grand Rialto websites,
- content from the Grand Rialto website, and
- ease of navigation from the Grand Rialto website.

We are confident that these recommendations will help Terrapin Enterprises Ltd. create an attractive, informative, and user-friendly website for The Vista Hotel.

We would like to thank Mark Baron for his feedback on the report's draft analysis. If you have any questions or concerns about the report, we would be pleased to speak with you. I can be reached by phone at 555-883-4723 or by email at bruce.wayne@webdesign.com.

Yours sincerely,

Bruce Wayne

Bruce Wayne
President

BW/jt

Table of Contents

List of Figures

List of Tables

Executive Summary

Based on the rise in Terrapin tourism and the success of its Silver Fork restaurant, Terrapin Enterprises has decided to build and open a new hotel, The Vista. The upscale hotel will be located next to the popular restaurant and it is scheduled to open on December 1, 2018.

Today, most hotel guests use the Internet to make accommodation choices. Thousands of hotels are available, all competing for new customers. Therefore, creating an effective website to attract potential guests is crucial for hotels.

Web Design Inc. was asked to analyze two hotel websites to serve as models for the construction of The Vista Hotel website. Because their standards and target audience are similar to The Vista's, we chose the websites of Aurora Hotels and Grand Rialto Hotels. The report recommends the most important features for an attractive, informative, and user-friendly webpage.

The two websites were analyzed using the following criteria:

- **Visual Appeal:** Attractive colour scheme, pictures, headings,
- **Content:** Simple language, ample information on rooms and availability, easy booking options, and
- **Ease of Navigation:** Reliable links, easy-to-use search engine, absence of pop-up ads.

In addition to the analysis, 100 hotel guests were surveyed on the two websites. In the survey, the Grand Rialto website scored the highest on all three criteria. These results supported our analysis, leading us to recommend that The Vista Hotel's website incorporate the following:

- visual appeal elements from both the Aurora and Grand Rialto websites,
- content from the Grand Rialto website, and
- ease of navigation from the Grand Rialto website.

We are confident that our recommendations will help The Vista Hotel attract new guests and achieve a high level of customer satisfaction.

Introduction

Over the past decade, Canadian tourism has increased, especially in the country's major cities. One of the largest increases was in Terrapin, BC, with a 67 per cent growth rate in ten years. This growth in tourism has caused hotel occupancy rates to rise (see Figure 1).

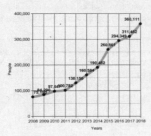

Figure 1: Increase in Terrapin hotel occupancy rate 2008–2018

For the past three years, Silver Fork restaurant has been a tourist favourite in Terrapin. Because of Silver Fork's success and the rise in tourism, Terrapin Enterprises Ltd. decided to build an upscale hotel, called The Vista, next to the restaurant (see Figure 2).

Today, most hotel guests use the web to help make accommodation choices, and a hotel's website usually forms users' first opinions about the establishment. These websites include pictures of rooms and amenities, discounts, and booking options. Over the last few years, the increase in accommodation choices has caused hotel competition to peak. Therefore, creating an effective hotel website to attract potential guests is vital.

Web Design Inc. was asked to analyze two hotel websites to help Terrapin Enterprises Ltd. construct the website for The Vista. The resulting report would recommend the most important features for an attractive, informative, and user-friendly webpage.

Web Design Inc. specializes in graphic design and marketing. Based in Toronto, we have been in business for 19 years. Our company has commissioned reports and built websites for a variety of businesses, including Pets West and Thrifty Foods.

For this report, we chose to analyze the Aurora Hotels and Grand Rialto Hotels websites. Each website was rated on three criteria: visual appeal, ease of navigation, and content.

In addition, an online survey was presented to guests at several hotels in Toronto, Vancouver, and Terrapin to get their opinions on the two websites. We sent out 150 surveys and received

Figure 2: Architect's concept for The Vista Hotel

100 responses, which is a large enough sample to reliably support our recommendations for The Vista Hotel.

1

Mode of Analysis

The Aurora and Grand Rialto websites were evaluated on three components necessary for an effective website:

- **Visual Appeal:** Attractive colour scheme, pictures, and headings
- **Content:** Simple language, information on rooms and availability, easy booking options
- **Ease of Navigation:** Reliable links, easy-to-use search engine, absence of pop-up ads.

As noted above, to support our analysis, 100 hotel guests in Toronto, Vancouver, and Terrapin completed an online survey with questions based on the three criteria.

Analysis of the Aurora Hotels Website

Hotel website: www.aurorahotels.com

Aurora Hotels is a global hotel company designed for business and leisure travellers. Under the Aurora brand, hotels range from midscale to upscale. Currently, there are over 5,300 locations across 106 countries. Its global headquarters is in Richmond, Virginia.

Visual Appeal

The Aurora Hotels website is simple and clear (see Figure 3). Information is displayed in a modular format, which makes the webpage reader-friendly. The homepage presents current deals and offers in bright boxes that immediately grab readers' attention.

The website has a blue theme. Pictures, toolbar headings, and text boxes follow this colour scheme, creating an overall cohesive look.

Headings on the homepage are bolded and white, an eye-catching contrast from the blue boxes. The large sans-serif font makes the information easy to read.

Figure 3: Aurora website homepage

Throughout the website, large high-quality pictures accompany the text. However, only one picture on the homepage is hotel-related, so that at first sight it is not clear exactly what the website is promoting.

Content

The Aurora website provides detailed information on the chain's hotels. For each establishment, information on rooms, amenities, and availability is listed. Additionally, the Aurora hotel that is closest to the user's browsing location is displayed. A hyperlink to the full hotel website is also included. However, a clear booking option is missing.

3

Trending deals are displayed on the homepage and "Offers" page. However, the descriptions of these deals are somewhat vague. Including the expiry date for the offers would be helpful. Finally, the website includes information about the company, including its mission statement, executive team, and corporate social responsibility. A hyperlink to the company brochure is also available.

Ease of Navigation

At the top of the page, a toolbar with drop-down menus allows users to find exactly what they are looking for. However, the website lacks a toolbar-heading for hotels—hotel information can only be found using the homepage search engine, although the search engine is in the centre of the homepage and easy to locate. After the search engine is used, pop-up ads that recommend hotels beyond the Aurora brand make the website appear disorganized.

Figure 4 shows that the Aurora website ranked second to the Grand Rialto in ease of navigation in our survey.

In summary, the Aurora homepage is attractive, if a bit unclear that it is promoting a hotel. The content is very comprehensive but lacks an easy booking option. The site is easy to navigate but could use a toolbar heading for finding hotels along with the search-box at the centre of the homepage.

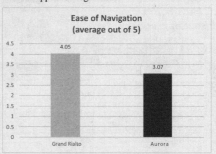

Figure 4: Ease of navigation survey results

Analysis of the Grand Rialto Hotels Website

Hotel website: www.grandrialto.com

Grand Rialto Hotels is a luxury hotel company with over 100 locations worldwide. In 2017, the Grand Rialto was included in *Travel + Leisure* magazine's Top 100 Hotels in the World. Its headquarters is in Toronto, Ontario.

Visual Appeal

The Grand Rialto Hotels website is sleek and sophisticated (see Figure 5). The company logo in the left upper corner gives the page a professional appearance. Throughout the website, a neutral colour scheme in blue and green creates a monochromatic look; additional colours could make the page more exciting.

Figure 5: Grand Rialto website homepage

In the centre of the homepage, a dynamic slideshow of hotels instantly catches users' attention. Under each image, the hotel location and the local time and temperature are displayed. Furthermore, the homepage's white background makes pictures stand out.

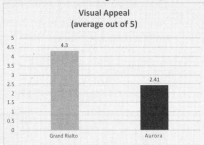

Figure 6: Visual appeal survey results

The website is divided into modular sections. Each section contains few words, making the page reader-friendly. High-quality pictures help break up sections that have more text.

Only three fonts are used throughout the website, creating a minimalistic but possibly boring look. Headings could also make more use of colour to help them stand out against the body text. Figure 6 shows our survey's result for visual appeal, with participants showing a strong preference for the Grand Rialto's design.

Content

The Grand Rialto website has thorough yet clear information for each hotel. Each description includes customer reviews, amenities, rates, and room pictures. In addition, numerous photos of each establishment, taken by professional photographers and previous visitors, accompany the description. A five-step booking option is also clearly presented.

In the centre of the homepage, a large title reading "Discover GRAND RIALTO HOTELS" clearly shows what the website is about for new users.

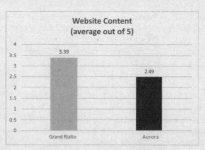

Figure 7: Content survey results

Figure 7 shows our survey results for content. Although the Grand Rialto did not score significantly high in content, it still surpassed the Aurora.

Ease of Navigation

On the homepage, a large search engine and toolbar with drop-down menus make the page easy to navigate. However, some of the main toolbar's headings are unclear. For example, users could easily mistake the "Residences" menu heading to mean information about hotels, rather than private condos or homes. That said, sub-headings within the page help clarify what the section is about.

In summary, the Grand Rialto site rates high in visual appeal, content, and ease of navigation.

6

Conclusions

Based on the rise in tourism in Terrapin and the success of its Silver Fork restaurant, Terrapin Enterprises Ltd. has decided to build a new hotel next to the restaurant. The upscale hotel, called The Vista, is scheduled to open on December 1, 2018. Aware of the need for an online presence, Terrapin Enterprises Ltd. asked Web Design Inc. to recommend features for an eye-catching and easy-to-use website for The Vista Hotel.

For our report, we analyzed the websites of Aurora Hotels and Grand Rialto Hotels. Both hotels are well-established and upscale, making them an effective basis for our analysis.

The websites were analyzed based on three criteria: visual appeal, content, and ease of navigation.

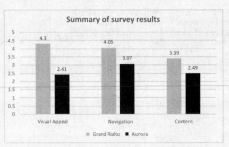

For further research, we conducted an online survey of hotel guests' opinions on the two websites (see Appendix A). Of the 150 surveys sent out, we received 100 responses. Figure 8 shows the average score out of 5 for each criterion in our survey.

Figure 8: Summary of survey results

Our study concluded that the Grand Rialto website (grey in the graph) surpassed the Aurora in all three criteria. However, although the Aurora website scored lower, it has many features of an effective hotel webpage.

We found both hotels used similar techniques to create an attractive and eye-catching website. Both websites' colour schemes look cohesive and professional. Additionally, both homepages use a modular format to grab users' attention. However, the Aurora lacks hotel-related pictures on its homepage, making it unclear what the website is about.

The Grand Rialto website was superior in content, as also shown by the survey results in Figure 8. Unlike the Aurora, its website presents clear booking options for each hotel. Both websites provide useful information on rooms, amenities, and offers. However, the Grand Rialto website adds unique details, such as guest photos and nearby tourist attractions, for each hotel.

We found both websites easy to navigate. Both hotels have a large search engine in the middle of the homepage that is easy for users to find. However, pop-up ads unrelated to the hotel make the Aurora's website slightly less user-friendly than the Grand Rialto website.

Overall, The Vista's website should combine visual-appeal elements from both hotels, including the Aurora's bold, modular look and the Grand Rialto website's dynamic homepage slide show, but follow the Grand Rialto in how The Vista site presents content and provides ease of navigation.

Recommendations

For The Vista Hotel's website, we recommend Terrapin Enterprises Ltd. do the following:

- Incorporate visual appeal elements from both the Aurora and Grand Rialto websites, including the Aurora's bold, modular look and the Grand Rialto's dynamic homepage slide show,
- Incorporate the content from the Grand Rialto website, and
- Incorporate the ease of navigation from the Grand Rialto website.

Appendix A: Hotel Website Survey

This survey has been created by Web Design Inc. to evaluate the visual appeal, user-friendliness, and content of hotel websites. Please look at the two websites provided and click on the answer that best fits your opinion of them. We appreciate your input.

<u>**Visual Appeal**</u>

1. The colours were eye-catching and attractive.

1	2	3	4	5
Strongly Disagree	Disagree	Neutral	Agree	Strongly Agree

2. There was a pleasing number of pictures.

1	2	3	4	5
Strongly Disagree	Disagree	Neutral	Agree	Strongly Agree

3. The headings were clear and concise.

1	2	3	4	5
Strongly Disagree	Disagree	Neutral	Agree	Strongly Agree

<u>**Ease of Navigation**</u>

4. I could easily find pictures of the rooms and facilities.

1	2	3	4	5
Strongly Disagree	Disagree	Neutral	Agree	Strongly Agree

5. The search engine was easy to locate and use.

1	2	3	4	5
Strongly Disagree	Disagree	Neutral	Agree	Strongly Agree

6. The links were reliable and accurate.

1	2	3	4	5
Strongly Disagree	Disagree	Neutral	Agree	Strongly Agree

Content

7. The language was simple and clear throughout the website.

1	2	3	4	5
Strongly Disagree	Disagree	Neutral	Agree	Strongly Agree

8. I found all the information I was looking for.

1	2	3	4	5
Strongly Disagree	Disagree	Neutral	Agree	Strongly Agree

9. Guidelines on booking a room were straightforward.

1	2	3	4	5
Strongly Disagree	Disagree	Neutral	Agree	Strongly Agree

Thank you for taking part in this survey about hotel websites. If you have any questions or comments, please email Natasha Ricole at nricole@webdesign.net.

10

Appendix B: Hotel Website Survey Results

Of the 150 online surveys sent out, 100 surveys were returned. The tables below show the breakdown of votes for each question. The figures in the report show the <u>average</u> of the responses in each of the three main criteria.

Visual Appeal

1. The colours were eye-catching and attractive.

Table 1: Visual appeal survey results on colours

	Strongly Agree	Agree	Neutral	Disagree	Strongly Disagree
Aurora	5	13	28	45	9
Grand Rialto	68	20	11	1	0

2. There was a pleasing number of pictures.

Table 2: Visual appeal survey results on number of pictures

	Strongly Agree	Agree	Neutral	Disagree	Strongly Disagree
Aurora	2	5	18	60	15
Grand Rialto	75	10	10	5	0

3. The headings were clear and concise.

Table 3: Visual appeal survey results on headings

	Strongly Agree	Agree	Neutral	Disagree	Strongly Disagree
Aurora	3	20	8	56	13
Grand Rialto	50	14	14	20	2

Ease of Navigation

4. I could easily find pictures of the rooms and facilities.

Table 4: Ease of navigation survey results on finding pictures

	Strongly Agree	Agree	Neutral	Disagree	Strongly Disagree
Aurora	25	20	10	36	9
Grand Rialto	60	20	5	10	5

5. The search engine was easy to locate and use.

Table 5: Ease of navigation survey results on search engine

	Strongly Agree	Agree	Neutral	Disagree	Strongly Disagree
Aurora	45	30	15	8	2
Grand Rialto	50	25	10	10	5

6. The links were reliable and accurate.

Table 6: Ease of navigation survey results on link reliability

	Strongly Agree	Agree	Neutral	Disagree	Strongly Disagree
Aurora	1	5	20	39	35
Grand Rialto	50	25	10	4	1

12

Content

7. The language was simple and clear throughout the website.

Table 7: Content survey results on language

	Strongly Agree	Agree	Neutral	Disagree	Strongly Disagree
Aurora	16	20	32	25	7
Grand Rialto	32	27	25	9	7

8. I found all the information I was looking for.

Table 8: Content survey results on quantity of information

	Strongly Agree	Agree	Neutral	Disagree	Strongly Disagree
Aurora	11	6	13	40	30
Grand Rialto	40	28	19	8	5

9. Guidelines on booking a room were straightforward.

Table 9: Content survey results on booking guidelines

	Strongly Agree	Agree	Neutral	Disagree	Strongly Disagree
Aurora	3	5	12	53	27
Grand Rialto	11	18	16	30	25

13

Appendix
Answers to Exercises

Exercise: Rewriting the Car Rental Ad (from page 22)

Added and eliminated words are in blue font; comments and named problems are in bold.

Thank you for asking XXX Car Rentals to quote on ~~for~~ [**more common preposition**] your car rental ~~requirements~~. [**redundant**] ~~We are pleased to say~~ [**goes without saying; a good company always aims to please the customer**] XXX Car Rentals has invested many ~~man-~~[**no woman-hours?**] hours~~,~~ [**no comma**] in gearing our ~~whole~~ [**redundant**] ~~rental~~ operation to work for our customers. [**Really, the whole sentence is redundant and can be deleted.**] We pride ourselves on our ~~the~~ high level of customer service ~~we achieve~~ [**revision to "our" makes this phrase redundant**], and [**must add the "and" to fix the comma splice; alternatively, the comma could be changed to a semicolon or period**] we are ~~also~~ [**redundant**] sure you will find us good value for money. [**Really, once the comma splice is fixed and the prose tightened up, we can eliminate the comma and the second "we."**]

~~At XXX Car Rentals we are aware know that~~ [**wordy and redundant**] ~~car~~ Car rental can be ~~a~~ stressful. ~~time for the best of us~~ [**wordy**]~~, that's~~ That's [**comma splice fixed by starting a new sentence**] why we have made our service very easy to use. In fact,[**comma**] we call it hassle free. [**The next sentence is incomplete (a sentence fragment) because what follows the "so" (a coordinating conjunction) is not an independent clause, as we would expect, but a participial phrase—that is, a phrase using a verbal.**] ~~So allowing~~ Thus, you ~~to~~ can [**Using a conjunctive adverb (followed by a comma) and adding a verb turns this into a sentence.**] start enjoying your holiday or ~~even~~ get~~ting~~ to that all-important [**hyphen needed for adjective**] business meeting ~~faster the moment you drive off in your rental car,~~ [**Doesn't this go without saying?**] sooner ~~or even getting to that all-important business meeting faster~~ [**reposition this idea to save words**]. If you need to cancel your trip for any reason, XXX Car Rental will refund your money ~~back~~ [**redundant**] in full, with no penalties. We are sure that, once you have tried our service, ~~;~~ [**should be comma, not semicolon**] you will ~~be delighted and will never look back.~~ [**What do you want your customers to do?**] return to us again and again. [**Really, sentence should be revised to focus on customer, e.g., "Once you have tried our service…."**]

~~Think of all the extras you are getting with XXX Car Rental, and~~ [**There aren't any extras listed.**] When comparing quotes from other rental agencies, ~~check that~~ be sure they include all that we offer, at no additional cost. ~~to you.~~[**redundant**]

Here's what the ad might look like corrected and without all the editing marks:

Thank you for asking XXX Car Rentals to quote on your car rental. We pride ourselves on our high level of customer service and are sure you will find us good value for money.

Car rental can be stressful. That's why we've made our service very easy to use. In fact, we call it hassle free. Thus, you can start enjoying your holiday or get to that all-important business meeting sooner. If you need to cancel your trip for any reason, XXX Car Rental will refund your money in full, with no penalties. Once you have tried our service, we know you will return to us again and again.

When comparing quotes from other rental agencies, be sure they include everything we offer at no additional cost.

CHAPTER 1

Exercise # 1 (from page 32)

You should notice that the second will, in plain language, is shorter, makes more and better use of bulleted lists (items are listed using parallel grammatical structures and punctuation of the list is correct), is clear, and uses concrete and specific language.

Exercise #2 (from page 32)

a. If you make a hole while freeing a stuck vehicle, you must fill the hole before you drive away.
b. After notification from NMFS, vessel operators must attend a skipper education workshop before each fishing season.
c. We will take two steps to look at this Medicare issue: we will find out if it was an error or fraud, and we will let you know the result.

CHAPTER 2

Identifying Transitions (from page 51)

In the past month, [*shows time*] our company's sales have gone down 30 per cent. **As a result,** [*causality*] our cash flow situation has become critical. **Worse**, [*contrast*] this loss of revenue could even threaten our company's future. **Therefore**, [*causation*] we need to take action to prevent bankruptcy, **including** [*illustration*] working harder to get sales and cutting our production costs.

Quiz on the Seven Cs (from page 60)

1. She decided to evaluate the program, which would take five months.—**Not clear**. The relative pronoun "which" is ambiguous; does it refer to the program or the evaluation? Which of these will take five months?
   Revised:
   Her evaluation of the program will take five months.
   She decided to evaluate the five-month program.

2. The entrance exam was failed by two-thirds of the applicants.—**Not clear or concise.** Use an active rather than a passive verb.
   Revised:
   Two-thirds of the applicants failed the entrance exam.

3. We will re-evaluate our marketing strategy after the new chairman is hired.—**Not courteous**. Use gender-neutral terms such as "chairperson" or "chair."

4. There is a steady flow of people crossing back and forth across the road while the cars are waiting in lines up to 300 metres.—**Not concise**.
   Revised:
   A steady flow of people crossed the road, causing 300-metre-long traffic jams.

5. A fair percentage of the company's tool-and-die stampers have developed mechanical problems.—**Not concrete/specific**. How many stampers are affected?
   Revised:
   Five of the company's nine tool-and-die stampers have mechanical problems.

6. If you can't use the new iPod, please return it back to me.—**Not concise**. "Back" is redundant.

7. Checkout procedures at the Luxor Hotel chain are especially designed for the businessman in a hurry.—**Not courteous**. Use gender-neutral terms such as "businessperson" or "executive."

8. In order to provide a mechanism by which customers may air their problems concerning product quality, the company has established the following procedure for registering grievances for all purchasers.—**Not concise**. Your revision would depend upon what you wanted to emphasize.
   Revised to emphasize how to complain:
   Use the following procedure for customer complaints.
   Revised to emphasize the company's care for customers:
   We care about customer satisfaction, so please use the following procedure to make a complaint.

9. There was a traffic accident at Bay and Main streets yesterday.—**Not complete**. All questions are not answered.
   Revised:
   Three people were injured, one seriously, when two cars collided at Bay and Main streets yesterday.

10. Belleville, Ontario, is a small city.—**Not concrete/specific.** What is a "small" city?
    Revised:
    Belleville, Ontario, is a small city of 50,000 residents.

11. Children under 42 inches tall cannot go on this ride.—**Not constructive.**
    Revised:
    Children over 42 inches tall can enjoy this ride.

12. Many English majors are skilled at reading and writing; however, commerce majors enjoy impressive salaries after graduation.—**Not clear and not complete.** Sentences should have only one idea. Also, the ideas connecting the two main points crammed into one sentence here are hinted at but not specified.
    Revised:
    Many English majors are skilled at reading and writing but have difficulty, at first, finding work. However, commerce majors often enjoy impressive salaries right after graduation.

13. Your speech shouldn't be too long.—**Not clear or complete.**
    Revised:
    You have ten minutes for your speech.

14. The owner's manual for your new Excelsior clock radio is enclosed herein to assist you in utilizing all the convenient and useful features of your new device.—**Not concise.**
    Revised:
    The owner's manual explains all the features of your new Excelsior clock radio.

15. The debate between the prime minister and his political opponent was about the merits of sweater vests.—**Not clear and not concise.** Avoid passive verbs and nominalizations ("debate" is a nominalization).
    Revised:
    The prime minister and his political opponent debated the merits of sweater vests.

16. We are pleased to inform you that we have selected you for an interview for the sales associate position.—**Not courteous.** Writing should be "you" centred.
    Revised:
    You have been selected to be interviewed for the sales-associate position.

17. Alicia's pet fish died yesterday. She went shopping.—**Not coherent and not complete**. The sentence needs a transition (we've used "therefore") and additional information.
    Revised:
    Alicia's pet fish died yesterday. Therefore, she went shopping for a new one.

18. Unfortunately, your order of plastic marmot figurines cannot be delivered before August 14.—**Not constructive**. Revise the use of negative language.
    Revised:
    Your order of plastic marmot figurines will be delivered on August 14.

19. He distributed annual reports to the audience bound in red and green covers.—**Not clear**. The misplaced modifier creates an incorrect if humorous picture—of the audience wrapped in red and green covers.
    Revised:
    He distributed to the audience annual reports bound in red and green covers.

20. A new photocopier is needed by the employees in our office.—**Not clear or concise**. Use an active verb.
    Revised:
    Our employees need a new photocopier.

CHAPTER 3

Quiz on Sentences (from page 78)

1. The three clauses are as follows:

   1. An independent clause can be a separate sentence; it contains a subject and a predicate (which usually comprises both a verb and an object).

      You (subject) don't have (verb) a heart (object).

   2. A subordinate clause (or dependent clause) depends on an independent clause for its meaning; it can't stand alone as a complete sentence, and begins with a subordinating conjunction.

      While you were sleeping

3. A relative clause relates information to a noun or pronoun; it begins with a relative pronoun, and it can provide either essential or non-essential information in a sentence.

> The girl _who played with fire_ [restrictive relative clause in italics; relative pronoun underlined]

2. The four ways of combining clauses correctly are by using

1. a coordinating conjunction (<u>You don't have a heart</u>, _so_ <u>I know you won't understand why I am angry.</u>),
2. a subordinating conjunction (<u>Melanie played a game on her iPad</u> _while_ <u>she waited for you to wake up.</u>),
3. a conjunctive adverb and punctuation (<u>You don't have a heart</u>; _therefore_ <u>I don't expect you to understand why I am angry.</u>), and
4. punctuation alone (<u>Doing things right is easy</u>; <u>doing the right thing is hard</u>.).

Quiz on Punctuation (from page 90)

1. Ten ways to use a comma correctly include
   a. after an introductory word, phrase, or subordinate clause (<u>Once upon a time</u>, three very different girls grew up to be three very different women.),
   b. before a coordinating conjunction (These women were very different, <u>but they had three things in common.</u>),
   c. to separate items (even clauses) in a list (<u>They were all beautiful</u>, <u>they were all brilliant</u>, <u>and they all worked for Charlie.</u>),
   d. to introduce dialogue or a quotation (I can hear you saying, <u>"Let's hope he's not talking about _Charlie's Angels_!"</u>),
   e. to set off interrupting elements (In the middle of winter, <u>when the flakes of snow were falling like feathers from the sky</u>, a queen sat at a window sewing.),
   f. to surround appositives (The queen had a little daughter, <u>Snow White</u>, whose skin was as white as snow.),
   g. before an end-of-sentence modifier (This queen was a beautiful woman, <u>but proud and haughty.</u>),
   h. to separate a series of coordinate adjectives (This <u>proud</u>, <u>haughty</u>, <u>beautiful</u> woman was jealous of Snow White.),
   i. to separate the elements of an address (Snow White can be contacted at <u>7 Dwarfs Lane</u>, <u>Great Forest</u>, <u>Disneyland</u>, <u>CA</u>.), and

j. after the salutation and closing in a personal letter (<u>Dear Woodsman</u>, Thank you very much for saving my life. <u>Yours sincerely</u>, Snow White.).

2. What is a comma splice?

A comma splice is two independent clauses joined by nothing but a comma.

Example: On Boxing Day, the stores are very busy, shoppers are returning presents they don't want.

Corrected: On Boxing Day, the stores are very busy **because** shoppers are returning presents they don't want. [Added subordinating conjunction **because**]

3. What are the two occasions when a semicolon is used?

    a. To separate independent clauses using either a linking/conjunction adverb or semicolon alone, assuming the two independent clauses are logically related. **Example**: I went to the store to return a Christmas gift; **however**, Mary was happy with her presents and stayed home. [Semicolon and linking adverb]

    b. When a long list contains internal punctuation. **Example**: While in London, we visited the British Museum, which was free of charge; walked through Piccadilly Circus, which was jammed with cars and buses; and attended a performance of *Les Misérables*, which has been running continuously in London since 1985.

4. What are the four occasions when a colon is used?

    a. To introduce a list or additional information. **Example**: While in London we did the following: visited the British Museum, walked through Piccadilly Circus, and saw a play.

    b. To introduce a quotation. **Example**: On his deathbed he proclaimed: "I am glad I could die for my country!"

    c. After the greeting in a business letter. **Example**: Dear Ms. Hartley:

    d. To separate a title and subtitle. **Example**: *Zen and the Art of Archery: A Master's Guide*

5. What types of punctuation are typically used *inside* quotation marks? What types of punctuation are typically used *outside* quotation marks?

    a. Most types of punctuation are normally used inside quotation marks. **Example**: "I am tired, now," he said. "Can we go home?"

    b. Semicolons and colons are normally found outside quotation marks. **Example**: You asked, "Can we go home?"; I wish we could.

    c. Question marks are used outside quotation marks when the question mark is not part of the quoted material. **Example**: Why did you say, "I'd like to go home"?

6. What is the difference between parentheses and brackets?
   a. Parentheses are used to insert additional, usually non-essential information into a sentence. **Example**: "My brother (who is listening, so I'll have to speak in a whisper) is a bit of a klutz."
   b. Brackets identify editorial insertions with additional or clarifying information from elsewhere in the text. **Example**: When Elvina [Roderick's sister] came into the room, everyone stopped talking.

Quick Quiz (from page 91)

We can count napkins, so the slogan should be this: Fewer napkins, less waste, less pollution.

Quiz #1 on Grammar (from page 93)

1. Suspecting fraud, the books were audited last month. **Dangling modifier**: Books can't suspect fraud. Add a subject that can suspect fraud.

   Suspecting fraud, *we* audited the books last month.

2. I hope you are pleased with the report, I would like to discuss it with you at your convenience. **Comma splice**: A comma alone cannot join two independent clauses. Add a coordinating or subordinating conjunction, a linking adverb, a relative pronoun (e.g., which), or some type of joining punctuation (e.g., a semicolon, in this case) or punctuate as two separate sentences.

   I hope you are pleased with the report, which I would like to discuss with you at your convenience.

   I hope you are pleased with the report; I would like to discuss it with you at your convenience.

3. Everyone deals with workplace stress in their own way. **Noun-pronoun disagreement in number**: "Everyone" is singular; "their" is plural. Make the pronoun singular or the noun plural.

   Everyone deals with workplace stress in *his* or *her* own way.

   People deal with workplace stress in *their* own way.

4. Employees, who work the late shift, will receive a 10 per cent bonus. **Essential clause doesn't take commas**: Only the employees *who work the late shift* will receive this bonus, so this relative clause is necessary to define the noun.

    Employees who work the late shift will receive a 10 per cent bonus.

5. The result of the tests are included in Appendix B. **Subject-verb disagreement in number**: "Result," the subject of the sentence, is singular, and the verb that relates to this subject ("are") is plural. (Some might think "tests" is the subject, but the sentence doesn't say that these "tests" will be included in the appendix.) Make the subject and verb agree in number.

    The *result* of the test *is* included....

    The *results* of the test *are*....

6. The 909 printer is our most popular model, it offers an unequalled blend of power and versatility. **Another comma splice**: Don't forget that a pronoun such as "it" can be the subject of an independent clause. Follow the advice given in question #2.

    The 909 printer is our most popular model because it offers an unequalled blend of power and versatility.

    The 909 printer is our most popular model; it offers an unequalled blend of power and versatility.

7. The truck, that ran into the ditch, had faulty brakes. **An essential clause doesn't take commas**: It's *that* truck that ran into the ditch and no other.

    The truck that ran into the ditch had faulty brakes.

8. I read the questions carefully, therefore, I did well on the exam. **Conjunctive adverbs (or transitional words) such as "therefore" and "however" can't link two independent clauses without a semicolon**: Add a semicolon or use a subordinating conjunction to make one clause dependent on the other.

    I read the questions carefully; *therefore*, I did well on the exam.

    Because I read the questions carefully, I did well on the exam.

9. If you find the plastic marmot that I've lost please phone me immediately. **Missing comma after introductory subordinate clause**: "If you find the plastic marmot that I've lost," because it comes in front of the independent clause, needs a comma after it.

> If you find the plastic marmot that I've lost, please phone me immediately.

10. The stewardesses made sure the passengers had blankets after the flight took off. **Does not use gender-neutral language**: Use "flight attendants."

> The flight attendants made sure the passengers had blankets after the flight took off.

Quiz #2 on Grammar (from page 94)

1. I try and minimize my travel. **As written, the sentence says the writer will both *try* something and *minimize* something, but the something that will be tried (or the complete object of the verb) is *to minimize my travel*.**

> I try to minimize my travel.

2. For example, Sunday school at the local church. **Sentence fragment**: There's no verb, so add one.

> For example, Sunday school *is held* at the local church.

3. We'd like to thank our list of volunteers and, if in error there is an ommission of a name, we apologize as we had so many this year. **Spelling error (omission) and complex, wordy writing that creates illogical statements and ambiguous pronoun references**: Do you thank a "list"? Isn't omitting a name an error by definition? And "so many" what? Volunteers or errors? Cut out unnecessary words and reorganize the parts of the sentence. It might also be useful to thank volunteers directly and to disconnect the apology from this expression of thanks.

> We'd like to thank our many volunteers this year and, because there were so many helping us, we apologize to those whom we didn't name.

> We thank all our many volunteers this year. If we didn't name you, because there were so many helping us, we apologize.

4. He said that if the federal government were serious about climate change, it would introduce a tax on carbon emissions, however, he applauded the tax on inefficient vehicles. **The conjunctive adverb "however" cannot link two independent clauses without a semicolon**: Use a semicolon in front of "however," use an appropriate coordinating or subordinating conjunction, or separate these two sentences. (You might think that the first independent clause has another error: subject-verb disagreement in number. Although it is true that "federal government" is singular and would usually take "was" as its verb, in this case, the "were" is correct. It indicates the subjunctive mood. The subjunctive is used in statements that do not describe known truths or that are contrary to fact: "If I were a rich man, I would….")

> He said that if the federal government were serious about climate change, it would introduce a tax on carbon emissions, but he applauded the tax on inefficient vehicles.

5. During Question Period, Mr. Dion and deputy leader Michael Ignatieff accused Mr. Harper of breaking several promises in the budget. Among them, a promise to create 250,000 day-care spaces. **Sentence fragment**: The last sentence isn't a full sentence because it has no verb and the idea is not complete. These sentence fragments are, however, sometimes allowed for effect in this type of journalistic writing. To fix this, join "among…." to the independent clause with a comma or add a verb.

> During Question Period, Mr. Dion and deputy leader Michael Ignatieff accused Mr. Harper of breaking several promises in the budget, among them, a promise to create 250,000 day-care spaces.

> During Question Period, Mr. Dion and deputy leader Michael Ignatieff accused Mr. Harper of breaking several promises in the budget. Among them **is** a promise to create 250,000 day-care spaces.

6. An office romance in Abbotsford between a manager and a female subordinate that turned nasty, cost the manager his job. **Comma error and (probably) misplaced relative clause**: Don't put a single comma between a subject ("romance") and its verb ("cost"). Also, is it the "romance" or the "female subordinate" that turned nasty? We assume the writer is following the rule of using "who" or "whom" for people and "that" for things, but the relative clause "that turned nasty" is too far away from the noun it relates to. Here are two ways to correct this sentence:

An office romance in Abbotsford between a manager and a female subordinate turned nasty and cost the manager his job.

In Abbotsford, a manager and female subordinate's office romance, which turned nasty, cost the manager his job.

7. Taking the ferry as a foot passenger results in less vehicles on the roads. **Incorrect choice of comparative adjective with countable noun**: Use "fewer" when referring to countable things (e.g., vehicles) and "less" when referring to things that are uncountable or too numerous to count (e.g., money or time). But note that this is correct: "We had fewer dollars to spend this year." Dollars can be counted, but money can't. Another example: "We had fewer accidents this year; therefore, there was less carnage on the roads."

Taking the ferry as a foot passenger results in fewer vehicles on the roads.

8. Along with a forgiveness of up to $2,000 on the B.C. provincial sales tax for hybrid cars the price premium for some hybrids has effectively disappeared. **Missing comma after introductory phrase**: "Along with … for hybrid cars" is an *introductory* prepositional phrase, so a comma should follow it for clarity.

Along with a forgiveness of up to $2,000 on the B.C. provincial sales tax for hybrid cars, [comma] the price premium for some hybrids has effectively disappeared. [Note that some style guides would require you to use "BC" rather than B.C., but the exercises and examples in this book use traditional abbreviations and acronyms.]

Quiz #3 on Clauses (from page 94)

The following paragraphs contain 15 subordinate or relative clauses. Subordinate clauses are shown by **bolding**; relative clauses are identified by underlining.

Plato versus Aristotle

Philosophy in the West ultimately boils down to two Greek thinkers from the fourth century BCE: Plato and Aristotle. One of Plato's most important ideas, which he expressed using Socrates as his source, was his Theory of Forms. Forms were idealized templates for everything that we can sense and think about. For example, horses are horses **because they reflect the Ideal Horse, dogs the Ideal Dog, chairs the Ideal**

Chair, and so on. For Plato, these Forms were not just abstract ideas; they actually existed, but beyond our senses.

Plato explains Forms with the parable of the Cave. A number of prisoners are chained in a cave. **Because they are facing away from the entrance**, they see on the back wall only shadows from the world outside the cave, and the prisoners believe <u>that the shadows are Reality</u>. However, one prisoner, <u>who is more curious than the others</u>, escapes from the cave, sees the reality <u>that is creating the shadows</u>, and returns to inform the others <u>that what they are seeing is only an illusion</u>. For Plato, then, **when we achieve full Wisdom**, we see the reality (the Forms) beyond our senses rather than mere shadows (the cave).

Aristotle, <u>who was a student of Plato</u>, rejected much of Plato's philosophy of Forms; he denied <u>that the "real world" was the Forms beyond the senses</u>. Instead, Aristotle believed <u>that we should learn more about the cave through intelligent use of our senses rather than trying to transcend the senses, which was Plato's preference</u>.

In the modern Western world, Plato's philosophy often appears as idealism: Plato's present-day followers, <u>who are usually not aware of their debt to Plato</u>, seek the ideal, the perfect, the permanent, the mystical. **While most of Aristotle's followers today are also not aware of their link to his ideas**, Aristotelians tend to be realistic and scientific, seeking <u>that which is possible in the world now rather than an idealized Form beyond the world</u>.

So, which philosopher do you prefer? **[In sentences that are questions, such as this one, "which" is not a relative pronoun but an adjective modifying "philosopher" and the sentence contains a complete idea. Therefore, this is not a relative clause.]**

CHAPTER 4

Here are the answers to the copy-editing exercise on page 106, showing how these would look if the exercise had been edited using Word's "Track Changes" feature. Of course, material in square brackets would not appear normally and has been added to explain the edited errors. You are looking for 22 errors.

Copy-editing is one of ~~most the~~ the most [<u>wrong word order</u>] important jobs in professional writing. You could think of the copy editor as a hunter, hidden in the foliage, waiting for ~~their~~ his or her [<u>noun-pronoun number agreement error</u>] ~~pray~~ prey [<u>wrong word</u>]—a spelling mistake, a grammatical or punctuation error, a problem in wording—to appear. Then, he or she ~~pounce~~ pounces [<u>subject-verb number agreement error</u>] and—lo!—the error is no ~~is~~ [<u>wrong word order</u>] more. [<u>run-on sentence; add missing period</u>] ~~it~~

It [capitalize "it"] is just as satisfying to take an immoderate spew of ~~verbaige~~ verbiage [spelling error] and, with a few ~~streaks~~ strokes [wrong word] of the keyboard, create instead a measured flow of words. The copy editor may also ~~redact~~ reduce [wrong word] five poorly chosen words to two or three~~;~~ [comma splice; needs semicolon or period] do we really have to say "in regard to" when we mean ~~"about".~~ "about"? [question mark] But the copy editor ~~be~~ must also be [wrong word order] ~~carefull~~ careful. [spelling error] Too much editing may ~~distract~~ detract [wrong word] from the meaning the writer is ~~not~~ [wrong word; delete it] trying to get across and even introduce new errors. Finally, [comma needed] the copy editor performs what can only be called a noble role in the ~~perservation~~ preservation [spelling] of proper English. Writers, even good ones, are constantly trying to change language by ~~braking~~ breaking [wrong word] the rules of grammar and by ~~concieving~~ conceiving [spelling error] new spellings or even entirely new words (words like "neologism," [comma before non-essential relative clause] which means "the practice of creating new words"). Copy editors are the ~~line last~~ last line [wrong word order] of defence against error and these barbaric practices. In other words, copy editors are the last bastion of ~~civiliized~~ civilized [spelling] discourse. May that bastion stand forever!

CHAPTER 5

Answers to List Exercise (from page 119)

Each of the lists below has something wrong with it. Identify what's wrong and make the correction.

1)
Not correct

The most important things in life are:

- Happiness
- Having good friends
- Making a good income

Correct

The most important things in life are [**No colon between verb and rest of the predicate**]

- being happy [**Original item not parallel; noun revised here to a participle**]
- having good friends .
- making a good income. [**We suggest a period at the end of every list.**]

Another correct version

The most important things in life are

- happiness,
- good friends, and [**Parallel nouns (with appropriate adjective and articles)**]
- a good income. [**Period at end of list; appropriate punctuation throughout**]

2)
Not correct

When you assemble a desk, be sure to do the following
  - Make sure all parts are in the box;
  - Use the correct tools; and
  - Keep your temper

Correct

When you assemble a desk, be sure to do the following: [**Full sentence takes colon**] [**Needs one space between introductory sentence and list**]

- Make sure all parts are in the box; [**Punctuation could be a comma, too**]
- Use the correct tools; and
- Keep your temper. [**Period at end of list needed for consistency.**]

3)
Not correct

My favourite movies are:

- My Friend Flicka
- Terminator 2
- Mamma Mia

Corrected

My favourite movies are [**Don't put a colon at the end of an incomplete sentence.**]

- *My Friend Flicka*
- *Terminator 2*
- *Mamma Mia*. [**Movie titles should be in italics; follow grammatical conventions in lists; we suggest a period at the end of every list.**]

CHAPTER 6

Memo Exercise (from page 140)

Take the following information and, using proper formatting and spacing, create the first and closing parts of 1) a formal memo on letterhead and 2) an emailed memo. You do not need to worry about the body of the email.

- The correspondence was sent by Penelope Anderson, the general manager of Terrapin Marmot Figurines, Ltd., on 24/1/19.
- The company's address is 2334 South Ripley Road, Terrapin, British Columbia, V8Q 2P5.
- The correspondence was sent to Bill Cleary, the company's financial manager, with a copy to company president Natalie Henstrick.
- The correspondence is about the possibility that Terrapin Marmot may invest in Rockcliffe Investment's family of mutual funds.
- The memo was typed by Anderson's secretary, Leslie King; the email was typed by Penelope Anderson.
- There is an enclosure (memo) or attachment (email) of financial figures for the fall quarter.

Formal memo on letterhead

Terrapin Marmot Figurines Ltd.
2334 South Ripley Road, Terrapin, BC V8Q 2P5

To: Bill Cleary, Financial Manager
From: Penelope Anderson, General Manager
Date: January 24, 2019
Subject: Terrapin Marmot Figurines investment in Rockcliffe funds

Text goes here.

Penelope

PA/lk

Enclosure: Financial figures for 2018
cc: Natalie Henstrick, President

Emailed memo

To: Bill Cleary, Financial Manager
From: Penelope Anderson, General Manager
Cc: Natalie Henstrick, President
Date: January 24, 2019
Subject: Terrapin Marmot Figurines investment in Rockcliffe funds

Good morning Bill,

Text goes here. I've attached the fourth-quarter financial figures.

Penelope

Attachment: Financial figures for 2018

Letter Exercise (from page 149)

Take the following information and, using proper block-letter style formatting and spacing, create the first and closing parts of a business letter. You do not need to write the body of the letter. Use spacing appropriate for a business letter.

- The letter was sent on company letterhead by Penelope Anderson, the general manager of Terrapin Marmot Figurines, Ltd.
- The company's address is 43 Oak Valley Road, Terrapin, British Columbia, V8Q 2P5.
- The letter was sent on Jan. 23, 2019, to Delwan Kuthrapalli, the president of Rockcliffe Investments Limited, at 223 Earnshaw Place, Toronto, Ontario, postal code M4P 2R2.
- The letter is about the possibility that Terrapin Marmot may invest in Rockcliffe Investment's family of mutual funds.

- The letter was typed by Anderson's secretary, Leslie King.
- Terrapin Marmot's 2018 annual report has been included as an enclosure.

Terrapin Marmot Figurines Ltd.

43 Oak Valley Road
Terrapin, BC V8Q 2P5

January 23, 2019

Delwan Kuthrapalli
President
Rockcliffe Investments Limited
223 Earnshaw Place
Toronto, ON M4P 2R2

Dear Mr. Kuthrapalli:

Subject: Terrapin Marmot Figurines investment in mutual funds

[Text of the letter goes here.]

Yours sincerely,

Penelope Anderson

Penelope Anderson
General Manager

PA/lk

Enclosure: Terrapin Marmot Figurines 2018 annual report

CHAPTER 8

Bad-News Letter Exercise: Air Canada Letters (from page 172)

A new letter blending the good-news and bad-news letter formats

Dear Mr._____:

Thank you for taking the time to write to us about this issue. It is very frustrating when luggage is delayed, leaving airline passengers without the clothing, toiletries, and other essentials they need to begin their much-anticipated holiday, family visit, or business trip. Please accept our sincerest apologies.

You wrote us requesting $400 in compensation for the expenses you incurred to replace some of these necessities when your luggage was not available until a week after you landed in London on July 12.

Delayed or missing luggage is a significant inconvenience, so every effort is made to ensure that our passengers' baggage arrives with them. Our newly designed routing label is normally easy to read, and bag-check computers are designed to automatically match tickets with baggage destination codes.

Still, many variables can affect luggage delivery. Sometimes computers do *not* work as they are designed to, and sometimes human error can also be a factor. There are also often variables outside of the airline's control; for example, a person catching a connecting flight may pick up the wrong bag and not recognize the mistake until this luggage has been separated from its rightful owner. Add to these circumstances the complications of travel delays as a consequence of weather or security checks, and it is clear why Airline Tariff regulations preclude liability for consequential claims if baggage is delayed.

As a gesture of goodwill, I am pleased to enclose our cheque for $240.99 in connection with your claim. This compensation represents an extension of airline policy.

If a passenger is away from home and his or her baggage is delayed more than 24 hours, Air Canada will contribute towards the cost of interim clothing and toiletry purchases, to a maximum of $100.00, when costs are substantiated with original purchase receipts.

This policy is common to all STAR Alliance partners as well as to our Connector carriers.

We hope this gesture will help recompense you for the inconvenience you experienced and the expense you incurred, and we hope as well that you will choose Air Canada again in the future.

Sincerely,

CHAPTER 12

Exercise on Writing a News Release (from page 241)

Follow-Up Questions on News Release Exercise (from page 242)

1) The key differences between versions 1 and 2 are as follows:

- Version 2 announces the news clearly and immediately, in the headline and in the first paragraph.
- Version 2 is much shorter: shorter sentences, shorter paragraphs, and shorter overall.
- Version 2 puts the product and its potential buyers first: quotations address what the audience would like to know rather than the university's philosophy or who at the university is being quoted, information that is not newsworthy is eliminated, and the opening and closing emphasize the important point: the guarantee.
- Version 2 follows the AIDA formula.
- Version 2 uses the conventional format for a news release.

For all of these reasons, version 2 is more effective than version 1.

Original draft news release.

EverQuest University

FOR IMMEDIATE RELEASE

EverQuest University Announces MBA Guarantee

EverQuest University is pleased to announce the introduction of the MBA Graduation Guarantee. It encourages undergraduates and executives to advance their skills and knowledge of business. The guarantee expresses confidence in EQU learning approaches. It is designed to encourage qualified, enthusiastic, and highly motivated candidates to invest in themselves at EQU. This is the first guarantee of its kind in Canada.

EverQuest University (EQU) believes that all students are active partners in learning and that we share jointly the responsibility for learning. As an equal partner, EQU is committed to providing environments that enable student success. Based on this commitment, EQU provides a graduation guarantee for any student accepted into the MBA Program. This guarantee is based on two principles:

1. EQU believes that all successful applicants are committed to self-improvement in order to gain an edge in the real business world.
2. EQU is confident in the curriculum and delivery systems available to students and is committed to provide the resources necessary to ensure graduation for every successful applicant.

The guarantee encourages success. Students need only be highly motivated to achieve their education goals. In fact the university is adamant that any applicant that meets the entrance requirements and follows the EQU Graduation Guarantee Contract will graduate. Simply put, if a qualified applicant agrees to and actively engages in the EQU learning model by committing his or her time and knowledge to the MBA program, EQU will guarantee graduation.

Flexible curriculum designs allow candidates to choose from one of three MBA offerings:

1. One year Online (includes a three-week residency) MBA for University Commerce and Business graduates;
2. Two year Online (includes a three-week residency each year) MBA for non-business graduates;
3. One year face-to-face intensive MBA.

A partnership in learning

EQU supports a learning-centred model wherein students become active partners in the university process. The EQU model engages students at the beginning of the learning process to ensure that each is prepared, ready and able to fully and actively participate. The guarantee sets out the university and student responsibilities to the learning model and when accepted, provides the pathway to graduation.

How the news release finally appeared (note that this release doesn't follow all the guidelines for the basic news release that we learned in Chapter 12).

EverQuest University

JULY 8, 2018 — FOR IMMEDIATE RELEASE

EverQuest University Announces MBA Guarantee

TERRAPIN, B.C.—Graduation guaranteed: that's what Canada's newest private university, EverQuest University, is offering students in its Master of Business Administration program.

"This doesn't mean students can enrol and then sit around drinking beer for a year or two," said Dr. Michael Corrigan, EQU's vice-president of academics at the Terrapin-based university, which will open in October.

Instead, MBA students will sign a "contract" to follow the university's innovative, learner-centred model of education. On its side of the contract, EQU will make sure that every successful MBA applicant has the resources and support she or he needs to graduate.

Extra support for learning, including learning teams backed by learning coaches and assistants, is a major part of EQU's approach for undergraduate and graduate degrees, said Dr. Corrigan. This support includes resources to help students "at risk."

As well, he said, the MBA program will be flexible enough to meet the needs of almost any student, with three options:

1. A one-year, face-to-face intensive MBA—a year less than most MBA programs at other universities;
2. A one-year, online MBA, including three weeks' residence on campus, for those who already have undergraduate commerce or business degrees;
3. A two-year online MBA, with three weeks' residence on campus each year, for non-business graduates.

"We believe that our students are here because they want to improve themselves and gain an edge in the business world," Dr. Corrigan said. "In other words, if they meet the entrance requirements and follow the graduation guarantee contract, we know they can succeed. Our job is to make sure that they do succeed — we guarantee it."

-30-

For more information, please contact Dr. Michael Corrigan
at EverQuest University, 555-555-1800, ext. 1210.

Permissions Acknowledgements

Leffler, Warren K. "Martin Luther King meets with President Johnson at the White House, December 3, 1963." Image courtesy of the Library of Congress.

Meza, Juan. "Sample 30 minute talk" from "Giving Good Talks Isn't as Hard as It Looks," PowerPoint presentation available as a PDF from Lawrence Berkeley National Laboratory: http://crd-legacy.lbl.gov/~meza/talks/Giving_Good_Talks.pdf. Reprinted with the permission of Juan Meza, Dean, School of Natural Sciences, University of California, Merced.

Nature's Path cereal box image. Copyright © Nature's Path Foods. Reprinted with permission.

Schrier, Dan. "Profile of the British Columbia High Technology Sector: 2017 Edition," cover image. Reprinted with the permission of the Province of British Columbia.

Index

From the Publisher

A name never says it all, but the word "Broadview" expresses a good deal of the philosophy behind our company. We are open to a broad range of academic approaches and political viewpoints. We pay attention to the broad impact book publishing and book printing has in the wider world; for some years now we have used 100% recycled paper for most titles. Our publishing program is internationally oriented and broad-ranging. Our individual titles often appeal to a broad readership too; many are of interest as much to general readers as to academics and students.

Founded in 1985, Broadview remains a fully independent company owned by its shareholders—not an imprint or subsidiary of a larger multinational.

For the most accurate information on our books (including information on pricing, editions, and formats) please visit our website at www.broadviewpress.com. Our print books and ebooks are also available for sale on our site.

broadview press
www.broadviewpress.com

The interior of this book is printed on 100% recycled paper.

100%

PERMANENT